THE CHURCHES OF SHROPSHIRE & THEIR TREASURES

THE CHURCHES OF SHROPSHIRE & THEIR TREASURES

by
John Leonard

With a Foreword by the Rt. Revd. Dr. John Saxbee,
formerly Bishop of Lincoln and Bishop of Ludlow

Logaston Press

LOGASTON PRESS
Little Logaston, Logaston,
Woonton, Almeley, Herefordshire HR3 6QH
logastonpress.co.uk

First published by Logaston Press 2004
This edition with colour photographs published 2013
Copyright text and photographs © John Leonard
(except where otherwise acknowledged)

ISBN 978 1 906663 78 0

Typeset by Logaston Press
and printed and bound in Poland
www.polskabook.pl

For the Shropshire Historic Churches Trust

Contents

Acknowledgments

This exploration of over 250 churches in Shropshire in the past two years would not have been possible without the patience, love and encouragement of my wife Marjorie. She drove me all over the county, and frequently noticed objects of interest in the churches that I had overlooked. We were immensely touched by the help and friendliness of many people whom we met – incumbents, churchwardens, and members of the worshipping community all conspired to make these visits a delight. There were, of course, frustrations to overcome, mainly due to locked churches and adverse weather. But these were minor irritations compared to the joy we experienced in seeing so many beautiful buildings and in meeting so many heart-warming people dedicated to serving God in their neighbourhood.

I thank the Shrewsbury Records and Research Library for permission to reproduce two paintings of the Revd. Edward Williams used in Figs.2.2 & 25.6. During his ministry in Shropshire, Dr. John Saxbee, then Bishop of Ludlow, and later Bishop of Lincoln, was an inspiration to many and a great supporter of the Shropshire Historic Churches Trust, and I am grateful to him for writing a Foreword, reproduced in this second edition. It is always a pleasure to work with Andrew and Karen Johnson of Logaston Press, who as usual provided much good advice and superb technical help.

Lastly, I wish to thank the Chairman and my fellow Trustees of the Shropshire Historic Churches Trust for their forbearance and encouragement. The Trust exists to support the churches of Shropshire of all denominations, and all royalties will be given to the Trust.

Preface to the second edition

Since the first edition was published nine years ago, there have been significant changes in Shropshire churches. Improvements have been made in many churches, notably the installation of toilets and kitchen facilities at the west end of many of our village churches. Holy Trinity, Much Wenlock, has been transformed by the opening up of the west doorway adorned with impressive Norman carving, which can now be readily appreciated for the first time since the 12th century. It is sad to report that several have closed – Woodcote, Sibdon Carwood, Linley – and the latter especially is a great loss. It is hoped that the building may reopen under the care of the Churches Conservation Trust.

I have taken the opportunity of using colour in this edition to re-photograph the churches and use digital photography for the first time: this has enabled greater appreciation of the excellent stained glass found in many Shropshire churches. The previous edition was concerned only with Anglican parish churches, though it did include the Greek Orthodox church in Shrewsbury (formerly the parish church of St. John Sutton). Now I have great pleasure in including the Roman Catholic Shrewsbury Cathedral, and the Methodist church of Broad Street, Ludlow. Also I have to apologise to the congregation of St. Luke's, Snailbeach for wrongly stating that this church has closed. On the contrary, it is alive and well, and has now been accorded its rightful place. Other errors of less significance have of course been silently corrected.

The problem of locked churches continues to frustrate many visitors, especially in the north of the county. Virtually every church now has its website, with useful contact telephone numbers. Prospective visitors should first consult the website if it is anticipated that the church may be locked. I understand, of course, the reasons for locking churches, but surely it is not too much to ask that a notice should appear in the porch of locked churches informing the public where the key may be obtained.

Finally, readers (and churches) are urged to consider joining the Shropshire Historic Churches Trust, which provides grants to churches in need; and to support the Trust in the Open Gardens scheme each summer, and in the Ride and Stride day each September. This will help to ensure that we can transmit to future generations this wonderful Christian heritage. Details of membership may be obtained from the website: www.shropshirehct.org. But of course, the buildings in the last analysis are less important than the people and the Christian message; and I conclude with the prayer that the Trust regularly uses:

> Almighty God, our heavenly Father, we remember before you now the churches
> in this county of Shropshire, and the houses of worship which they use. Make

the doors of our churches wide enough to receive all who need human love and fellowship and a Father's care, and narrow enough to shut out all envy, pride and lack of love. In them may the tempted find help, the sorrowing receive comfort, the careless be awakened to repentance, the penitent be assured of your mercy. And there may all your children renew their strength and go on their way in hope and joy. Through Jesus Christ our Lord, Amen.

Foreword

John Betjeman observed that 'scenery is more memorable in Shropshire than buildings', but in this excellent and informative work, Dr. Leonard takes us on a tour of Shropshire churches which effectively challenges us to think again. By tackling the county region by region, he encourages systematic exploration of its architectural treasures found in more than 300 parish churches, and his starring system enables the visitor to make best use of available time.

Dr. Leonard wears his learning lightly, and he provides a clear and concise account of how churches came to be where they are, and how the hand of history has impacted upon their form and contents. Furthermore, his delight in craftsmen's art expressed through a wealth of architectural treasures and artefacts in churches great and small is truly infectious. Because the county is so rich in medieval churches, it is easy to overlook or even disparage later contributions to our ecclesiastical heritage, so Dr. Leonard's careful attention to Victorian churches is particularly welcome.

For ten years I was privileged to live and work in Shropshire, and many of my memories centre on these parish churches and those who love and care for them year on year. Such commitment must not be taken for granted, and Dr. Leonard is right to wonder just how long some of these churches can continue to remain open and available to those seeking God's presence and peace in beautiful buildings hallowed by centuries of prayer and praise. This book of wise words and wonderful photographs will surely help these churches to find new friends, who will come to know them better and love them more.

Rt. Revd. Dr. John Saxbee
formerly Bishop of Ludlow and of Lincoln

Outline map of Shropshire, showing the areas into which the gazetteer of churches is divided, and the approximate location of 96 three- and two-starred churches (see p.4)

Fig.1.1 Shrewsbury, St. Mary: the roof over the nave, chancel arch and east window

Introduction

Shropshire is a county of three distinct zones: in the north, the rural landscape is gentle and undulating, with a few low hills to vary the pastoral scene; the central belt comprises the ancient country town of Shrewsbury and the new town of Telford; in the south, hills dominate the scene, and here is the finest scenery in the county. Parish churches are everywhere abundant – over 300 in all, half of them medieval. Their variety is astonishing, and apart from the town churches of Shrewsbury and Ludlow, few are well-known or much visited. Furthermore, they are under threat, and it is likely that during the next 20 years there will be a drastic reduction in the number of churches open for public worship. When Dean Cranage completed his masterly survey of Shropshire's churches a hundred years ago, he described a total of 311, of which at least 279 were then used for worship. Since then, I calculate that 23 churches have closed, but this has been partly compensated for by the building of at least 12 new churches – so that the number in use has changed very little during the course of the 20th century. This will change.

During the past few years, I have visited 320 churches which are described in these pages. Of these, 304 are still used for worship; 8 are closed for worship but are regularly open to the public under the care of the Churches Conservation Trust or English Heritage, (including St. Mary, Shrewsbury); Old St. Chad may be visited by application to the Shrewsbury Tourist Information Office. The remaining 8 churches are privately owned and may not be visited. The congregations of many of the surviving village churches struggle to maintain their buildings, and the Shropshire Historic Churches Trust exists to help them preserve this heritage for the future. Royalties from the sale of this book will be donated to the Trust, but needless to say, opinions expressed here are solely the author's and may not represent the views of the Trust.

Visitors throng the town churches of Shrewsbury (Fig.1.1) and Ludlow (Fig.1.2), but nearly all the other churches are largely neglected. The one exception is Heath chapel (Fig.1.3), the perfect example of a Norman church virtu-

Fig.1.2 Ludlow, St. Laurence

Fig.1.3 Heath chapel

Fig.1.4 The Norman tympanum at Aston Eyre

ally unaltered for 800 years; it is justly celebrated, and finds a place in nearly every book about English parish churches. Yet there are countless other little-known gems: the Norman carving in Edstaston, Upton Cressett, Stirchley, Aston Eyre (Fig.1.4) and Stottesdon; the medieval and later monuments at Kinlet, Pitchford, Quatt and Tong; the medieval altar frontal at Alveley; the half-timbered church at Melverley (Fig.1.5); the Georgian furnishings and fittings at Petton; the Victorian churches at Chetwynd, St. George's and Leaton (Fig.1.6); the stained glass at Meole Brace and Whitton; the 20th-century church at Harlescott (Fig.1.7); the humble remoteness of Mindtown and Bettws-y-Crwyn (Fig.1.8); the eccentricity of Llanyblodwel (Fig.1.9). All these,

Fig.1.5 (above) The half-timbered church at Melverley
Fig.1.6 (right) The Victorian church at Leaton

and many others, would delight the visitor; and I hope that this book will prove a useful guide.

Specific sources of information about the churches are listed in the bibliography and references at the end of the book; these exclude the many church guides which have often proved useful, and one or two booklets. General sources are few, but the following have proved extremely helpful.

Fig.1.7 *The Holy Spirit, Harlescott, Shrewsbury: the finest 20th-century church in Shropshire?*

The oldest is the collection of over 300 watercolours by the Reverend Edward Williams in the Shropshire Records and Research Library. Most of these were painted between 1785 and 1794 and provide an invaluable guide to the appearance of parish churches before the restorations of the 19th century. Williams was an accurate observer, and comparison of his paintings with the present-day appearances of the buildings gives confidence that where changes have occurred, his depiction of their previous appearance is to be trusted.

Then there are Sir Stephen Glynne's *Church Notes for Shropshire*, recently published by the Centre for Local History, University of Keele. These record Glynne's observations made during his visits to Shropshire churches between 1829 and 1872. Glynne visited 131 churches and his records constitute an invaluable description of churches in Victorian times. He was a true antiquarian – often scathing about work of the 18th century and frequently deploring the work of many of the Victorian restorers. In his assessment of medieval buildings he is usually reliable, though some of his judgments do not accord with modern taste and knowledge.

Fig.1.8 *Bettws-y-Crwyn*

Fig.1.9 *Llanyblodwel*

D.H.S. Cranage's *The Churches of Shropshire* appeared in instalments between 1892 and 1911. This massive work will never be equalled and Shropshire is very lucky that an architectural historian of his distinction laboured for 20 years on its ecclesiastical heritage. The medieval fabric of the churches was described with loving care and devotion to detail, and few of his conclusions have been disturbed by later scholarship. He was less interested in work of the 18th century, and even less in that of the 19th century – frequently using the word 'debased' to describe modern (i.e. Victorian) work; and indeed Victorian churches get scant mention.

Sir Nikolaus Pevsner's *Shropshire* in *The Buildings of England* series published in 1955 includes nearly all the parish churches and is held in the highest regard. Pevsner was a great architectural historian and a scholar, and his description of churches is invariably succinct and nearly always accurate. He provided an invaluable account of parish churches. Yet to some extent he shared the prejudices of the 1950s against Victorian architecture and few churches of the 19th century get more than a perfunctory assessment. This has been corrected in the new 'Pevsner' by John Newman, published in 2006.

Finally there are the volumes so far published of *The Victoria County History of Shropshire*. Volume II (published 1973) dealt with the monastic foundations of the Middle Ages. Volumes VIII (1968), X (1998) and XI (1985) describe in detail the parishes of central Shropshire, of Wenlock, Upper Corvedale and the Stretton Hills, and of Telford respectively. These volumes give invaluable information on the parish churches in their respective areas, a total of 59 parishes having been analysed. It is greatly to be deplored that funding for this work has recently stopped, at a stage when only about one quarter of the county has been covered.

The purpose of the present work is to describe the current state of the churches and to help people who love parish churches to visit those buildings which are most rewarding. Locked churches are a common problem, especially in the urban centres. But almost every parish church now has a website where the telephone numbers of parish administrators, churchwardens and clergy may be found. I have used a starring system to indicate which churches are especially worth visiting; as in the old Michelin guides, *** indicates a church worth a special journey; ** a church worth a detour; and * a church worth a visit *en passant*. Visiting parish churches is increasingly popular, as people seek to explore our heritage – religious, architectural, historic, artistic. After an historical survey of the origins of the church in Shropshire, medieval churches, monastic foundations and post-Reformation churches are described in turn. The next part of the book presents a summary of the treasures which may be found, dealing in turn with towers, porches, roofs, sculpture, fonts, memorials and monuments, stained glass, woodwork etc. The third part deals with the churches themselves, arranged in the regions of the county. Throughout, I have consciously tried to give due emphasis to the Victorian churches which have largely been neglected in other works.

As previously indicated, many of Shropshire's churches face an uncertain future. I hope that this book will encourage both the residents of Shropshire and those who visit the county to explore the treasures in our midst, and at the beginning of the third millennium to appreciate anew the wonders of our Christian heritage.

The Origins of the Church in Shropshire

In the 17th century, Thomas Fuller (in *Fuller's Worthies*) described Shropshire as 'a large and lovely county generally fair and fruitful, affording grass, grain and all things necessary for man's sustenance'. It was not always thus. In ancient times, Shropshire was heavily wooded and settlements were sparse. By the 7th century BC, Celtic peoples from central Europe had settled in the Severn valley[1] and in the central Marches left a series of impressive Iron Age hillforts. The dominant tribe in the area was the Cornovii, but these were overwhelmed by the arrival of the Romans in the first century AD. They established their base at Wroxeter (*Viroconium*), and at one time this was the fourth largest town in Roman Britain. Almost certainly, it was in Wroxeter (Fig.2.1) in the 4th century that the first Christian presence in Shropshire became established, but firm evidence for this is elusive:[2] 'Perhaps the clearest proof of Wroxeter's Christianisation comes from the demise of its temples which excavation has shown were abandoned within the 4th century and were despoiled. Even more intriguingly, a possible early Christian congregational church has been detected within the city centre.'

The Roman soldiers departed in the early 5th century, but White and Barker have shown that *Viroconium* persisted for a long time thereafter before the site was finally abandoned in the early 6th century. The withering of Roman rule allowed the Celtic tribes of the area to resume their independence, and by the 6th century the old tribal groups in Wales and the Marches had been transformed into petty kingdoms. The 5th and 6th centuries are shrouded in uncertainty and documentary evidence for this period is scanty indeed. Clearly, however, Christianity was slowly spreading through the Celtic tribes: British bishops attended the council of Arles in 314 and the council of Ariminum in 360; and monastic communities were arising by the middle of the 6th century. One of these was at Bangor-on-Dee halfway between the Roman cities of Chester and Wroxeter. The leading historian of the period was Gildas, a monk who wrote his *De Excidio et Conquesta Britanniae* shortly before 548 and whose work was largely incorporated by the Venerable

Fig.2.1 Roman pillars at St. Andrew, Wroxeter

Bede in his *Ecclesiastical History* written *c*.731. In Wales, the 6th century has been aptly called 'the age of the saints', and prominent among these are David and Samson; the latter claimed Gildas among his pupils[3] and was commemorated in the dedication of the church at Cressage (Fig.2.2). Gildas described the early pagan Saxon invasions and stated that the Saxons originally came to Britain as hired mercenaries to fight northern enemies rather than as invaders.

Fig.2.2 Medieval church of St. Samson at Cressage

It was probably early in the 7th century that Saxon Mercians began to push westwards into the area covered by the present counties of Shropshire and Herefordshire. Under the Britons, the northern part of Shropshire had come to be part of the petty kingdom of the Wroecensaetan (the people who dwell by the Wrekin), while the southern part and most of Herefordshire constituted the kingdom of the Magonsaetan. It is said that the boundary between the Magonsaetan and the Wroecensaetan still demarcates the limits of the dioceses of Lichfield and Hereford in Shropshire. To the east lay the kingdom of the Hwicce, later centred on Worcester. The Magonsaetan appear to have been conquered by Penda, the pagan king of Mercia, in 628 and in 641 he defeated and slew the Christian King Oswald of Northumbria at the battle of Maserfelt which some believe to have been where Oswestry (St. Oswald's Tree – Fig.2.3) now stands. In 655 Penda was slain in battle by Oswald's brother Oswy; his son and heir Peada was converted to Christianity, and the formal conversion of Mercia rapidly followed – Mercia was the last of the Anglo-Saxon kingdoms to embrace the faith.

Meanwhile, during these times of change in western Mercia, the Christian faith was also spreading from the south-east. In 597 Pope Gregory had sent St. Augustine to Kent, whence the faith spread through neighbouring areas. So by the middle of the 7th century two forms of Christianity existed side by side in much of England – the Celtic church which had spread from Ireland, Wales and Scotland into northern and western England, and the Roman church derived from St. Augustine's mission. It was an

Fig.2.3 St. Oswald, Oswestry

Fig.2.4 Wenlock Priory

unstable situation – these two ecclesiastical systems could not co-exist for long – and matters came to a head at the famous Synod of Whitby in 664, which confirmed the victory of Canterbury and Rome; the casting vote was given by the king of Northumbria.

The reign of King Peada was short, and he was succeeded as king of Mercia by his brother Wulfhere (659-675); during his reign Chad (Ceadda) became the first bishop of Mercia, fixing his see at Lichfield in 669. Wulfhere was succeeded by a second brother, Aethelred (675-704). A third brother, Merewalh, ruled only over the Magonsaetan, but he was a pivotal figure, for he was converted *c*.660 by Eadfrith, a missionary from the Celtic church in Northumbria. He founded the first Christian church in the English part of Herefordshire at Leominster, placing Eadfrith in charge. Merewalh was also responsible for the establishment in 680 of Wenlock, the first Christian foundation in Shropshire (Fig.2.4). This was a convent for monks and nuns and originally was a daughter establishment to the monastery at Icanhoe (usually identified as Boston in Lincolnshire), founded by St. Botolf. Merewalh's daughter Mildburga became the first abbess. She was later canonised, and her name survives in Stoke St. Milborough. Wenlock was granted extensive estates in Shropshire, especially around the Clee Hills and in Corvedale, and also in Wales. Eventually the whole of Shropshire became part of the kingdom of Mercia, which reached its pinnacle of power under kings Aethbald and Offa in the 8th century.

The diocese of Lichfield initially covered an enormous area, but it appears that within 20 years of its foundation, the dioceses of Lindsey (based on Lincoln and amalgamated with that of Dorchester in the 11th century), Leicester, Worcester and Hereford were created out of it. It has traditionally been accepted that the first bishop of Hereford was Putta. He

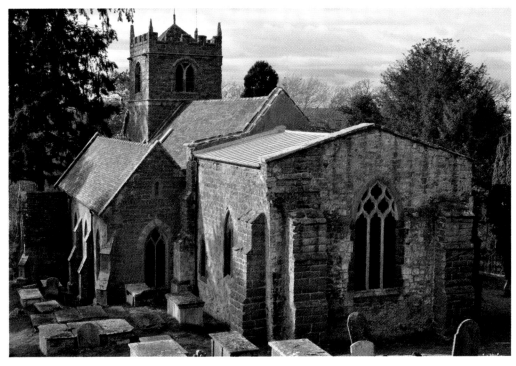

Fig.2.5 St. Mary Magdalene, Quatford: near to a Danish encampment

Fig.2.6 The Norman tower at Clun: note the double pyramid roof

had been consecrated bishop of Rochester in 669, but when, seven years later, Kent was ravaged by the forces of Aethelred, it was believed that Putta fled and established his see at Hereford and remained as bishop until his death in 688, when he was succeeded by Tyrthel. However, in a scholarly review, Hillaby persuasively demolished this scenario, and concluded that Tyrthel was the first authenticated bishop of Hereford, c.693, and that Putta sought sanctuary with Seaxwulf (who had succeeded Chad as bishop of Lichfield).[4] Chad, according to Bede, 'granted him a church and a small estate, where he ended his life in peace'.

Offa's Dyke was constructed in the 8th century at the height of Mercian power to delineate the frontier between Mercia and Wales. It follows fairly closely the western border of present-day Shropshire. In the 9th century, after the reign of Offa (757-796), Mercia was in decline, and Wessex finally emerged as the greatest kingdom of Anglo-Saxon times. Shropshire was largely peripheral to the prolonged campaigns waged by

Alfred the Great (871-899) against the Danes – although the Danes did succeed for a time in establishing an encampment at Quatford (Fig.2.5) on the river Severn south of Bridgnorth. But Danish power was steadily reduced by King Edward the Elder (son of Alfred, reigned 899-924) and his sister Aethelflaed.

The town of Shrewsbury, five miles from Wroxeter, was first mentioned in a document in 901, when a transaction was recorded '*in civitate Scrobensis*'. The name may mean Scrobb's burg, or alternatively it may be derived from a word relating to English 'shrub' and meaning 'brushwood'.[5] Established on a hill almost encircled by the river Severn, it early became an important administrative centre and the site of a royal mint during the reign of Edward the Elder. The county of Shropshire came into being at some time in the 10th century or early 11th century, the name *Scrobbesbyrigscir* (meaning the shire with Shrewsbury as its head) being first recorded in 1006.[6]

During the Anglo-Saxon centuries it is now apparent that many more churches were founded than was previously believed. Those that have survived are but a minuscule proportion of the total. Nearly all the churches were built of wood, and so have perished without trace. Stone was used only for cathedrals and monasteries until *c*.950 (but for exceptions in Shropshire, see p.11); thereafter it was used increasingly for some parish churches. But it was not until one hundred years later that large-scale building in stone was undertaken for local churches.

The organisation of the church in Saxon times was relatively loose. Originally a number of minsters arose, usually serving a very wide area, and being staffed by a variable number of canons. Some of these became collegiate churches. In the later Saxon centuries, many village churches were founded by laymen, with only a tenuous relationship with the local bishop. These churches were often regarded by the local thane as part of his personal property, almost as a capital investment; for ownership of a church increasingly brought in revenue in the form of tithes. Thus the larger areas served by the older minsters became progressively subdivided as parishes multiplied.

In contrast to Herefordshire, where Welsh influence predominated over nearly half the county, Welsh influence in Shropshire was largely confined to the western

Church only	Priest(s) only
Baschurch	Astley
Corfham (in Munslow)	Chetton
Great Ness	Chetwynd
Hodnet	Child's Ercall
Stottesdon	Cleobury Mortimer
	Condover
Church(es) and priest(s)	Glazeley
Abdon	Ightfield
Berrington	Leighton
Bitterley	Lilleshall
Burford – 2 priests	Lydham
Chirbury – 2 churches	Market Drayton
Holdgate	Munslow
Lydbury	North Myddle
Maesbury	Onibury
Morville	Petton
Rodington	Prees
Shawbury	Rowton
Stanton Lacy	Wellington
Stanton-upon-Hine-Heath	Westbury – 2
Stoke on Tern	Wotherton (near Chirbury)
Stretton (Church)	Woolston (in Wistanstow)
Wrockwardine	Yorton (near Pimhill)
Wroxeter – 4 priests	

Table I Shropshire churches and priests recorded in the Domesday survey[8]

margin, and turbulence continued in the border area until the end of the 15th century. The Welsh presence was felt mainly in the north-west, around Oswestry, and in the south-west, around Clun (Fig.2.6). For over 200 years after the Norman Conquest there were frequent Welsh incursions into Clun Forest, and Clun changed hands several times before finally becoming English in the 13th century. Even after that, there were further Welsh incursions in the 14th and 15th centuries, notably under Owain Glyndwr; the latter's rebellion reached the peak of its territorial gains around 1405, when defeats in Monmouthshire combined with war weariness led to a falling off in his support and by 1409 the rebellion was all but over.

Twenty years after the Norman Conquest (1066), William I instituted the Domesday survey, a detailed statement of lands held by the king and by his tenants and of the resources which went with those lands.[7] The survey was clearly invaluable for fiscal purposes, but its record of churches and priests was seriously deficient. The absence of any record of a church in a particular manor cannot be taken as meaning that no church was then in existence. In Shropshire, 23 churches were recorded in 22 manors (Chirbury had two); and the presence of priests was recorded in 40 manors (Table I).

3
Medieval Churches

At least 230 churches were built in Shropshire during the Middle Ages; for the sake of readers who may be unfamiliar with medieval churches, a brief description of the styles used may be helpful.

An unknown number of Saxon churches were built in the county; the great majority of these were of timber and so have not survived. As mentioned previously, the use of stone for the construction of parish churches was most unusual before *c*.950. There were, however, exceptions: at Wroxeter, for example, the adjacent Roman ruins provided a ready source of stone, and the north wall of the church has been dated to the 7th or 8th century. By the 11th century, stone was being used increasingly, and the nave and north transept at Stanton Lacy is a fine example of work of that period.

There are a number of characteristic features which identify Saxon stonework. At corners, slabs were often set alternately vertically and horizontally – long-and-short work – a feature not found in Norman building. In the north wall at Wroxeter, traces of long-and-short work can be discerned at the junctions between the Saxon and Norman portions (Fig.3.1). Herring-bone masonry consists of rows of stones applied diagonally, each row leaning alternately to the right and the left. Saxon masonry of this type may be seen at Diddlebury (Fig.3.2), though not all such work dates from before the Norman Conquest. For decoration, very typical Saxon features are tall strips made of thin stones set vertically against walls (pilasters) –

Fig.3.1 Wroxeter: traces of long-and-short work in Saxon masonry

Fig.3.2 Diddlebury: a Saxon window and herring-bone masonry

Fig.3.3 Stanton Lacy:
Saxon pilasters and doorway

Fig.3.4 Diddlebury:
a Saxon doorway

best seen at Stanton Lacy (Fig.3.3). Saxon windows are small, usually high up, and sometimes splayed equally both inside and outside (Norman windows are splayed internally only). They may be round-headed, as at Barrow and Diddlebury, or triangular-headed, as possibly at Atcham (see p.178). Saxon doorways are plain (Fig.3.4).

The arrival of William the Conqueror in 1066 swept away Saxon England, and the Normans introduced their own style of so-called Romanesque architecture. But this did not happen overnight and buildings dating from the last 30 years of the 11th century often show features of both Saxon and Norman influence, making it difficult, sometimes impossible, for experts to assign a date with any confidence. The fact is that Norman influence was making itself felt in England before 1066, and Saxon influence persisted after that watershed year. But from 1100 onwards, Saxon styles are extinguished.

I have retained the traditional names for the medieval styles introduced in Rickman's classification. This dates from 1817, when Thomas Rickman published his *Attempt to discriminate the Styles of English Architecture* which for the first time analysed medieval buildings in terms which, though perhaps not ideal, have stood the test of time and have survived until the present day. He divided medieval styles into four groups – Romanesque or Norman (1066-1200), and three Gothic styles, Early English (1200-1300), Decorated (1300-1350) and Perpendicular (1350-1550). These dates are approximate, and must be treated with considerable caution. In Shropshire, most medieval churches date from the 12th or 13th centuries – the Norman and Early English periods; the amount of building declined early in the 14th century. There are relatively few Decorated or Perpendicular churches, though there are some notable exceptions, (e.g. Ludlow). Decorated or Perpendicular towers, however, occur quite frequently.

The Norman or Romanesque style lasted from the time of the Conquest until the end of the 12th century. Early Norman building (say until *c.*1120) is sometimes characterised by herring-bone

12

Fig.3.5 Culmington:
early Norman herring-bone masonry

Fig.3.6 Quatford:
characteristic pitted appearance of tufa

masonry as at Clee St. Margaret, Culmington (Fig.3.5), Pitchford, Rushbury, Sidbury and Stanton-upon-Hine-Heath. Another sign of early Norman building is the extensive use of tufa, a form of limestone in which new rocks have been formed by spring-water bubbling through sphagnum moss laden with calcium carbonate. This is deposited in the form of a precipitate and gradually hardens. When the rock dries out, it develops a characteristic pitted appearance (Fig.3.6), like a petrified sponge.[1] The church at Quatford is largely built of tufa. The use of tufa declined during the second quarter of the 12th century.

The 12th century witnessed a tremendous programme of church building throughout the entire country: cathedrals, monastic houses and especially parish churches were built in abundance. The smaller parish churches were usually built in a simple one- or two-cell form.[2] The length of single-cell churches exceeded their breadth, so that the building could accommodate both nave and chancel. Two-cell churches had a structurally separate nave and chancel. In general, single-cell churches were chapels rather than parish churches, while those with parochial status usually were of the two-cell form; but numerous exceptions occur. Single-cell churches include Hadnall, Leebotwood and Lydham; two-cell churches include Heath, Hope Bagot and Clee St. Margaret. Mercer also points out that single-cell churches hardly appear before the second half of the 12th century; all churches which can be securely dated before 1150 were of the two-cell kind.

The larger Norman churches are characterised by solidly built arcades and towers: the arches are rounded, the cylindrical columns supporting the arcades massive (Fig.3.7). The columns or piers are surmounted by square-edged capitals, as at Shawbury (Fig.9.7), which effect the transition from the round column to the square

Fig.3.7 Kinlet: massive piers and round-headed arches in the south arcade

Fig.3.8 Hope Bagot: a small Norman window, deeply splayed internally

abacus above which supports the arch. The inferior surface of the capital is often carved into various shapes (see p.55).

As we have seen, the smallest churches began as just a nave and chancel – this is to be seen in its purest form at Heath chapel (Fig.1.3) – a building perfectly preserved and virtually unaltered for over eight hundred years. The population steadily grew throughout the 12th and 13th centuries, and it was often necessary to enlarge the two-cell churches. This was frequently done by lateral enlargement of the nave in the form of aisles, separated from the nave by arcades of semicircular arches supported by massive piers or columns. Norman arcades are not very frequent in Shropshire – many have been replaced in later centuries – but may be seen in, for example, Shawbury and Clun. For Norman building on a grand scale, there is nothing to compare with the 12th-century nave at Shrewsbury Abbey.

Semicircular arches are the hallmark of Norman or Romanesque building, and in addition to the arcades are found above doors and windows. They were often decorated by geometric designs, especially the ubiquitous chevron or zigzag (see p.53) which was introduced very early in the 12th century. Norman windows are usually small, round-headed, and deeply splayed internally to maximise the provision of light (Fig.3.8), glass being expensive.

The introduction of the pointed arch, which ushered in Gothic architecture and which was to revolutionise church building, was primarily for structural reasons, such an arch being able to transmit a larger proportion of the thrust directly to the ground.[3] It appears to have been first used at Autun Cathedral, France, around 1120-1130. In England, it may be seen from about 1160-1200 side by side with semicircular arches and massive Norman columns (the Transitional period); examples of Transitional arcades may be seen at Clun (Fig.3.9) and elsewhere. After about 1200 semicircular

Fig.3.9 Clun: the north arcade. Transitional between Norman and Early English. The piers are still massive, but the arches are pointed (except the easternmost one in the foreground, which is round-headed). Chevron decoration of the arches and scallop under the capitals

Fig.3.10 Cleobury Mortimer: Early English arcade.
The piers are less massive, the arches acutely pointed

Fig.3.11 Aston Botterell: note the lancet windows

Fig.3.12 Monkhopton: Y-tracery

arches are seen no more, the columns become less substantial, and the Early English style is said to have begun. This lasted throughout the whole of the 13th century. Arches are acutely pointed; the less massive piers at first remained mostly cylindrical (Fig.3.10), but later octagonal or multi-shafted piers may be seen. Capitals are now usually rounded rather than square, and are sometimes decorated with 'stiff-leaf' foliage (Fig.9.18) – more exuberant than water-leaf, the leaves often being multilobular. A frequent ornamental motif in the 13th century is dogtooth (p.57). The other major characteristic of the Early English style is the lancet window – until later revivalists imitated it, a sure indication of the 13th century. The lancet is a tall narrow window with an acutely pointed upper end (Fig.3.11). Often they may be paired, or grouped in a series of three or more, sometimes provided with a common hood-mould to throw rainwater clear of the window. Later in the century, the area enclosed by a common hood-mould was often pierced, resulting in plate or Y-tracery (Fig.3.12); from this germ, the development of complex tracery seen in the next century evolved.

The Decorated style was introduced around 1300, and lasted for about fifty years. The most complete example of Decorated architecture is probably at Chelmarsh. Decorated arches are not so acutely pointed, and the piers are now much more often octagonal (Fig.3.13) or multi-shafted in cross-section. Carvings on the moulded capitals are freer and more elaborate, and when foliage is seen it is more realistic than the stiff-leaf carving of the previous century. Y-tracery developed into intersecting tracery (Fig.3.14) in which each vertical mullion branches into two curved bars. The most characteristic Decorated feature,

Fig.3.13 Lilleshall: the piers of the arcade are octagonal

introduced very early in the 14th century, is the ogee arch – two shallow S-shaped curves meeting upwards in a sharp point (p.58). There was nothing functional about the ogee arch – it was an exuberant artistic fancy. In windows it led to complicated patterns of flowing tracery (Fig.3.15), some of which may be described as geometrical, curvilinear or reticulated (Fig.3.16). Leaf patterns – trefoil, quatrefoil, cinquefoil, even sexfoil – were frequent in Decorated adornments, the leaves often separated by much cusping. Another characteristic motif of the Decorated age was ball-flower ornamentation (p.58).

Fig.3.14 Kinlet: intersecting tracery with cusps in the east window

Fig.3.15 Albrighton: more complex tracery in this Decorated window

Fig.3.16 Battlefield: the window on the left is Perpendicular, that on the right has reticulated tracery (Decorated)

Fig.3.17 Edgmond: tall Perpendicular arcade, the piers are octagonal. The east window is Decorated

Around 1350 the Black Death engulfed the country, and a quarter, perhaps a third, of the entire population died. Some authorities have believed that the emergence of the Perpendicular style may have been related to this disaster; it was pointed out that the first evidence of Perpendicular appeared to be at the choir at Gloucester Cathedral, *c*.1350. It was also believed that Perpendicular was the only medieval style to have originated in England, and to have been confined there. Recently, however, the origins of Perpendicular have been traced earlier, to the 1330s, eliminating any connection with the Black Death. Wilson believes that the first appearance of Perpendicular was in the chapter house and cloister of Old St Paul's (now destroyed) and in the remodelling of the south transept of Gloucester;[4] both buildings were begin in the early 1330s. Dispelling another English illusion, he traces the style back to the triforia of certain French churches built in the mid- and late 13th century Rayonnant style. However, there is no doubt that within a few decades of its introduction, the sterner, plainer style of Perpendicular had completely replaced Decorated. This was in contrast to France, where Decorated became ever more extreme, producing the Flamboyant style. In Perpendicular building, the emphasis throughout is on verticality; straight lines replace the sinuous tracery of the Decorated style; the pointed arches become flatter. This alters the proportions of the arcade: a large part of its height is now taken up by the piers. The piers being both taller and thinner (Fig.3.17) make the arcade appear loftier and produce the impression of height and lightness of structure that is so characteristic of the Perpendicular style … the preference for straight lines shows particularly clearly in window tracery. There the vertical mullions that divide a window into its lights rise almost without interruption to the head of the window, ruling its tracery into tiers of vertical compartments.[5] The steeply sloping roofs of earlier centuries were now often replaced by low-pitched roofs (Fig.3.18), thus enabling the side walls of the nave to be heightened and allowing for the insertion of a clerestory. In Shropshire there is relatively little Perpendicular building. This is in marked contrast to Cheshire and to areas of the country enriched by the trade in wool, where glorious Perpendicular churches may be found, e.g. in the Cotswolds and East Anglia. The inference must

Fig.3.18 Ludlow: tall Perpendicular arches in the crossing

be that Shropshire in the 15th century remained relatively poor, with a static population, and it was therefore not necessary to extend many churches. A notable exception is, of course, Ludlow, where the wealth of the Palmers' Guild produced a noble parish church. The other main example of the Perpendicular style in Shropshire is Edgmond. For Perpendicular towers, see p.42.

4

Monastic Foundations

Although this book is primarily concerned with parish churches, a number of churches had close links with monastic foundations. It seems artificial to ignore these – so a brief account here of Shropshire's religious houses is appropriate.

Monastic foundations were not, of course, so numerous as parish churches. Nevertheless Shropshire eventually possessed over 20, and of these, 12 date from the Norman period (say 1066-1200 – Table II). The major foundations in Shropshire were the abbeys at Shrewsbury, Haughmond, Buildwas and Lilleshall and Wenlock Priory. Priories tended to be smaller than abbeys (Wenlock was an exception), and many of the priory cells were very small, often housing only two or three monks sent from the owning house to exploit a distant estate. The alien priories were so called because they were founded by French religious

Foundation	Order and status	Founded	Dissolved	Subject to
Wenlock	Nunnery	c.680		
	Cluniac priory	1080-81	1540	La Charité
Shrewsbury	Benedictine abbey	1083-86	1540	
Haughmond	Augustinian abbey	1130-35	1539	
Buildwas	Savignac; later Cistercian	1135	1539	Savigny
Wombridge	Augustinian priory	1130-35	1536	
Morville	Benedictine priory	1138	1540	Shrewsbury
Lilleshall	Arroasian, later Augustinian, abbey	1148	1538	
Church Preen	Cluniac priory cell	1150	1539	Wenlock
Bromfield	Benedictine priory	1155	1540	Gloucester
Chirbury	Augustinian priory	1190-95	1536	
Whiteladies	Augustinian canonesses priory	?1190	?1538	
Ratlinghope	Augustinian priory cell	1200-09	1538	Wigmore
Halston	Knights Hospitaller	1221	1540	
Stanton Long	Knights Templar	1225	1308-12	
Alberbury	Grandmontine alien priory	1228	1441	Grandmont
Shrewsbury	Dominican friars	1231-34	1539	Oxford
Bridgnorth	Franciscan friars	1244	1538	Worcester
Shrewsbury	Augustinian friars	c.1254	1538	Lincoln
Ludlow	Augustinian friars	1254	1538	Lincoln
Woodhouse	Augustinian friars	c.1250	1538	Lincoln
Ludlow	Carmelite friars	1350	1538	

Table II The Monastic Foundations of Shropshire

houses; later in the Middle Ages, at the time of the wars with France, they became very vulnerable, and most of them were suppressed in the 15th century; some escaped by purchasing naturalisation.

The earliest religious foundation in Shropshire was Wenlock Priory (Figs.2.4 & 4.1), established as a convent for monks and nuns in 680. Originally Wenlock was a dependency of the monastery at Icanhoe (usually identified as Boston in Lincolnshire) founded by St. Botolf. The site was given by Merewalh, son of Penda and king of the Magonsaetan, and his daughter Mildburga became the first abbess. She was later canonised, and her name survives in the area in Stoke St. Milborough. Wenlock was granted extensive estates in Shropshire, especially around the Clee Hills and in Corvedale, and also in Wales. In the later Saxon centuries Wenlock fared badly, perhaps as a result of Danish raids, and it appears to have been re-founded by Leofric, earl of Mercia during the reign of Edward the Confessor (1050), and then again by Roger, earl of

Fig.4.1 Wenlock Priory:
intersecting arcading in the chapter house

Montgomery after the Conquest (1083); he arranged for monks from the leading Cluniac house at La Charité-sur-Loire to go to Wenlock. The story goes that the monks found St. Mildburga's shrine empty; later they found documents telling them where to dig for it. The bones were then found, washed and laid with reverence in a new shrine upon the altar. Miracles at once began.[2]

Most of the orders of religious houses were represented in the county, the Benedictine and Augustinian foundations being most numerous (Table II). Benedictine houses followed the Rule laid down by St. Benedict in the 6th century. For five hundred years they were the dominant influence in monasticism, and for much – and especially the early part – of this period, they were the major repositories of learning and literature throughout western Europe. The Benedictines did not, however, constitute a single religious order, for each monastery was autonomous. In Shropshire the major Benedictine establishment was the great abbey at Shrewsbury (Fig.4.2), at first known as St. Peter's church (p.185). This was founded by Earl Roger in 1083 as a daughter house of Séez in Normandy, and endowed with much property. A priory cell was established at Morville as a dependency of Shrewsbury Abbey in 1130. The remaining Benedictine foundation in Shropshire was Bromfield (Fig.4.3), a priory cell established in 1155 and dependent on St. Peter's Abbey at Gloucester.

The loose Benedictine monopoly was not challenged until 910 when a Benedictine abbey was established at Cluny, and here was instituted a stricter

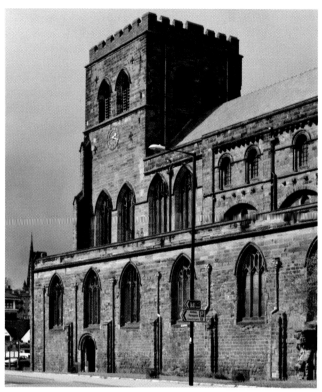

Fig.4.2 Shrewsbury Abbey

Fig.4.3 Bromfield: a priory cell was established here in 1155. Some ruins remain

observance of St. Benedict's Rule. Furthermore, the abbey sponsored an extensive series of subsidiary houses, known generally as priories. These were often favoured by the aristocracy, and many Cluniac foundations became wealthy. In England, the leading Cluniac priory was at Lewes in Sussex, closely followed by the priory at Wenlock. Being ultimately subservient to Cluny, these ranked as alien priories; in common with most other Cluniac foundations, Wenlock purchased naturalisation (thus it became 'denizen') in 1395. A small priory cell, dependent on Wenlock, was founded at Church Preen *c*.1150.

By about 1100, there was a general desire for reform of monasticism: the Benedictines were seen as too lax, the Cluniacs as too wealthy. To meet this situation, three orders were founded at about the same time: the orders of Tiron, Grandmont and Citeaux. The first two remained relatively small, with only a handful of dependencies in England. There was, however, a Grandmontine foundation in Shropshire, at Alberbury, one of only three in England; this was a late establishment, founded only in 1228, and as an alien foundation it was suppressed early, in 1441. The Cistercians, from Citeaux, became large and extremely influential, transforming the face of monasticism in the 12th century; they had a major foundation in Herefordshire at Dore Abbey (founded in 1147) and in Shropshire they took over Buildwas Abbey. Their great expansion was largely the work of Bernard of Clairvaux (1090-1153); Cistercian monasteries were characterised by extreme asceticism, combined with hard physical labour on their estates. Their architecture, at least at first, was plain and elegant, eschewing decorative sculpture. Buildwas had been founded by Roger de Clinton, bishop of Coventry and Lichfield, in 1135 as a daughter house of Furness Abbey, for monks of the Savigniac order; in 1147 it became Cistercian when the establishments of Savigny were merged in the order of Citeaux.

The remaining major movement of reform in the 12th century was that instituted by followers of St. Augustine's Rule. St. Augustine of Hippo (392-430) had never laid down a strict Rule like St. Benedict, and his precepts could be widely interpreted. The Augustinian canons (sometimes known as Austin canons) lived together under a moderate rule: asceticism was discouraged, and they were much given to good works – 'They ran hospitals and retreats for the aged and for lepers; they were schoolteachers, chaplains ... above all, they assumed the responsibility for the parish churches.'[3] The major Augustinian house in Shropshire was Haughmond Abbey; this was probably founded *c*.1130-35 by William fitzAlan of Clun, although some authorities date it earlier (to 1110). It was responsible for dependent hospitals in Oswestry and Whitchurch. The Augustinian abbey at Lilleshall began life at Lizard in 1143, moving the next year to Donnington Wood, and to Lilleshall in 1148. It was responsible for the hospital at Bridgnorth, and in *c*.1221-26 it founded Alberbury which shortly after became Grandmontine (see above). Other Augustinian foundations were the priory at Wombridge (founded *c*.1130-35), Chirbury (founded 1190-95) and the priory cell at Ratlinghope (a dependency of Wigmore Abbey, founded 1200-09). Whiteladies Priory at Boscobel was an establishment for Augustinian canonesses; this was founded *c*.1199.

By 1200 the majority of religious houses in Shropshire had been established, and in the following century some of the impetus for expansion was lost. Instead, the early 13th century was characterised by the arrival in England of two orders of mendicant friars – the Dominicans and the Franciscans. The friars relied mostly on charity for subsistence and on wealthy donors for the cost of their buildings. They preached a more personal faith, bringing men and women directly to God rather than relying on the intercessory roles of the monks. Such an approach suddenly became more in tune with the times (more 'relevant' in today's parlance), and the friars soon established themselves in almost every cathedral city and county town in England. The Franciscans (the grey friars) came to Bridgnorth in 1244. St. Francis of Assisi (c.1182-1226) founded an order based on poverty, chastity, and obedience, renouncing all idea of property, which spread very rapidly during the last years of his life. The Dominicans (the black friars) arrived in Shrewsbury c.1231-34, following the teachings of St. Dominic (c.1170-1221); they imitated the Franciscans in eschewing property, and living a life of rigid poverty. Augustinian friars arrived in Shrewsbury and Ludlow c.1254, and at Woodhouse, near Cleobury Mortimer at about the same time. Much later, the Carmelites (the white friars) also settled in Ludlow c.1350. The orders of mendicant friars expanded rapidly throughout the 13th century, and by 1300 their establishment was virtually complete.

The remaining religious houses in Shropshire were those of the Knights Hospitallers and the Knights Templars. The Knights Hospitallers (the knights of the Order of St. John of Jerusalem) were founded in the 11th century to care for pilgrims in Jerusalem, and after the capture of that city by the crusaders in 1099 they guarded Christian possessions in the Middle East. By the middle of the 12th century, the manor at Halston (q.v.) had come into the hands of the Knights Hospitallers who built there a preceptory, c.1221; the hospital at Oswestry was assigned to them. The Knights Templars were founded in the early 12th century to protect pilgrims on their way to the Holy Land and they held land in Stanton Long from c.1225. In 1312 the Templars were overthrown by King Philip IV of France, and the property in Stanton Long passed to the Knights Hospitallers. Other hospitals established in Shropshire during the Middle Ages are listed in Table III.

From the 14th century onwards, the story of monastic establishments in England was one of decline in vigour and influence, an increasing laxity of spiritual observance, loss of reputation, and reduced numbers of monks and nuns. During the wars with France most of the alien priories were either suppressed or else escaped by purchasing naturalisation. By the time of the Reformation the remaining religious houses were weak and demoralised, and Henry VIII brought this chapter of religious history to a close by the Dissolution of the Monasteries in 1536-40.

After the Dissolution, the religious houses passed into private hands and over the centuries most have crumbled into ruin. Substantial remains, which are well worth visiting, survive at Haughmond, Buildwas and Lilleshall Abbeys and at Wenlock and Whiteladies Priories. Less impressive ruins survive at Alberbury and Bromfield, and there are fragments of St. Giles Hospital, Ludford, St. John's Hospital, Ludlow and St. James' Hospital, Bridgnorth. Some major monastic churches survived the Dissolution by being transformed into parish churches: to this category belong the magnificent Holy Cross, Shrewsbury (formerly Shrewsbury Abbey), and the parish churches of Bromfield, Chirbury and Morville (q.v.).

The foundations at Wombridge, Halston, Stanton Long, Church Preen and Ratlinghope and the friaries at Bridgnorth, Ludlow, Shrewsbury and Woodhouse have disappeared completely.

Place	Name of hospital	Founded	Subject to
Ludlow	St. John the Evangelist	?11th century	Palmers' Guild
Bridgnorth	Holy Trinity and St. John the Baptist	1199	Lilleshall
Oswestry	St. John the Baptist	1200-10	Haughmond, later Halston
Ludford	St. Giles (for lepers, 1216 later for almsfolk)		
Ludlow	Holy Trinity, the Virgin Mary and St. John the Baptist	1221	
Bridgnorth	St. James (and for lepers)	1224	
Bridgnorth	Vetus Maladeria (for lepers)	1231	
Nesscliff	St. Mary	c.1250	
Meole Brace		1277	
Bridgnorth	St. Leonard	1278	
Whitchurch		13th century	Haughmond
Newport	St. Giles	1337	
Tong	St. Bartholomew almshouses	1410	
Ludlow	St. John the Baptist	1411	(?the same as 5 above)
Newport	St. Nicholas	1446	
Ludlow	Hosyer's almshouses	1486	
Cleobury Mortimer	?St. Giles		

Table III Medieval Hospitals in Shropshire

5
Post-Reformation Churches

The 16th and 17th Centuries

Ludford aisle *c.*1555
Langley chapel** 1564/1601
Sutton Maddock tower 1579
Shipton chancel** 1589
Loughton 1622
Ratlinghope ?1625
Astley Abbots** chancel 1633
Myddle tower 1634
Adderley aisle 1635-36
More transept 1640

Shrawardinc* 1649
Stokesay** 1654
High Ercall restoration 1658-62
Sheriffhales 1661
Condover*** (most) 1662
Benthall* 1667
Little Berwick** 1672
Minsterley ** 1689
Great Bolas chancel – late 17th century

The building of churches in Shropshire, as in the rest of the country, came to an abrupt end at the Reformation. During the reign of Elizabeth I (1558-1603), only two new buildings were recorded: the chancel of the medieval church at Shipton (1589) and the Puritan chapel at Langley, variously dated 1564 and 1601. It is surprising that the chancel at Shipton was built not in Perpendicular but in Decorated style (Fig.5.1) – and interesting to note that a new window in Astley, dated 1568, is also Decorated. Furthermore, the chancel at Astley Abbots, dated 1633, is also Decorated in style.

But these were probably just exceptions to the general rule that during the 17th century a 'debased' form of Perpendicular was prevalent. Seven churches were certainly built during the course of the century – including Stokesay (Fig.5.2) and Benthall, rebuilt following damage to the medieval churches during the Civil War. There was also extensive rebuilding of Condover between 1662 and 1679 following the

Fig.5.1 Shipton: the chancel was built in 1589

collapse of the tower. How much of the masonry of Ratlinghope dates from the 17th century is quite unknown. A feature of 17th-century interiors was the hammer-beam roof, seen at Condover (Fig.8.15), Benthall, Sheriffhales and elsewhere (p.51). In all these churches the Gothic style prevailed, providing evidence of Gothic survival until the second half of the century; in none is there any trace of the classical architecture currently in vogue. Inigo Jones had built St. Paul's, Covent Garden in 1630,

Fig.5.2 The church at Stokesay was rebuilt after the Civil War

the first English church in classical style; and even a generation later when Sir Christopher Wren was building St. Paul's Cathedral and the City churches in Renaissance style, Shropshire was still wedded to outmoded Perpendicular.

But in 1689 came a sharp break with the past. Minsterley was the first Shropshire church built on classical lines, an essay in rural Baroque (Fig.21.10). It was also the first Shropshire church to be built in brick,

The 18th Century 1700 – *c.*1790 (architects in brackets)

Selattyn tower 1703
Whitchurch, St. Alkmund** 1712 (Barker)
Leighton** 1714
Hinstock* 1719
Buildwas 1720
Fitz* 1722
Great Bolas 1726-29 (Willdigg)
Petton*** 1727
Eaton Mascott 1735
Montford 1737 (Cooper)
Preston-upon-the-Weald Moors 1739
Stirchley** 1740
Sibdon Carwood 1741

Longdon upon Tern 1742
Eyton-upon-the-Weald Moors 1743
Myddle 1744 (Cooper)
Cardeston *1748
Shrewsbury, St. Julian** 1749 (Pritchard)
Coreley 1757
Quatt*** 1763
Hopton Cangeford 1766
Kinnerley* 1773 ?Pritchard
Cockshutt 1777
Great Wollaston 1788
Moreton Say** 1788
Weston-under-Redcastle 1790

As the table shows, there was a steady stream of new churches built throughout the 18th century, the majority being in the north of the county – only seven out of 28 are in the diocese of Hereford. The new churches were, of course, built for Protestant worship, with much greater emphasis on the preaching of the Word. There was less emphasis on the sacraments, so the chancel was often of modest size. The altar was often flanked by boards on which were inscribed the Ten Commandments, the Apostles' Creed and the Lord's Prayer. In towns, galleries were provided to accommodate large congregations; and even in village churches, galleries were often added as the century progressed. Most of the galleries in village churches have since been taken down, but a fair number remain. Many of the village churches were built of brick, often with stone dressings (e.g. Eyton-upon-the-Weald Moors [Fig.6.11]). The windows are wide, round-headed, usually with a keystone at the apex. Towers were usually topped with a balustrade and adorned with pinnacles or urns. Not all the churches listed were totally new builds – Quatt and Moreton Say were encased with brick and appear Georgian on the outside, but the interior reveals their medieval origins. Sometimes a Georgian tower was added to a medieval church – e.g. Chelmarsh, Westbury; in other places, the converse occurred, a Georgian nave being added to a medieval chancel (Stirchley) or tower (St. Julian's and St. Alkmund's, Shrewsbury [Fig.5.3] and Kinnerley).

Georgian architecture was unpopular in the 19th century. It is regrettable, but not surprising, that the Victorian restorers often drastically altered the character of the buildings by 'gothicising' the windows. After the High-Church revival, the chancels of Georgian churches were frequently extended or rebuilt to reflect the increased emphasis on the 'correct' administration of the sacraments. The greatest churches of this period are Whitchurch, and St. Julian, Shrewsbury; Leighton, Petton and Quatt earn their stars by the outstanding quality of their monuments or furniture and fittings. Details of the architects of the 18th and 19th centuries are summarised in Table IV.

Fig.5.3 The towers of St. Alkmund's (left) and St. Julian's, Shrewsbury. The towers are medieval, the naves 18th-century.

Architects	New Churches	Restorations and Extensions
Baddeley, J.	Tibberton 1842	
Barker, John (1668-1727)	Whitchurch, St. Alkmund 1712	
Blomfield, Sir Arthur (1829-99)	Jackfield 1863	Linley 1858
	Neenton 1871	Alveley 1878
	Glazeley 1875	Willey 1880
	Ludlow, St. John 1881	Bridgnorth, St. Mary Mag. 1875
Carline, John, sen. (1761-1835)	Shrewsbury, St. Alkmund 1793	Wrockwardine 1808
Carline, John. jun. (1792-1862)	Shrewsbury, St. Michael 1829	
	Grinshill 1839	
	Albrighton, near Shrewsbury 1840	
Cooper, William	Montford 1735	
	Myddle 1744	
Curzon, Henry (1839-91)	Norbury 1880 and 1892	
	Boraston 1884-87	
	Wentnor 1885	
Ebbels, Robert (?-1860)	?Priorslee 1836	
Eginton, Harvey (1809-49)	Broseley 1845	
	Dawley 1845	
Ferrey, Benjamin (1810-80)	Fauls 1856	
	Sambrook 1856	
	Chetwynd 1865	
Griffiths, R.	Dawley Parva 1845	Quatford 1857
	Farlow 1858	
Hamilton, George Ernest	Woore 1830	
Harrison, Thomas	Whittington 1805	
Hawkins, Rhode (1820-84)	Pradoe 1860	
Haycock, Edward sen. (1790-1870)	Shrewsbury, St. George 1829	Church Pulverbatch 1852
	Tilstock 1835	
	Whitchurch, St. Catherine 1836	
	Cruckton 1840	
	Cressage 1843	
	Chapel Lawn 1843	
	Bayston Hill 1843	
	Hope 1843	
	Middleton-in-Chirbury 1843	
	Dorrington 1843	
	Newcastle-on-Clun 1848	
	Shelton 1854	
Haycock, Edward jun. (1830-82)	Weston Lullingfields 1857	
	Welsh Frankton 1858	
	Yockleton 1861	
	Meole Brace 1867	
	Newtown 1869	
	Shrewsbury, All Saints 1875	
Kennedy, Henry (fl.1840-97)	Weston Rhyn 1878	
Lloyd, Rev. Alban	Hengoed 1849	
Lloyd-Oswell, Arthur	Bicton 1885	
	Shrewsbury, Holy Trinity 1886	
	All Stretton 1902	

Architects	New Churches	Restorations and Extensions
Nesfield, William Eden (1835-88)	Calverhall 1872	
Nicholson, Thomas (1823-95)	Llanfair Waterdine 1854 Bishop's Castle 1860 Hopton Castle 1871 Cleeton St. Mary 1878 Sutton Maddock 1888	
Owen, Thomas (1804-64)	Hadley 1856	
Parker, Rev. John	Llanyblodwel 1847	
Pearson, John L. (1817-98)		Shrewsbury Abbey 1886 Cheswardine 1888
Penson, Thomas (1790 1859)	Oswestry, Holy Trinity 1835 Llanymynech 1843	
Pritchard, Thomas Farnolls (1723-77)	Shrewsbury, St. Julian 1749 Kinnerley 1769	
St. Aubyn, James (1815-?)	Tuck Hill 1865	Clunbury
Scott, Sir George Gilbert (1811-79)	Donnington Wood 1843 Welshampton 1863 Ludlow, St. Leonard 1870	Ludlow, St. Lawrence 1839 West Felton 1841 Ellesmere 1849 Cleobury Mortimer 1874 Shifnal 1876
Shaw, Richard Norman (1831-1912)	Peplow 1879 Richard's Castle 1891	
Slater, William (1818/9-72)	Bridgnorth, St. Leonard 1860	
Smith, S. Pountney (1811/2-83)	Harley 1846 Little Drayton 1847 Uffington 1856 Leaton 1859 Shrewsbury, St. Giles 1860 Hope Bowdler 1863 Preston Gubbals 1866	Cound 1862 Church Stretton 1866
Smith, Samuel	Wrockwardine Wood 1833	
Smith, Thomas	Ironbridge 1835 Wellington, Christ Church 1838 Eaton Constantine 1847	
Steuart, George (c.1730-1806)	Wellington, All Saints 1788 Shrewsbury, St. Chad 1790	
Street, George Edmund (1824-81)	St. George's 1861 Waters Upton c.1865 Church Aston 1867 Whixall 1867 Lyneal 1870 Withington 1874	Upton Magna 1856 Oswestry, St. Oswald 1872 Clun 1877
Telford, Thomas (1757-1834)	Bridgnorth, St. Mary Magdalene 1792 Madeley 1794 Malinslee 1805	
Whitling, Henry John	Cwm Head 1842	
Willdigg, John	Great Bolas 1726	

Table IV Architects of the 18th and 19th centuries

The Greek Revival, *c.*1790-1836

Wellington, All Saints** 1790 (Steuart)
Shrewsbury, St. Chad*** 1790 (Steuart)
Bridgnorth, St. Mary Magdalene** (Telford)
Madeley** 1796 (Telford)
Adderley* 1801
Whittington 1804 (Harrison)
Malinslee* 1805 (Telford)
Frodesley* 1809

Trefonen 1821
Hopton Wafers 1827
Shrewsbury, St. Michael 1829 (Carline)
Woore 1830
Wrockwardine Wood 1833
Tilstock 1835
Whitchurch St. Catherine 1836

The relatively short-lived Greek Revival dates from a visit to Athens (then part of the Ottoman Empire) between 1751 and 1755 by two young architects, James Stuart (Athenian Stuart) and Nicholas Revett. There they studied Greek architecture, and after their return they published *Antiquities of Athens* in successive volumes. Enthusiasm for the Greek style was rather slow in developing until late in the 18th century when established architects such as George Dance the Younger and Henry Holland became interested. Lord Elgin, British Ambassador at Constantinople from 1799-1803, studied the ruins of the Parthenon in Athens and brought the Elgin marbles to England because they were in great danger of neglect and destruction. This augmented the public interest in all things Greek, and encouraged leading architects such as Sir John Soane, Sir Robert Smirke and John Nash. In the 1820s the Greek struggle for independence caught the public imagination, especially when Lord Byron became involved – he died during the Greek war of independence in 1824. But by the mid-1830s the Greek revival was over, the style lacking staying power and being swept away by enthusiasm for Gothic.

During this time Greek churches were built in relatively small numbers up and down the land, the best being in London. Few of the Shropshire churches listed above really show many of the characteristics of the Greek revival, yet they are different from the Georgian churches earlier discussed. All show some classical features, and they are emphatically not Gothic. The finest churches were all built in the 1790s – Steuart's churches at Shrewsbury and Wellington, and Telford's at Bridgnorth and Madeley. These are described in the gazetteer. The last Anglican churches to be built in the Classical manner were two by Edward Haycock sen. – Tilstock (1835), and St. Catherine, Whitchurch (1836) – though the Congregational church at Whitchurch dates from 1846.

The Gothic Revival

During the whole of the reign of Queen Victoria (1837-1901), nearly every Anglican church was built in the Gothic style – a choice which would have seemed unaccountable to Sir Christopher Wren and his immediate successors in the 18th century. But from about 1750 choice spirits such as Thomas Gray (of the famous 'Elegy') and Horace Walpole were growing dissatisfied with Classical forms and were beginning to regard medieval architecture with greater enthusiasm than their contemporaries. Walpole (1717-97) bought a former coachman's cottage near Twickenham and gradually converted it into the stuccoed and battlemented Strawberry Hill. This influential building started a fashion for Gothic amongst some aristocrats, who delighted in building sham castles, follies, and sometimes more substantial edifices. But 'Gothick' in the last half of the 18th century was not the preserve only of eccentric plutocrats – a handful of churches were built in the picturesque version of the style which had involved, including Shobdon (Herefordshire) and Croome d'Abitot (Worcestershire). The earliest Shropshire church which can claim to derive from the incipient Gothic revival is St. Alkmund's, Shrewsbury, designed by John Carline and John Tilley (1793-95) – the Decorated tracery of the windows being combined with a rather barn-like interior. Only two other churches followed in the first 30 years of the 19th century – Longford (1802-06), now closed, and the rebuilding of the tower and nave at Pontesbury by John Turner (1829). Here, before the Revival got fully under way, was a masterly essay in Gothic, complete with arcades and windows exhibiting both Y- and intersecting tracery.

The years of the Napoleonic Wars brought church-building virtually to a halt throughout the country, and Shropshire was not exempt from this: very little was built between Telford's churches of the 1790s and Pontesbury. But social unrest and dissent were growing, especially in the newly-industrialised cities (including the area in Shropshire which later became Telford); the establishment, both government and ecclesiastical, looked nervously across the Channel and was keen to avoid similar troubles at home. From the established church's point of view, dissent was rampant as the Methodists moved steadily away from the Church of England and set up their own organisation. So, in 1818, the Church founded the Church Building Society and in the same year Parliament passed the Church Building Act. This provided £1m to be spent by the Commissioners, and the churches resulting from the Act were known as Commissioners' Churches. It has been estimated that between 1818 and 1833, the Commissioners actually spent £6m, and 214 churches were built throughout the country. Very few of them were in Shropshire, and on the whole Commissioners' Churches were not highly regarded. Many of them were in a starved Early English style, and some of Edward Haycock senior's churches of the 1830s and 1840s were probably influenced by them.

At this time more serious study of Gothic building was being undertaken; in 1817 Thomas Rickman published his *Attempt to discriminate the Styles of English Architecture* (see p.12). As a result of this, architects began consciously to look back to medieval styles, now formally described as Norman (or Romanesque), and the three styles of Gothic: Early English, Decorated and Perpendicular. Then, under the influence of Augustus Pugin, a revolution in taste was rapidly accomplished.

Augustus W.N. Pugin (1812-52) was born in London, the son of a French refugee from the Revolution and an English Presbyterian mother. Pugin *père* became a draughtsman in John Nash's office and specialised in the study of Gothic architecture. Pugin junior early developed a passion for Gothic, and this became an *idée fixe* throughout his short and tumultuous life. It led him in 1833 to convert to the Roman Catholic Church, then newly emancipated, in which he doubtless hoped to be able to express his love for Gothic. Not the least irony of Pugin's life is that his ideas made little headway in the Roman church, which by and large remained wedded to Italianate forms, yet they were taken up uncritically and enthusiastically in the church he had forsaken, the Church of England. Pugin analysed the various styles of Gothic and decided that in the Decorated style, Gothic had attained perfection. After initial experimentation with Early English, this was later held to be immature, while Perpendicular was regarded as 'decadent', or worse, tainted with Protestantism. It was Pugin who first propounded an idea which seems incomprehensible to us, that good architecture can come only from good men – a thesis taken up by a greater writer than Pugin, the staunchly Protestant, if somewhat sceptical, John Ruskin.

In the same year that Pugin converted to Roman Catholicism, life began to stir in the established church. It cannot be denied that the Church of England at this time was at a low ebb. Morale had suffered as its earlier monopoly was assailed by Methodists and other dissenters on the one hand and Roman Catholics on the other. But regeneration was at hand which ensured that by the end of the 19th century much of the lost ground would be reclaimed; the Anglican church in 1900 was much more confident of its future than it had been 70 years earlier – in fact, over-confident in the light of the century that was to follow! The vehicles for this transformation were the Oxford Movement and the Cambridge Camden Society.

In Oxford in 1833, John Keble preached a famous sermon on National Apostasy, and he was joined by Pusey, Newman and others in launching the Oxford Movement, intent on reviving Anglican worship by a greater insistence on correct liturgical and sacramental observance. But it was at Cambridge that the trend towards Gothic architecture became most effectively underpinned. There, in 1839, a group of undergraduates, including J.M. Neale (now remembered chiefly for his hymns), formed the Cambridge Camden Society, dedicated to the reform of church architecture and ritual. In 1841 they started to publish the monthly magazine *The Ecclesiologist*, which lasted until 1868 and which achieved a dominating, some would say a tyrannical, influence over the design of churches. In its pages, new churches were regularly reviewed, and every detail of architectural and liturgical significance was assessed. The aim throughout was to influence the building so that it could readily express High-Church ritual which was held to be essential to the gospel.

The years of Queen Victoria's reign witnessed an explosion of church building in Shropshire unequalled since the 12th century. A total of at least 85 completely new churches was built, and a number of others were rebuilt, retaining only the medieval tower (as at Bishop's Castle and Cheswardine). Nearly every other church was 'restored', for better, or sometimes for worse, and the scale of restoration was sometimes so huge that virtually a new church resulted (as at Ellesmere, by Sir George Gilbert Scott). As the table below shows, the number of new churches was fairly evenly distributed through the decades 1830-79, but from 1880 onwards there was a notable slackening of the rate of new building.

1830-39	13	1870-79	15
1840-49	20	1880-89	6
1850-59	15	1890-99	2
1860-69	14	Total	85

It will be convenient to divide these churches into three arbitrary groups: early Victorian (1830-49); high Victorian (1850-79); and late Victorian (1880-99).

Early Victorian Churches (1830-49)

Classical	4
Neo-Norman	5
Early English	20
Perpendicular	2
Part N/N, part E/E	2

The 1830s and 1840s were on the whole bleak years for the architecture of Shropshire churches. Not one of these churches is really distinguished, and only one (Donnington Wood – an early work of Sir George Gilbert Scott, see below) is by an architect with a national reputation. Of the 33 churches built between 1830 and 1849, 20 are in a very plain Gothic style, nearly always Early English, with lancet windows. Four churches were built in the fast-disappearing Classical style (see p.30), the last being St Catherine, Whitchurch in 1836. Five are in the neo-Norman style (Grinshill 1839, Albrighton near Shrewsbury 1840, St. Luke, Dawley Parva – now disused; Cwm Head; and Llanymynech, all started in 1845). This style was a footnote to the Gothic Revival, a short-lived fashion for the revival of Romanesque styles, either Norman or Italian. Of the Shropshire examples, Llanymynech and Grinshill are the best. Two churches, Doddington (1849) and Ketley (1838), show some neo-Norman features but are predominantly Early English. So the neo-Norman style was only briefly in favour, being confined mainly to the 1840s.

The most prolific of the local architects in these decades was Edward Haycock senior (1790-1870), who was responsible for about 13 churches, the best of which are probably Cressage and Dorrington. Colvin's assessment was not flattering: 'He was a Greek Revivalist of some merit [Tilstock, St. Catherine Whitchurch], but his numerous Gothic churches, mostly in the lancet style, are however routine productions of their time.'[1]

John Carline jun. (1792-1859) built St. Michael, Shrewsbury (Fig.19.28) in the Greek style in 1829, and two of the neo-Norman churches, Grinshill and Albrighton near Shrewsbury.

Thomas Penson (*c.*1790-1859) built Holy Trinity, Oswestry in the Early English style, and a few years later the neo-Norman Llanymynech (Fig.15.10).

The best church of the 1840s is Broseley (Fig.23.6) built by Harvey Eginton. This is a stately town church, much more substantial than the Early English examples and, unusually for its time, built in the Perpendicular style. It is very correct, with its lofty arcades, high clerestory, and tower with rather top-heavy battlements. Holy Trinity, Dawley, just a few miles away, was built in the same year by the same architect, but is much less impressive.

High Victorian Churches (1850-79)

Early English	16
Decorated	26
Perpendicular	2

During the 1840s, while Shropshire churches were being built in an uninspired and plain Early English style, more ambitious designs were being built in London and elsewhere.[2] The

Gothic Revival was by now firmly established and, as we have seen, these years were dominated by the opinions of *The Ecclesiologist* which favoured the Decorated style. In London, Richard Carpenter built St. Mary Magdalene, St Pancras (1849), and Benjamin Ferrey built St. Stephen, Rochester Row (1847), both in an expensive Decorated style. Then, in 1850, came Butterfield's All Saints, Margaret Street, the church which has remained the symbol of the High-Church movement and which became enormously influential. Butterfield was the first to bring structural polychromy into churches, bringing back colour to English church interiors for the first time since the Reformation.

Shropshire duly followed suit, after an appropriate interval. Of the 44 churches built between 1850 and 1879, only 16 were Early English, while 26 were in the Decorated style. Analysis of the figures decade by decade confirms that Early English was steadily passing out of fashion, and Decorated was increasingly favoured, in conformity with the views of Pugin and *The Ecclesiologist*. During these decades, architects with a national practice were building up to one-third of Shropshire churches, as set out below:

Sir George Gilbert Scott	3
Benjamin Ferrey	3
George Edmund Street	6
Sir Arthur Blomfield	4
Richard Norman Shaw	2
John Loughborough Pearson	2 (part)

Sir George Gilbert Scott (1811-78) is by far the best known of the Victorian architects, and of course he was a great populariser of Gothic. Moreover, in his reading of Pugin in 1840 he experienced something akin to a religious conversion. 'I was awakened from my slumbers by the thunder of Pugin's writings. I well remember the enthusiasm to which one of them excited me, one night when travelling by railway, in the first years of their existence. I was from that moment a new man. What for 15 years had been a labour of love only, now became the one business, the one aim, the one overmastering object of my life. I cared for nothing as regarded my art but the revival of Gothic architecture.' John Wesley could not have phrased it better.

And yet, in spite of the earnestness of his conviction, he fails to convince us of the grandness of his vision: his reputation today is probably less than that of his contemporaries, Butterfield, Street and Pearson, all of whom had a streak of originality which was denied to Gilbert

Fig.5.4 Welshampton by Sir George Gilbert Scott (1863)

Scott. Having said that, there is no doubt that Scott's 1861 church at Welshampton (Fig.5.4) is distinguished (see p.123). By contrast, his churches at Donnington Wood (1843) and Ludlow St. Leonard (1870; now closed) are simpler and much less impressive. Scott also built the chancel at West Felton and restored many churches, notably Ellesmere, Cleobury Mortimer, Ludlow St. Laurence and Shifnal.

Benjamin Ferrey (1810-80) built three churches in Shropshire: Fauls (1856), Chetwynd (1856) and Sambrook (1865). He was a pupil of Pugin, and so closely influenced by him that he subsequently wrote *Recollections of A.N. Welby Pugin* (1861). All his churches show a great attention to detail, with a concern accurately to reproduce Gothic architecture. He was not, however, an architect of genius, nor was he a striking innovator. Chetwynd (Fig.5.5) is by far the best of his Shropshire churches, though Sambrook also is pleasing.

G.E. Street (1824-81) was an outstanding architect, perhaps his most famous church being St. James the Less, Vauxhall Bridge

Fig.5.5 Chetwynd by Benjamin Ferrey (1865)

Road, Westminster. In early life he was an assistant to Scott, but outshone his master in originality and boldness of effect. In the early 1850s he travelled in France, Germany and Italy and in 1855 he published *Brick and Marble Architecture in Italy*. He was closely associated with Butterfield and The Ecclesiological Society, and had clearly been influenced by All Saints, Margaret Street, where he was a churchwarden for many years. In Shropshire, he extensively restored Upton Magna and Clun, and all but rebuilt St. Oswald, Oswestry. He

also built six new churches in the county: St. George's near Telford (Fig.20.14) is the outstanding Shropshire church of the mid-century, and deserves to be much better known. Withington, Lyneal (Fig.5.6) and Church Aston are also rewarding; Waters Upton and Whixall perhaps less so.

Sir Arthur Blomfield (1829-99) was the son of the Right Reverend C.J. Blomfield, bishop of London, and he designed a great number of rather conven-

Fig.5.6 Lyneal by G.E. Street (1870)

Fig.5.7 Jackfield by Sir Arthur Blomfield (1863)

tional Victorian churches, notably the nave of Southwark Cathedral. His Shropshire churches are not outstanding: they comprise Jackfield (1863, the best, Fig.5.7), Neenton (1871), Glazeley (1875) and St. John, Ludlow (1881).

Of the other Victorian architects of the first rank, William Butterfield (1814-1900) designed no churches in Shropshire, but his polychromatic influence may be seen at Jackfield. But John Loughborough Pearson was an architect of distinction who designed Truro Cathedral and St. Augustine, Kilburn – possibly the finest Victorian church in England. In 1886 he came to Shropshire, where he rebuilt the east end of Shrewsbury Abbey, displaying his special expertise in vaulting (Fig.19.14). In the same year he designed Cheswardine church, retaining the medieval tower and meticulously re-locating the Early English north chancel chapel. Cheswardine is a marvellous example of mid-Victorian architecture at its best – Pearson sensitively retained much of the medieval masonry of the Norman south arcade and the Early English north arcade, and the work has a sense of proportion and nobility which is hard to match. And yet for its date (1886) it is essentially conservative, being characteristic more of the 1860s than the 1880s (which is why I have included it under the High Victorian phase). Seven years earlier, a younger architect, Richard Norman Shaw at Peplow, was pointing the way forward (see below).

Several regional architects designed Victorian churches of some character. S. Pountney Smith (1812-83) was responsible for seven churches, including Little Drayton (1847), Uffington (1856), Leaton (1859) and Hope Bowdler (1863). Leaton (Fig.1.6) is excellent – an essay in Early English and Decorated – and ranks with Meole Brace (below) as the finest Victorian church in the county by a local architect.

Edward Haycock jun. was rather more adventurous than his father, and in particular Meole Brace is excellent, worth visiting for its architecture and for its stained glass. Other good churches by this architect are All Saints, Shrewsbury, Welsh Frankton and Yockleton.

Another little-known mid-Victorian church worth noticing is Pradoe, by Rhode Hawkins. Madge Moran has called the roof 'a Gothic pastiche of 13th-century design'.

Late Victorian Churches (1880-1901)

From 1880 onwards, there was a noticeable slackening in the rate of building of new churches, and only eight completely new churches were constructed during the last 20 years of Queen Victoria's reign. Only one of these is outstanding – and it was the last church to be built in Shropshire in the 19th century.

Richard Norman Shaw (1831-1912) had been a pupil of G.E. Street and built a number of churches and many domestic buildings, including several in Shropshire, notably Adcote, a country house near Baschurch. He blended with great freedom an interest in Gothic, particularly Perpendicular, architecture and, especially in his domestic buildings, features of the 17th and 18th centuries (the 'Queen Anne' style). Like Butterfield, Street and Pearson, he had a general loyalty to the High-Church movement in the Anglican church. By the last 20 years of the century, the floridities found in the 1860s when the Decorated style was dominant were less apparent, and both Shaw and his contemporary Bodley favoured Perpendicular. In 1879 he built the Chapel of the Epiphany at Peplow (Fig.16.18) which although a humble church, is significant for already there are signs of the changes to come. It is not Gothic at all – the windows are plain and horizontal – and the design is notable for the half-timbering with brick infilling, known as 'nogging'.

Twelve years later came the much more substantial church at Richard's Castle (Fig.5.8), a village which bestrides the Herefordshire/Shropshire border. The massive south-west tower stands away from the south aisle, and there is an imposing entrance next to the tower. The interior is spacious and light-filled, with windows in the Decorated and Perpendicular styles. Compared with earlier Victorian architects there is no escaping that Shaw's church is restrained and highly effective.

Fig.5.8 Richard's Castle by Richard Norman Shaw (1891)

In some ways, Norman Shaw was a transitional figure, because from his work at Richard's Castle came the commission for his former pupil William Lethaby for the new church at Brockhampton-by-Ross, Herefordshire (1901), where the beginnings of modern architecture are plain for all to see. And so at the end of Queen Victoria's reign, the Gothic Revival was already passing into history. But Gothic took a long time to die – in Shropshire as late as 1928 a 'Perpendicular' church was built at Gobowen which owed nothing to the modern movement, and over the country as a whole a sort of stripped Gothic persisted until after the Second World War. The wheel has now come full circle: Victorian churches in Shropshire, as elsewhere, have long been underestimated, but, freed from ecclesiological controversy, they can now be appreciated at their true value.

20th-Century Churches

All Stretton 1902	Harlescott, The Holy Spirit** 1961
Little Stretton 1903	Brookside 1967
Gobowen 1928	Stirchley, All Saints 1976
Wattlesborough 1931	Bayston Hill 1983
Harlescott, The Holy Spirit, Roseway 1936 (closed)	Muxton 1997
Monkmoor 1939	Harlescott, Emmanuel* 2001

In comparison with the 18th and 19th centuries, the contribution of the 20th century to Shropshire churches is meagre. After the Second World War, all the new churches were in outer Shrewsbury and in the new town of Telford. The best two churches were built in Harlescott, a northern suburb of Shrewsbury (Fig.1.7). It is disappointing that no outstanding church has yet been built to grace Telford – an area with a great many undistinguished churches of the 18th and 19th centuries. I hope that this deficiency may be made good in the 21st century. A first-class modern church, preferably ecumenical, might do much to reach the unchurched population of Telford. In the south of the county, the town which is in greatest need of a new church is Craven Arms: this is recognised as a centre for growth – at present, there are two parish churches on the outskirts (Stokesay and Halford), both remote from the centre of population.

6
Towers and Spires

Medieval towers

To the world outside, the tower is the most obvious and accessible part of the village

Fig.6.1 An Early English tower with a Perpendicular top at Atcham

church, often visible for miles around. Shropshire towers are modest in comparison with those, say, of Somerset or East Anglia, but nevertheless they are a familiar and much-loved element in the village scene. Of the 320 churches reviewed here, at least 186 (58%) have towers. Eighty-six survive from medieval times, spread fairly evenly from the 12th to the 16th centuries. One difficulty in dating towers is that windows were often later inserted into an earlier structure: thus an Early English window may be found in a Norman tower, causing considerable confusion. Another difficulty in classification is that parts of some towers were built at widely different periods: the lower storeys might be Norman or Early English, and the belfry Perpendicular (e.g. Atcham [Fig.6.1]; Shrewsbury, St. Julian [Fig.5.3]). Another source of confusion is the number of towers built during the transition period between successive medieval styles (e.g. Norman/Early English, for towers built *c*.1200, and Early English/ Decorated for towers built *c*.1300). After trying to take all these factors into consideration, I classified the surviving towers as follows (with Cranage's figures placed in parenthesis):

Norman	20 (23)
Early English	30 (21)
Decorated	11 (14)
Perpendicular	25 (27)

When one recalls that only a handful of Shropshire churches are mainly Perpendicular, it is obvious that there must be many churches in which a Perpendicular tower has been added to a much earlier structure.

39

Fig.6.3 *The corbel-table above the belfry windows at Linley*

Fig.6.2 *The heavily buttressed central tower at Wrockwardine*

By far the commonest site for the tower is at the west end of the nave, and the ground floor of the tower usually opens into the nave through a tower arch. Of the 82 medieval towers in Shropshire, 64 (79%) are western. Cruciform churches, with a central tower and transepts, are unusual in villages, but tend to occur more frequently in small towns; there are only ten in Shropshire (Church Stretton, Ellesmere, Ludlow, Neen Sollars, Shifnal, St. Mary Shrewsbury, Stanton Lacy, Tong, Wistanstow, Wrockwardine [Fig.6.2]). Five churches have a north or north-western tower (Alberbury, Bromfield, Clungunford, Hodnet and Worfield) and seven have a south, south-western or south-eastern tower (St. Leonard Bridgnorth, Child's Ercall, Claverley, Cleobury North, Eaton-under-Heywood, Oswestry and Worfield).

There are no Saxon towers in Shropshire (though the bases of Diddlebury and Stottesdon are probably partly Saxon), so the earliest structures date back to Norman times: squat, sturdy, solidly-built, with thick walls. In the west of the county, (e.g. at Clun [Fig.2.6]), some may have been built partly to offer refuge to the people in times of border warfare (as in Northumberland). At belfry level, there are usually two round-headed windows divided by a shaft, with a large round-headed arch surmounting both. At Linley (Fig.6.3) there is a corbel-table above the belfry windows with carved heads

Fig.6.4 *The saddleback tower at Alberbury as painted by Mary Parker in 1835*

Fig.6.5 Clasping buttresses at the lower part (Norman) of the tower at Albrighton. The top is Perpendicular

Fig.6.6 Early English tower at Tugford. Corner buttresses at right-angles to each other and sloping set-offs to shed rainwater

Fig.6.7 Decorated tower and recessed spire at Worfield

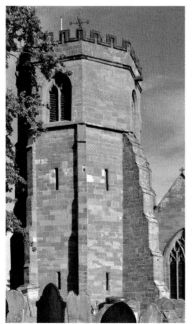

Fig.6.8 Octagonal tower at Hodnet

in the Kilpeck manner. The roof may be flat and plain, but can be pyramidal. Clun, Hopesay and More have a double-pyramid roof. Alberbury (Fig.6.4) is unique in the county in having a gabled roof known as a saddleback. Buttresses in the 12th century usually clasp the angles of the tower (e.g. Albrighton, near Shifnal [Fig.6.5]).

Early English towers have pointed lancet windows, and the belfry windows become more prominent, in the later part of the 13th century often showing Y-tracery.

Buttresses were usually placed at each corner, at right-angles to each other. The projection of the buttresses diminishes towards the top of the tower, and was reduced stepwise with a sloping set-off to shed rainwater (e.g. Tugford [Fig.6.6]).

Decorated towers were typically of four storeys: the ground floor opened into the nave through the tower arch; above this, a ringers' gallery with small windows; then the belfry with prominent windows; and at the top, the roof sometimes surmounted by a spire (e.g. Worfield [Fig.6.7]). Buttressing in the 14th and later centuries was

Fig.6.9 Perpendicular tower with decorated frieze, battlements, and corner pinnacles at Shawbury

Fig.6.10 The central tower at Church Stretton. The lower part is Early English. Is the Perpendicular top before or after the Reformation?

usually diagonal, placed at the corners of the structure. The tower at Hodnet (Fig.6.8), octagonal from bottom to top, is unique in Shropshire.

In the Perpendicular period towers are usually topped by a battlemented parapet, and below this, in the north of the county, is often a decorative frieze (e.g. Cheswardine [Fig.16.3]; Shawbury [Fig.6.9]; Ightfield [Fig.16.11]). This may take the form of a band of quatrefoils or saltires; the most southerly examples in Shropshire are Donington and Wroxeter, but they are frequent in the neighbouring part of Staffordshire and may represent a local school of masons.[1] Parapets were developed when lead roofing was introduced and necessitated the lowering of the pitch of the roof. Previously the roof may have been supported at the eaves by a corbel-table, (as at Linley [Fig.6.3]) overlapping it so that rainwater was thrown clear of the walls. When the roof became flatter, it ended in a gutter behind the parapet from which the water then escaped through spouts (gargoyles), often fantastically carved into grotesque shapes, which project from the wall just below the parapet (Fig.16.11). There are numerous churches in Shropshire with Perpendicular battlements and parapets added to a Norman or Early English tower (e.g. Atcham [Fig.6.1]).

Fig.6.11 Georgian tower and nave at Eyton-upon-the-Weald Moors

Fig.6.12 Victorian tower added to a medieval nave at Hadnall

Fig.6.13 Broach spire at Yockleton

Post-Reformation Towers

At least six towers were built in the 17th century, all except Minsterley being in late Perpendicular style. Indeed it is sometimes impossible to say whether a late Perpendicular tower is before or after the Reformation (e.g. Church Stretton [Fig.6.10]). Minsterley broke new ground (see p.223) and instituted a totally different style, which was taken up enthusiastically in the 18th century.

There are 32 Georgian towers, a few of which were added to medieval naves (e.g. Chelmarsh [Fig.24.11]), but most were an integral part of a new 18th-century church (e.g. Eyton-upon-the-Weald Moors [Fig.6.11]). They usually display classical features – wide arched windows, often with a keystone, and sometimes with pediments and pilasters; at the top there is often a balustrade with urns or pinnacles at the corners.

In the 19th century there was an explosion of church building, and there are at least 57 towers from this period in the county. During the first 30 years, the style adopted was usually classical, but from 1840 onwards as the Gothic Revival came into full swing, towers were built in Early English, Decorated, Perpendicular, or even in a few cases neo-Norman, styles. Usually the rest of the church was built or rebuilt at the same time as the tower (e.g. Dorrington [Fig.6.15]), but occasionally a 19th-century tower was added to a medieval or 18th-century nave (e.g. Acton Burnell, Aston Botterell, Clungunford, Hadnall [Fig.6.12]). I have found only five towers constructed in the 20th century – Gobowen, Kemberton, St. George's and the two churches of The Holy Spirit, Harlescott, Shrewsbury.

Spires

Spires are not common in Shropshire; in compiling this survey I noted 30, of which only 11 are certainly medieval. In addition, there are numerous 'spirelets'. Spires may be of stone or timber, and timber spires are usually covered with shingles or, sometimes, lead.[2] The construction of spires presented a problem: spires were usually octagonal, and it was difficult to effect a transition between this and the four-sided tower. At least three types of spire may be recognised. In broach spires, semi-pyramidal pieces of masonry are used to buttress the spire at each corner of the tower (e.g. Yockleton [Fig.6.13]). In the chamfered, or splayed-foot spire, instead of broaches the lower part of the octagonal spire is pared down; the cardinal faces of the spire in effect are extended outwards at the foot to meet at the corner angles of the top of the tower (e.g. Ditton Priors [Fig.26.9]; Norbury [Fig.6.14]). This is the commonest type of spire in Shropshire. In recessed spires, the spire is set within a parapet (e.g. Dorrington [Fig.6.15]). Most of the spires from the Early English or Decorated eras were broach or chamfered spires; following the introduction of lead in the Perpendicular period, recessed spires evolved. Details of Shropshire spires are summarised in Table V.

Fig.6.14 Chamfered or splayed-foot spire at Norbury

Fig.6.15 Recessed spire within a parapet at Dorrington

Broach	Chamfered	Recessed	Unclassified
Astley Abbots	Ashford Bowdler (M)	Clive	Llanyblodwel
Bitterley (M)	Bedstone (M)	Dorrington	Oswestry, Holy Trinity
Culmington (M)	Boningale	Leaton	Pradoe
Yockleton	Chetwynd	Shrewsbury, St. Alkm. (M)	Welsh Frankton
	Cleobury Mortimer (M)	Shrewsbury, St. Mary (M)	Withington
	Ditton Priors (M)	Tong (M)	
	Nash (M)	Worfield (M)	
	Neen Sollars (?M)		
	Norbury		
	Sambrook		
	Sidbury		
	Smethcott		
	Stowe		
	Woolstaston		

Table V Shropshire Spires (M = medieval)

7
Porches

In the Middle Ages many ceremonies took place at the church door. Here was performed the early part of the baptism and marriage services; penance, the churching of women and pronouncements of outlawry were also made there.[1] In general it was not until the 14th century that porches were erected to give shelter, usually, but not always, over the south door. A high proportion of Shropshire churches have porches, and a few are of special significance or beauty. Wooden porches are found in many village churches, while town churches usually have porches of stone.

The finest medieval timber-framed porches are at Billingsley and Munslow (Fig.7.1). The date of the former is uncertain: Pevsner says probably *c.*1500, while Cranage ascribes it to the middle of the 14th century. Dendrochronology is needed! The bargeboarding of the gable displays quatrefoiled panelling, and the sides have pierced tracery, with ogee arches on the east and round arches on the west. Munslow is also splendid – the open sides display ogee tracery on the west and Y-tracery on the east. This also has been thought to be 14th-century. Other handsome medieval porches are at Lydbury North, Neen Savage and Onibury.

Two fine 17th-century wooden porches are at Cardington (1639) and Worthen. At the former (Fig.7.4), the timber-framed gable has a cross-beam and semicircles, and the sides

Fig.7.2 17th-century porch at Worthen, with open woodwork at the sides

Fig.7.1 Medieval timber-framed porch at Munslow

and gate are balustered. The sides are also balustered at Worthen (Fig.7.2). Barrow has a brick porch, dated 1705 (Fig.23.1).

Stone porches are found in most of the medieval town churches, and several are two-storeyed (Claverley [Fig.7.3], Clun, Ludlow, Much Wenlock, Shifnal [Fig.7.5], Shrewsbury St. Mary). The porch at Shrewsbury Abbey is three-storeyed. The porches at Ludlow, Shifnal and Shrewsbury St. Mary are rib-vaulted with a central boss. The earliest stone porch is probably that at Shrewsbury St. Mary (*c*.1200), and Much Wenlock (Fig.23.18) and Shifnal are also Early English (13th-century). The porches at Clun and Ludlow are Decorated. That at Ludlow is truly remarkable – one of only three hexagonal porches in England (the others are at St. Mary Redcliffe, Bristol, and Chipping Norton, Oxfordshire). There are windows with Decorated tracery on either side. Embattled Perpendicular porches may be seen at Claverley and Ightfield. The three-storeyed porch at Shrewsbury Abbey is also Perpendicular.

Fig.7.3 Embattled two-storey porch at Claverley

Fig.7.4 St. James, Cardington

Fig.7.5 Early English two-storeyed porch at Shifnal

8
Roofs and Vaults

In medieval churches, the timber framework of the roof supports the actual waterproofing material. In the earliest days, the latter consisted of primitive thatching with turf or heather (or occasionally reed), but by the end of the 12th century in eastern England clay roofing tiles had been introduced. Alternatively, long pointed tiles made of split wood (shingles) were used and pegged to boarding beneath. In the early Middle Ages, the pitches of roofs in northern countries were steep to prevent lodging of vast amounts of snow in winter. Following the widespread introduction of lead as a roofing material later in the Middle Ages, it became necessary to lower the pitch to prevent sheets of lead 'creeping' down the roof.

Church roofs may be divided into two basic types: either single-framed roofs, in which there are no principal rafters, all rafters being the same size, each pair being pegged together at the apex; or double-framed roofs, divided into bays by the principal rafters. Simple single-framed roofs developed relatively early in the Middle Ages, the earliest surviving example in Shropshire probably being in the north transept at Wistanstow (Fig.8.1). Cranage said that this type of simple trussed-rafter roof became common in the latter part of the 12th century.[1] His view has now been triumphantly confirmed by denrochronology, giving a date for Wistanstow of 1192-1226. This is the earliest dendrochronological dating yet obtained in any Shropshire building – see Table VI.[2] Another early example of a trussed-rafter roof is the north aisle at Westbury (Fig.21.15); this has been dated to 1342. Such a roof consisted of a longitudinal beam (the ridge-piece) which extended along the whole length of the apex of the roof, supported at each end by the gables. From either side of the ridge-piece, pairs of rafters extended laterally to the wall plates which were laid along the tops of the side-walls. Each pair of common rafters, trussed or not, is an independent unit of the roof, and is sometimes supported by transverse collar-beams, short horizontal timbers placed below the ridge-piece. Occasionally scissor-beams were used: these support the common rafters above

Wistantstow north transept	1192-1226
Clungunford chancel	1329
Clungunford nave	1338-39
Westbury north aisle	1342
Shrewsbury Abbey	
bell-chamber	1365-95
tower	1380-95
Halston	1437
Clunbury nave	1494-95

Fig.8.1 Wistanstow: the roof over the north transept (dated 1192-1226)

Table VI Dendrochronological dating of medieval church roofs

Fig.8.3 Seven-canted trussed-rafter roof at Longnor

the level of the collar-beams, and were placed diago-nally between opposite rafters (as, for example, in the Victorian church at Pradoe). There are a good number of single-framed trussed-rafter roofs in Shropshire, not all of them medieval. Some of the best examples may be seen at Chelmarsh (Fig.8.2), Church Stretton, Kinlet, Longnor (Fig.8.3), and Neen Sollars.

In double-framed roofs, principal rafters occur at intervals between the common rafters, dividing the roof into a series of units (Figs.8.4 & 8.5). The commonest types of double-framed roofs employ tie-beams, or collar-beams; both tie-beams and collar-beams are often supported by arched braces. Tie-beams were transverse timbers inserted to tie the wall-plates together to prevent them slipping off

Fig.8.2 Single-framed trussed-rafter roof at Chelmarsh

Fig.8.6 Tie-beams and queen-posts at Onibury

Fig.8.7 Collar-beams on arched braces and three tiers of wind-braces at Bettws-y-Crwyn

48

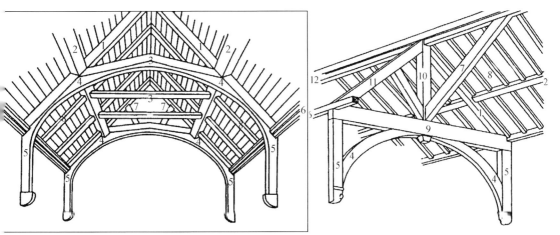

Figs.8.4 & 8.5 The Timbers of a Roof: On the left is an example of an arch-braced roof and on the right a king-post roof construction. Various timbers are identified thus:
1. Principal (sometimes Principal Rafter) 2. Purlin 3. Collar-beam 4. Arch-brace
5. Wall-post 6. Wall-plate 7. Longitudinal strut 8. Common rafter 9. Tie-beam
10. King-post 11. Transverse strut (queen-posts if there is no king-post)
12. Ridge-piece or -board

the tops of the side-walls. A series of tie-beams may stretch from wall to wall; from the centre a king-post may rise vertically to support the ridge-piece. Alternatively, the same function may be provided by a pair of queen-posts, one on either side. Purlins are longitudinal timbers carrying the common rafters; they lie parallel to the ridge-piece and the wall plates, halfway between the two. Tie-beams are frequently seen in Shropshire, for example at Atcham, Eaton-under-Heywood, Ightfield, Lydham, Neen Savage and Onibury (Fig.8.6).

Later in the medieval period, the arch-braced roof was developed. Curved timbers were used to support the tie-beams, but often instead of a tie-beam the principal rafters were supported by curved arch-braces springing from wall-posts. The arch-braces were linked towards the top of the roof by a collar-beam, and this is the commonest type of roof seen in medieval Shropshire churches. Cranage estimated that there are nearly 100 collar-braced roofs in the county. A further development that was especially characteristic of south Shropshire was the use of wind-braces to strengthen the side of the roof. These were often carved into quatrefoil patterns, and arrayed on each side in one, two or even three tiers. Good examples of this kind of roof may be seen at Alberbury (Fig.21.1), Bettws-y-Crwyn (Fig.8.7), Hopesay (Fig.8.8)

Fig.8.8 The roof at Hopesay, with ornamented panelling above both walls

and Mainstone. At Clunbury (Fig.8.9), where there is one tier of wind-braces on each side, the roof has been dated dendrochronologically to 1495-96. Of the 28 churches with wind-braces in the county, 22 are in the south (diocese of Hereford).

Lead was readily available in medieval England and gradually replaced thatching or wooden shingles for roofing. This led to a reduction in the steepness of slope of the roof, to avoid the tendency of the lead to slide down the slope. This enabled the nave and aisles to be roofed separately, thus clearing the way for clerestories with taller windows. Roofs of low pitch were developed, and frequently panelling appeared between the beams, with carved bosses at the intersections. This type of roof was especially, but not exclusively, associated with Perpendicular architecture, of which there are not many examples in Shropshire. Roofs of this type may be seen in the nave at Claverley, the chancel at Eaton-under-Heywood (Fig.8.10), the south chapel at Ellesmere (Fig.8.11), in the nave at Newport (Fig.8.12), and above all in the nave at St. Mary's, Shrewsbury (Fig.1.1). There is a spectacular example in the chancel at Selattyn (Fig.8.13). An unusual feature at Claverley is the extra embellishment over the former site of the rood screen forming a ceilure; at Clun, the ceilure is over the altar.

Sometimes in roofs of low pitch, a wagon-roof was formed by using soft-wood boards to cover the undersides of the rafters, collars and bases. Such roofs are characteristic of the west country,

Fig.8.9 The roof at Clunbury, dated 1495-96

Fig.8.10 Low-pitched panelled roof at Eaton-under-Heywood

Fig.8.11 Ornate panelled roof over the south chapel at Ellesmere

Fig.8.12 Low-pitched panelled roof with bosses at Newport

Fig.8.13 Intricately decorated roof over the chancel at Selattyn

Fig.8.14 Wagon-roof over the chancel at Little Berwick

Fig.8.15 The fine hammer-beam roof at Condover

but are infrequent in Shropshire. Examples may be found at Little Berwick (Fig.8.14), St. Martin's (Fig.15.16) and Stockton.

Hammer-beam roofs were evolved in the late 13th century as a mechanical device for supporting complex roofs,[3] and were used in the 1390s in Westminster Hall. They were not used in Shropshire until the 16th and 17th centuries. Hammer-beams are short beams which project at the level of the wall-plate supported by an arched brace arising from a corbel. Vertical posts rise from the inner ends of the hammer-beams and are secured to collar-beams and purlins.[4] Occasionally there may be two tiers of hammer-beams, as, for example, at Donington. The finest hammer-beam roof spans the very wide naves at Condover (Fig.8.15) and at Battlefield (Fig.8.16); others may be seen at Astley Abbots, Benthall, Ford, High Ercall, Rushbury, Sheriffhales, Sheinton (Fig.8.17) and Shifnal. At Sheinton there is a second tier of hammer-beams, forming a double hammer-beam roof.

The provision of a stone vault was beyond the means of the great majority of parish churches in the Middle Ages, and there is no church in Shropshire with a vaulted nave (though the chancel at St. Mary's, Shrewsbury was at one time vaulted). At Tong (Fig.11.10), there is a chapel with exquisite fan-vaulting, a rare feature in a parish church; and there are several churches with vaulted porches. At Shrewsbury Abbey, the Victorian architect, J.L. Pearson, used vaulting to cover the roof of the choir (Fig.19.14).

Fig.8.16 The Victorian hammer-beam roof at Battlefield

Fig.8.17 Double hammer-beam roof at Sheinton

9
Sculpture

Compared with the neighbouring county of Herefordshire, Romanesque sculpture in Shropshire is fairly limited in extent. Fragments of Anglo-Saxon carving are found at Diddlebury and Wroxeter, in each case appearing to be part of a cross. At Diddlebury, two fragments are displayed in a window-niche on the north wall, while at Wroxeter (Fig.9.1) the fragment is embedded high up on the outside of the south wall. In each case there is evidence of interlace and foliage scrolls, and at Wroxeter also a dragon.

Following the arrival of the Normans, various geometric designs were introduced. Very early in the Norman period (the last 30 years of the 11th century) a sunken star pattern may be seen, together with rosettes and other motifs. Other Norman motifs included beakhead (the repeated use of stylised heads of birds or mammals with long beaks [Fig.9.2]), billet (short raised rectangles repeated at regular intervals [Fig.24.16]), nailhead (small pyramids similarly repeated), cable (Figs.10.11 & 10.13), and linked chains (Fig.9.3).

But it is the ubiquitous use of chevron decoration, introduced very early in the 12th century, which has come to symbolise Norman building. The Courtauld Institute of Art

Fig.9.1 Part of a Saxon cross at Wroxeter

Fig.9.3 Chain links around a window at Monkhopton

Fig.9.2 Beakhead and other Norman motifs over the south doorway at Holdgate

Fig.9.4 Chevron decoration in
two planes at Lilleshall, with
water-leaf on the capitals

Fig.9.6 Varieties of chevron and chain on the chancel
arch at Stirchley

Fig.9.7 Scallop carving on the inferior surface of a
capital at Shawbury

Fig.9.5 Chevron over a window
at Edstaston

Fig.9.8 Volute (spiral scrolls) on a capital
at Linley

is currently working on a Corpus of Romanesque Sculpture in Britain and Ireland, and is analysing the great variety of chevron ornament. Chevron is defined as 'a form of three-dimensional architectural ornament consisting of zigzags formed by a roll or rolls'. It is most commonly found decorating the orders of an arch. It may be found on the face or on the soffit (underside) of the arch, or occasionally on the edge. The chevrons may point in various directions with respect to the surface on which they are carved, most commonly projecting at right angles to the face or carved in the plane of the face (Fig.9.4). Chevron is extremely common in Shropshire churches – the most spectacular displays occur at Edstaston (over doorways and windows [Fig.9.5]) and over the chancel arches at Upton Cressett (Fig.24.24) and Stirchley (Fig.9.6).

In Norman architecture, cylindrical columns supporting the arcades or shafts flanking doorways are surmounted by capitals which effect the transition from the round column to the square abacus or impost above. The inferior surface of the capital is often carved into a cushion (a rounding-off of the lower angles into the cylindrical shaft below), scallop (a further modification in which the surface is elaborated into a series of truncated cones [Fig.9.7]), or volute (spiral scrolls [Fig.9.8]). Sometimes a variant of the scalloped capital may be seen in which each scallop assumes a concave or trumpet shape. Towards the end of the 12th century a few capitals were enriched with decoration known as water-leaf (Fig.9.4) – a broad leaf turning up towards the angle of the abacus. The base of a pier or shaft may be as informative as the capital. Norman bases have very simple mouldings, but they may be carved.

Fig.9.9 11th-century tympanum at Stottesdon

The tympanum is the space between the lintel of a doorway and the arch above it, and this area was sometimes filled with sculpted designs. There are several such decorated tympana in Shropshire, the earliest probably being those at Stottesdon and Uppington; these are from the 11th century, though it is doubtful whether they date from before or after the Norman Conquest. At Stottesdon (Fig.9.9) is a bearded head at the apex of the triangle, with a pattern of crosses on the tympanum below. On the lintel are strange beasts, two of which are upside down. At Uppington (Fig.9.10) the

Fig.9.10 A dragon on the 11th-century tympanum at Uppington

tympanum is rudely carved with a dragon biting a twisted tail. At Barrow (Fig.9.11) the late 11th-century tympanum is carved with rows of simple geometrical patterns. At Linley there are carved tympana above both the north and south doors: the south tympanum (Fig.9.12) is simply carved with zigzags, but on the north there is a 'green man', a pagan fertility symbol (Fig.9.16). Geometric carving may also be seen on a tympanum at Billingsley (Fig.9.13) while above the priest's door at Tugford, the tympanum is carved with an unusual floriated pattern. Lastly, at High Ercall, a remarkable tympanum (Fig.9.14) is set in the inside of the north wall of the nave; it represents the Tree of Life, and has been dated by Gethyn Jones to *c*.1110-15.

But all these works are clumsy indeed compared with the superb tympanum at Aston Eyre, the greatest Norman sculpture in the county (Fig.1.4). This was once thought to be the work of the Herefordshire School, but none of the common themes of the School is here depicted: there are no dragons, no beasts of prey nor malevolent serpents. Instead the work is calm, almost devotional. The theme is the Entry into Jerusalem, with Christ riding on an ass, a man with palm leaves before him and a disciple with a foal behind.

Corbels are blocks, usually of stone, projecting from a wall; if under the

Fig.9.11 Geometrical patterns on the 11th-century tympanum at Barrow

Fig.9.12 Geometrical carving on the south tympanum at Linley

Fig.9.13 Geometrical carving on the tympanum at Billingsley

Fig.9.14 A 'Tree of Life' on the tympanum at High Ercall

eaves they may support roof beams. A corbel-table is a row of such corbels, and occasionally they were carved with a great variety of subjects – grotesque, humorous, rarely religious. The finest example is at the well-known church of Kilpeck in Herefordshire. In Shropshire the best examples of a corbel-table carved with heads etc. are at Acton Burnell, Bromfield and Linley (Fig.6.3). Isolated heads of uncertain age may be seen at Cound, Little Ness, Much Wenlock and Pitchford. Sheila-na-gigs (fertility symbols) are at Church Stretton, Holdgate (Fig.9.15), Linley (Fig.9.16) and Tugford. At Alveley the south capital of the tower arch displays carving which is probably the work of the Herefordshire School: at the angle of the capital is a head, and issuing from the mouth on each side are stems ending in trilobed leaves.

In the 13th century (the Early English period) a frequent ornamental motif is dogtooth – a row of four-cornered stars placed diagonally and raised pyramidally – though occasionally the dogtooth may be seen in late Norman building (Fig.9.17). Capitals are sometimes decorated with 'stiff-leaf' foliage (Fig.9.18), more exuberant than water-leaf, the leaves often being multi-

Fig.9.15 Holdgate: sheila-na-gig

Fig.9.16 Green man on the north tympanum at Linley

Fig.9.18 Stiff-leaf carving on a capital at St. Mary's, Shrewsbury

Fig.9.17 Dogtooth on the late Norman doorway at Wistanstow

lobular. At the base, there may be a 'water-hollow' moulding around the shaft or pier. In the Decorated period (early 14th century), the ogee arch was introduced (Fig.9.19) – two shallow S-shaped curves meeting upwards in a sharp point, often embellished with crockets and other ornamental features. In window tracery and elsewhere, the ogee often led to reticulated forms and to cusping (Fig.3.14). A characteristic motif of the Decorated age was ball-flower ornamentation – a small ball enclosed by three petals forming a globular flower (Fig.9.20); this was often set in rows on mouldings on windows (Fig.9.21), above tomb-recesses and elsewhere. In the Perpendicular period (*c*.1350-1550), a sterner, plainer style emerged. Crockets and finials were eschewed and Perpendicular carving on fonts etc. often displayed plain quatrefoils (Fig.10.18).

Fig.9.19 Ogee-arched tomb-recess at Acton Burnell

Fig.9.20 Ball-flower on a capital at Chelmarsh

Specific examples of medieval carving in Shropshire churches include: from the 14th century, the remarkable representation of the Trinity at Kinlet, and the figure of a scrivener at Ellesmere; and from the 15th century, alabaster panels of the Trinity and Virgin and Child, with donor, at Shrewsbury St. Mary.

The finest carving in wood is the Pieta at Battlefield, dating from the 15th century. Also notable are the wooden carvings of the 17th century representing the four Evangelists at Morville.

Carving on fonts and monuments, pulpits and benches is discussed elsewhere.

Fig.9.21 (right) Exuberant ball-flower on a window at St. Laurence, Ludlow

10

Fonts

Baptism is the rite of admission to the Church, and in medieval times the first part of the service was conducted in the porch, or at the entry into the church. The traditional site for the font was centrally at the west end of the nave. The earliest fonts were probably constructed of wood, but none of these survives.

The Table below offers an analysis of 129 Shropshire fonts dating from before the 19th century; it shows an impressive number of 12th-century fonts, with the remainder spread fairly evenly from the 13th to the 18th centuries. I have not attempted to count 19th-century fonts. Cranage's analysis was broadly similar.[1]

	Shropshire fonts before 1800	
'Roman'		3
Norman	63	
Early English	8	
Decorated	11	
Perpendicular	18	
Medieval, but uncertain style	8	
Total medieval		108
17th-century	16	
18th-century	5	
Total 1600-1800		21
Grand total		132

Fig.10.1 Wroxeter: the font may be the base of a Roman column

The earliest fonts in Shropshire may well be at least partly of Roman origin. Three fonts in the vicinity of the Roman town of Wroxeter may be based on material removed from that site. At the church of St. Andrew, Wroxeter (Fig.10.1), the font is probably the base of a Roman column; at Woolstaston (Fig.10.2), the plain Norman font is set within a large bowl which could be of Roman origin; and at Shrewsbury Abbey the font appears to be made from a Roman capital.

The styles of medieval fonts mirror the characteristics of the parish churches, and they may be approximately dated using similar criteria to

59

Fig.10.2 Woolstaston: a plain Norman font set within a ?Roman bowl

Fig.10.3 Shawbury: a Norman font with beading, cable and flattened zigzag

Fig.10.4 Edgmond: (?) various Norman geometrical patterns

Fig.10.5 Upton Cressett: cable moulding at top and foot of bowl, with a Norman arcade between

those used in dating architectural features (see chapter 3). Thus Norman fonts, if adorned at all, may display a variety of geometrical patterns – zigzag, plain and cable mouldings, saltire crosses, scallops and other Norman motifs. If arcades are present they are round-headed, and sometimes intersecting. Human figures are not frequent, but when present may be rude and sometimes bizarre. Dragons and serpents, perhaps symbolising evil, and various beasts and birds may be depicted. Drake has recently analysed a vast number of Romanesque fonts in Britain and north-western Europe and has shown the great variety of themes used in the 12th century.[2]

In the 13th century (the Early English era), arcades become pointed, following the general adoption of the Gothic arch, and sculpture became more realistic. In the 14th century (the Decorated era), arcades may exhibit ogee patterns and cusping, while later Perpendicular fonts are frequently octagonal and may display quatrefoil panels, inverted fleurons etc.

Norman fonts

Of the 108 medieval fonts in Shropshire, 63 (58%) probably date from the 12th century. Of these, more than half (35) are plain unadorned tubs, so interest centres on the remaining 28 which include the finest fonts in the county.

The simplest form of adornment is a plain moulding around the middle of the bowl, as at Bedstone, or a single band of cable moulding at the foot of the bowl, as at Quatt. The fonts at Pontesbury and Shrawardine are also plain, with some scalloping below. Aston Botterell has a single band of nail-head. The font at Quatford shows geometrical patterning around the lower part of the bowl; the upper part has been carved much later with quatrefoils. The upright font at Shawbury (Fig.10.3) has a series of bands of carving, with beading, cable, and flattened chevron. At Old St. Chad, Shrewsbury, the font has a diaper pattern. The most complex font with geometrical patterning is at Edgmond (Fig.10.4). There is interlace and geometrical motifs, the whole bearing a striking resemblance to the Staffordshire fonts at Church Eaton and Bradley a few miles away.[3]

Fig.10.6 Lilleshall: cable, vertical bars and arches

Norman arcades with round-headed arches, sometimes intersecting, feature on six fonts. The simplest is at Heath, where there is a frieze of incised arches. Bitterley displays arches, with some foliage above. At Upton Cressett (Fig.10.5) there is cable moulding at the top and bottom of the bowl, and in between a series of tall arches. At Lilleshall (Fig.10.6) there is around the rim a cable moulding, and then a band of vertical bars above and below a series of short arches, some of which enclose various geometrical patterns. The

Fig.10.7 Claverley: patterned columns in arcade, and above inverted fleurs-de-lis

Fig.10.8 Adderley: rosettes and volutes beneath a Latin inscription

Fig.10.9 Cound: a series of rosettes around the bowl, and a rim of foliage above

Fig.10.10 Bucknell: 11th-century font with a human head and linear patterns

beaker font at Claverley (Fig.10.7) displays patterned columns in the arcade, and above the columns are inverted fleurs-de-lis. Below is a band of beading. At St. Giles, Shrewsbury, there is chevron below the rim, and around the bowl an arcade with capitals, and various patterns within the arches.

Various combinations of rosettes, volutes and foliage appear on several fonts. At Adderley (Fig.10.8) there are rosettes with two upright volutes, and around the rim is a Latin inscription. The font at Albrighton near Shrewsbury has nail-head and zigzag, above a petal motif. At Cound (Fig.10.9), there are rosettes in beaded medallions, with a strip of foliage above.

The remaining seven fonts exhibit more complex carvings, with representations of beasts, both real and mythical, and human heads or figures. The very old font at Bucknell (late Saxon or very early Norman [Fig.10.10]) shows interlace, with one head. The old font at Sidbury (destroyed by fire in 1911) showed spiral work and foliage above and intersecting arcading below.[4] At Berrington (Fig.10.11) the crude font has cable around the rim, and a plain moulding below. Around the bowl are seven fairly naïve heads, wide above and pointed at the chin, while between are represented a lion, a hen and a lighted candle. The elaborate font at Holdgate (Fig.10.12) stands on a square plinth, with animals' heads at the corners. Above this is a raised circular platform in the centre of which is a roll-moulding around a shaft decorated with chevron. The rim of the bowl has a thick cable moulding and around the bowl are animals and leaves, intermingled with formal ornaments including a ring and saltire crosses. The beaker font at Morville (Fig.10.13) has cable around the rim, and below this a series of concentric beaded medallions enclosing

Fig.10.11 Berrington: cable around the rim, with seven heads, a lion, a hen and a candle

Fig.10.12 Holdgate: complex Norman carving, including serpents and interlace

rosettes or leaves, some of which are separated by lions' masks; above the medallions are leaf-forms, and below a pattern on criss-crossing lines. The font at Linley (Fig.10.14) is described by Drake as a poor relation of Morville, being of lower quality.[5] Again there is cable around the rim, with leaf ornaments below. Then again is a series of medallions

Fig.10.13 Morville: cable around the rim, and beaded medallions separated by lions' masks

Fig.10.14 Linley: 'a poor relation of Morville'

Fig.10.15 Stottesdon: the finest font in Shropshire. Vivid carving of the Herefordshire School

Fig.10.16 Dawley: arcades around the sides, chevron decoration below, and a Tree of Life on one side

with rosettes and leaves, some tied with lions' masks. Drake remarks that because of poor preparation the pattern of the rings is varied as it moves around the bowl: some of the rings overlap and two butt against each other.

Fig.10.17 Acton Burnell: an elegant octagonal font with cusped arches

Fig.10.18 Ryton: a Perpendicular font with quatrefoils

No such doubts about quality surround the font at Stottesdon (Fig.10.15), for here is the finest font in the county, the work of the Herefordshire School.[6] The sides and upper parts of the base have a continuous vine tendril. On the shaft is a band of undulating triple parallel lines, and this pattern is repeated at the top of the bowl. Where two lines cross each other there is a three-stranded ring. Around the bowl is a series of beaded rings wrapped together by lions' masks; between the rings are fleurs-de-lis, inverted above and upright below. In the rings are an Agnus Dei, a lion, a looped cross, a cross of four linked rings, a 9-petal rosette, a lion biting its tail, a winged dragon and, most characteristic of the Herefordshire School, a bird of prey pecking at the head of a smaller bird.

The font at Dawley (Fig.10.16) is late Norman; it has arcades around the sides, chevron decoration below, and a Tree of Life on one side.

Gothic fonts

In contrast to the 12th century, there appear to be only three which can be firmly dated to the Early English period: Acton Burnell, Cleobury North and Selattyn. At Acton Burnell (Fig.10.17) is an elegant octagonal font, showing a tectonic arcade with cusped arches and chaste Early English capitals. The font at Cleobury North is also octagonal, with a band of dogtooth around the base. The font at Selattyn has a band of foliage around the rim.

Octagonal fonts became very common in the Decorated and Perpendicular eras, and plain fonts of this shape may be seen at Acton Round and Child's Ercall. Other octagonal fonts from the 14th or 15th centuries have more elaborate designs. These typically include cusped arches on the stem, with quatrefoils filled with flowers or shields in panels around the sides of the bowl. Among the best of this group are Beckbury, Burford, Church Stretton, Diddlebury, Ellesmere, Munslow, Ryton (Fig.10.18), St. Mary's Shrewsbury, Stockton and Tong.

Post-Reformation fonts

It is not possible to do more than to draw attention to some of the best of the numerous post-Reformation fonts in the county. In the 17th century, late Perpendicular styles prevailed in fonts, as in churches, and examples of this may be seen at, for example, Llanyblodwel, Whitchurch and Whixall. Fonts from the late 17th and 18th centuries often take the form of a graceful bowl on an elegant stem, and fonts of this character may be seen at Longden, Loughton, and Petton (Fig.10.19). The font at Preston-upon-the-Weald Moors (Fig.10.20) looks as though it should be 18th-century, but actually dates from 1905. I have made no attempt to count the numerous fonts from the 19th century, but those at Lawley, Leaton (Fig.10.21), Lyneal, Meole Brace, Middleton Scriven, and Welshampton are noteworthy. Unsurpassed for elegance is the font at Peplow designed by Norman Shaw (Fig.10.22).

Fig.10.19 Petton: an elegant 18th-century font

Fig.10.20 Preston-upon-the-Weald Moors: a Georgian style font, dating from 1905

Fig.10.21 Leaton: a Victorian font

Fig.10.22 Peplow: a very fine font designed by Norman Shaw

11

Memorials and Monuments 1250-1870

Shropshire is an excellent county in which to study memorials and monuments, and a number of churches have truly impressive assemblies. The finest is at Tong, but Ludlow, Badger, Condover, Hodnet, Kinlet, Moreton Corbet and Shrewsbury Abbey all have significant collections.

Medieval monuments

Relatively few Shropshire parish churches have medieval memorials or monuments to the dead – the number with post-Reformation memorials is far greater. The earliest memorials are coffin-lids. These were the carved lids of stone coffins which were allowed to remain exposed on the floor of the church to provide a permanent memorial to those buried beneath.[1] This practice apparently began early in the 12th century and persisted for about 200 years. Examples in Shropshire may be found at Cheswardine, Eaton-under-Heywood, Quatford, Ruyton XI Towns, Shifnal and Shrewsbury Abbey. Most of these coffin-lids are incised with a foliated cross of varying complexity, and they commemorate unknown persons.

In some of the early coffin-lids elsewhere in England, an effigy of the deceased was carved in low relief on the lid, one of the earliest examples being at Westminster Abbey (Abbot Crispin, c.1118). The earliest effigies in the 12th century were of ecclesiastics, but later, effigies of knights, civilians, and ladies became increasingly frequent. Gradually during the 12th, 13th and early 14th centuries, some effigies instead of being carved out of the slab were fashioned in low relief by cutting back the surrounding slab. Later there was progressive undercutting of the sides of the effigy until finally the effigy was freed from the underlying slab.

Fig.11.1 Berrington: oaken effigy of a knight, c.1285

Some of the earliest effigies, however, were carved of oak, and there are four examples in Shropshire out of only about a hundred in the entire country. The oldest examples are at Berrington (Fig.11.1) and Pitchford (Fig.11.2). At Berrington there is a knight in 13th-century armour, his head resting on cushions and his crossed legs resting on a lion.

67

It probably dates from *c.*1285. At Pitchford, again from the late 13th century, is an effigy 7 feet long and carved from a single piece of oak. The knight is shown in full armour, in the act of pulling the sword-blade from the scabbard. His feet rest on a lion. The other oaken effigies are later: at Eaton-under-Heywood the effigy of a civilian rests in a Decorated tomb-chest adorned with ball-flower (Fig.23.13); this

Fig.11.2 Pitchford: effigy 7ft long, carved from a single piece of oak, late 13th century

dates the tomb-recess to the first half of the 14th century, but whether the effigy is of the same date is uncertain. Finally at Burford is a much later wooden effigy to Edmond Cornwall, d.1508; there are two angels by the pillow and a large dog at the feet (Fig.11.3).

The earliest stone effigies in Shropshire are at Leighton and Shrewsbury Abbey. At Leighton, there is a very fine effigy of a knight in full armour dating from the late 13th century (Fig.20.10). The head rests on two pillows and there is a lion at the feet. Considerable traces of colour remain, especially on the shield which displays the Leighton arms. Of approximately the same date is the headless effigy of a knight in Shrewsbury Abbey; this has traditionally been believed to be the effigy of Earl Roger of Montgomery, but this is not now accepted. A further effigy in the abbey of about the same date is of a cross-legged knight with his hand on a sword; this originally came from Wombridge. Also in the abbey are two further monuments, *c.*1300: one of a lawyer, from old St. Chad, Shrewsbury; and the other of a priest, with a chalice and bell, book and candle, and above a coffin-lid with a floriated cross. This was formerly in St. Giles, Shrewsbury.[2]

From the 14th century are effigies of knights at St. Mary's, Shrewsbury and at High Ercall. The knight at St. Mary's is clad in armour, his head rests on a cushion, and the crossed legs press against a lion. The effigy at High Ercall is similar, and both are dated *c.*1325. Of about the same date is a remarkable slab at Preston Gubbals (Fig.11.4): this bears in low relief the bust of a man with a foliated cross on his breast. At Ellesmere is an unusual effigy – a lawyer (Cranage) or a knight (Pevsner). The pair of effigies at Shrewsbury Abbey, previously in St. Alkmund's church, Shrewsbury, are dated later in the 14th

Fig.11.3 Burford: oaken effigy of Edmond Cornwall (d.1508)

Fig.11.5 Tong: effigies of Sir Fulke de Pembrugge (d.1409) and his wife, Dame Isabella (d.1446)

Fig.11.4 Preston Gubbals: 14th-century slab with a man with a foliated cross

century: here are two effigies on one slab, the head of one against the feet of the other. Both are clad in long robes, but in one there is clearly armour underneath.

From the 15th century the identity of effigies and the date of death is usually known; but it is necessary to sound a note of caution about dates. In the Middle Ages it sometimes happened that the effigy was made during the lifetime of the person concerned, but on other occasions the effigy was not made until some decades after death. So the date of death may not always correspond to the date of construction of the memorial. In Burford is the painted alabaster effigy of Princess Elizabeth, daughter of John of Gaunt, duke of Lancaster. She died in 1426; the head of the lady rests on a cushion supported by angels, and at her feet is a dog. At Whitchurch is the memorial to John Talbot, first earl of Shrewsbury, who was killed in battle near Bordeaux in 1453. The effigy lies on a tomb-chest panelled with quatrefoils; above is a pointed arch and a crocketed canopy. Sir John wears a coronet and the Order of the Garter. There are two notable memorials of the 15th century at Tong: the earlier is that to Sir Fulke de Pembrugge, d.1409 (Fig.11.5) and his wife Dame Isabella (d.1446). These are recumbent alabaster effigies on a tomb-chest, the sides of which are decorated with arches; angels are present on the east side only. The second is the very fine memorial to Sir Richard Vernon (d.1451) and Benedicta of Ludlow (Fig.11.6). Sir Richard

Fig.11.6 Tong: effigies of Sir Richard Vernon (d.1451) and Benedicta of Ludlow

is depicted in full armour, wearing the SS collar of the House of Lancaster; his wife is elegantly clad in a long cloak with richly carved brooches. Around the sides of the chest are canopied niches in which stand saints and angels. At Kinlet is an alabaster effigy of an unknown lady from the early 15th century; she lies recumbent, with angels at her pillow. Also at Kinlet is the first of the Blount memorials – to Sir Humphrey Blount (d.1477) and his wife. Their effigies (Fig.11.7) lie on a tomb-chest, and around the sides are mourners under ogee-headed arches.

Fig.11.7 Kinlet: effigies of Sir Humphrey Blount (d.1477) and his wife

For the first 30 years of the 16th century monuments continued to be entirely medieval in character. Thus at Moreton Corbet (Fig.11.8) the memorial to Sir Robert Corbet (d.1513) and his wife displays recumbent effigies on a tomb-chest, and around the sides mourners are placed under crocketed and ogeed arches – Decorated rather than Perpendicular in form. At Tong is the tomb of Sir Henry Vernon (d.1515) and his wife Anne (Fig.11.9). This monument is under a panelled ellip-tical arch – a big superstructure with four brackets and crocketed canopies for images, with vaulting typical of the Perpendicular era. On the west wall of the chantry chapel is a bust of Sir Henry's son Arthur (d.1517; Fig.11.10), depicted in academic robes.

Fig.11.8 Moreton Corbet: memorial to Sir Robert Corbet (d.1513) and his wife

Fig.11.9 (right) Tong: effigies of Sir Henry Vernon (d.1515) and his wife. Beyond is the Stanley tomb

Fig.11.10 Tong:
bust of Arthur Vernon
(d.1517)
in academic robes

Fig.11.11 Pitchford:
incised alabaster slab to
William Ottley (d.1529)
and his wife Margery

Fig.11.12 Claverley:
slab to Francis Gatacre
(d.1599) and his wife,
Elizabeth

Less costly than memorial effigies were incised slabs of stone or alabaster. These came into favour for about 150 years from *c*.1450. The best collection is at Pitchford (Fig.11.11), where there are four 16th-century examples, dating from 1529 to 1587; these vividly portray the changes in costume of the period – the early ladies have a pedimental head-dress, the later ones a full Elizabethan ruff. Also instructive are the three at Claverley (Fig.11.12), dated 1448, 1557 and 1599 respectively. Other incised slabs may be seen at Aston Botterell (1479), Atcham (1524), Beckbury (1505), Leighton (1520), Tong (1542) and Woodcote (1485). Of an entirely different character is the incised slate slab at Munslow, dated 1602.

Monumental brasses evolved in the 13th century, the oldest brass in England being at Stoke d'Abernon, dated 1277; the earliest in Shropshire is dated 1370. The material used is latten, an alloy of copper and zinc, with a small amount of lead.[3] Brasses were more durable than incised slabs of stone and they became exceedingly popular during the second half of the Middle Ages, especially in the eastern parts of England. Brasses from the 14th and 15th centuries are usually the finest; these were engraved more deeply, whereas from the Tudor age onwards they tended to be poorly engraved on thin metal.[4] They may be seen at 16 Shropshire churches (Table VIII, overleaf); the brass at Ludford is illustrated (Fig.27.8).

Post-Reformation Monuments

For the remaining years of the 16th century, memorial effigies continued to be displayed recumbent on a tomb-chest, the hands clasped in prayer. But from the 1530s onwards, signs of Renaissance influence can often be detected, especially around the sides of the tomb-chest and in the architectural surrounds of the monument. Thus twisted colonettes may appear between the mourners around the sides or at the corners of the tomb-chest; while ribbon-work, strapwork, obelisks and other Renaissance motifs become increasingly evident. The earliest sign of impending change in Shropshire may be the 1531 tomb of Sir John and Lady Blount at Kinlet (Fig.11.13). Mourners with shields are displayed infor-mally around the sides, and above the figures scrolls have replaced Gothic arches. Twisted colonettes may be seen on tomb-chests at Albrighton near Shifnal (1555), Claverley (1558) and Stoke upon Tern (1566). The monu-ment to Chief Justice Bromley (d.1555) and his wife at Wroxeter (Fig.11.14) is an excellent example of the new trend: the side of the chest is divided by pilasters into three panels – the outer two contain shields, the central one a young woman with scrolls above. The later tomb at Wroxeter to Sir Richard Newport (d.1570) and his wife displays twisted colonettes at the corners (Fig.11.15). At Moreton Corbet the monument to Sir Richard Corbet (d.1567) and his wife has panels round the sides separated by colonettes, and beneath the heraldic shields are elephants and owls. This contrasts with the purely medieval monu-ment to Sir Robert Corbet in the same church. The Stanley tomb at

1370	Burford	Elizabeth de Cornewayle
1382	Acton Burnell	Sir Nicholas Burnell
1390	Adderley	abbot
1467	Tong	Sir William and Lady Vernon
1475	Harley	knight and lady
1495	Ightfield	Dame Margery Calverley
1497	Ightfield	William Maynwaryng
1510	Tong	Reverend Ralph Elcott
1512	Withington	John Onley and wife
1517	Tong	Arthur Vernon
1530	Withington	Reverend Adam Grafton
1533	Edgmond	Francis Yonge and wife
1554	Ludford	William Fox and wife
1557	Plowden Hall	H. Plowden and wife
1560	Adderley	Sir Robert and Lady Nedeham
1564	Myddle	Arthur Chambers and wife
1571	Acton Scott	Thomas Mytton and wife
1580	Market Drayton	Rowland Corbet
1592	Much Wenlock	Richard Ridley
1599	Glazeley	Thomas Wylde and wife
1616	Alveley	John Grove
1640	Upton Cressett	Richard Cresset and wife
1673	Alveley	Reverend John Podmor

Table VII Monumental Brasses in Shropshire

Fig.11.13 Kinlet: tomb of Sir John Blount (d.1531) and his wife. Scrolls instead of Gothic arches on the sides

72

Fig.11.14 Wroxeter: the tomb-chest of Chief Justice
Bromley (d.1555) and his wife

Tong shows Sir Thomas Stanley (d.1576) and his wife lying on a slab, while beneath lies their son Sir Edward (just visible in Fig.11.9). The whole is a large monument in two tiers (irreverently termed 'the bunk bed' by a group of visiting schoolboys). There are allegorical figures above and obelisks at the corners. At Condover, the tomb-chest of Thomas Scriven (d.1587) and his wife has mourners around the sides separated by Ionic columns (Fig.11.16).

The change to a more florid style is most marked at Acton Burnell (Fig.11.17) where the monument to Sir Richard Lee (d.1591) and his wife shows the effigies on a tomb-chest, and behind them a row of nine

Fig.11.15 Wroxeter: tomb of Sir Richard Newport
(d.1570) and his wife. Twisted colonettes at the corners

Fig.11.17 Acton Burnell:
monument to Sir Richard Lee
(d.1591) and his wife

Fig.11.16 Condover: the tomb-chest of Thomas Scriven
(d.1587) and his wife

Fig.11.18 Aston Botterell: monument to John Botterell (d.1588) and his wife

Fig.11.19 Kinlet: gigantic monument to Sir George Blount (d.1584) and his wife

Fig.11.20 Bitterley: kneeling figure of Timothy Lucye (d.1616)

Fig.11.21 Acton Burnell: monument to Sir Humphry Lee (d.1632) and his wife, by Nicholas Stone

Fig.11.23 Condover: above, Jane Norton and her husband, Bonham; below her father Judge Owen and her brother Sir Roger Owen

Fig.11.24 Moreton Say: kneeling figures of three Vernon sisters, erected by their sister Jane

kneeling children. Above is a colossal architectural surround, with pillars, an arch, coats of arms, caryatids etc. – an overt display of wealth which would have been unthinkable 50 years earlier. Much less accomplished technically, but of comparable size, is the monument to John Botterell (d.1588) at Aston Botterell (Fig.11.18).

The last of the Blount monuments at Kinlet introduces a new theme which becomes increasingly frequent during the next half-century – couples are shown not recumbent, but kneeling, often in prayer on either side of a prayer-desk. This became a popular theme for memorials in late Elizabethan and Jacobean times – and was intended to be a demonstration of Protestant piety. It fell out of favour in the latter part of the 17th century – the latest example in Shropshire is dated 1642. The memorial at Kinlet is unusual in its ostentatious display – Sir George Blount (d.1584) and his wife are depicted kneeling frontally (Fig.11.19), while below them is a cadaver as an emblem of mortality. Again there is an enormous architectural surround, with arches and coats of arms above. Later examples of kneeling figures are more modest and appealing; they may be seen at Bitterley (1616 [Fig.11.20]), Oswestry (1616), Berrington (1628), Burford (1630), Acton Burnell (1632; [Fig.11.21]), Ludlow (1635; [Fig.11.22]), Condover (1640 [Fig.11.23]) and Moreton Say (1642; [Fig.11.24]). The accomplished monument at Acton Burnell (Fig.11.21) is the earliest work in Shropshire by a known sculptor, Nicholas Stone (*c*.1587-1647). He 'emerged as the leading mason-sculptor by about 1625'.[6]

Fig.11.22 Ludlow: kneeling figures of Edward Waties (d.1635) and his wife

Recumbent effigies on a tomb-chest retained their popularity in Shropshire for the first four decades of the 17th century, but after 1640 there are just two late examples, at Ludford (1697) and Shifnal (1698). Several from the earlier years of the century are worth noting. At Norton-in-Hales there is an excellent monument to Sir Rowland and Lady Cotton (Fig.11.25); the latter died in childbirth in 1606. The effigies are of alabaster, and Lady Cotton holds her infant in her arms. There is an ornately deco-

Fig.11.25 Norton-in-Hales: monument to Sir Rowland and Lady Cotton (d.1606)

rated architectural surround, with columns, garlands and arabesque patterning. Rather plainer is the monument at Quatt to Francis Wolryche (d.1614) and his wife (Fig.24.20); around the chest are kneeling children. At Wroxeter the monument to John Barber and his wife (1618) has a tomb-chest with Tuscan columns and shields with strapwork. The

Fig.11.26 Cardington: Chief Justice Leighton (d.1607)

Fig.11.27 Ludlow: Dame Mary Eure (d.1612)

memorial to Sir Edward Bromley (1626) and his wife is imposing, with alabaster effigies in a heavy six-post edifice.

As the 17th century progressed there was a trend towards more ostentation and less piety: instead of recumbent effigies with the hands clasped in prayer, the deceased were sometimes shown reclining languidly, often in apparently uncomfortable postures. The earliest example is at Cardington (Fig.11.26), where Chief Justice Leighton (d.1607) is depicted in a rather stiff posture, still with the children kneeling against the tomb-chest. Then came the alabaster semi-reclining effigy of Dame Mary Eure (d.1612) at Ludlow (Fig.11.27). Rather freer is the grandiose memorial to Humfrey Conyngsby (d.1624) at Neen Sollars (Fig.11.28), where the deceased is shown semi-reclining, his head propped up by his right hand. At Upton Magna, Walter Barker (d.1644) reclines on a mat against a background of Corinthian pilasters, an open segmental pediment above (Fig.19.31). The memorial at Lilleshall to Sir Richard and Lady Leveson (d.1661 and 1674 respectively [Fig.11.29]) presages the 18th century in its sophistication and Baroque influence, with putti standing outside the columns. There are two reclining figures, Sir Richard being depicted above and behind his wife. Finally, there is the memorial at Quatt to Lady Mary Wolryche (d.1678 [Fig.11.30]) – a remarkable monument in white marble, showing the deceased loosely robed, semi-reclining and holding a lute. There are Baroque twisted columns on each side, and above an open segmental pediment

Fig.11.28 Neen Sollars:
Humfrey Coningsby (d.1624)

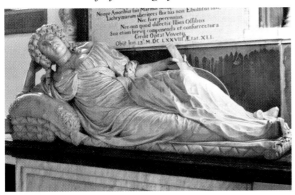

Fig.11.30 Quatt: monument to
Lady Mary Wolryche holding her lute (d.1678)

Fig.11.29 Lilleshall: the memorial
to Sir Richard and Lady Leveson
(d.1661 and 1674 respectively)

Fig.11.31 Benthall: wall memorial to Ralph Brown (d.1707)

Fig.11.32 Acton Round: Richard Acton (d.1703) and his wife, by Edward Stanton

containing a vase. Lady Wolryche appears almost saucy – perhaps it is not surprising that this monument was erected in the reign of Charles II.

Half-figures or busts were sometimes used instead of full-length effigies to commemorate the deceased. At Shrewsbury Abbey there is the half-figure of John Loyd (d.1647), while busts may be seen at Condover (1641), Ludford (1658) and Moreton Corbet (1691). Hanging wall-tablets, which became very common in the 18th century, made an early appearance at Longford (1686), Alberbury (1691) and Tong (1696). Another foretaste of change to come was the use of marble in tomb-chests at Ludlow (1637) and Quatt (1688).

In the second half of the 17th century the English Baroque evolved, to be followed in the next century by rococo (both rather restrained in England compared with the extravagancies seen on the Continent). There was a vogue for standing wall-monuments with urns, obelisks and sarcophagi, without effigy but often with scrolls, cherubs, and displays of flowers and foliage. Good examples of these wall-monuments may be seen in a number of Shropshire churches. From the reign of Queen Anne (1703-14) there are elegant memorials to Anne and Richard Cresswell at Sidbury, and to Ralph Brown at Benthall (Fig.11.31). At Acton Round is an excellent monument to Richard Acton (d.1703 [Fig.11.32]) and his wife, who are shown holding hands in a horizontally oval frame; this is by Edward Stanton (1681-1734).

In the 18th century, tomb-chests and kneeling figures at prayer-desks are no longer seen, and effigies are distinctly uncommon. The enthusiasm for urns, cherubs and sarcophagi

Fig.11.33 Acton Round: memorial to
Sir Whitmore and Lady Acton, c.1769,
by T.F. Pritchard

Fig.11.34 Cound: memorial to Edward
Cressett, bishop of Llandaff (d.1755),
probably by T.F. Pritchard

continued and as the century proceeded there was an increasing use of pyramids or obelisks as a background instead of architectural surrounds with columns and pediments. As an alternative to effigies, busts in medallions or later on pedestals were sometimes employed. The memorial at Hodnet to Henrietta Vernon (d.1752) – attributed to Sir Henry Cheere – was described by Pevsner as 'an exquisite rococo piece': a wreathed urn on a pedestal against an obelisk, with two wreathed urns on each side, and three cherubs' heads above. Other good rococo monuments may be seen at Baschurch (1754) and Wrockwardine (1765 [Fig.20.20]), by T.F. Pritchard. The finest mid-18th-century monument is that to Sir Whitmore and Lady Acton at Acton Round also by Pritchard (Fig.11.33). It is celebrated for combining rococo motifs with unmistakable Gothick features[7] – one of the earliest works of the Gothic Revival, a little later than the church at Shobdon in Herefordshire. There is a sarcophagus in an architectural frame, the side-columns have Corinthian capitals and there are garlands and lamps; but in addition the frieze has pseudo-Perpendicular lozenges, with foliage surmounted by a row of cinquefoiled Gothic arches. Probably by the same sculptor is the fine wall-monument at Cound to a former rector, Edward Cressett, later bishop of Llandaff (1755 [Fig.11.34]).

There are two 18th-century monuments in Shropshire by sculptors with a national reputation: Michael Rysbrack and Louis Francois Roubiliac. At Llanyblodwel is a minor work by Rysbrack (1694-1770). He arrived in England from Flanders c.1720, and for the next 20 years was the leading sculptor in England. He set 'a standard which his rivals failed to reach during those years, achieving a style which combined the best features of late Baroque with the classical elements so attractive to his English patrons'.[8] The monument at Llanyblodwel commemorates Sir John Bridgman (d.1752); above is a large urn flanked by volutes, with a cartouche and further volutes below. At Condover is the much more impressive monument to Roger Owen

Fig.11.35 Condover: monument to Roger Owen (d.1746), possibly by Roubillac

(d.1746 [Fig.11.35]) and his wife Catherine, possibly by Roubiliac. Owen is portrayed semi-reclining, with his wife seated at his feet. Roubiliac (1702/5-62), born in Lyon, 'was probably the most accomplished sculptor ever to work in England'.[9] He worked here from about 1735.

The end of the 18th and the first half of the 19th centuries witnessed the Greek revival (see p.30), which replaced the penchant for things Roman in the Baroque and rococo eras. Colour was eschewed, and the use of white marble was almost universal. Figures were often carved in relief, and the depiction of angels ministering at the point of death was a frequent theme. Women mourning over the deceased were also commonly depicted. Two monuments in Shropshire (at Market Drayton [1778] and at Tong [1780]) may be early indicators of Greek influence: at Market Drayton the memorial to Sir J.J. Markham by Joseph Wilton shows a seated lady with an anchor by an urn; and at Tong the memorial to George Durant (probably by John Bacon the elder) again shows a seated lady mourning below an urn. Joseph Wilton (1722-1803) – 'an uneven artist'[10] – worked in the Baroque and rococo style when it

Fig.11.36 Burford: monument to Revd George Rushout (d.1842), attributed to the Westmacott school

Fig. 11.37 Hopton Wafers: monument to
Thomas Botfield (d.1843) by E.H. Baily

was passing out of fashion, yet he seemed unable fully to absorb the neo-classical style which replaced it. John Bacon (1740-99) also never fully adopted neo-classical styles – his English patrons were seemingly 'well-contented with a combination of sentiment with rococo charm'.[11]

Work of the three leading sculptors of the early 19th century, John Flaxman (1755-1826), Sir Richard Westmacott (1775-1856) and Sir Francis Chantrey (1781-1841) may be seen in Shropshire. At Badger, Flaxman's memorial to Henrietta Browne (d.1802 [Fig.18.3]) shows the deceased standing, with a spirit hovering above. Whinney's assessment of Flaxman is as follows: 'His sentiment is that of his age, drenched with nostalgia for the past ... but ... applied to the present with a freshness, a lack of self-consciousness that gives him a special place among neo-classical artists, for few have his innate sincerity and charm.' Also at Badger is a fine work, Chantrey's memorial to Henrietta's husband Isaac Hawkins Browne, MP, FRS (d.1819) – a large seated memorial with Browne holding a large book (Fig.18.2). Further work by Chantrey may be seen at Hodnet (Fig.16.10), Little Berwick, and St. Chad's, Shrewsbury. At Burford are three works by Sir Richard Westmacott and his son – Lady Caroline Rushout (d.1818) (by Westmacott sen.) is shown reclining, with an angel standing by. A later monument at Burford is the memorial to the Revd George Rushout (d.1842 [Fig.11.36]) showing an angel blessing a kneeling clergyman. This is also said to be by the Westmacott school.[12]

Several works by less well-known artists deserve mention. Thomas Carline's memorials at Prees and Hadnall are unusual: at Prees the memorial to Sir John Hill (d.1824) shows a funeral procession of small figures 'in a style much influenced by the Elgin marbles';[13] at Hadnall the memorial to Viscount Hill shows a mourning grenadier and tenant, with a lion between them. The memorial at Hopton Wafers to Thomas Botfield (d.1843 [Fig.11.37]) is by E.H. Baily; the deceased is shown lying in bed, with his wife kneeling beside him. John Gibson was responsible for two monuments at Badger, each depicting an angel; the memorials are to Harriet Cheney (d.1848) and Harriet Pigot (d.1852). Finally two monuments at Condover are worthy of notice. The kneeling figure in the chapel is Sir Thomas Cholmondeley by G.F. Watts, said by Esdaile to be 'not unworthy of the masterpiece by Roubiliac hard by'. Just to the west of this is the monument to

Alice Cholmondeley, who died in childbirth in 1868; the monument is the work of her husband Reginald.

By the 1860s, however, the fashion for depicting the deceased in memorial form was everywhere falling out of favour, the Greek revival had expired, and the Gothic revival, then in full swing, did not find expression in memorials and monuments; instead, the affluent deceased henceforth were frequently commemorated in stained glass.

Stained Glass and Wall-Painting

At a time when few could read, painted windows and walls were invaluable methods used by the Church to reinforce teaching, to encourage reverence and awe and love of beauty, and to rebuke and warn of sin and the Last Judgment. Wall-paintings, in particular, were ubiquitous in churches. Doubtless the general artistic standard was low, and the colouring to our eyes garish. Stained glass evolved more slowly: glass was expensive in the Middle Ages, and the techniques which needed to be mastered spanned many centuries.

Stained glass

The three basic ingredients for making glass are silica (usually in the form of sand), an alkali (potash or soda) and an alkaline earth (lime). Potash was obtained from the ashes of beech trees, which contained a balance of metallic oxides such as iron and manganese necessary for colour; other colourants could be added such as cobalt (blue) and copper (red). Thus was produced 'pot-metal glass' which was cut into shapes required for a design, each colour requiring a separate piece of glass to compose a mosaic pattern. Glass of the 12th and 13th centuries was predominantly red and blue. Pot-metal glass was coloured throughout by the metallic oxides and enlivened by surface painting in brown and black. The earliest glass in Shropshire (13th-century) is in the heads of four windows in the south wall of St. Mary's, Shrewsbury.

Silver staining was introduced *c*.1310; it had been developed in Islamic art, and gradually spread from Islamic Spain to France, and then to England. A solution of silver nitrate or oxide was applied to the reverse of white glass, and on firing produced colours ranging from pale yellow to deep orange; when fired onto blue glass it produced green. Silver staining thus greatly increased the range of colours available and the 14th century witnessed the golden age of English medieval stained glass.

English medieval glass

Only two parish churches in Shropshire have extensive displays of English medieval glass – St. Mary, Shrewsbury and St. Laurence, Ludlow; Donington and Prees have some attractive windows, and about 20 other churches have fragments, as noted in the gazetteer. In St. John's chapel at St. Laurence, Ludlow, are several examples of 15th-century glass; one window (Fig.12.1) depicts on the left St. Catherine with her wheel, in the centre, St. John the Baptist holding a lamb, and on the right St. Christopher carrying the Christ child over a stream. Both Shrewsbury and Ludlow have Jesse windows, in which Christ's descent from Jesse, the father of King David, is depicted. Below lies the recumbent figure of Jesse, and from him arises a tree peopled with figures from the Old Testament, culminating at

Fig.12.1 Ludlow: St. Catherine,
St. John the Baptist and St. Christopher
(15th-century)

Fig.12.2 Donington: the
Coronation of the Virgin
(14th-century)

the top with the figure of Christ. Both the Shrewsbury and Ludlow windows were restored in the 19th century, but much of the glass in each is medieval – see pp.197-198 and 328-333 for a fuller description. At Donington (Fig.12.2) there is 14th-century glass depicting the Coronation of the Virgin. At Prees are fragments of medieval glass including representation of a donor a prayer.

Continental glass

A great deal of continental glass was imported into England during and after the Napoleonic Wars. The finest collection is at St. Mary's Shrewsbury where the Reverend William Rowland, vicar from 1828-52, imported glass from Germany, Belgium and the Netherlands. At Battlefield is some excellent glass from Normandy, depicting a king, a monk and ?a soldier (Fig.12.3). Small roundels from Flanders and Germany were imported in large numbers into England. They mostly date from the 16th century and may be seen at Badger, Bromfield, Church Stretton, Cleobury North, Hope Bowdler, Knowbury, Monkhopton, Munslow, St. Mary's Shrewsbury, Uffington and Upton Cressett. A Flemish representation of the Last Supper is at Coalbrookdale.

Post-Reformation glass – the 'pictorial' style

The production of stained glass virtually ceased in England at the Reformation, and very little was made during the next 200 years. Also, from about 1500, the supply of pot-metal

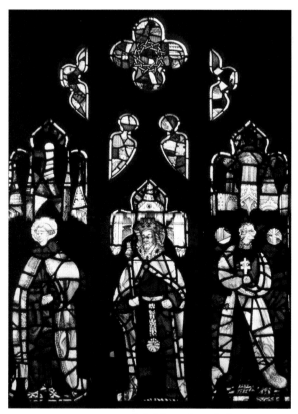

Fig.12.3 Battlefield: medieval glass from Normandy

Fig.12.4 Shrewsbury St. Alkmund: painted glass by Francis Eginton (c.1795)

glass rapidly declined, and ultimately knowledge of its means of production was lost. Its place was taken by enamel colours which could be painted and fired directly onto clear glass. This meant that it was no longer necessary to cut coloured glass to the shapes required for a mosaic assembly; instead enamels were painted onto large pieces of clear glass so that 'stained' glass became much closer to oil-painting, producing a 'pictorial' style which lasted until the Gothic Revival of the 19th century. So when in the 18th century artists again turned their attention to this medium, glass of quite a different character was produced. By the 1750s a few members of the aristocracy became interested in stained glass and began importing Continental glass to adorn their stately homes. These works often reproduced well-known pictures by artists such as Raphael. The earliest, and best, example of the pictorial style in Shropshire is the magnificent east window of St. Alkmund's, Shrewsbury (Fig.12.4). This is by Francis Eginton (1737-1805). He revived the art of glass painting and from his factory in Birmingham he issued a long series of works. The window at St. Alkmund's is a copy of Guido Reni's Assumption of the Virgin (see p.191).

The major practitioner of the pictorial style in Shropshire was to be David Evans (1793-1861), of the Shrewsbury firm of Betton and Evans which dated to the 18th century. John Betton sen. (1730-75) was admitted to the Shrewsbury Glaziers' Co. in 1752. His son, also

Fig.12.5 Shrewsbury St. Julian: east window by David Evans

John Betton (1765-1849), continued the business from premises in Gibbon's Mansion, a half-timbered building just behind Wyle Cop. He was knighted in 1817, and retired from the firm in 1825. David Evans became Betton's apprentice in 1808 and partner in 1815, and later sole owner. After Betton's retirement, Evans continued to make glass in very bright colours, and his work may be seen in many Shropshire churches (see Table VIII). The aim was still to achieve a pictorial effect, and Evans remained immune to the influence of Pugin and the Ecclesiologists. It is generally accepted that his greatest work is the east window at St. Julian's, Shrewsbury, a representation of Raphael's Transfiguration (Fig.12.5); for a detailed description, see p.195. The main window at St. Chad's Shrewsbury is also by him and depicts Rubens' Deposition (Fig.19.22). Further examples of Evans' work may be seen in St. Mary's, Shrewsbury and at West Felton (Fig.12.6). Although some of his work is too garish for modern taste, much of it is excellent, and Shropshire is fortunate in having such a wide range of his works.

Fig.12.6 left) West Felton: east window by David Evans

Aikman, William	Shrewsbury Holy Trinity
Arnold, Hugh	Coalbrookdale
Baillie, E.	Pitchford, Wroxeter
Ballantine and Son	Oswestry St. Oswald
Barnett, H.M.	Hopton Castle, Kenley
Bell, Joseph	Hopesay, Ludlow St. John, Shelve
Betton and Evans	Berrington, Church Stretton, Kinlet, Shrewsbury Abbey
Bourne, Swain	Bishop's Castle, Farlow, Stottesdon
Brown, Ford Madox	Meole Brace**, Newport
Bryans, Herbert	Cound, Holdgate, Lydham
Burlison and Grylls	Albrighton near Shrewsbury, Beckbury, Bicton, Chelmarsh, Church Aston, Church Stretton, Donington, Edstaston, Ellesmere, Ford, Little Ness, Market Drayton, Middleton Scriven, Montford, Newport, Quatford, Shifnal, Silvington, Stottesdon*, Upton Magna, Wistanstow
Burne-Jones, Sir Edward	Calverhall, Meole Brace**, Newport, Whitton**
Burrow, F.	Llanymynech
Camm, T.W.	Donnington Wood, Oakengates, Rodington, Sutton Maddock, Wrockwardine Wood
Chance brothers	Prees
Chaplin, Graham	Preston-upon-the-Weald Moors
Cholmondeley, R.	Condover
Clayton and Bell	Bitterley, Bridgnorth St.Leonard, Oldbury, Calverhall, Cheswardine, Clive, Hadnall, Ludlow St. Laurence, Moreton Corbet, Myddle, Newport, Oswestry St. Oswald*, Pontesbury, Quatford, Rodington?, St. George's, Stowe, Trefonen, Upton Magna, Wentnor, Westbury, Withington
Clutterbuck	Cleobury Mortimer
Comere and Capromier	Little Berwick
Comper, Sir Ninian	Moreton Corbet*, Stanton-upon-Hine Heath
Cooper-Abbs, George	Gobowen. Wombridge
Cox and Son	Coreley, Oldbury
Cox, Trena	Shrewsbury Cathedral
Curtis, Ward and Hughes	Little Berwick, Clun, Culmington, Newtown, Oswestry Holy Trinity, Petton, St. George's, Shrewsbury St. George
Davies, A.J.	Claverley, Tuck Hill
Davies, John	Clive, Condover, Dawley, Marton, Newcastle on Clun, Norbury, Sambrook, Shrewsbury St. Chad, Stanton Long, Wellington Christ Church, Wentnor, Whitchurch Methodist, Wistanstow
Davis, Louis	Ludlow St. Laurence
Dix, A.J.	Ightfield, Kemberton, Ruyton XI Towns
Done, W.	Bridgnorth St. Leonard, Prees, Waters Upton
Done and Davies	Bishop's Castle, Chirbury, Cwm Head, Diddlebury, Dorrington, Eaton-under-Heywood, Eyton-upon-the-Weald Moors, Much Wenlock, Ruyton XI Towns, Sibdon Carwood, Stanton Long, Sutton Maddock, Wombridge

Table VIII 19th- and 20th-century stained glass in Shropshire (cont. overleaf)

Eden, F.C.	Whittington*
Edmondson, R.B.	Ludford, Ludlow St. Laurence
Eginton, Francis	Shrewsbury St. Alkmund
Evans, Charles	Cleobury North, Hanwood, Newtown, Prees, Shrewsbury St. Mary
Evans, David	Alberbury, Astley, Badger, Broseley, Claverley, Cleobury North, Cressage*, Diddlebury, Edstaston, Hanwood, Harley*, Hodnet, Hope, Hope Bowdler, Ironbridge, Leebotwood, Little Ness, Longdon-on-Tern, Ludlow St. Laurence, Middleton, Middleton Scriven, More, Moreton Corbet, Munslow, Newcastle on Clun, Oswestry St. Oswald, St. Martin's, Shrewsbury St. Chad*, Shrewsbury St. George, Shrewsbury St. Giles*, Shrewsbury St. Julian*, Shrewsbury St. Mary, Stanton Lacy, Stockton, Stoke-on-Tern, Stoke St. Milborough, Tuck Hill, West Felton*, Woolstaston
Evans, Everall and Dodson	Lawley, Shrawardine
Evans, Samuel	Sutton Maddock
Forster, J.W.	Glazeley
Gibbs, Charles	Caynham, Sambrook*, Wheathill, Worfield
Gordon, Bronwen	Oakengates
Gray, Jane	Badger, Shrewsbury Abbey
Hall, John and Sons	Bitterley
Hardman	Ashford Carbonell, Berrington, Chetwynd*, Church Stretton, Claverley, Cleeton St. Mary, Clunbury, Clungunford, Condover, Diddlebury, Donington, Edgmond, Highley, Hopton Castle, Lilleshall, Ludlow St. Laurence, More, Morville, Much Wenlock, Neen Savage, Pradoe, Rushbury, Ruyton XI Towns, Sheriffhales, Shifnal, Shrewsbury Abbey, Shrewsbury St.Chad, Shrewsbury Cathedral, Telford Hadley, Upton Magna, Wentnor, Whittington, Worfield, Wrockwardine
Heaton, Butler and Bayne	Bucknell, Church Aston*, Ellesmere, High Ercall, Jackfield**, Loppington, Oswestry St. Oswald, Peplow*, Prees, Shrewsbury Holy Trinity, Telford Coalbrookdale, Uppington, Welshampton*
Hemming, A.E.	Oldbury, Shrewsbury All Saints
Holiday, Henry	Bishop's Castle*, Calverhall*, Cleobury Mortimer, Hordley*, Quatt
Holland, William	Upton Magna
Horwood brothers	Rushbury
Hughes, H.	Sambrook, Sheinton
Jones and Willis	Leighton, Lydham, Oswestry Holy Trinity, Tibberton
Kempe, C.E.	Alveley, Baschurch, Bedstone*, Bicton*, Bromfield, Broseley, Caynham, Chelmarsh*, Cheswardine*, Chirbury, Clunbury, Cockshutt, Cound, Donnington Wood, Dudleston*, Dudleston Heath, Easthope, Edgmond*, Fitz, Ford, Glazeley*, Hadnall, Hope Bowdler, Hopesay, Kinnerley, Market Drayton*, Melverley, Meole Brace, Middleton, Middleton-in-Chirbury, Moreton Say*, Newport, Quatt, Selattyn*, Shrewsbury All Saints, Shrewsbury St. Giles, Tong, West Felton, Woore, Wrockwardine*, Yockleton*
Lavers, Barraud and Westlake	Atcham, Battlefield, Chetton, Edstaston, Milson*, Nash, Neen Sollars, Ruyton XI Towns, Sambrook, Tuck Hill

Lee, Lawrence	Gobowen
Lister, Sophia	Weston Lullingfields
Lobin *et fils*	High Ercall
Mayer and Co	Cleobury North, Dawley, Knowbury, Shrewsbury St. Mary, Wellington All Saints
Moore, A.L.	Acton Scott, Cardeston, Hopton Wafers, Wistanstow, Woolstaston
Morris, William	Meole Brace**
Morris and Co	Bitterley, Calverhall, Church Aston, Edgmond, Frodesley, Meole Brace**, Neenton*, Newport, Ruyton XI Towns, Shifnal, Shrewsbury All Saints*, Whitton*, Willey, Wroxeter
Newbery, R.J.	Ash
Newill, Mary	Hopesay, Ludlow St. Laurence, Wrockwardine
Nicholson, A.K.	Acton Burnell, Pitchford, Sibdon Carwood, Stoke-on-Tern, Woodcote
Nuttgens, J.E.	Newport
O'Connor	Bishop's Castle*, Church Aston, Ellesmere, Fauls, Lilleshall, Longdon-on-Tern, St. George's, Shrewsbury St. Giles, Wellington All Saints, Wrockwardine
Payne, Edward	Cardington
Payne, Henry	Stokesay
Pearce, William	Newport, Pontesbury, Wrockwardine Wood
Pilkington	Oswestry St. Oswald
Powell's	Bettws y Crwyn, Bishop's Castle*, Oldbury, Burford*, Calverhall, Cardeston, Cardington, Chirbury*, Clee St. Margaret, Cleobury Mortimer*, Coreley, Farlow, Hadnall, Hodnet, Hopesay, Hordley*, Llanfair Waterdine, Mainstone*, Market Drayton, Meole Brace, More, Norbury*, Onibury, Prees, Quatt, Ratlinghope, Shrewsbury All Saints, Shrewsbury St. Giles, Shrewsbury St. Mary, Sidbury, Stockton, Stokesay, Stowe, Telford Madeley, Tibberton, Welsh Frankton, Worthen
Pownall, L.A.	Child's Ercall*
Preedy, Frederick	Church Preen, Claverley. Eaton-under-Heywood, Habberley, Stockton
Price, Claude	Newport
Pringle, Evelyn	Newport
Reyntiens, Patrick	Malinslee
Robinson, John	Greete
Rope, Margaret	Shrewsbury Cathedral**, Wistanstow*
Saunders and Co	Newtown
Seward and Co.	Little Berwick
Shrigley and Hunt	Dawley, Market Drayton, Newtown, Shrewsbury All Saints
Skeat, Francis	Chetwynd*, Clungunford
Smith, G.E.R.	Montford, Sambrook
Sotheby, Barbara	Alberbury
Stephens, Francis	Wrockwardine Wood
Taylor, W.G.	Claverley
Thomas, Brian	Ford

Wailes, William	Atcham, Bridgnorth St. Mary Magdalene, Bucknell, Ellesmere, Hodnet, Llanymynech*, Middleton Scriven, Myddle, Shifnal
Wailes and Strang	Beckbury
Ward and Hughes	Leaton, Shrewsbury St. Giles, Wem, Whitchurch St. Alkmund, Whittington
Warrington, William	Albrighton near Shifnal, Boraston, Broseley, Ellesmere, Hodnet*, Linley, Norton-in-Hales, Whitchurch St. Alkmund*
Webb, Geoffrey	Munslow, Quatford, Selattyn
Whall, Christopher	Newport
Willement, Thomas	Cleobury Mortimer, Hopton Wafers, Ludlow St. Laurence*
Woodroffe, Paul	Hadley
Younger, Alan	Newport

Table VIII 19th- and 20th-century stained glass in Shropshire
(The information in this Table has been largely compiled from Newman and Pevsner, 2006.
Asterisked windows are recommended)

Gothic Revival

At the same time that Pugin and his associates were launching the Gothic Revival in architecture and church ritual, a parallel movement transformed the design of stained glass. Artists such as William Wailes, William Warrington (1786-1869), Thomas Willement (1786-1871) and John Hardman (1811-67) (all of whom are represented in Shropshire – see Table VIII) began to recapture the style of medieval glass and revived the mosaic craft technique of the Middle Ages. Examples of windows by Willement (Fig.27.10) and Warrington (Fig.12.7) are shown. The revival of medieval techniques was largely made possible by the work of a lawyer, Charles Winston (1814-64). For many years he studied stained glass from the Middle Ages, the Renaissance and later, and his work *An Inquiry into the Difference of Style observable in Ancient Glass Paintings, especially in England: with Hints on Glass Painting, by an Amateur* (1847) achieved an influence comparable to Rickman's analysis of medieval architecture (see p.12). Winston favoured the mosaic system used in the Middle Ages, in which each colour of the design, except yellow, brown and black, must be represented by a separate piece of glass, yellow and brown being excepted because of the possibility of staining. Winston rediscovered the chemical components of medieval pot-glass and persuaded the London firm of James Powell and Sons to make antique glass to his recipes. He found, for example, that the blue colour in 12th-century glass was due to cobalt, and not to lapis lazuli; within a few years he was able to produce red, green, yellow, white and purple according to medieval methods. The result was astonishing: the pictorial system was rapidly superseded, and by 1860 a revolution in the art of stained glass was accomplished.

Among the artists who applied Winston's discoveries in the ensuing years, two names stand out: William Morris (1834-96) and Edward Burne-Jones (1833-98). In the mid-1850s Burne-Jones had become linked with the Pre-Raphaelite brotherhood, and in 1857 in association with Powell's, Burne-Jones designed his first cartoon for stained glass. Burne-Jones also worked for a time with another firm, Lavers and Barraud, but then, in 1861, William Morris founded the firm which bore his name; the original partners

Fig.12.7 Hodnet: east window by William Warrington (1849)

*Figs.12.8 & 12.9 Meole Brace: south aisle windows, Faith (left) and Hope (right)
by Burne-Jones and Ford Madox Brown*

*Figs.12.10 & 12.11 Whitton: east window 'Saviour of the World' (left) and south window
'Angels' (right) by Morris and Co. (1893 and 1912 respectively)*

Fig.12.12 Church Aston: St. Paul preaching in Athens (1901), by Morris and Co.

Fig.12.13 Dudleston: Noli me tangere (1904) by C.E. Kempe

included Burne-Jones, Ford Madox Brown and D.G. Rosetti. The work of this firm may be seen in about a dozen Shropshire churches, notably Meole Brace, Newport and Whitton (Figs.12.8-12.12 and Table VIII). Morris was an outstanding colourist: his 'chords of deep green, dull ruby, blue and pale gold have a boldness of contrast and a subtlety of tonal balance which are ... entirely personal'. After the deaths of Morris and Burne-Jones, the firm of Morris and Co. continued to operate along the same lines, the cartoons being drawn by J.H. Dearle. The firm finally closed in 1940.

C.E. Kempe (1837-1907) (and his firm Kempe and Co., which lasted until 1934) produced a vast amount of stained glass which appears in at least 45 churches in Shropshire. He was an early associate of the architect G.F. Bodley, and he was trained in stained glass work at the firm of Clayton and Bell. By 1866 Kempe had started his own glassworks; eventually he ran one of the largest stained glass studios, employing at one time over 100 men. He was a deeply religious man who regarded his art as his vocation, and evolved a style based on French and English 14th-century Gothic, little influenced by his contemporaries in the Pre-Raphaelite movement. It is generally held that the earlier Kempe windows display greater inventiveness than his later output, although as they do not have the characteristic wheat-sheaf 'signature' which he adopted in 1895 they are harder to identify (Fig.12.13). One of Kempe's later pupils was Sir Ninian Comper (1864-1960).

Powell's was a glass-making firm based in the City of London dating back to the 17th century, which continued in operation until 1973. Their work may be seen in a number of Shropshire churches (Table VIII), most notably the Piers Plowman window in Cleobury Mortimer. Henry Holiday is one of their most notable designers.

It is not possible to review here more than a small selection of Victorian stained glass in the county; some other Victorian artists whose work may be seen are listed in Table VIII, but this list is by no means exhaustive. Nearly every Shropshire church contains Victorian glass, much of it uninspired, but I hope that the Table will guide readers to the most rewarding glass. Two examples of later Victorian glass are shown (Figs.12.14 & 12.15). A later Shropshire-born artist who produced excellent stained glass was Margaret Rope (1882-1953). Her work is best seen in Shrewsbury Cathedral (Figs.12.16 & 12.17), and there is a delightful figure of St. Wystan by her at Wistanstow (Fig.12.18). There is very little in the county of the Arts and Crafts movement – Christopher Whall is represented at Newport, but there is nothing by Walter Crane, and just one window at Alberbury could be said to exhibit Art Nouveau. Furthermore, the stock of later 20th-century glass is not impressive. Work by Comper may be seen at Moreton Corbet and Stanton-upon-Hine Heath, and there is the Jesse window by F.C. Eden (1864-1944) at Whittington. Modern glass from the later 20th century may be seen at Badger, Chetwynd, Gobowen, Newport and Weston Lullingfields.

Fig.12.14 Child's Ercall: The Ascension (1895) by L.A. Pownall

Wall-paintings

It is now difficult to appreciate that medieval churches were full of colour, all the walls being frequently covered with paintings designed to impress the parishioners. The painting was done in distemper (colour with water as a medium, and bound with white of egg or size – a gluey material) on dry and finished plaster-work (in contrast to frescoes, in which painting was done on wet plaster and permanently incorporated with it). Sometimes painting was repeated. 13th-century painting could be executed on fresh plaster applied over the paintings of the

Fig.12.15 Peplow: memorial window by Heaton, Butler and Bayne (1903)

94

Fig.12.16 Shrewsbury Cathedral, window by Margaret Rope

previous century or so. Because distemper was fugitive and easily damaged, very few good examples remain. Their number was further depleted when at the time of the Reformation many paintings were destroyed, or more fortunately covered over – sometimes to remain hidden for hundreds of years.

The commonest subject for medieval wall-painting was the figure of St. Christopher. Another frequent subject was the Doom, or Last Judgment, painted over the chancel arch; remains of this may be seen at Claverley and Cound. Doom paintings usually showed Christ in Majesty presiding over the Last Judgment, where the souls of the dead were weighed by St. Michael and received either into eternal paradise by angels, or into the mouth of hell by devils.

Fig.12.17 Shrewsbury Cathedral, window by Margaret Rope

Fig.12.18 Wistanstow: St. Wistan, by Margaret Rope, 1925

The finest wall-paintings in Shropshire are those at Claverley which are thought to depict the Battle of the Virtues and Vices (Fig.24.12), described on p.277. At Heath chapel there are remains of a painting said to represent St. George and the dragon; currently most of this is obscured by plaster and the paintings await skilled conservation. In St. John, Sutton (now the Greek Orthodox church) are remains of a painting of the murder of Thomas à Becket in Canterbury Cathedral. Remains of other medieval wall-paintings may be seen at Upton Cressett, Leebotwood (Fig.22.14) and the south transept of St. Laurence, Ludlow.

After the Reformation it became common practice to exhibit the Ten Commandments, Apostles' Creed and the Lord's Prayer. These might be painted on boards on either side of the altar, or sometimes on walls (as at Stokesay and Wistanstow). Stokesay has a particularly good display of all three texts set in decorative frames. At Lydbury North the texts are inscribed on a very large tympanum mounted over the rood screen, and dated 1615 (Fig.25.8).

13

Rood screens and lofts

In the later Middle Ages screens had two functions, firstly to act as a partition between the nave and chancel, and secondly to support the great rood – the image of Christ crucified, flanked by the figures of the Virgin Mary and of St John the Evangelist. The rood loft was a gallery above the screen, to which access was frequently provided by means of a stone stair-case; these stair-cases sometimes survive and may now be the sole evidence of the previous existence of a loft. Sometimes the rood loft housed an altar, in which case a piscina high up on the south wall may remain to indicate its past location (as at Church Stretton). Normally the rood screen and rood loft were part of the same fabric, but this was not universally the case, and in some churches they were independent structures. At the Reformation the great rood and the rood lofts were almost universally destroyed; in Shropshire there are no medieval rood lofts surviving, though it is known that the loft at Selattyn survived until 1751.[1] Many screens (or partitions as they were then termed – the word 'screen' appears to have come into general use only at the end of the 16th century) were also destroyed, but a fair number were spared. Where they were destroyed in the 16th century, they were often replaced in the High-Church revival from the 1840s onwards, so Victorian screens greatly outnumber medieval survivals. Above the great rood, extra decoration was occasionally applied to the roof, to act as a canopy of honour, or ceilure; at Clun, the ceilure is above the altar.

Good medieval screens may be found almost anywhere in England, but those in Devon and East Anglia are recognised as of outstanding quality. The earliest screen to survive in Shropshire may possibly be the rustic one at Melverley – a plain structure connected vertically with one of the tie-beams of the roof (Fig.15.12). This may be as early as the 15th century, but dendrochronology would be necessary to establish this. Nearly all the remaining medieval screens exhibit features of late Perpendicular work and date from the first half of the 16th century. There are fine medieval screens at Badger, Bettws-y-Crwyn (Fig.13.1), Llanyblodwel

Fig.13.1 Bettws-y-Crwyn: a fine Perpendicular screen

Fig.13.2 Neen Savage: another fine Perpendicular screen

(Fig.1.9), Ludlow, Lydbury North (Fig.25.8), Neen Savage (Fig.13.2), Tasley and Tong; but the best is the outstanding screen at Hughley – a wonderful structure dating from the early 16th century (Figs.13.3 & 13.4). It consists of three arches on either side and two central ones, the tracery in the arches being varied and delicate. The upper part of the dado is also beautifully carved. Above there is vaulting with the underside of the curved coving being adorned with birds, grapes and flowers. The ribs of the coving display a stellar pattern, similar to the screens at Aymestrey (Herefordshire), Astbury (Cheshire), and Denbigh and Gresford (north Wales).[2] Parclose screens are used to screen off a subsidiary chapel or aisle, and may be seen at Cleobury North (Fig.26.6), Ludlow and Tong.

After the Reformation, the art of fine carving in wood appears to have been lost for some time, and the only screen of the 17th century worth mentioning is that at Adderley,

Fig.13.3 Hughley: the finest screen in Shropshire

Fig.13.4 Hughley: stellate patterns on the underside of the coving

where there is a massive Jacobean screen in the Kilmorey chapel. It has slim columns, arches above, and is surmounted by a shield and phoenix centrally, and by spear-like finials laterally. Victorian screens are too numerous to be mentioned here, but some of the best are at Bitterley, Chelmarsh, Chetwynd, Clun, Doddington (Fig.13.5), Hopton Wafers, Market Drayton and Stottesdon. The unusual 19th-century screen at Nash (Fig.26.17) came from Louvain. The 19th-century screens at Newtown and Petton are made of wrought iron.

Finally, there is the remarkable structure at Middleton chapel, near Ludlow. This is a rood screen and loft (Fig.13.6), reconstructed at some time before 1854, being an amalgam of late Perpendicular and 19th-century work. The original Perpendicular work consists of the horizontal bars above the dado, the mullions and most of the tracery in the

Fig.13.5 Doddington: a Victorian screen

*Fig.13.6 Middleton: the reconstructed rood screen and loft,
part Perpendicular and part Victorian*

lights on either side of the central opening. Above the lights is upward coving, then at the base of the loft are original cornice beams in three rows, with vine-leaf carving. Most of the loft itself is early Victorian, but above is a Perpendicular rood-beam.

14

Pulpits, Pews and Chancel Furnishings

Pulpits

Pulpits surviving from the Middle Ages are not common in England, and there is only one surviving in Shropshire. This is the celebrated refectory frater pulpit which stands in the open to the south of Shrewsbury Abbey (Fig.14.1); originally scriptural passages would be read from here as the monks consumed their meal in silence. It dates from the early 14th century and is an octagonal structure, with tall trefoil-headed lancet openings. Above the pulpit is a domed roof, and on the central boss is carved a Crucifixion, with the figures of the Virgin Mary and St. John.

Fig.14.1 Shrewsbury Abbey: refectory pulpit

After the Reformation much greater emphasis was placed on the preaching of the Word and every parish church was required to provide a pulpit. There is a small group of churches in the south of the county whose pulpits probably date from the second half of the 16th century – these are at Greete (Fig.14.2), Middleton chapel, and Onibury, all within a few miles of each other. The plainest pulpit is at Greete – two tiers of panels with a plain cornice above and no decoration of any kind. Middleton is similar, but the cornice is carved with a series of plain arches. At Onibury there is linenfold panelling, and on the door two tiers of cusped tracery of dubious antiquity.

From the 17th century onwards surviving pulpits suddenly become numerous – there are well over 50 'Jacobean' pulpits dating from the reigns of James I and Charles I, some of which are dated – e.g. Shawbury 1612, Quatt 1629, Petton 1635, and Church Preen

Fig.14.2 Greete: late 16th-century pulpit

Fig.14.3 Bourton: Jacobean pulpit   *Fig.14.4 Cressage: another Jacobean pulpit*

Fig.14.5 Clun: a stately   *Fig.14.6 Petton: Jacobean*   *Fig.14.7 St. Martin's: the county's*
Jacobean pulpit with tester   *pulpit with carved tester*   *grandest three-decker pulpit*

Fig.14.8 Easthope: a 17th-century hourglass to restrain prolix preachers

1641. Some Jacobean pulpits are plain but many are decorated, as at Bourton (Fig.14.3), Cressage (Fig.14.4) and Melverley (Fig.15.12). Short blank arches are characteristic, and in addition there are often arabesques, balusters, caryatids (Cleobury North, Stottesdon), flowers (Astley Abbots, Stockton) or even mermen (Cardington, Much Wenlock). The pulpit at Cleobury North has an upper tier with blank arches separated by caryatids, and below arches with a lozenge ornament between. Several Jacobean pulpits retain their testers or sounding-boards, as at Clun (Fig.14.5), Kenley, Petton (Fig.14.6), Pitchford (Fig.22.18), and Stokesay. Pulpits from the later 17th century may be seen at Little Berwick, and at Eaton-under-Heywood and Minsterley (both with tester).

Reading-desks may often be seen adjacent to the pulpit, and may be carved in a similar style. From the desk, the minister would take the service or sometimes the clerk would lead the congregational responses. Examples may be seen at Bourton, Quatt, Shelve, Stockton and elsewhere.

In the 18th century pulpits tended to be plainer. They include Albrighton near Shrewsbury, Great Bolas, Halston (Fig.15.4) and Stirchley (all with tester), Longden, Longnor, and Selattyn. It was in this century that the three-decker pulpit really came into its own. It is a stately sight, especially when crowned by the sounding-board which amplified the voice of the preacher. The lowest tier is the reading-desk, from which the clerk led the responses. From the middle tier the minister conducted the service, and he then ascended into the top tier from which he would deliver his weighty, and usually lengthy, sermon. The grandest three-decker pulpit in Shropshire is at St. Martin's (Fig.14.7), assembled in 1810 but containing some re-used Jacobean panels.

To restrain the eloquence of verbose preachers, hourglasses were sometimes placed beside the pulpit; there is a fine example at Easthope (Fig.14.8).

Under the influence of the High-Church movement, there was less emphasis on preaching in the Victorian period and greater insistence on the correct ordering of sacramental worship. Wooden Victorian pulpits are very frequent in Shropshire, far too numerous to be listed here; among the best may be mentioned those at Meole Brace (complete with sounding-board) and at Woolstaston. There are a number of stone pulpits in the county, including three by the architect G.E. Street – Lyneal, St. George's and Withington. Other pulpits of stone or marble may be seen at Beckbury, Caynham, Farlow, Sambrook and Welshampton. At Wem is a pulpit of wrought iron, dated 1887.

Fig.14.9 Ludlow: choir-stalls

Choir-stalls

In medieval cathedrals and the larger parish churches, stalls for the clergy were arranged on either side of the chancel. Each stall was provided with a hinged seat, and the under surface of this had a bracket, or 'misericord', to support the clergy during prolonged standing.[1] The misericords were usually carved, with subjects often domestic, grotesque or satirical; few were of religious themes. There are two notable sets of choir-stalls in Shropshire – at Ludlow and Tong, both Perpendicular churches. The 32 stalls at Ludlow (Fig.14.9) date from the mid-15th century and were provided at the expense of the Palmers' Guild. The woodwork is, however, not all of the same period. The complete set of misericords is one of the finest in England; one is illustrated here (Fig.14.10).

The 16 stalls at the collegiate church of Tong (Fig.14.11) also date from the 15th century; they have been skilfully restored but contain much original work. Of the misericords, the finest is possibly the representation of the Annunciation.[2] The stalls have tall backs, with exquisitely rich tracery, and there are poppyheads at the ends of the benches.

Fig.14.10 Ludlow: misericord – a kitchen scene, with a stew-pot on the fire

Fig.14.11 Tong: choir-stalls

Fig.14.12 Worthen: box-pews on either side, and a central series of benches, some medieval

Pews and benches

On a lower level of workmanship, two churches in Corvedale (Holdgate and Munslow) have rustic pews of medieval origin, while more have benches or pews dating from the 17th century (e.g. Clee St. Margaret, Langley [Fig.22.13]). At Worthen there is a remarkable series of benches displayed in the middle of the nave (Fig.14.12), with box-pews on either side. At least some of these benches may well be medieval. An unusual series of Victorian pews is at Bettws-y-Crwyn (Fig.14.13), where

Fig.14.13 Bettws-y-Crwyn: benches inscribed
with the names of local farms

the names of local farms are inscribed on the
bench-ends.

Larger pews for the local squire and his family,
or occasionally for churchwardens and clergy,
may be seen in a number of churches. The finest
is undoubtedly the canopied pew at Stokesay
– an elaborate late-17th-century structure of two
compartments, with seats on three sides (Fig.14.14).
Such pews were satirised by Jonathan Swift:

Fig.14.14 Stokesay: 17th-century
canopied pew

A bedstead of the antique mode,
Compact of timber many a load,
Such as our ancestors did use,
Was metamorphosed into pews;
Which still their ancient nature keep
By lodging folks disposed to sleep.[3]

Fig.14.15 Cleobury North:
Jacobean family pew

Fig.14.16 Lydbury North: carved box-pews

On a lesser scale of luxury are two big square pews below the gallery at Halston, and the Forester family pew at Willey. At Cleobury North is a fine Jacobean family pew, with a high back and pedimented top, decorated with vine leaves, fruit, etc. (Fig.14.15). The pew at Holdgate is similar, but unfortunately somewhat damaged. At Ditton Priors are two double-seats in Jacobean style, dated 1714. Squire's and/or vicar's pews may be seen at Heath, Longnor and St. Martin's.

Sets of box-pews were almost universal during the 18th century, but many were destroyed during Victorian restorations so that today only a precious few survive. These may date from the 17th (Wroxeter, Heath, Edgton) or 18th century (Longnor, Stirchley). The finest sets are preserved at Worthen (Fig.14.12), Stokesay, Leebotwood and Lydbury North (Fig.14.16). They may also be seen at Church Pulverbatch, Frodesley, Little Berwick, Petton, St. Martin's and Sheinton. At Halston (Fig.15.4), they are arranged facing each other, as in a college chapel.

Fig.14.17 Priorslee: the gilt reredos

Chancel furnishings

A reredos is a decorative screen placed behind the altar. Most medieval reredoses were destroyed after the Reformation, and none survives in Shropshire. At Pitchford and Quatt, however, parts of the late Perpendicular screen were fashioned into a reredos. Jacobean panelling and other 17th-century work may be seen at Ford, Halston, Petton and Stapleton. Distinguished Victorian reredoses, often of stone or marble, may be seen in a number of Shropshire churches – among the best are Chetwynd, Dorrington, Lyneal and Welshampton. Well-known Victorian architects designed the reredos in various Shropshire churches – G.E. Street at Church Aston (Fig.18.8), Oswestry, Pontesbury and Withington (a notable chancel); Bodley and Garner at Edgmond and Ruyton XI Towns; Pearson at Cheswardine and Shrewsbury Abbey; Comper at Moreton Corbet. The reredoses at Stowe and Chirbury are composed of mosaics of multicoloured stone, while the gilt reredos at Priorslee (Fig.14.17) is unique.

Other chancel furnishings of note in Shropshire include the sedilia at Stottesdon, the Easter sepulchre at Billingsley (Fig.24.7) the candlesticks at Lydbury North and the candlesticks and the altar composed of Jacobean panelling at Stapleton (Fig.14.18).

Fig.14.18 Stapleton: the handsome altar

15

The north-west – Oswestry and Ellesmere

Cockshutt
Criftins (Dudleston Heath)
Dudleston**
Ellesmere***
Gobowen
Halston***
Haughton
Hordley*
Kinnerley*
Knockin*
Llanyblodwel**
Llanymynech*
Loppington*
Lyneal**
Maesbrook

Maesbury
Melverley**
Morton
Oswestry, Holy Trinity
Oswestry, St. Oswald*
Pradoe*
St. Martin's**
Selattyn**
Trefonen
Welshampton**
Welsh Frankton*
West Felton*
Weston Rhyn
Whittington*

St. Simon and St. Jude, Cockshutt
There was a medieval church here dedicated to St. Helena, but this fell into disrepair and was replaced in 1777 by the present plain, brick building, consisting of a nave and apse, with a western tower. Its most attractive feature is the glass in the lancet windows of the apse by C.E. Kempe (1896), showing the Crucifixion in the central window, flanked by figures of St. Helena and St. Chad on the left, and St. Simon and St. Jude on the right.

The church clock is notable: it was made in 1789 by Bullock and Davies, an apparently unique collaboration between two well-known Shropshire clockmakers.

St. Matthew, Criftins (Dudleston Heath)
This is a conventional red-brick Victorian church, built in 1874 to the design of W.G. MacCarthy. The sole interesting feature is the stained glass in the apsidal windows by Kempe.

St. Mary, Dudleston**
The earliest description of this church (a chapel to Ellesmere) is the Williams painting of 1789; this shows a stuccoed building with no evidence of timber-framing, but with an engaging wooden bell-turret and above an open lantern stage and quite a tall balustrade enclosing a short spirelet. This building was radically altered in 1819 when the upper

octagonal stage of the tower was added, together with north and south aisles. It is likely that as far as possible the old masonry was re-used.

The church (Fig.15.1) now consists of a nave with north and south aisles, chancel, and western tower. The nave at least is old, for it is covered with a fine late Perpendicular roof, with two tiers of cusped half-wind-braces. The pulpit is Jacobean. There is an ancient chest at the west end

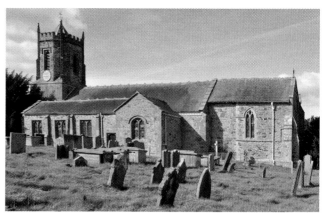

Fig.15.1 St. Mary, Dudleston

of the church. There is excellent stained glass by Kempe in the westernmost window of the north aisle (Fig.12.13); this depicts the Resurrection, and has Kempe's wheatsheaf 'signature' in the corner. The glass in the east window is probably also by Kempe. At the west end of the church are an impressive series of benefaction boards.

St. Mary, Ellesmere***

At the time of the Domesday survey there were two manors at Ellesmere, one of which was exceedingly prosperous and worth £20 per year. The presence of two priests was recorded. The manors were held by Earl Roger; after the rebellion of his sons they passed to the Crown. When Henry II's sister married the Welsh prince Dafydd ap Owain in 1174,

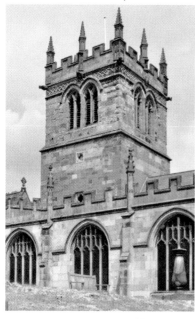

Fig.15.2 St. Mary, Ellesmere: the tower

and King John's natural daughter married Llywelyn the Great early in the 13th century, Llywelyn became possessed of both manors. In 1225 Llywelyn gave Ellesmere to the Knights of St. John, who held it until the Dissolution. The knights had a major preceptory at Halston (q.v.) nearby, and it was they who rebuilt and adorned the medieval church. Apart from the tower and the chancel chapels, very little of the medieval church remains; for, by the 1840s, the church was in a sorry state.

Sir George Gilbert Scott was asked to advise, and he reported that he had never seen so many galleries cluttering the nave and one of the side-chapels. The nave was in such a decayed and dilapidated state that he recommended that it should be entirely rebuilt and considerably enlarged by the addition of spacious aisles. His advice was accepted, and the present church is largely the result of his work.

The church occupies a commanding position above the mere, with lovely views. The central tower (Fig.15.2) is Early English below, but Perpendicular above, with a quatrefoil frieze above the belfry, battlements, pinnacles and gargoyles. The chancel is mostly medieval, but the east wall was rebuilt in 1888. There are Perpendicular sedilia in the south wall, with Victorian black marble columns between the seats. On the north side of the chancel, an arcade of two bays opens into St. John's chapel, which is entirely Perpendicular. On the south side, an arcade of three bays opens into St. Anne's chapel, which is also Perpendicular. The roof of this chapel (Fig.8.11) is the finest in the church: low-pitched, with panelling between the beams and rafters, and bosses at the junctions. The crossing, transepts, nave and aisles are the work of Gilbert Scott; all is competent and correct, if a little conventional, and done in the Decorated style. Medieval work remains only in the east side of the east arch of the crossing, and in the door opening into the north transept.

There are two fonts: the original Perpendicular font, with octagonal bowl carved with the Instruments of Christ's Passion, is placed unobtrusively in the north transept. A 19th-century replica is in the baptistry at the west end of the south aisle. In the south chancel chapel is the monument to Francis Kynaston (d.1581) and his wife – alabaster effigies on a tomb-chest. Also in this chapel, high on the west wall, is an excellent carving, believed to be of a scrivener, discovered in 1849. The man's head rests on a cushion, his hands hold a book, and his feet rest against a dog. The sculpture probably dates from the 14th century. There is plentiful stained glass in the church; among the best examples are the windows in the south transept and south aisle by Wailes (1845); in the north window of the chancel by David Evans (1833); in the east window of the chancel by Heaton, Butler and Bayne (1888); and in the south chapel by Burlison and Grylls (1872).

All Saints, Gobowen
All Saints was built in 1928 because the expanding village of Gobowen was relatively distant from the parish church of Hengoed, which has now been demolished. The architects, Messrs Freeman and Ogilvie, designed a very conservative building in the Perpendicular style, without a trace of influence of the 20th century. The only unusual feature is the presence of blind arcading inside and out between the windows of the south wall of the nave. Yet it is attractively built of Caen stone – unfortunately the nave was gutted by fire in 1979 and the stonework has been replaced by plaster. There is good modern stained glass in the east window by Lawrence Lee, who designed some of the glass in Coventry Cathedral. The font and priests' stalls came from a redundant church in Birmingham.

Halston chapel***
This chapel in the grounds of Halston Hall is not, and never has been, a parish church, but it demands inclusion in any book on Shropshire churches because of the quality and rarity of its furnishings.

After the Norman Conquest, Halston manor was held from Earl Roger by Rainald the Sheriff, according to the Domesday Book, but by the middle of the 12th century it had come into the hands of the knights of St. John of Jerusalem, who owned it until the Dissolution. By 1551 it belonged to the Mytton family, but was briefly restored to the knights by Queen Mary. Elizabeth confirmed the Myttons in their ownership and it remained with this family for 300 years. The original Hospitallers' preceptory was probably adjacent to the site of the present chapel, but the Myttons moved their dwelling to drier ground 400 yards away in 1690, when the present Halston Hall was built and the preceptory was demolished.

The chapel (Fig.15.3) therefore stands alone in pleasant parkland, surrounded by yews. There is an incongruous 18th-century brick tower, but the remainder of the building is half-timbered and very attractive to the modern eye.

Fig.15.3 Halston chapel: 15th-century half-timbered nave and 18th-century brick tower

When was it built? Until recently, no-one knew, and guesses ranged from the late 14th to the mid-16th centuries. But dendrochronology has come to the rescue, and the result is surprising: the date of the roof timbers was 1437,[1] earlier than most experts had predicted. So Halston has proved to be a 15th-century church.

But attractive though the exterior undoubtedly is, it is the interior which is truly breathtaking because of the remarkable range of Jacobean and Georgian fittings. The pews are

Fig.15.4 Halston: pews and pulpit

Fig.15.5 Looking west from the pulpit

displayed facing each other, as in a college chapel, with panelling on both sides and at the east end (Fig.15.4); all this probably dates from the 17th century. The two-decker pulpit is later, dated 1725, and the reredos is of the same era. As was customary in the late 17th and 18th centuries, there are paintings of Moses and Aaron, and the Ten Commandments, Lord's Prayer and Creed. The west gallery (Fig.15.5), bearing the Hanoverian Royal Arms, is carried by the westernmost tie-beam. The roof-trusses are moulded and the spandrels carved with various figures, including a bishop, a fox and the Bear and Ragged Staff symbol of the Greville family with whom the Mytton family had intermarried in 1552.[2] There is a fine brass chandelier carrying candles (electricity is not installed), and family hatchments adorn the north and south walls. This is a privately owned chapel; applications to visit should be made to Mr. R. Harvey of Halston Hall.

St. Chad, Haughton
A small church built in 1886 in the parish of West Felton.

St. Mary, Hordley*

Fig.15.6 St. Mary, Hordley

St. Mary's is a small Norman village church consisting of nave and chancel, with a picturesque timber-framed belfry (Fig.15.6). The blocked Norman north doorway is wide and plain. The masonry (red and yellow sandstone) of the north and west walls looks original, but the east wall has clearly been rebuilt, and possibly also the south wall. All the windows (Decorated and Perpendicular) have been restored.

Inside there is an attractive set of box-pews on the north; the names and coats of arms of some of the owners are recorded. The plain pulpit is probably late 17th-century. All the stained glass was made by Powell's; the east window is especially good, and was designed by Henry Holiday.

St. Mary Kinnerley
The combination of a Perpendicular west tower and Georgian church, often incongruous, is at Kinnerley quite attractive – possibly because both parts are built of red sandstone and thus harmonise reasonably well. The tower is truly Perpendicular only in its lower stages (including the fine west window), for the Williams painting of 1786 shows a wooden bell-cote with pyramidal roof. So the present belfry, battlements and gargoyles came later.

The rest of the church is attributed to T.F. Pritchard because of entries in the church-wardens' accounts, but Ionides[3] fails to find many clues about the architect. The wide round-headed windows are capped with keystones, as in many other Georgian churches in Shropshire. The interior is rather barn-like. Behind the altar is a panel inscribed with the Creed, Lord's Prayer and Ten Commandments. Perhaps the most interesting feature is the stained glass by Tower in the chancel, depicting the Annunciation and the Adoration of the Magi; it is said to be an imitation of Holbein, and is as late as 1932; this is just before the demise of Kempe and Co., which was run by Tower after Kempe's death. Outside the church stands a rather battered but very ancient font; I presume that this is the same structure described in Cranage as having formerly resided in a garden at Dovaston, and being inscribed with a Greek palindrome. At the base is some linear carving.

St. Mary, Knockin

Fig.15.7 St. Mary, Knockin

Fig.15.8 Knockin: the north arcade now embedded in the north wall of the nave

The place-name is of Welsh origin, meaning 'a small hillock'.[4] There was a Norman castle, the remains of which still constitute a prominent mound just east of the church. The church probably developed as a chapel to the castle, for it was founded between 1182 and 1195 by Ralph l'Estrange, the patronage being given to Haughmond Abbey.

Knockin church (Fig.15.7) today presents a curious aspect, being almost entirely Victorian, with a few Norman survivals. The latter consists of a north arcade, now embedded in the north wall (Fig.15.8), the north aisle having been demolished; the round-headed priest's door in the south wall of the chancel (this has chevron decoration at right-angles to the plane of the door); and a plain Norman font, with a single band of moulding around the bowl. Some of the capitals of the arcade have water-leaf carving. All the windows are Victorian, a few neo-Norman, but mostly lancets. The very weathered red sandstone porch looks old, but in fact dates from the early 20th century.

St. Michael the Archangel, Llanyblodwel**

St. Michael's has in the past had a poor press from architectural historians. 'One cannot help smiling at the absurdity of Llanyblodwel', says Dean Cranage. 'Everything is incorrect here', pronounces Pevsner a little loftily, 'and little is beautiful'. But times and tastes change and recent writers have looked more favourably on St. Michael's, in spite of the church's obvious eccentricities. 'A high flight of Victorian whimsy', says Harbison,[5] not unkindly; and Simon Jenkins also writes sympathetically of this 'eccentric rebuilding'.[6]

Fig.15.9 St. Michael the Archangel, Llanyblodwel

The setting of the tiny village is enchanting, with the old stone arched bridge over the river Tanat and the half-timbered Horseshoe Inn. The church is along a lane on the north bank of the river, and is of medieval origin – though the present evidence for this is largely confined to the Norman south doorway and the Perpendicular arcade and east windows. The old church was recorded by Williams in 1790. Sir Stephen Glynne visited it in 1845: he was not favourably impressed. There was no tower, but a slated belfry over the west end of the nave. The porch was 'a bad one built in the 17th century'. He found 'several late and poor Perpendicular windows'. The altar 'is elbowed by a hideous new aristocratic pew'. In the north chancel there was 'a frightful and stupendous monument'; was that Rysbrack's? – see below. By the late 1840s, the south wall was becoming ruinous, and the vicar, the Reverend John Parker of Sweeney Hall took a hand. He was a man of tremendous energy, and a proficient water-colourist – his sister Mary even more so (see figs.6.4 & 21.3).

The church as it stands now is Parker's memorial – entirely loveable and characteristic of the early Victorian age. The octagonal tower and spire (Fig.15.9), semi-detached from the church, is a local landmark. Based on that of Freiburg Cathedral, it has a slight convexity, and there are narrow vertical windows on each face, diminishing in height from below upwards. The south wall is entirely Parker's design, and has two dormer windows and a porch with wavy wooden timber ribs.

The interior (Fig.1.9) is a feast of colour, with the painted Perpendicular arcade, many texts, and a bizarre arrangement of roof timbers with pendants and bosses. There is a west gallery, and an organ gallery in the north aisle. The fine screen extends across the whole breadth of the church, some of it is original Perpendicular, and some Victorian. There is an octagonal font of uncertain age, and a hatchment on the north wall of the nave. Of several monuments, the best is that of 1752 to Sir John Bridgman by J.M. Rysbrack (1694-1770); above is a large urn flanked by volutes, with a cartouche and further volutes below. This is a minor work of the great sculptor, who was famous for his busts and reclining figures.

St. Agatha, Llanymynech*

Eight years after he built Holy Trinity, Oswestry, Thomas Penson designed Llanymynech in the neo-Norman fashion – a style which achieved a brief vogue in the 1840s. Pevsner was severe: 'a crazy demonstration of the neo-Norman fashion'.

There had been a medieval church dating perhaps from the late 13th century. This was painted by Williams in 1790 and shows a twin-gabled building of nave and chancel, with north aisle and a western bell-turret. By the 1840s the building was in a poor state of repair and it was demolished and

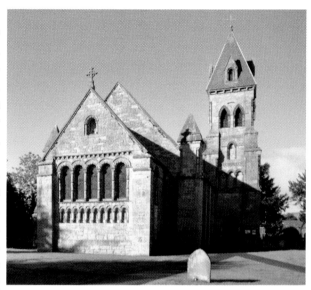

Fig.15.10 St. Agatha, Llanymynech

replaced by the present church, which consists of nave and shallow chancel and a north-western tower. The neo-Norman features are present throughout the building – round-headed windows and blind arcading, all decorated with rather heavy chevron motifs. Both the west (Fig.15.10) and the east façades are heavily adorned. The church is built of local grey limestone, but all the mouldings, jambs and ornamental parts are of yellow terra-cotta.[7] The only exceptions to the round-headed windows are some lancets high on the west façade and on the tower, and again these are decorated incongruously with chevron (perhaps this is what Pevsner thought was crazy?). Despite this quibble, the overall effect is pleasing, and St. Agatha's must rank as the best neo-Norman church in the county.

Inside, there are no monuments of any note, but the octagonal font is good: apparently it came from Beachampton church, Buckinghamshire, and was found by Lord Dungannon in a lane being used as a drinking-trough for cattle. Some of the stained glass is good: the colourful east window depicting in five panels the Nativity, Baptism, Crucifixion, Resurrection and Ascension of Christ is by William Wailes (*c.*1853), whose work may also be seen at Ellesmere.

St. Michael and All Angels, Loppington*

Loppington church has undergone many changes over the centuries, including damage sustained during the Civil War, and it is not always easy to piece together its history. In 1190 the church was given to Wombridge Priory, but no part of the present building dates from the 12th century. The church now consists of a western tower, nave with south aisle and south porch, and chancel. The tower and south aisle are built of a warm, attractive yellow sandstone, but the north wall of the nave is of red sandstone and was clearly built at a different period: the explanation appears to be that there was formerly a north aisle which was later demolished, the north wall being rebuilt at some time after the Reformation.

Fig.15.11 St. Michael and All Angels, Loppington

In the north wall, however, there is a genuine Decorated doorway and a Decorated window, which must have been inserted. The tower (Fig.15.11) and the south aisle are Perpendicular, with three-light windows with head-stops, now badly weathered. Below the window in the south aisle are vertical marks, possibly arrow cuts. In the west wall of the tower is a doorway, and above a Perpendicular window. Over this, the clock conceals what was once a niche for an image, with a canopy over it. The south doorway appears to be Victorian. The porch is dated 1658. The chancel was rebuilt at some time in the 19th century, but the south Perpendicular window was retained and the reticulated east window is a Decorated insertion.

The best features of the interior are the roofs over the nave and the south aisle; these are similar and consist of collar-beams on arched braces, and ogee-curved wind-braces. They probably date from the 17th century. Both the arcade and the chancel arch look Victorian, and this is confirmed by Sir Stephen Glynne. He visited Loppington in 1851 and described a wooden arcade and mentioned that the chancel arch had been destroyed. He also wrote of a west gallery and ugly pews; all this was clearly swept away later in the 19th century. The octagonal font is plain, but probably not medieval. The panelled pulpit is probably 18th-century.

St. John the Evangelist, Lyneal with Colemere**

The church stands on elevated ground with a lovely view through an avenue of yews to Colemere. Lady Alford paid for the church to be built in memory of her son who had died of tuberculosis in 1867. She held High-Church views, and naturally chose an architect of similar persuasion. The result is one of the most attractive of Street's village churches, all the more so for being understated and modest in its pretensions.

The church consists of nave and chancel, with a bellcote at their junction (Fig.5.6). It is built of buff-coloured stone from Cefn, with a few transverse red bands providing a little polychromy. There is some trellis work in the west gable, now nearly hidden by a tree. The south doorway is contained in a buttress-like projection, as at Whixall. The windows are mostly cusped lancets.

The interior is beautifully proportioned, with the stone exposed, and above is a trussed-rafter roof. Street was a stickler for details, and most of the fittings are to his design. The font is restrained and distinguished, the pulpit bold with open-work tracery of pointed quatrefoils. A low stone screen separates nave from chancel as at Withington. In the chancel are encaustic tiles, with representations of birds and lions.

The reredos (1880) is outstanding – a terracotta Crucifixion panel flanked by corn and vine motifs. The artist is George Tinworth (1843-1913), whose work in terracotta was patronised by the Prince of Wales (later Edward VII) for Sandringham church and exhibited in the Paris Exhibition of 1878.

St. John, Maesbrook
A small church built in 1878 in the Decorated style; the architect was Mr. Hancock, from Shrewsbury. It has a nave and chancel, and a western bell-turret.

St. John the Baptist, Maesbury
A sweet little church of corrugated iron, painted white, with a spirelet at the west end. The interior is wooden. Its activities would put to shame many a grander building.

St. Peter, Melverley**
Melverley means 'meadow by the mill-ford',[8] and St. Peter's church stands perilously close to the river Vyrnwy, near to its confluence with the Severn. In February 1990 the foundations of the church were seriously threatened by flooding and extensive works were instituted to protect the church from further hazard. The medieval church was burnt by Owain Glyndwr in 1401, and it appears that the present church was built soon after.

St. Peter's (Fig.1.5) is famous for being one of only 27 half-timbered churches in the country (see also Halston). Clifton-Taylor wrote about such churches: 'All were doted on by the Victorian ecclesiologists, but the truth is that every one of them has been so drastically restored as to offer today only very limited pleasure.'[9] Although that may be true for connoisseurs of church architecture, ordinary folk will indeed get a great deal of pleasure from a church such as Melverley.

The church is divided into three compartments by two timber frames disposed north/south. The eastern frame divides the chancel from the nave, and its downward continuation forms a screen (Fig.15.12). The western frame is modified by the gallery. The entire structure is pegged together without nails. It is noticeable that the width of the wattle-and-daub between the timbers is less than the width of the timbers – a sign of a relatively early date of construction. There is a south porch and a western bell-turret. In the roof are collar- and tie-beams, and, in the chancel, arched braces. The gallery and pews probably date from 1718 (though the gallery, in particular, may be earlier); it slopes markedly from south to north, giving a very quaint appearance, enhanced by the uneven steps leading up to it. The pulpit is

Fig.15.12 St. Peter, Melverley: the interior, looking south-west

Jacobean. The octagonal font may be 15th-century; it bears a palindromic Greek inscription, which is translated 'Cleanse your sin, not your face only'. The glass in the east window is by Kempe and Co. *Pace* Clifton-Taylor, the entire church is a delight, which should not be missed.

St. Philip and St. James, Morton
Morton church was built in 1872-73, the architect being S. Pountney Smith. It is a surprisingly large church, with nave and chancel and a south aisle. The arcade of four bays has rounded piers and plain rounded capitals, in contrast to the chancel arch which has florid leafy capitals on corbels, the arch itself being decorated with dogtooth. There are plain arches leading from the chancel to the vestry and organ-chamber. There is a circular stone pulpit with some carving, and a plain octagonal font. The windows on the south side consist of groups of three cusped lancets under trefoils, with a straight top; on the north, paired taller lancets with quatrefoils above.

Holy Trinity, Oswestry
This church was built in 1837 because St. Oswald's could not accommodate the growing population of the town. The architect chosen was Thomas Penson 'the Younger' (1790-1859), a local man who also built Llanymynech and various churches in Wales. It is a large hall church, with a Lady chapel to the south added in 1894. At the same time a north-west tower with a timber spire was added by Eustace Frere. The windows are very tall lancets, and the apse has rib-vaulting and dogtooth ornament. There is a flat ceiled roof, with fan-vaulting rising from corbels. An unusual feature is the lancet window filled with stained glass in memory of Queen Victoria. The font is a marble baluster.

St. Oswald, Oswestry*
Oswestry is an attractive border town, but the church has had rather an unfortunate history. It was severely damaged in the Civil War; after this catastrophe, it was almost completely rebuilt in a 'debased' Perpendicular style. Sir Stephen Glynne visited Oswestry before 1840, and predictably he was not impressed: 'the interior has a clumsy appearance'. G.E. Street was responsible for an extensive restoration in 1872-74; perhaps he was constrained by the existing building for the interior still looks 'clumsy', with a veritable forest of arcades.

The church consists of a nave with wide north aisle, double south aisle into which the tower cuts, and chancel with north and south chancel chapels. The heavily buttressed south-west tower is impressive

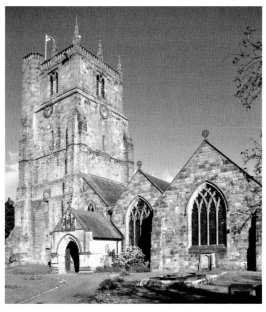

Fig.15.13 St. Oswald, Oswestry

119

(Fig.2.3), and the lower part dates from the 13th century; the upper part was rebuilt after the Civil War and has a balustrade and pinnacles. The rest of the exterior (Fig.15.13) is a composite of rebuildings in the 17th and 19th centuries, mainly the latter. Nearly all the windows are Victorian, though some are said to be accurate reproductions of the originals.

The interior is confusing, with its three arcades dividing the nave and aisles, the west end of the middle arcade running parallel and very close to the north wall of the tower. The best part of the church is the chancel, which is colourful and attractive; the reredos is by Street. To the north (beyond the organ) is the chapel of St. Catherine, recently refurbished and set aside for private prayer. To the south is the Lady chapel, with an excellent 18th-century reredos. There are two fonts – a Victorian one just inside the main door (? by Street) and another dated 1662 in the north aisle. At the west end of the north aisle is a large, rather coarse Jacobean monument to Hugh Yale (d.1616) and his wife.

Pradoe Church*

This attractive chapel of ease (Fig.15.14) has been awarded extraparochial status, and its survival as a place of worship is largely due to the tenacity of its congregation. Pradoe prides itself on being always open, and on being devoted to the Book of Common Prayer. The church was built in 1860-65, the architect being Mr. Rhode Hawkins. It consists of a nave and chancel, undivided, with a short arcade of three bays dividing the chancel from a north vestry. The piers of the arcades have florid foliated capitals, commonly found in the

Fig.15.14 Pradoe church, by Rhode Hawkins

1860s. There is a north tower. The roof of the nave is an unusual scissor-braced trussed-rafter. Moran[10] describes it as a Gothic pastiche of mid-13th-century design – a six-canted, ashlared, scissor-braced roof.

St. Martin, St. Martin's**

Gelling[11] groups St. Martin's with the obviously Welsh names of Shropshire parishes – Llanyblodwel, Llanymynech, Llanfair Waterdine and Bettws-y-Crwyn – implying that St. Martin's is an anglicised form of an originally Welsh name; all five are near to the Welsh border.

The church is worth visiting mainly for its excellent roofs and woodwork. The building consists of a nave with north aisle, chancel and a west tower. The structure of the church is a great hotchpotch of styles, but the overall result is successful, especially from the south

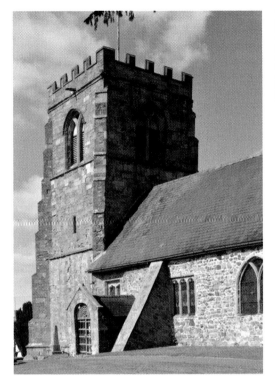

Fig.15.15 St. Martin, St. Martin's   Fig.15.16 St. Martin's: the interior

(Fig.15.15). The chancel is basically Early English, though the east wall and window were rebuilt in 1862. The south doorway is probably Decorated. The nave is separated from the north aisle by a Perpendicular arcade, the eastern bays of which are earlier than the western. The windows in the south wall of the nave and chancel are later Perpendicular insertions. The tower is also late Perpendicular, and according to Cranage may be as late as 1632.

The nave roof (Fig.15.16) is made of collar-beams, with queen-posts giving additional support. The chancel roof is boarded, ribbed and embossed, giving the effect of a wagon-roof. Unfortunately, the previous set of box-pews has gone, the ends of the pews now panelling the east wall of the chancel. The show-piece of the church is the complete three-decker pulpit (Fig.14.7) now standing at the west end of the building. Though assembled only in 1810, some Jacobean pieces were re-used. On the south wall of the nave hangs a fine wooden carving of St. Catherine, said to be of Celtic origin. Two of the aisle windows have stained glass by David Evans. There is a monument to Richard Phillips (d.1824) by C.M. Seddon, showing a kneeling woman with an urn.

St. Mary, Selattyn**

The place-name is based on Acton – oak settlement – the name being modified by Welsh influence;[12] the first part of the name is from *sulh* – a gully. The village is attractively situated in the hilly country west of Oswestry, and St. Mary's church is worthy of its setting. Sir Stephen Glynne is alone amongst writers in not responding favourably to Selattyn

– he gave a very dyspeptic account following his visit in 1845.

The church (Fig.15.17) consists of a western tower, with nave, north aisle, south transept and chancel. The upper stage of the tower is dated 1703, but the lower stages may be older; certainly the lower of the two pairs of windows on the south face seem older. The west window is a Victorian insertion. At the junction of the nave and the south transept are the remains of a Norman doorway, the siting of which puzzled Cranage. There are straight-headed Perpendicular windows in the south wall of both nave and chancel, but the east window is Victorian. The north aisle and porch were built in 1892.

Fig.15.17 St. Mary, Selattyn

The best feature of the interior is the lovely roof of the chancel (Fig.8.13) – this has curved panelling and a cornice with a frieze of quatrefoils. Some of this is Victorian, but Cranage ascribed the main part of the roof to the 15th century. On either side of the apex is a band ornamented with leaf-scrolls. The roof of the nave has collar-beams on arched braces, with two tiers of cusped wind-braces. The medieval rood loft survived until 1751,[13] and a long beam from this is mounted at the east end of the aisle; further remnants are in the south transept. All these show Perpendicular tracery. The bowl of the font is Early English, with a band of foliage around the rim. The pulpit, communion rail and panelling in the chancel date from the 18th century. The panelling in the north aisle consists of the bench-ends and doors of the former box-pews. There is good glass by Kempe in the east window.

All Saints, Trefonen

Externally, the church, built in the 1820s, is a rather depressing building of grey stone. In 1876 the chancel and apse were added and the windows converted to Gothic. Inside, a low stone screen divides nave from chancel. There is a stone pulpit and a west gallery.

St. Andrew, Welsh Frankton*

St. Andrew's church, built in 1858, is one of the best of the High Victorian village churches. It occupies a precipitous site commanding panoramic views over north Shropshire. The architect, Edward Haycock jun., took full advantage of this: access to his church is up a steep flight of steps flanked by gabled walls, and the visitor then passes through the base of the tower, acting as a porch, into the west end of the nave. The church is built of stone from Cefn, and the exterior is enlivened with bands of Shevloke red stone. The handsome spire is a landmark for miles around.

The interior is relatively simple: the chancel is raised five steps above the nave, and there are three further steps eastwards. The chancel arch has marble shafts resting on capitals adorned with foliage. The fittings are all High Victorian, and of good quality.

St. Michael and All Angels, Welshampton**

The place-name is recorded as *Hantone* in Domesday Book, meaning 'high settlement'.[14] The present church was preceded by at least three buildings – a Saxon or Norman church, a second medieval building dating from 1391, and an ugly brick cruciform church with an octagonal western tower built in 1788. This fell into disrepair and became inadequate for the needs of the parish, so in 1861 a new building was commissioned from the leading architect of the day, Sir George Gilbert Scott. It is instructive to compare the two High Victorian churches of Lyneal (1870) by Street and Welshampton – just two miles apart. Street's design is the more restrained – signalling perhaps the transition from High Victorian to late Victorian.

Scott was a more conventional architect than Street, but there is no doubt that Welshampton is a very impressive building. The church (Fig.5.4) consists of a nave with south aisle, apsidal chancel and north porch, with a bell-turret over the chancel arch. Like Lyneal, it is built of buff-coloured stone from Cefn Mawr, though here there is no polychromy. A distinguishing external feature is the band of foliage at cill level round the apse, with a corbel-table above. The roof is patterned with blue and green slates.

The interior is expensively adorned; the plastered walls contrast with the black marble columns of the south arcade, and in the chancel with the marble nook-shafts of the windows. The windows are lancets, some with plate tracery. The boarded roof of the chancel is divided into rectangles, and at the intersections of the ribs are carved bosses. There is a distinguished alabaster reredos by William Farmer, with a central panel of the Crucifixion; this is flanked by panels moulded and inlaid by various marbles. Farmer was also responsible for the font and pulpit – both made of Caen stone with marble columns and splendidly carved with floral patterns. The very good stained glass in the chancel is by Messrs. Heaton and Butler. In the north wall of the nave is a memorial window to a Basuto prince by Hardman.

St. Michael, West Felton*

Situated attractively, away from the village centre and the former A5 which courses through it, St. Michael's church (Fig.15.18) has a Georgian tower, a Victorian chancel, and a medieval nave and aisles which were modified externally in Victorian times. This sounds like a prescription for disappointment, but the disparate parts have become moulded by the passage of time into a

Fig.15.18 St. Michael, West Felton

Fig.15.19 West Felton; the arcade

harmonious unity. The medieval tower fell down in 1782 and the present edifice was built two years later. The Norman arcades have circular piers; the north is a little earlier, and here the capitals and abaci are square (Fig.15.19) On the south, the piers are less robust, the capitals circular and the abaci octagonal. There is an excellent roof, with arched braces, collar-beams and queen-posts.

The major attraction of St. Michael's is the 19th-century stained glass. The east window is outstanding (Fig.12.6), probably by David Evans of Shrewsbury, and there is a further window by the same artist in the north aisle. These were presented to the church by the Kenyon family in 1841-42.[15] Another window in the north aisle is by C.E. Kempe.

St. John the Divine, Weston Rhyn

The church was built in 1878, the architect being H. Kennedy of Bangor. It is a conventional building, with mainly Decorated window tracery.

St. John the Baptist, Whittington*

Whittington, on the former A5 near Oswestry, was previously a place of some importance. The Welsh form of the place-name is *Drefwen*, meaning 'white homestead'; the English *Wititone* has the same meaning. Opposite the church stand the ruins of the medieval castle. The medieval church has long since disappeared, and it was replaced in the 18th century by the plain brick edifice which stands today.

The tower was built in 1747, the nave following in 1804 (Fig.15.20). The architect of the latter was Thomas Harrison of Chester. Further changes followed in 1894 when Eustace Frere altered the windows to Venetian style, panelled the walls with oak and improved the ceiling. The result is a rather sombre interior, enlivened by some stained glass, especially the Jesse east window designed by F.C. Eden in 1934. In the porch is a plain old font, possibly Norman.

Fig.15.20 St. John the Baptist, Whittington, viewed from across the lake

16

The north-east – Whitchurch and Market Drayton

St. Peter, Adderley**

In the Middle Ages, Adderley was a substantial market town, larger than Market Drayton, but today it has shrunk to a parish of some 300 souls, set in tranquil scenery in the far north of the county. The church (Fig.16.1) is an astonishing tripartite building, erected in three stages – in 1635-37, 1712-13, and 1801. It is quite a large cruciform building – nave, chancel, north and south transepts, and a western tower. The oldest part is the north transept, the Kilmorey chapel, built in 1635-37 in a rather debased Perpendicular style. The western tower dates from 1712-13 – a handsome edifice, the belfry windows with Y-tracery, the corners clasped by angle pilasters.

The main body of the church – the nave, chancel and south transept – was erected in 1801 in late Georgian style. The wide windows display late Perpendicular tracery executed in cast-iron. Because of the total absence of stained glass, the interior is brilliantly lit. Unfortunately, the nave has been divided from the transepts and chancel by an unattractive plasterboard partition – this undoubtedly makes the church

Fig.16.1 St. Peter, Adderley

more suitable for worship for a small congregation, but at the expense of eliminating what must once have been a remarkable spatial experience. Some idea of what has been lost may be obtained from Cranage, where a photograph of the old interior is shown. The excellent 12th-century font (Fig.10.8) is carved with rosettes, scrolls and volutes, and has a Latin inscription around the rim.

Beyond the partition, the church is under the care of the Churches Conservation Trust. To the north is the Kilmorey chapel, with its massive Jacobean screen. It has slim columns, arches above, and is surmounted by a shield and phoenix centrally, and by strange spear-like finials laterally. The chapel has a low roof, decorated with many bosses. To the south of the screen is a plain panelled pulpit, probably of 1801. The south transept contained the pews of the Corbet family. The church guide gives an entertaining account of the feud between the Corbets and the Needhams which lasted for decades in the 17th century (Sir Robert Needham was created Viscount Kilmorey in 1625). In the south transept is the memorial by John Carline and Son to Sir Robert Corbet (d.1823). The old chancel is notable for some fine brasses on the floor to the north of the altar: the older brass (c.1390) is to an abbot or bishop whose head is missing. The other brass displays Sir Robert Needham (d.1556) in Tudor armour, his wife, seven sons and two daughters.

Fig.16.2 Christ Church, Ash

Christ Church, Ash

There was no medieval church here, Ash being part of the parish of Whitchurch. The present building (Fig.16.2) is of brick, built in 1836, the architect being George Jenkin. It is in the Gothic style, with broad lancet windows, between which are prominent buttresses. The church consists of a western tower, a nave with a west gallery and a chancel added in 1901. All the panelling around the chancel is the work of villagers, who also carved the pulpit. The attractive glass in the east window is a memorial to the victims of the First World War.

Holy Trinity, Calverhall*

Holy Trinity was built of stone in 1878, the architect being Eden Nesfield (1835-88). It presents a distinctly unusual aspect to the village street: its south wall directly abuts the village almshouses of 1724, and the west end is dominated by an enormous Perpendicular window of seven lights. Next to this is the very prominent tower, with an even more prominent stair-turret. Entrance to the church is through a porch and on either side is some decorative stonework. The best feature of the interior is the stained glass in the chancel: the south window is by Sir Edward Burne-Jones, depicting the Virgin Mary and St. Elizabeth; the glass in the north window was designed by Henry Holiday for Powell's; and that in the east window is by Clayton and Bell.

St. Swithun, Cheswardine***

At the time of the Domesday survey, Cheswardine was in the Bradford hundred of Staffordshire; Ekwall tentatively suggested that the place name means 'cheese farm'. The attractive village is crowned by the church of St. Swithun, built on a knoll overlooking the surrounding streets. The church is a fascinating and attractive amalgam of three different styles – Early English, Perpendicular and Victorian.

The medieval church was already falling into dilapidation by the 18th century, and the nave and chancel were replaced by an ugly building in 1808. Sir Stephen Glynne visited Cheswardine in 1862 and has left an interesting description of the church at that time. 'The outer walls have been rebuilt in an ugly modern fashion ... the interior too has but a bad effect with its flat modern ceiling, high pues and west gallery ... the chancel is modern and very poor.'[1] The building that disappointed Glynne was demolished in 1887 and replaced by the present church.

Fig.16.3 St. Swithun, Cheswardine: Perpendicular tower, Victorian church

The Perpendicular tower, however, survived and has many features of interest (Fig.16.3). It was built around 1470 and has diagonal buttresses, battlements and pinnacles. Below the battlements is a quatrefoil frieze. Below each belfry window is a knot with a dog on each side: the dog is the badge of the Talbots, and the knot is the badge of the Staffords. This has led to the suggestion that the tower was built to commemorate the marriage of John Talbot, third earl of Shrewsbury to Katherine Stafford, daughter of the first duke of Buckingham and sixth earl of Stafford in 1467.[2] On the west face of the tower is a large Perpendicular window of four lights, flanked by niches for images. Below the window is another frieze. The tower is adorned with a rather loveable lion on the south-east buttress, and a renewed dragon on the north.

Even more impressive than the tower is the north chancel chapel, which is Early English. This was taken down in 1886 and rebuilt stone for stone 13 feet further east. There are four windows consisting of groups of lancets, one on the east wall and three on the north. The roof of this chapel is very fine: it is a low-pitched Perpendicular panelled roof, with bosses at the intersections.

John Loughborough Pearson (1817-98) was an architect of distinction (see p.36), who came to Cheswardine (and Shrewsbury Abbey) with tremendous experience. He here produced an outstanding church, showing his skill in so many ways. The meticulous translocation of the north chancel chapel is typical of his deep concern for medieval architecture, and this is also evident in his treatment of the arcades: the south arcade is 'Norman', with round arches, while the north is Gothic. Glynne confirms that this difference between the arcades was present in 1862, and Pearson clearly retained some of the original masonry.

The capitals are florid but well-carved, in style more like 1866 than 1886 (Fig.16.4); in the second pier in the south arcade, part of the original capital with early stiff-leaf carving has been retained. Above the nave is a clerestory with lancet windows. The vigorous tracery of the windows in the aisles is amazingly different. The chancel is divided from the north and south chapels by Gothic arcades.

There is some excellent Victorian glass, including eight windows by Kempe. The reredos is a triptych reminiscent of the one in Shrewsbury Abbey which was designed by Pearson. There are some excellent Minton tiles in the chancel. The only monument of note is a foliated 13th-century coffin-lid in the north chancel chapel. In the south aisle is a carved Hanoverian Royal Coat of Arms. In the tower are 18th-century paintings of Moses and Aaron.

Fig.16.4 Cheswardine: the north arcade and chancel

St. Michael, Child's Ercall*

Ercall (pronounced Arkle) is said to be an old Welsh name for the district.[3] High Ercall and Child's Ercall were *Archelou* and *Arcalun* in the Domesday Book respectively; in the 13th century they were called *Magna* and *Parva Ercalwe*. The presence of a priest at Child's Ercall was recorded in Domesday Book, so presumably there must have been a Saxon church here. The churches at both High Ercall and Child's Ercall are dedicated to St. Michael.

The church (Fig.16.5) consists of a nave with north and south aisles, porch, south-western tower and chancel – built at various periods. The nave is the earliest part, though how old is open to question. Both arcades date from the 13th century, the south being earlier than the north (Fig.16.6). The south arcade has round piers and plain Early English moulded capitals, with only slightly chamfered arches. Note that the west respond of the north arcade is similar, but the remainder of the north arcade has octagonal piers and more obviously chamfered arches. It is concluded that the south arcade was built *c*.1200, and the north about 50 years later. The south aisle was rebuilt in the 14th century, with Decorated windows of that period; note the squint from the east end of the aisle into the chancel, enabling people at the south doorway to see the priest officiating at the

Fig.16.5 St. Michael, Child's Ercall

Fig.16.6 Child's Ercall: the nave and chancel

altar. The south-western tower is late Perpendicular (*c*.1500), with straight-headed west windows both here and in the west wall of the nave. The tower opens into the south aisle with a very tall tower arch. The north aisle and the chancel were rebuilt in 1879, but the priest's door in the south wall of the chancel is late Norman, being reset here at the rebuilding; it features a prominent hood-mould ending in large round volutes.

The plain octagonal font is medieval but difficult to date. The good glass in the east window of the chancel portrays the Ascension; it was inserted in 1895, and is said to be the work of L.A. Pownall (Fig.12.14).

St. Mary, Edstaston**

Edstaston (meaning 'Eadstan's settlement') is recorded in Domesday Book as *Stanestun*. The church of St. Mary deserves to be much better known, for it has the finest Norman doorways in Shropshire, remarkable in a building which was only a subsidiary chapel in the parish of Wem until 1850. Why was it so lavishly adorned?

Fig.16.7 St. Mary, Edstaston:
the north doorway

The church consists simply of a nave and chancel, with a 19th-century bellcote. Both nave and chancel are Norman and under the eaves of the north and south walls of the nave and chancel is a complete Norman corbel-table of trefoil arches. A large Norman window may be seen in the north wall of the nave. The east wall of the chancel was rebuilt in the Decorated era, and the windows in the south wall of the nave are Perpendicular insertions.

The simplest of the three Norman doorways is the priest's door in the south wall of the chancel. This has one order of shafts, with capitals showing upright leaves. The jambs are decorated with dogtooth. The arches above have dogtooth, a rather coarse zigzag, and a hood-mould with geometric patterning. The north door (Fig.16.7) has a carved head in the middle of the dripstone; below this is a plain hollow, then a band carved with dragons and heads, and then a band with zigzag. Again there is one order of shafts, but the

129

capitals are much more richly carved with leaves. The third Norman doorway is spectacular – the finest in Shropshire (Fig.16.8). The hood-mould has a double dogtooth pattern, with three original carved heads, one at the apex, and one on either side. Within this are three orders of complicated zigzag, and then the innermost arch is embattled. The doorway has four orders of shafts, with fine capitals displaying foliage almost of the stiff-leaf type. On one of the eastern capitals is a head.

The doors themselves are worth examining: all three have fine Norman iron-work, and except for the priest's door, the doors themselves are original. The windows also are worthy of inspection before entering the church. There is an

Fig.16.8 Edstaston: elaborate Norman carving over the doorway – the finest in Shropshire

unusually large Norman window in the north wall of the nave; this has nook-shafts on each side, and chevron decoration above (Fig.9.5) The east window of the chancel is an excellent Decorated window, with intersecting tracery and a sexfoiled light at the top, similar to the east windows of Kinlet, Chelmarsh and Stottesdon. On the south side, there is one Decorated window in the chancel, and three Perpendicular windows in the nave.

The interior has less excitement to offer. Below the Norman window in the north wall of the nave is a round-arched recess; Cranage suggested that there may have been a piscina here serving a nearby altar. There is a good nave roof, with tie-beams and king-posts. The pulpit is Jacobean. There are some fragments of medieval glass in one of the south windows of the nave and traces of medieval wall-paintings in both nave and chancel.

Holy Immanuel, Fauls

Fauls church was built in 1855-56 to serve a new parish carved out of the parish of Prees. It is an unpretentious and relatively inexpensive brick building designed by Benjamin Ferrey (see p.35). It consists of nave and shallow chancel only, with a later porch and north organ chamber. There was originally a spirelet over the junction of nave and chancel, but this has been removed. The exterior is rescued from dullness by transverse bands of black brick, which is also displayed around many of the windows. In addition, there are bands of projecting brickwork at various heights around the church. In the roof are bands of diamond-shaped slates. The interior is plain, with a west gallery, and above this a rose window. The stone pulpit can be entered only from the vestry.

St. Oswald, Hinstock*

Hinstock is recorded in the Domesday Book as *Stoche*, and by 1242 the prefix '*hine*' had been added. The place-name may mean 'cell or monastery of the monks'[4] as in Hine Heath.

The medieval church here was demolished and the new church was completed by 1720. This refers to the present nave; the date of the tower is disputed: Pevsner wrote that it 'looks *c*.1800', yet Cranage ascribed it to the 17th century. The present

Fig.16.9 St. Oswald, Hinstock: the Georgian interior

south aisle was added in 1853, producing in effect a twin-naved church. Perhaps the most remarkable thing about Hinstock is that the Victorians succeeded in matching so closely their south aisle with the Georgian nave, and resisted the temptation to 'gothicise' the entire church by adding lancet windows.

So the windows of both nave and south aisle are wide-arched, and the church is built of stone, giving it a dignified aspect, and making it one of the best Georgian village churches in Shropshire. Inside (Fig.16.9), the church is light. Nave and aisle are divided by a plain round-arched arcade. There is an attractive pulpit of *c*.1800, and an enormous organ at the west end of the nave.

St. Luke, Hodnet***

Hodnet (meaning 'pleasant valley' from Old Welsh) is an uncommon example of a pre-English name in Shropshire.[5] It was clearly an important manor in pre-Norman times, for the Domesday Book mentions the presence of both a priest and a church; church and manor (worth £8) were held by St. Peter's church, Shrewsbury (the Abbey).

St. Luke's church stands in the centre of the small town, at the entrance to the famous gardens. It is a stately church, remarkable architecturally for its tower, the twin 'naves', the long seven-bay arcade and the three gables of the east end. The western tower (Fig.6.8) is octagonal from bottom to top, the only such in Shropshire, and it dates from the Decorated era – though the battlements are probably Perpendicular. The tower opens into the nave by a multishafted Decorated arch, the finest architectural feature of the church. It has six recessed orders of alternating wave moulds and sunk chamfers.[6] It has been suggested that these features resemble those found in Edwardian castles of north Wales.[7] The twin naves are divided by an unsatisfactory arcade: the two eastern bays have an original Decorated octagonal pier, the rest of the arcade dates from the 19th century, probably from the restoration of 1846. It is not known what happened to the rest of the original arcade. The original nave was what is now the south aisle, but there is very little medieval work remaining; all the 'Decorated' windows are Victorian. The north aisle (now the nave) is also largely

Victorian, and in 1870 a mortuary chapel (the Heber chapel) was added, providing the third gable to the east end.

The octagonal font poses as many problems as the church. At first sight, it appears to be Norman, but some of the carving is suspicious. The carving on each face is varied, and some of the motifs are more convincingly Norman than others. Perhaps the truth is that the bowl was originally Norman, but that some, at least, of the carving is much later. To the west of the south door is an offertory box inscribed 'Remember the poore. H.F. 1685 R.B.'. The stained glass in the east window of the chancel is by William Warrington (1849 *cf* Whitchurch) and depicts scenes from the Passion among foliage; that in the south chancel is by David Evans, and dates from 1846. Also in the south chancel is a remarkable collection of chained books, including a 'Breeches' Bible and a Book of Hours.

Fig. 16.10 St. Luke, Hodnet: the fine portrait in marble of Bishop Heber (d.1826), by Sir Francis Chantrey

There is an impressive series of monuments:
1) Richard Hill (d.1726) – west wall of south aisle. Two vases against a tall obelisk.
2) Sir Richard Hill (d.1808) – south wall of south aisle. Urn in front of an obelisk by John Carline senior.
3) Henrietta Vernon (d.1752) – north wall. An excellent monument by Sir Henry Cheere (1703–81) featuring wreathed urns with cherubs' heads and an obelisk.
4) John Hill (d.1814) – north wall. Mourning woman and child by a sarcophagus by John Carline.
5) Bishop Heber (d.1826) – in the Heber chapel (Fig.16.10). Portrait in marble by Sir Francis Chantrey (1781-1841 *cf* Badger, p.160).
6) Blanche Heber (d.1870) – in the Heber chapel. Recumbent effigy on a tomb-chest by Reginald Cholmondeley of Condover.

No account of Hodnet can omit reference to Bishop Heber, rector here from 1807-23, and author of well-known hymns. He left Hodnet to become bishop of Calcutta and died there three years later. His descendant, Algernon Heber-Percy is the patron of the living and resides in Hodnet Hall.

St. John the Baptist, Ightfield**

The first element of the name is believed to be derived from *Giht*, an ancient British river name.[8] The church is nicely situated at the edge of the village, with good views over the surrounding country. It consists of a western tower, with nave, south porch, north aisle and chancel. Unusually for Shropshire, it is mainly a Perpendicular church, adorned with battlements and pinnacles. At the top of the tower is a quatrefoil frieze below the battlements, with gargoyles perched precariously (Fig.16.11). The nave is also crenellated. The Perpendicular porch is unusually imposing for a village church. The south windows have rather unusual Perpendicular tracery, and at the sides of the eastern window are carved

*Fig.16.11 St. John the Baptist, Ightfield:
the tower and gargoyles*

*Fig.16.12 Ightfield: Perpendicular
window with carved animals*

animals (Fig.16.12). The chancel is Victorian, but retains the original priest's door with ogee mouldings. The north arcade has short octagonal piers and plain capitals (Fig.16.13). There is a tie-beam roof, and an excellent brass to Dame Margery Calverley (late 15th-century).

Fig.16.13 Ightfield: the nave and chancel

Christ Church, Little Drayton

Little Drayton now comprises the western part of Market Drayton, but originally it was a hamlet quite distinct from its larger neighbour. The church was built of red sandstone in 1847 to the design of the Shrewsbury architect S. Pountney Smith. The building consists of a north-west tower, a south porch, a nave with north and south aisles and a fairly shallow chancel, and is in the Early English style, as was usual in the 1840s. There is a western gallery. The arcades are of four bays, the piers being circular, with plain moulded capitals.

St. Mary, Market Drayton**

The presence of a priest here is recorded in the Domesday Book, but no trace remains of a Saxon or early Norman church. The earliest part of the present building is the west doorway at the base of the tower. This is late Norman, and the doorway originally consisted of two orders of shafts, with lozenges going down the jambs. The shafts have disappeared, but the capitals remain with round abaci. The rest of the tower (Fig.16.14) is Decorated, with tracery of that style in the west and belfry windows. Internally, the tower has arches on the north, east and south sides.

The rest of the church has been so modified in turn by the Georgians and the Victorians that very little of the original remains. In the 18th century the south aisle was rebuilt, and later both aisles were given two tiers of windows;[9] the Williams painting of 1790 depicts the truly awful result of these changes. Fortunately all this was swept away in the 19th century. In particular, both aisles were then totally rebuilt, and all the aisle and clerestory windows now date from the 19th century. The arcades appear to be Decorated, (octagonal piers and double-chamfered arches) but are largely Victorian. An exception is the western-most pier of the north arcade where there is a capital carved with 15 heads, three crowned and 12 mitred. The fine rood screen, designed by Kempe, was formerly between nave and chancel, but has now been moved to the west end of the nave. This welcome change has opened up the spacious chancel beautifully. Kempe was also responsible for six of the stained glass windows – the east window, two in the north aisle and three in the south. The small wheatsheaf, which is Kempe's hallmark, is visible in each. The difference in quality between his work and the other windows is immediately apparent.

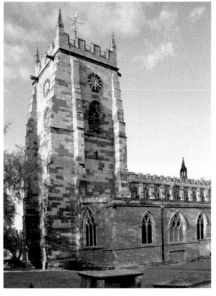

The best monument is that to Sir J.J. Markham (d.1778), by Joseph Wilton. It shows a woman seated by an urn, with an anchor, and is of good quality. Joseph Wilton (1722-1803) was 'a most uneven artist',[10] but achieved fame with such works as the monument to General Wolfe in Westminster Abbey. Other artefacts to note are the large painting in the chancel after the style of the 16th-century Spanish painter, Ribera; the modern triptych in the north aisle by Nicholas Parry; and the Victorian reredos in the south chancel chapel.

Fig.16.14 St. Mary, Market Drayton

St. Margaret, Moreton Say**

Moreton means the homestead ('tun') by the moor; the second component of the name is from the local lords of the manor, the de Say family (*cf* Hopesay, Stokesay). At first sight, St. Margaret's appears a typical Georgian brick church (Fig.16.15). The tower was built in 1769; and the rest of the church (dated 1788) appears to epitomise the end of the 18th century; but step inside, and the doorway at the west end of the nave leading to the base of the tower is clearly late Norman,

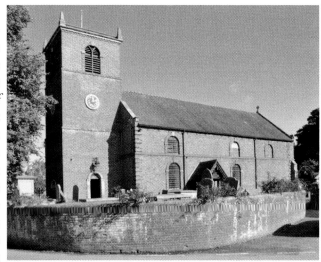

Fig.16.15 St. Margaret, Moreton Say

with early stiff-leaf capitals, and has been dated *c*.1190. So what happened in 1788 was that the medieval building, apart from the east wall, was encased in brick. The east wall is of stone and was rebuilt in 1742; it contains a Perpendicular window.

Inside, the 17th century is at least as important as the 18th, largely due to Jane Vernon. In 1623, she erected a huge monument in the north wall of the chancel, where in front of an impressive architectural surround she is seen flanked by stone effigies of her two husbands (Fig.16.16). In 1634 she built the west gallery, one of the finest in Shropshire; and in 1642 a charming wooden memorial to three of her sisters was placed in the north wall of the chancel (Fig.11.24).

But Moreton Say is perhaps best known because of its connection with Robert Clive, founder of the British Empire in India. His family came from Styche Hall nearby, and he was baptised in St. Margaret's in 1725 and buried here in 1774. There are several Clive memorials in the church and churchyard. The stained glass in the east window is very good: it is by C.E. Kempe, commemorating Sir Percy Herbert, a descendant of Robert Clive. It portrays the Crucifixion, flanked by the Virgin Mary and St. John, and by St. Chad and St. Margaret of Antioch.

Fig.16.16 Moreton Say: monument of Jane Vernon between her two husbands

King Charles the Martyr, Newtown

After the Civil War, the people of Newtown, Wolverley and Northwood desired to have a chapel of ease (as they lived at a great distance from the parish church of Wem), and a private house was brought into use; after the Restoration this was consecrated by the bishop of Lichfield and Coventry. This building was demolished in 1836 and replaced by a brick church. By 1861 the parish was formed, and the brick church replaced in 1869 by the present stone church designed by E. Haycock jun. It is an unremarkable building, redeemed by a good wrought-iron screen and a lovely altar frontal.

St. Chad, Norton-in-Hales**

The church (Fig.16.17) is worth visiting for the sake of its outstanding monument. It consists of a Perpendicular tower, a restored Early English chancel, and a nave, north transept, baptistry and vestry which date from a restoration in 1864-72. The western entrance at the base of the tower is apparently Victorian, but based on genuine Norman fragments.[11] There is extensive Jacobean panelling in the chancel.

The tomb-chest to Sir Rowland Cotton and his wife who died in childbirth (Fig.11.25) is incongruously placed just to the right of the entrance. The monument was apparently designed by Inigo Jones, Surveyor of the King's Works, whose drawings survive.[12] The monument

Fig.16.17 St. Chad, Norton-in-Hales

was originally in the chancel, and was moved to its present site by the western entrance during the Victorian restoration. The effigies are of alabaster, and Lady Cotton is depicted nursing her dead infant. The inscription records that she 'dyed on Sondaye a daye of rest beinge the 23rd daye of November anno domini 1606'.

Chapel of the Epiphany, Peplow**

The place-name means 'pebble tumulus or hill',[13] and it is recorded in the Domesday Book as *Papelaw*. In spite of its ancient origin, there is no village here: the chapel stands alone near to a farmhouse, and at the gate of Peplow Hall.

This relatively humble church by Norman Shaw broke new ground in the story of Shropshire churches. It was built in 1877, the first Victorian church in Shropshire to break with the Gothic tradition; but Shaw progressed from here to his greater church at Richard's Castle (1890; p.334), which is Gothic. Because of Shaw's work there, his former pupil William Lethaby obtained the commission to build a new church at Brockhampton-

Fig.16.18 Chapel of the Epiphany, Peplow

by-Ross, Herefordshire, where the beginnings of modern architecture are plain for all to see.

The chapel of the Epiphany is built of brick, with half-timbering with brick infill above (Fig.16.18). It has been compared with the church of St. Michael, Great Altcar, Lancashire, which John Douglas built in the same year,[14] and which is also timber-framed. A continuous tile roof sweeps down low on each side, and at the junction of nave and chancel is a small bellcote. The horizontal windows are straight-headed and owe nothing to Gothic tradition. The interior is simple but pleasing. The imposing screen, pulpit and font (Fig.10.22) are all by the architect, and in the chancel is an enormous mural of the Epiphany by Douglas Strachan (1903), now badly in need of renewal by removal of varnish. There is some good Victorian stained glass, especially the south windows by Heaton, Butler and Bayne (1901; Fig.12.15).

St. Chad, Prees**

Prees is thought to be an ancient Celtic name meaning brushwood or grove.[15] St. Chad's church (Fig.16.19) is a strange mixture of styles: Gothic nave, 18th-century tower, and Victorian chancel. It appears that the whole church was rebuilt in the early 14th century, though the south wall of the nave may survive from an earlier structure;[16] even so there are Perpendicular windows in this wall. The best feature externally is the Perpendicular north porch. Inside, there is a single north arcade, with short octagonal piers and plain capitals. The unusually-shaped west window was inserted in 1857.

In the north chapel are pieces of medieval stained glass transferred here from Battlefield; the best is the figure of Richard Sandford, the donor, kneeling in prayer. There is also good Victorian glass elsewhere in the north chapel and in the chancel. The best monument is by Thomas Carline in the north wall of the chancel; it is to Sir John Hill, d.1824, and is in the Greek style representing a funeral procession of figures.

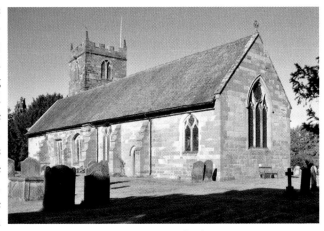

Fig.16.19 St. Chad, Prees

St. Peter, Stoke on Tern**

At the time of Domesday, the manor of Stoke on Tern was prosperous, being valued at £7 – much more than most Shropshire manors. There was a mill, and the presence both of a church and a priest was recorded.

By 1872 the medieval church (pictured by Williams in 1790) was in need of such restoration and repair that a faculty was granted for rebuilding and the architect chosen was Charles Buckeridge (1833-73). He had studied with Sir George Gilbert Scott and was well known to both Street and Ferrey, who jointly proposed him for his A.R.I.B.A. Unfortunately Buckeridge died suddenly before the church was completed and his friend J.L. Pearson took over his practice, day-to-day supervision being delegated to Matthew Holding. It seems that the church was rebuilt on the original plan.

Fig.16.20 St. Peter, Stoke on Tern, seen across the flooded river

St. Peter's (Fig.16.20) consists of a nave and chancel, with a south aisle and a south chancel chapel, and a tower unusually sited in the south-west. The style is less florid than in the High Victorian era of the 1850s and '60s, and some of the furnishings, especially the poppy-heads on the choir-stalls, are very attractive. There is also some good stained glass by Kempe in the chancel and the south aisle. But the greatest treasure is the Corbet monument in the south chancel chapel, which was not moved at the time of the rebuilding. This is to Sir Reginald Corbet (d.1566) and his wife; they are represented by alabaster effigies on a large tomb-chest, with standing figures and colonettes round the sides.

Christ Church, Tilstock

Tilstock was a chapelry of Whitchurch until 1844, but in 1835 the present building was erected because of donations from the late earl of Bridgewater. The architect was Edward Haycock sen. The brick-built church looks Georgian and on the north and south of the nave are five large round-headed windows. At the west end is a tall

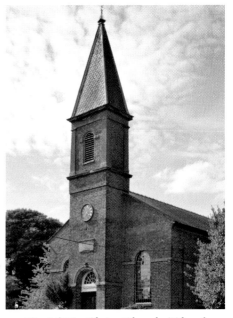

Fig.16.21 Christ Church, Tilstock (1835)

slender tower with a steeply pyramidal roof (Fig.16.21). Inside, the church is airy and bright. There is a handsome west gallery. The good Victorian glass in the east window depicts Moses lifting up the serpent in the wilderness.

St. Peter and St. Paul, Wem*

The unusual place-name derives from OE *wemm* (filth) but both Ekwall and Gelling[17] assert that here it means 'marshy ground'. Of the medieval church, only the Perpendicular tower survives, the remainder being damaged in a fire which swept through the town in 1677. This part of the church was demolished between 1809 and 1813, when the present nave was built, the chancel following in 1886. So we have in Wem a medieval tower, a late Georgian nave and a Victorian chancel – a not altogether happy combination.

The tower is very good: an Early English doorway with four roll and fillet mouldings has been inserted, but the rest of the tower is Perpendicular (late 14th-century), with battlements and pinnacles (Fig.16.22). The lower west window was inserted in 1667. High on the west wall is a statue, possibly of Lord Greystock, baron of Wem when the tower was built; and on the east wall is a further figure thought to be St. Chad.

The interior is Georgian in character, with north, south and east galleries supported on iron columns.

Fig.16.22 St. Peter and St. Paul, Wem: the Perpendicular tower

The nave was given windows of Gothic character in 1840. There is a notable pulpit of wrought iron, dated 1887, and a brass chandelier given to the church in 1733. The Victorian chancel is built of red sandstone.

St. Luke, Weston under Redcastle

The church is attractively situated in a village near Hawkstone Park. Weston was anciently a chapelry in the parish of Hodnet, and there was a medieval church here recorded by Williams in 1781. Within ten years, that church had been demolished and replaced by the present building, constructed of large blocks of red sandstone. The west tower alone looks Georgian, the rest of the church having lancet windows, some with plate tracery. The chancel was added in 1879.

St. Alkmund, Whitchurch**

Whitchurch arose in Roman times as *Mediolanum* ('the place in the middle of the plain') and was situated halfway along the road between Wroxeter and Chester. In the Domesday Book it was known as *Westune* (indicating that it was on the western border of England), and it presumably acquired its present name after the construction of a Norman church in stone, possibly replacing a wooden Saxon predecessor. The dedication to St. Alkmund is unusual (see p.190). Later in medieval times, the Norman church was extended, for according to a surviving picture there were Early English windows and finally a Perpendicular tower. Tower and church collapsed on Sunday, 31 July 1711. So now in Whitchurch is the very fine Queen Anne church, surpassing in elegance all the other 18th-century churches in Shropshire, with the exception of the much later St. Chad's, Shrewsbury.

The design of the new church was by John Barker (1668-1727), who a few years earlier had probably designed St. Ann's church, Manchester.[18] The builder was William Smith (1661-724), brother of 'Smith of Warwick'.[19] It was built in red sandstone in 18 months from March 1712. There is a large west tower with balustrade and pinnacles (Fig.16.23); on the west face there are two niches, and above them twin round-headed belfry windows under a common arch. The arms of the earl of Bridgewater (patron of the church) are carved

Fig.16.23 St. Alkmund, Whitchurch (1713)

on the south face. On the south side of the church, a prominent semicircular porch with balustrade above is attached to the tower. The porch had to be rebuilt in 1925 and replicates the original. Along each side of the nave and at the west end are tall round-headed windows. The apsidal chancel is relatively small.

The interior (Fig.16.24) is distinguished. A fine staircase leads up to the west gallery: below there is a sense of space and dignity, with arcades of tall Tuscan columns and arches dividing the nave from the aisles. The north and south galleries have been removed. At the east end, the apse is lit by three tall windows; in between are Corinthian pilasters with full entablature above, the cornice alone being continued round the whole apse.[20] To the north of the apse is the organ, with a fine original case, adorned with scrolls, cherubs and an angel with trumpet at the top. Behind the organ is the effigy of Sir John Talbot (d.1550), founder of the local grammar school. To the south of the apse is the Lady chapel containing the monument to John Talbot, first earl of Shrewsbury (d.1453); he was killed in battle at Castillon after recapturing Bordeaux from the French. Both effigies came from the original church, but the arches above were erected in 1874.

Fig.16.24 Whitchurch: the apsidal sanctuary

The stained glass in the apse depicts the Ascension, and is by Warrington. The octagonal font dates from 1661. The chandelier is contemporary with the church.

St. Catherine, Dodington, Whitchurch

St. Catherine's was built in 1836 by the widow of the seventh earl of Bridgewater, and it is the last Anglican church in the county built in the classical style; the architect was Edward Haycock sen. It has a stone-built façade, with Ionic columns on each side of the entrance; above is the belfry and an open octagonal turret with Tuscan columns. Behind, the sides and east end are of brick, with large rectangular windows; at the east end is a Venetian window.

The church was closed for worship about 40 years ago, and has recently been converted into residential accommodation, retaining the façade.

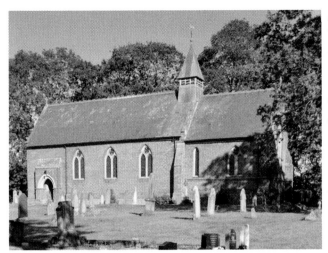

Fig.16.25 St. Mary, Whixall, by G.E. Street (1867)

St. Mary, Whixall*

Whixall was formerly a chapelry of Prees, and Cranage recorded the remains of a chapel about half a mile from the present church. The present church (Fig.16.25) was built in 1867 by G.E. Street, replacing the older chapel. The architect's inventiveness is shown most clearly in the variety of window tracery – mostly paired lancets, with trefoils or quat-refoils above. The east window has a wide central lancet flanked by two narrower lancets, and above a large rose window. The building is of brick, with stone dressings, and consists of a nave, north aisle and chancel, with a bell-turret over the entrance to the chancel. The aisle is divided from the nave by a plain arcade. The most interesting artefact is an old font, apparently dated 1608, from the previous chapel: it consists of a hexagonal bowl carved with various creatures, a scallop shell, fleurs-de-lis etc. There is also a four-lobed Victorian font on four shafts, presumably designed by the architect.

St. Leonard, Woore*

The parish of Woore occupies a projecting tongue of Shropshire jutting out between Cheshire and Staffordshire; it is situated on high ground forming the watershed between streams draining in the north to the river Weaver and thence to the Mersey, and to the south to the river Tern and thence to the Severn. An attractive village, Woore boasts an unusual church (Fig.16.26), a striking Classical edifice built in 1832 at the very end of the Georgian period – and thus in a style which was fast becoming obsolete. It was built of brick, later stuccoed, and it replaced an earlier chapel of ease. Woore was originally a chapelry in the Staffordshire parish of Mucklestone.

The architect was George Hamilton of Stone; ten years later the same architect built Pelsall church in Staffordshire in the Gothic style, reflecting the triumph of Gothic over Greek styles which had finally been consummated in the 1830s. But in 1832 at Woore there is no hint of Gothic, nor of the coming High Church revival. The chancel is shallow, the church plain and chaste, unnecessary decoration spurned. All is done in a seemly fashion. Over the west door is a balustrade, and behind rises the tower. The windows are large and round-headed. The chancel was rebuilt in 1887, and the tower was added in 1910. There is late Victorian glass in the east and north windows, including one by Kempe and Co. The screen was added in 1918.

Fig.16.26 St. Leonard, Woore, by George Hamilton (1832)

Central Shropshire – Baschurch and Myddle

Albrighton, near Shrewsbury*
Astley*
Baschurch*
Broughton
Clive*
Fitz*
Great Ness*
Grinshill
Hadnall*
High Ercall**
Leaton**

Lee Brockhurst
Little Ness*
Moreton Corbet***
Myddle*
Petton***
Preston Gubbals*
Ruyton XI Towns**
Shawbury**
Stanton-upon-Hine Heath*
Weston Lullingfields*

St. John the Baptist, Albrighton, near Shrewsbury*

The manor of Albrighton is mentioned in the Domesday Book as one of the extensive holdings of Reginald the Sheriff under Earl Roger, and in medieval times the church was a chapelry of St. Mary's, Shrewsbury. Cranage mentions that in Albrighton Hall there was a sketch of the old church; and the Williams painting of 1786 records the then church as a chapel to St. Mary's Shrewsbury.

The present church was built in 1840-41 (Fig.17.1) the nave being in the neo-Norman style then briefly in vogue. Thus the windows of the nave are all round-headed, as is the south doorway, but the west window is Decorated. The apsidal chancel, with lancet windows, was built 30 or 40 years later. The Norman font has a circular bowl carved with V patterns, with some beading enclosed; the lower part of the bowl has a series of round-headed arches or horseshoes. The plain, panelled pulpit, complete with sounding-board, probably dates from the later 17th century. There is good Victorian glass in the apsidal windows.

Fig.17.1 St. John the Baptist, Albrighton near Shrewsbury

St. Mary, Astley*

The Domesday Book records that the manor of Astley was held by St. Mary's, Shrewsbury, and mentions the presence of a priest. The earliest part of the present church dates from about 100 years after Domesday – this is the unusual and rather good blocked south doorway (Fig.17.2). The hood-mould over the doorway shows some dogtooth, and below this is a combination of chevron and battlements motifs. The inner order has round billet. The capitals of the shafts are carved with early stiff-leaf foliage. The tower was built in the Gothic style in 1837, and the rest of the church largely rebuilt in 1887. In the lower part of the south wall are abundant marks left by men sharpening their swords and arrow-heads. One window to the west of the south doorway is cusped (Fig.17.3) and bears the date 1568 – an example of Elizabethan Decorated (*cf* Shipton).

Fig.17.2 St. Mary, Astley: the blocked south doorway, and vertical 'arrow marks'

Fig.17.3 Astley: 'Decorated' window, dated 1568

All Saints, Baschurch*

The *Canu Heledd* is a cycle of Welsh poems celebrating the deeds in the 7th century of a prince of Powys named Cynddylan; their date is uncertain, but may be around 900.[1] The poems contain a reference to Baschurch (translated into Welsh as *Eglwysseu Bassa* – 'the churches of Bassa'), said to be the burial place of Cynddylan. 'The poet's choice of this settlement as Cynddylan's resting-place may have been partly due to the presence in the parish of the great earthwork called the Berth.'[2] Baschurch's antiquity as a place of Christian worship is confirmed by the entry in the Domesday Book recording that St. Peter's church (i.e. Shrewsbury Abbey) held 2½ hides of this manor and the village church from the Earl (Roger).

The church now consists of a western tower, with nave, chancel and south aisle. The tower (Fig.17.4) is impressive: Early English below, with later belfry and battlements. The arcade dividing the nave from the south aisle looks Norman (Fig.17.5), with circular piers and semicircular arches, but it is so scraped that it is difficult to tell how much is original. The medieval church also had a north aisle but in 1789 because of the ruinous state of the church Thomas Telford directed its removal. Towards the east end of the south aisle are three tomb recesses, one enriched with three rows of ball-flower decoration. In the south wall

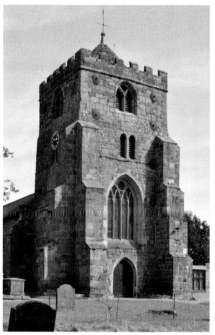

Fig.17.5 Baschurch: the nave and chancel

Fig.17.4 All Saints, Baschurch: the tower

of the chancel are the remains of a segmental arch, apparently dating from the end of the 13th century; it is probably the remains of a sedile for the priest. The stained glass in the east window is by Kempe (1886). In the north wall of the nave is a wall-monument commemorating William Basnett (d.1754)

St. Mary, Broughton
Built in 1858, this church has a continuous nave and chancel in the early Decorated style.

All Saints, Clive*
Clive (OE for 'cliff') is appropriately named, for the village has an impressive situation on the edge of Grinshill; and the spire of All Saints church (Fig.17.6) is seen from miles around. For many years Clive church was a chapel in the parish of St. Mary, Shrewsbury; but in 1885 it was radically rebuilt to the design of C.J. Ferguson. The north doorway, however, was preserved from the original church, and there is a little medieval masonry surviving in the north wall of the nave. The doorway is late Norman, with one order of shafts and stiff-leaf capitals. There are two orders of chevron decoration in the arch, one of them at right-angles to the wall.

The church is built of red and grey stone, and the recessed spire is superb – crocketed and pinnacled, with two tiers of dormer windows. The interior is rather conventional, but the furnishings are of high quality. The window tracery is mostly in the Decorated style, and the church is certainly rather conservative for its date.

Fig.17.6 All Saints, Clive

St. Peter and St. Paul, Fitz*

The place-name has undergone some extraordinary changes. It is OE *Fitteshoe*, the hoe (literally the heel) being a long low ridge of land above the river Severn;[3] the first element is probably an Anglo-Saxon personal name. In the Domesday Book it is recorded as *Witesot*. Later the second element was dropped and the name shortened to *Fittes*.

There was a medieval church here, and Cranage described a late Norman capital and some tiles which had survived from the original building. The present church was built in 1722, of red brick with stone quoins and dressings (Fig.17.7). A south aisle was added in 1842 and the chancel was rebuilt in 1905 by Sir Aston Webb. The west tower has Y-tracery in the belfry windows and in the lower west window, and at the top there is a parapet and corner pinnacles. The wide Georgian windows have projecting keystones, and fortunately the windows of the later extensions have harmonised with the original ones in the nave.

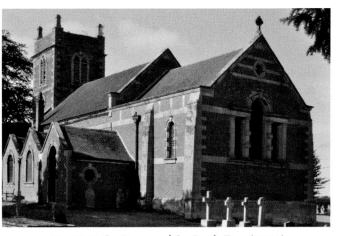

Fig.17.7 St. Peter and St. Paul, Fitz (1722)

The interior (Fig.17.8) is plain but attractive, marred somewhat by a heavy wooden screen on a stone base which partly obscures the excellent glass in the east window. This is by Tower (*cf* Kinnerley) and dates from 1915. There is a west gallery, with a Royal Coat of Arms.

Fig.17.8 Fitz: the nave and chancel

St. Andrew, Great Ness*

The OE *naess* refers here to an inland hill,[4] the hill now being called Nesscliffe. At a short distance to the east of the hill lie the villages of Great and Little Ness. The Domesday Book refers to two settlements here: *Nessham*, now called Great Ness, and *Nesse*, now Little Ness. Nessham was held by Earl Morcar from Earl Roger, and the church (one of only 22 Shropshire churches mentioned in Domesday) was held by St. Peter's church, Shrewsbury (the Abbey).

Today, St. Andrew's stands in an attractive cul-de-sac near the village, and is a church of some interest. It consists of a western tower and nave, built of red sandstone, and a chancel of contrasting grey stone. The tower and nave are Early English, the chancel Decorated.

Fig.17.9 St. Andrew, Great Ness: above and behind the door are vestiges of arches of uncertain significance

Fig.17.10 Great Ness: the chancel, with a hatchment on the right

One feature has puzzled antiquaries: on the south wall of the nave internally, above and to the west of the door, are two well-marked arches which look like an arcade (Fig.17.9); there are fainter traces of a third arch just to the east of the door. However, there is no other evidence of a former south arcade, and the arches are not visible externally. Cranage suggested that perhaps a south aisle was intended at one stage, and the project later abandoned. It is surprising that Sir Stephen Glynne, who visited the church in 1862, did not comment on these arches: were they hidden by plaster at this time? The east window of the chancel has reticulated tracery of the Decorated era (Fig.17.10). The roof of the nave is excellent: arched braces, collar-beams, wind-braces laterally and diagonal queen-posts.

All Saints, Grinshill

This pretty village, commanding extensive views to the south and west Shropshire hills, keeps its unusual parish church a closely guarded secret: it is hidden behind trees and houses along a lane, and the notice to the church is inconspicuous and easily missed. This is a pity, for All Saints is a rare example of a neo-Norman church built of red sandstone.

It was built in 1839-40 by John Carline jun. The aspect from the south (Fig.17.11) is impressive – pairs of shafts on either aside of the south doorway, and nook-shafts on the side of each window. The north aspect is plainer, without the nook-shafts. All the windows are round-headed except for three lancets in the east wall. The interior is light and airy, the

Fig.17.11 All Saints, Grinshill (1839-40), by John Carline jun. A neo-Norman church

nave being separated from the chancel by a screen erected in celebration of the Diamond Jubilee of Queen Victoria.

St. Mary Magdalene, Hadnall*

The place-name means 'Headda's nook' (or hollow),[5] and the village, a few miles north of Shrewsbury, was anciently a chapel of ease in the parish of Myddle; Richard Gough in *The History of Myddle* describes how in 1693 the inhabitants, being 'three long myles distant from the Mother church of Myddle' unsuccessfully petitioned the bishop of Lichfield and Coventry to order the present incumbent to provide a competent curate to read divine service and administer the holy sacrament. They were clearly aggrieved that the rector of Myddle was not providing them with adequate pastoral care, but the bishop replied that he had no power to order the rector to do as the petitioners asked.

Hadnall church (Fig.6.12) is a pleasing mixture of medieval and Victorian styles. The oldest parts are the north and south doorways, with plain Norman round-headed arches. The nave may have been rebuilt in the 14th century; there is some Decorated tracery in one of the nave windows, and further rebuilding occurred three hundred years later. The west tower was built in the 1830s, replacing the wooden turret shown in the Williams watercolour of 1787. The chancel was built in 1874.

The finest monument is that to Rowland Hill (d.1842), the duke of Wellington's second-in-command at Waterloo; it depicts the Hill coat of arms, flanked by the figures of a soldier and a shepherd.

There is some excellent Victorian stained glass: the east window, showing angels adoring Christ, is the work of C.E. Kempe, and further glass by Kempe is in the north and south windows of the nave.

St. Michael, High Ercall**

At the time of the Domesday Book, High Ercall was one of the most prosperous manors in the county, being worth £20. It was held by Earl Edwin, and by custom when the Countess came to the manor, 18 ora of pence were brought to her.

St. Michael's (Fig.17.12) is attractively situated next to the Jacobean hall, and is mainly a church of the end of the 12th century (i.e. the Transitional period when circular Norman piers co-existed with pointed Gothic arches; this building probably replaced an earlier church built at the end of the 11th century). There has been controversy concerning the extent of the rebuilding which took place after damage sustained during the Civil War. Cranage was strongly of the opinion that the rebuilding between 1657 and 1662 was almost total, whereas Pevsner stated that all

Fig.17.12 St. Michael, High Ercall

Fig.17.13 High Ercall: the north arcade, with carvings on the capitals

the architectural evidence was in favour of the almost complete survival of the medieval church. Interpretation is complicated by the extensive restoration undertaken by G.E. Street in 1864-65. Reference to the painting by Williams (1787) shows that the windows in the tower have been renewed since 1787; the painting also shows two dormer windows in the south of the nave, and no protrusion between the chancel and the nave on the south side. Sir Stephen Glynne described the church in 1853, before the restoration; he confirms the dormer windows, and mentions the west gallery.

The church consists of a nave with aisles, a chancel with a north chapel, a south porch and a west tower. The arcades (Fig.17.13) between the nave and the aisles are very good, with capitals decorated with scrolls and leaves; on the third north pier are two human heads and two rams' heads. It is uncertain how much of the carving is Norman – even Pevsner says it is 'very much renewed'. Both the chancel arch and the tower arch are Transitional. The chancel and the north chapel are Decorated; the east window of the chancel has reticulated tracery, that of the north chapel is Perpendicular (a later insertion?). Most of the other windows are straight-headed Perpendicular – so-called Tudor windows – but these were commonly used also in the 17th century. The roofs of the nave, chancel and chapel are all double hammer-beams of the sort employed after the Civil War (*cf* Condover). The tower is Perpendicular, with battlements and a frieze.

There are some interesting artefacts. Older than any part of the church is the early Norman tympanum (Fig.9.14) now built into the wall of the north aisle. This has been dated to *c*.1110-25.[6] The tympanum consists of the Tree of Life, with a border of six-leaved rosettes; at the base of the tree are two volutes. Under the arch connecting the chancel and the chapel is an effigy of a cross-legged knight, *c*.1320. There is some good Victorian glass in the east window of the chancel. On the north wall of the tower externally is embedded a fragment of early carving: a crowned figure on horseback, inscribed ST'S EDWARDUS. This presumably refers to the original dedication of the Norman church to Edward the Confessor, probably built *c*.1090.

Holy Trinity, Leaton**

Although the manor of Leaton is ancient, being recorded in the Domesday Book as *Letone*, it did not become a parish until 1859 when the present church was built by S. Pountney Smith at the expense of John Lloyd of Leaton Knolls. And expense was certainly not spared, for the building is lavishly endowed.

Not that the church has been universally admired. Pevsner, who in general did not like High Victorian building, called the façade 'as crazy as any of this High Victorian phase', although he conceded that the tower, added in 1872, was far more reasonable. Times and tastes have changed, and today we can admire Leaton unreservedly: I believe it is one of the finest Victorian churches in Shropshire by a local architect.

The church consists of a tower and spire, nave with north aisle, and chancel, and in general is built in Early English and Decorated styles, as was usual in 1859. The north-west tower and spire, a landmark for miles around, has paired lancet windows in the belfry, battlements and pinnacles above, and the spire is adorned with crockets and tall lucarne windows (Fig.1.6). The west end of the nave has a bellcote set diagonally on a diagonally projecting buttress standing on a flying buttress (this seems particularly to have disturbed Pevsner!).

The interior (Fig.17.14) is impressive, especially the sanctuary (Fig.17.15) with good tiling, and behind the altar there is blank arcading filled with a series of paintings recently restored. There are three lancet windows at the east end, separated by shafts of Purbeck marble, and filled with good stained glass. Especially attractive is the small south window of the sanctuary, with glass portraying Christ the Light of the World (after Holman Hunt). There is also a small vesica window high in the gable above the altar with a Christ in Majesty. The font, rather oddly placed at the east end of the north aisle, is of high quality (Fig.10.21); the bowl stands on marble pillars and is carved with the Baptism of Christ. The arcade dividing the nave and north aisle has plain cylindrical piers, with four fillets running longitudinally.

Fig.17.14 Holy Trinity, Leaton: the north arcade

Fig.17.15 Leaton: the chancel

St. Peter, Lee Brockhurst

'Brockhurst' implies a hill frequented by badgers, and 'Lee' refers to the wooded nature of the area. St. Peter's church is small and consists of a nave basically Norman, with a Victorian chancel. The nave has a small round-headed internally-splayed window in both the north and south walls. The south doorway is clearly Norman for there are two bands of zigzag in the arch, one at right-angles to the other. The capitals are carved with scallop, and internal to the eastern capital is a short band of cable. There is one shaft on either side of the doorway, the eastern renewed. In the west wall of the nave is a straight-headed window, probably a Perpendicular insertion, and a large rectangular window in the south wall which is probably later still.

St. Martin, Little Ness*

Throughout the Welsh Marches, it frequently happens that a motte-and bailey castle and a parish church are found side by side. Little Ness is a good example of this, and there are indeed Norman features in the church. In the Domesday Book, Little Ness (recorded as *Nesse*) was held by Siward from Earl Roger. The castle probably followed, some time in the 12th century.

Fig.17.16 St. Martin, Little Ness

It is a small church (Fig.17.16), built of sandstone on a knoll adjacent to the motte, consisting of an undifferentiated nave and chancel, with a western bellcote. The south doorway is Norman, and the shafts have scalloped capitals. The arch is decorated with four rows of zigzag, and above the dripstone has pellet decoration and at the apex a grotesque head. Above this is a larger head, probably a green man. To the east of the porch is a straight-headed Perpendicular window. The font is a plain Norman tub, with cable moulding connecting the bowl with the stem. There is one stained glass window by Kempe in the south wall of the nave.

St. Bartholomew, Moreton Corbet***

Fig.17.17 St. Bartholomew, Moreton Corbet

'Wayfarers welcome – from an open road to an open church', says the notice on the lane; and the visitor then walks along a short avenue of yews to a perfect Shropshire country church. It is worth travelling many miles to see – the church (Fig.17.17) has a lovely situation, with the extensive Norman and Elizabethan ruins of the castle next door; there is good architecture of several different styles; and an outstanding group of monuments. The Corbets were one of the families of great Marcher lords who dominated Shropshire for centuries. The founder of the family, Roger Fitz Corbet, came from Caux in Normandy, and he was given extensive lands in the west of Shropshire at the end of the 11th century.

The Norman church at Moreton was founded about 1140 as a chapel attached to Shawbury, and the manor was held by Richard Corbet *c.*1200. Some parts of the north wall of the Norman church remain, and there is a Norman window in the north wall of the chancel. The greater part of the church dates from the 14th century, when the south aisle was added (*c.*1330-40). The east window of the aisle shows Decorated tracery (Fig.17.18); but at the west end is a most unusual triangular window, very similar to one of about the same date in Alberbury, which was another of the Corbet family's possessions. The arcade dividing the aisle from the nave is of three bays with multishafted piers. There is both an aumbry and a piscina in the south wall of the south aisle. A hagioscope allows views of the altar

Fig.17.18 Moreton Corbet: a Decorated window

from the aisle. In the 18th century, a squire's pew was added as an offshoot of the south aisle. The western tower was started in 1539 (see the Tudor-style west doorway), but was not finished until 1769.

There are numerous monuments, but the best are the two 16th-century memorials to Sir Robert and Sir Richard Corbet and their wives respectively. The earlier one, dated 1513, is purely medieval (Fig.11.8); the effigies lie on a tall tomb-chest, and round the sides are small figures below ogee arches. The second memorial, dated 1567, shows clear signs of Renaissance influence: around the sides the panels are divided by colonettes, and in the panels are shields with the Elephant and Castle (the badge of the Corbets). There are also owls, and in the centre a baby wrapped in swaddling clothes, from which arises a tree. Such an assembly would never have been produced in the Middle Ages.

There are two good later monuments: a Baroque monument to Richard Corbet (d.1691), with a bust in a recess between fluted pilasters carrying an open segmental pediment; and a memorial to Charlotte Corbet (d.1774), depicting an urn with cherub in front of an obelisk.

Both the pulpit and reader's desk are Jacobean. The Victorian stained glass in the east window of the south aisle is very good. Even more striking is the glass in the chancel, which was the work of Sir Ninian Comper in 1905. He also designed the canopy or baldacchino over the altar, adorned with heraldic shields.

St. Peter, Myddle*

Myddle is another parish where the church is situated next to a medieval castle. It is named in the Domesday Book as *Mulleht*, and the presence of a priest (but not a church) was recorded.

It is unique among Shropshire villages in being propelled to fame by the writings of one man, Richard Gough (1634-1723). In 1700-1702, he compiled *The History of Myddle*. The first part of the book describes the 'Antiquityes and Memoryres of the Parish of Myddle', a competent but unremarkable account; but in the second part, Gough wrote his 'Observations concerning the Seates in Myddle and the familyes to which they belong'. He drew a seating-plan of the church and wrote the history of each family in turn. The result is a fascinating commentary on 17th-century village life. One lesson of his work is that nearly all the problems that afflict urban life in England today were present in Myddle three hundred years ago – problem families, marriage breakdown, alcoholism, petty crime, promiscuity – human nature has clearly changed little over the centuries!

It is good to see that Richard Gough's legacy is widely appreciated in Myddle today, for the church now houses an excellent millennium exhibition of his work. Perhaps some thought should be given to providing a permanent memorial to him in St. Peter's church.

Of the present church, Richard Gough would recognise only the tower – which looks medieval but is not. Here is part of Gough's account: 'As to the time when, and by whom, this church was built, these things are long since buried in the depth of antiquity that it is impossible to make any other discovery of them; but yet the steeple was built in our Fathers' time or about the beginning of my time, for I believe it was about the year of our Lord 1634. The steeple was at first built of stone as high as the walplatt [the wall-plate – the top of the outer wall of the nave] of the church, and upwards it was built of timber. In the time that Mr. Ralph Kinaston was rector of Myddle, the timber part of the steeple was ruinous, and the said Mr. Kinaston did desire the parishioners to take it wholly down, and rebuild it, and offered that at his own charges he would lay the ground work and would build above ground the height of his stature, and there place a stone in the wall to show how high hee had built at his own charge. But the parishioners not agreeing, Mr. Kinaston died, and soon after part of the steeple did fall, and then the parishioners of Myddle parish were forced to rebuild it, and I doubt had little or noe assistance from Mr. Moore then rector.'

The tower is built in Perpendicular style, and is a good example of how deceptive post-Reformation towers can be (Fig.17.19). It is built of a local Triassic sandstone, which

Fig.17.19 St. Peter, Myddle: the post-Reformation Perpendicular tower (c.1634)

could be quarried only in large blocks.[7] The tower, in fact, is the best part of the church, the nave and wide south aisle being built in 1744 in a rather uninspired Georgian style, later gothicised by the Victorians. There is a brass to Arthur Chambre of Petton (d.1564) and his wife, and a further brass to the above-mentioned Rev. Kinaston (d.1629). On the north wall of the nave are several memorials to the Atcherley family of Marton – Richard Gough says that Mr. Andrew Atcherley owned part of three pews in the north 'isle' of the church, with a further pew towards the rear reserved for his servants.

Petton Church***

'Never was ... so sweet a kernel in so poor a husk' was Francis Bumpus' comment on Wren's magnificent church St. Stephen Walbrook in the City of London. It could be applied with equal justification to Petton. For here, in a quiet setting in rural north Shropshire, stands a plain brick early Georgian church (Fig.17.20). It is quite small, just nave and chancel, with a western bellcote, and few people are aware of its existence. This is a shame, for the interior, compact as a jewel-case, is exquisite, filled with woodwork of the 17th and 18th centuries.

Fig.17.20 Petton church

Petton church stands alone in farmland, with only the farm for company. The manor at the time of the Domesday Book was part of the holding of Robert Butler under Earl Roger. There was a church here by 1159, and the knoll beside the church indicates the former presence of a motte and bailey.

The medieval church was replaced in 1727 by the present building. Though plain without, the interior overwhelms the visitor: for here is a store of treasures collected from sundry places at home and abroad. At the west end of the church is an ancient stone basin, which may have been a holy water stoup. The font (Fig.10.19) is an early 18th-century piece, ornamented by Corinthian foliage; the cover came from Bridgnorth. Also from Bridgnorth is an ancient Dutch carving of the Resurrection, mounted on the north wall of the chancel. The box pews, arranged in squares, probably came from Cockshutt when that church was rebuilt in 1777. The Jacobean pulpit, resplendent with its tester, is dated 1635; this came from St. Giles, Wrexham (Fig.14.6). The complex reredos also came from Wrexham. There is a further small carving of St. Martin sharing his cloak with a beggar; this came from Ellesmere. The west gallery stands on carved wooden pillars from the Council House in Shrewsbury; and much oak panelling came from Stanwardine Hall nearby. There are Minton tiles in the chancel, and an Italian mosaic floor by the altar. The candle sconces and wrought-iron screen were installed to celebrate the diamond jubilee of 1897; these were designed by Emma Brooke Cunliffe. Most of the stained glass was made by Messrs. Ward and Hughes; the east window is a copy of Holman Hunt's painting The Light of the World.

The church owes this fantastic assembly of treasures to the families who lived in Petton Hall nearby: the Chambres, the Sparlings and the Brooke Cunliffes. Especially active was Emma Florence Sparling, who inherited Petton Hall in 1890 and married Ellis Brooke Cunliffe of Wrexham. Petton church is usually locked, but the key can be obtained from the farm nearby.

St. Martin, Preston Gubbals*

The Domesday Book records that St. Alkmund's church (Shrewsbury) 'held and holds Preston, and Godbold from it'. 'Preston' means 'priest's tun or homestead', and Gubbals is a corruption of Godbold the priest.

Sir Stephen Glynne came here in 1864 and found 'a small and somewhat neglected church having only a single nave and undivided chancel, with a south porch and a wooden belfry over the west end'. This church had been painted by Williams in 1788. Within two years of Glynne's visit, the church was transformed by S. Pountney Smith, who added a new nave and chancel to the north of the old building, together with a massive tower. When the church was declared redundant in 1973, his building was demolished, leaving the original medieval structure. There is a plain round-headed priest's doorway in the south wall of the chancel (presumably 12th-century), and a Decorated window in the east wall of the chancel. The straight-headed window in the south wall of the chancel is probably late Perpendicular. The other windows in the nave date from the Victorian rebuilding, as does the rose window in the west wall.

The most remarkable feature is a rare 14th-century slab bearing in low relief the figure of a man with a foliated cross on his breast (Fig.11.4). Above is a crocketed ogee gable. The font is a plain octagonal bowl of uncertain date. Most of the woodwork – pulpit, lectern, reading-desk, communion table etc. – were carved by the Reverend E.D. Poole, an incumbent in the 19th century. The church is now in the care of the Churches Conservation Trust.

St. John the Baptist, Ruyton XI Towns**

The manor originally consisted of 11 townships, only six of which were in the parish. The church was originally a chapelry in the parish of Baschurch. The castle, immediately next to the church, was built in the early 14th century and now lies in ruins. Both church and castle occupy a prominent site above the Perry valley.

The church is built of red sandstone. The oldest part of the church is the chancel, dated by Cranage to c.1140. Two Norman windows remain in both the north and south walls, and low down in the south wall a small wooden door leads to a tiny chamber, which may have been an anchorite's cell. In the south wall is the priest's doorway, a plain Norman structure. The chancel was extended eastwards in the Decorated period, and the fine east window consists of three lights with foiled sub-arches and cusped spherical triangles above. The dormer window in the chancel was built in 1903, and the chancel arch is Victorian.

The nave is also Norman, the main south doorway again being round-headed and plain. The straight-headed windows in the south wall are later insertions, as is the Decorated window west of the main doorway. The late Perpendicular roof of the nave has collar-beams on arched braces, and two tiers of wind-braces. One of the corbels supporting the roof on the north side is of carved stone.

The arcade dividing the nave and north aisle is mainly Early English: at the west end is a narrow arch, with Victorian dogtooth decoration on it. The pillars are octagonal and on the second pillar is a horned head, possibly representing the Devil! In the respond at the east end a Perpendicular niche has been carved for an image. Above may be seen an aperture which once led to the former rood loft, and remains of the staircase are also visible. The north aisle was originally Decorated, and the fine east window shows reticulated tracery. The aisle was rebuilt in 1845. The western tower is Perpendicular (Fig.17.21), with diagonal buttresses and battlements.

There are two rather unimpressive 17th-century wall-monuments in the north wall of the chancel. The fine reredos (Fig.17.22) is an example of late Victorian art; it was designed by Bodley and Garner in 1892, and depicts the baptism of Christ – as is fitting in a church dedicated to

Fig.17.21 St. John the Baptist, Ruyton XI Towns: the west tower and castle ruins

Fig.17.22 Ruyton XI Towns: the reredos, designed by Bodley and Garner

John the Baptist. The best stained glass in a window in the north aisle, dated 1928, resembles the work of Morris and Co. (p.90). Another good window is the Hunt window, at the east end of the aisle; it is German glass of 1855 showing Christ blessing little children, and the window commemorates the four children of the vicar and his wife, all of whom died in 1831-32. Leaning against the wall below is a 13th-century coffin lid carved with a foliated cross. There are several hatchments in the church.

St. Mary, Shawbury**

The elegance of Shawbury's tower, seen from afar when approaching from Shrewsbury, should ensure plenty of visitors to this lovely village church. The place-name means 'settlement by a small wood', and the presence of both church and priest are noted in the Domesday Book.

Fig.17.23 St. Mary, Shawbury: the south doorway

St. Mary's consists of a nave with aisles, chancel, west tower and north porch. It is a good example of a parish church with representation of every medieval building style from the Norman era onwards. Perhaps it would make for clarity if we proceeded chronologically. The north doorway is late Norman, having been moved to its present position when the north aisle was built; the arch has a roll moulding and nail-head ornament, and the capitals carved with foliage. The south doorway (Fig.17.23) is also Norman. The round-headed arcades in the nave are late 12th-century; notice how the westernmost arch has been truncated by the later building of the tower, resulting in an arcade of two and a half bays. The piers are circular, but not perhaps as massive as those from earlier in the Norman era. The capitals are well carved with a variety of scallop (Fig.9.7), nail-head, faces and foliage.

The chancel was rebuilt in the Early English period (13th century); there are two blocked lancet windows, and the chancel arch is pointed. The Decorated period (14th century) is represented by the east window of the south aisle. To the Perpendicular age (15th and early 16th centuries) belong the north aisle, with its eastward extension opening into the chancel, and the tower (Fig.6.9). The latter is one of the best in Shropshire – a fine edifice, opening into the nave by a very tall tower arch. At the top are battlements and eight crocketed pinnacles, and below this an ornamental frieze of quatrefoils. The belfry windows are two-light Perpendicular, and the buttresses are at right-angles to the corners, with many set-offs. There is a staircase turret at the south-eastern corner. The porch dates from the late 17th or early 18th century.

The Norman font (Fig.10.3) displays a band of beading below the rim, then cable, and then a broad band of lattice-work. Above the font is an 18th-century brass chandelier. The Jacobean pulpit is dated 1612. In one of the south windows in the chancel are some fragments of 15th-century stained glass

St. Andrew, Stanton-upon-Hine Heath*

The churchyard here is not only circular, but is notably raised above the surrounding ground. Gelling speculates that these features may represent an early Irish/Welsh tradition which persisted to influence the sites chosen for churches or monasteries in later centuries;[8] she cites similar examples in Shropshire at Abdon, Coreley, Diddlebury, Easthope and Eyton-on-the-Weald Moors. Further evidence of Stanton's antiquity comes from the entry in the Domesday Book, which records the presence of both a church and a priest. The courses of herring-bone masonry in the north wall of both nave and chancel likewise also indicate an early Norman church (either late 11th or early 12th century). Near to the herring-bone masonry are internally-splayed Norman windows, two in the chancel and one in the nave. The nave also has two Norman doorways – that in the south wall is plain, that in the north has one order of shafts, and capitals bearing upright leaves. The west tower is Early English below, and Perpendicular above. It

Fig.17.24 St. Andrew, Stanton-upon-Hine Heath

is supported by two huge diagonal buttresses (Fig.17.24) which were added in 1666 to prevent the tower slipping down the mound.

Internally remains of an arcade persist in the south wall of the nave, indicating that at one stage there was a short south aisle. The chancel arch is Victorian. The pulpit is late 17th-century, and the panelling in the chancel probably came from the former box-pews in the nave. The reredos of carved wood depicts Christ and the disciples fishing, and dates from 1896. The communion rails were from the balustrade of the 18th-century gallery pulled down in 1892. The present west gallery dates only from 1913. The stained glass in the east window, depicting the Feeding of the Five Thousand, was designed by Sir Ninian Comper; he also worked at the nearby church of Moreton Corbet.

Holy Trinity, Weston Lullingfields*

This church was built in 1857 to serve a new parish carved out of the parish of Baschurch. The architect was Edward Haycock jun. and the style is mainly late Early English. The chancel is quite deep, reflecting the influence by the late 1850s of the High-Church movement. The church is light and airy, and there is some attractive glass in the east window by Sophia Lister (1992). On the south side, the church is connected by a corridor to the vicarage.

East Shropshire – Newport and Shifnal

Albrighton, near Shifnal**
Badger**
Beckbury*
Boningale
Chetwynd**
Church Aston*
Crudgington
Donington*
Edgmond**
Great Bolas*
Kemberton
Kynnersley
Lilleshall**
Longford Talbot chapel*

Muxton
Newport**
Rowton
Ryton*
Sambrook*
Sheriffhales
Shifnal***
Stockton*
Sutton Maddock
Tibberton
Tong***
Waters Upton
Woodcote*

*Fig.18.1 St. Mary Magdalene,
Albrighton near Shifnal: the chancel*

St. Mary Magdalene Albrighton, near Shifnal**
Albrighton church has had its share of alterations
and rebuildings over the years, but it is pleasant to
record that its recent re-ordering is a resounding
success. The church is now a model for any parish
that is seeking to rid itself of Victorian pine pews
– for here they have been replaced by good-
quality chairs, disposed in a semicircular fashion
around the nave altar. The gain in appearance,
and in flexibility of use, is considerable.

The church goes back to Norman times, as
evidenced by the tower (Fig.6.5). For here, in
the second storey, is quite a large round-headed
window, with nook-shafts; a similar window, now
blocked, is present at about the same height in the
west wall of the nave. Below the Norman window
in the tower is an Early English lancet, which must
be a later insertion. There are clasping buttresses
at the corners of the tower, and Perpendicular
battlements. The chancel (Fig.18.1) is Decorated,

and has a fine five-light window (Fig.3.15). There are sedilia and a piscina on the south side. The roof of the chancel has trussed rafters supported by collar-beams and arched braces. The nave and aisles were rebuilt in 1853; the south aisle is unexceptional, but the north is built of an incongruous yellow stone.

During the rebuilding, an impressive 13th-century tomb-chest was found under the floor of the south aisle, and is now placed at the west end of the north aisle. The lid is carved with many heraldic designs and around the sides of the chest are pointed trefoiled shafts. Pevsner dates this monument to *c*.1260-70. In the chancel is the late medieval memorial to Sir John Talbot (d.1555) and his wife. There are two alabaster effigies on a tomb-chest, and around the sides are family figures between twisted colonettes – a Renaissance motif. Sir John wears the SS collar. There is a good Victorian marble font.

St. Giles, Badger**

The place-name has nothing to do with badgers; in the Domesday Book, it is recorded as *Beghesovre*, which means 'Baecg's hill-spur', Baecg being a personal name and OE *ofer*

Fig.18.2 St. Giles, Badger: monument to Sir Isaac Hawkins Browne (d.1819), by Sir Francis Chantrey   *Fig.18.3 Badger: monument to Henrietta Browne (d.1802) by John Flaxman*

meaning a bank or hill-spur.[1] In the Middle Ages the parishes of Badger and Beckbury formed a detached area of the diocese of Hereford, reflecting the historical association of these parishes with Wenlock Priory.[2]

The tiny village is picturesque, and St. Giles has a wonderful situation beside a large pool. There was a medieval church here, but this was demolished and replaced by the present building in 1834. The base of the western tower is, however, old. The architect was Francis Helley but the church is really just an oblong preaching box, with no distinction of nave and chancel – a late date for such an arrangement. The windows are wide lancets. A north chapel was added in 1886, the architect being F. Francis. Fortunately, some treasures were included from the earlier church, and it is these which give Badger some distinction.

The finest artefact is probably the screen which now divides the north chapel from the nave; it is late Perpendicular, resembling the very fine screen of Hughley. The screen was moved to its present position when the north chapel was built. Then there are four monuments of more than ordinary merit: the largest is the seated memorial of Isaac Hawkins Browne, MP, FRS (d.1819) by Sir Francis Chantrey (Fig.18.2), singled out for special praise by Whinney.[3] To the right of this memorial in the north chapel is the monument by John Flaxman to Browne's wife Henrietta (d.1802); she is depicted standing, with a spirit hovering above (Fig.18.3). Chantrey and Flaxman were two of the leading sculptors during the Greek Revival in the early 19th century – the last great age of English church sculpture. To the left is a monument to Harriet Pigot (d.1852) by John Gibson; a further monument by the same sculptor is that to Harriet Cheney (d.1848) in the north wall of the nave. The stained glass in the east window is contemporary with the church, but above are some Flemish roundels of the 16th or 17th century. At the west end is some modern stained glass in memory of Margaret Dix and her father; the artist is Jane Gray, and the window was dedicated in April 1995. Finally, two paintings embellish the church – a copy of Titian's Ecce Homo, and a copy of Guido's Annunciation.

St. Milburga, Beckbury*

The parishes of Badger and Beckbury, on the Shropshire/Staffordshire border, for centuries constituted an enclave of the diocese of Hereford east of the Severn, surrounded by parishes which were in the diocese of Lichfield. This was because they were part of the estates of Wenlock Priory from at least 1120, and it was not until 1905 that they were transferred to Lichfield. The dedication to St. Milburga reflects the link with Wenlock.

Beckbury is an attractive village, enhanced by its sweet little church (Fig.18.4). This presents an unusual combination

Fig.18.4 St. Milburga, Beckbury

of medieval chancel, Georgian tower and nave, and Victorian aisles. The nave and tower were built in 1731, with well-marked quoins at the corners and rustication around the west door; the tower has a pyramid roof. There is a clerestory of small quatrefoil windows on the south side only of the nave. The south and north aisles and arcades were added in 1856 and 1879-80 respectively. The chancel is Decorated, but as can be seen from the east wall externally it was raised by four feet in 1884. On the outside of the south wall of the chancel is an unusual arch – probably a tomb-recess, but some have believed it to be an entrance arch. Another unusual feature is the pair of narrow windows, low down at the west end of the chancel, one on the north and one on the south side. There is a Perpendicular font and a Victorian stone pulpit.

The great treasure is the incised alabaster slab to Richard and Margaret Haughton (d.1505), with figures of their children at the foot of the slab. This is now mounted on the south wall of the chancel, having previously been part of an altar tomb. There are graffiti dated 1708 and 1724 on the figure of Richard Haughton – evidently vandalism is no new phenomenon! The slab (like the one at Aston Botterell) is almost certainly the work of alabasterers based at Burton on Trent,[4] and the costume of the lady is an excellent depiction of fashion in the early 16th century.

St. Chad, Boningale

Boningale was an ancient chapelry in the parish of Stockton. St. Chad's church (Fig.18.5) consists of a nave, with a narrow south aisle, chancel and a western weather-boarded belfry with a short spire. There is a Norman window in the north wall of the nave, and another, now blocked, in the north wall of the chancel just beyond the vestry. The east window of the chancel is Decorated and the south windows square-headed Perpendicular. The south aisle was built in 1861, and the low solitary pier has a very florid capital. The roofs of nave and chancel are good: they are of low pitch, panelled and embossed. The pulpit is relatively plain, and probably dates from the mid-17th century.

Fig.18.5 St. Chad, Boningale

St. Michael and All Angels, Chetwynd**

Although the present church dates only from 1865, the parish of Chetwynd has a long and distinguished history. It is recorded in the Domesday Book as *Catewinde*, the manor being held by the Countess Godiva. There was a mill with two fisheries and 64 sticks of eels. More notably, there was a priest, and therefore, one must assume, a Saxon church. This

*Fig.18.6 St. Michael and All Angels,
Chetwynd (1856) by
Benjamin Ferrey:
the florid capitals of the arcade*

disappeared without trace and was succeeded by a medieval church probably built in the 13th century. This in turn was pulled down in 1735 and a Georgian church built, like its two predecessors, next to Chetwynd Park Hall. Its appearance was recorded by the Rev. Williams in 1791. By the 1850s, population and attendance at church were increasing, and the owners of the great house felt that the nearness of the parish church interfered with family life; so it was decided to demolish the building and build a new church away from the hall. Benjamin Ferrey was appointed architect.

The splendid result was the present building (Fig.5.5), the best of Ferrey's three churches in Shropshire. No expense was spared, most of the cost being borne by the Borough family who lived in the great hall. The church is built of red sandstone quarried locally, and the building consists of a north tower with spire, nave, chancel and south aisle. The tower has twin windows on each face of the belfry, and above is a tall broach spire, with lucarnes. The prevailing style is Decorated, as enjoined by *The Ecclesiologist* (and of course Ferrey was a great admirer of Pugin – see pp.35 and 31-32). The piers of the arcade are of polished Devonshire marble, and the capitals are exceedingly florid (as was common in the 1860s at the height of the High Victorian phase). They are, however, beautifully carved (Fig.18.6), as are two heads in the south-west corner of the nave. Curl comments that although continental Gothic (from Germany and France) dominated English church architecture in the 1860s, here at Chetwynd there is no trace of this: Chetwynd is a thoroughly English church.[5] He also points out that the tower and spire are modelled on the limestone churches of Rutland, and is of the opinion that the church is curiously old-fashioned for its date. Perhaps that should not surprise us, for Ferrey was not an adventurous *avant-garde* architect. At any rate, it was thought highly of when it was built, and it was described and illustrated in Eastlake (1872).

The chancel is separated from the nave by a good screen. In the north and south chancel walls are paired lancets, separated internally by marble shafts. Further shafts are supported by corbels behind the screen. There is a fine reredos consisting of an upper band of majolica tiles displaying the symbols of the Passion, and below a series of Gothic terracotta panels. There is good Victorian glass by Hardman in the east window of the chancel, and some attractive modern glass by Francis Skeat depicting St. Guthlac in one of the windows in the north wall of the nave. The font, a stone bowl supported by marble pillars, is octagonal, alternate faces being sculpted with the symbols of the four evangelists.

St. Andrew, Church Aston*

Church Aston is now virtually a southern suburb of Newport, but in medieval times it was a chapelry in the parish of Edgmond. The old chapel was apparently demolished in 1803 and replaced by a 'neat brick structure'; this in turn was replaced in 1867 by the present building designed by G.E. Street. The church is one of Street's happier creations in Shropshire – not so grand as St. George's, and not so intimate as Lyneal, but showing plenty of inventive touches.

Fig.18.7 St. Andrew, Church Aston (1867) by G.E. Street

The church consists of an undivided nave and chancel, with a lead *flèche* over the nave (Fig.18.7). Street employed the Decorated style mainly for the windows, but, as ever, he never slavishly copied medieval styles. The arcade has round piers and plain rounded capitals. Between the nave and chancel is a low stone partition, as in other churches designed by Street. The pulpit and font are both of stone. In the chancel is a reredos (Fig.18.8), almost certainly by Street, featuring the symbols of the four evangelists.

The church is noted for its stained glass. In the splendid east window by Heaton, Butler and Bayne is Christ in Majesty, with the Crucifixion and Last Supper below. The glass in one of the south windows features St. Paul in Athens; the design is by Burne-Jones (Fig.12.15).

St. Mary, Crudgington

Crudgington is a sweet little Victorian church, built in 1863. It has a western bell-turret of wood, with a spirelet above, and a series of three-light horizontal windows, with longer windows in two tiers at the western end. The roof comes low down on each side, giving the church a picturesque look.

Fig.18.8 Church Aston: the reredos by Street

St. Cuthbert, Donington*

It is often surprising to find how close medieval churches can be to each other, and not only in urban centres, for Donington church is only about a quarter of a mile from Albrighton. Donington today is clearly less important than its larger neighbour, yet the Domesday Book valued the manor at Donington at £9, while Albrighton was worth only 16s. No part of Donington church goes back to the time of the Normans – the oldest part of the church is the 14th-century chancel. Here the east window shows uncusped intersecting tracery (Fig.18.9), and on the south side, there is a low-side window. In the north window of the chancel is some excellent 14th-century stained glass, depicting the Coronation of the Virgin (Fig.12.3). There is a piscina in the south

Fig.18.9 St. Cuthbert, Donington: 14th-century chancel

wall, and an aumbry in the north. The best feature of the nave is the double hammer-beam roof, which is dated 1635. Cranage maintained that the nave was rebuilt at this time. In 1879 the church was restored and a north aisle added. A few days before the church was due to re-open, the medieval tower fell into the churchyard and was rebuilt the following year. The Victorian tower closely reproduces the earlier tower.

St. Peter, Edgmond**

Edgmond (meaning 'Ecgmund's hill') is situated at the summit of a low hill (200-250 feet above sea-level) on the eastern side of the marshy land around the Weald Moors.[6]

At a first glance, Edgmond appears to be that rarity, a Shropshire Perpendicular church. But as one walks along the path through the well-kept church-yard, a glance at the chancel to the right immediately reveals that all is not of one period; for there are clear Decorated windows contrasting with the Perpendicular windows of the south aisle (Fig.18.10).

The church therefore consists of a Perpendicular western tower, south porch, and nave with north and south aisles, and a Decorated chancel. The fine

Fig.18.10 St. Peter, Edgmond: Decorated chancel and Perpendicular nave

tower has Perpendicular windows, and a quatrefoil frieze below the battlements; there are also battlements on the porch and south aisle. Tall, slender octagonal columns separate the nave from the aisles (Fig.3.17); but the bases of the columns are round, and these, as Cranage recognised, are the remains of an earlier Early English arcade. Glynne had noted in 1858 that the eastern responds (the half-columns bonded into the wall carrying the easternmost arches) were circular, not octagonal. Cranage amplified this by pointing out that on the north side the lower 5 feet of the respond above the plinth was part of the earlier arcade. The spacious Decorated chancel has an east window showing curvilinear tracery and a double piscina in the south wall.

There are some excellent artefacts. The fine font (Fig.10.4) is Norman, older than any part of the church: there is a ring of cable around the rim, then a row of billets, then square motifs with pairs of right-angled triangles, and at the bottom a mixture of Nordic interlacing and chevron.[7] In the chancel is a brass to Francis Yonge (d.1533) and his wife; he is shrouded, she normally clothed. The very good stone reredos was designed by Bodley and Garner (1889 – *cf* Ruyton XI Towns); at the centre is the Crucifixion. There is good Victorian glass by Powell's in the south window of the chancel, and by Kempe in the east and north windows.

St. John the Baptist, Great Bolas*

The name 'Bolas' indicates a site on a flood-plain,[8] and Great Bolas is indeed on the confluence of the rivers Meese and Tern. There was a medieval church here, but no trace of it survives. The present attractive building consists of a Georgian west tower and nave (Fig.18.11), dated 1726, and an earlier chancel which looks medieval but in fact was built in the late 17th century. Nave and tower are of brick, with stone quoins, and vases on the top of the tower. The windows are wide and round-arched, with a

Fig.18.11 St. John the Baptist, Great Bolas: tower and nave (1726), the chancel late 17th-century

keystone at the top. The builder (and presumably the designer) of the nave and tower was John Willdigg and his accounts survive.[9]

The interior is authentic Georgian, with a full set of 18th-century box-pews, pulpit with sounding-board, communion rails etc. There is a west gallery.

St. Andrew and St. John the Baptist, Kemberton

Kemberton is mentioned in the Domesday Book (*Chenbritone*), and there have been several churches before the present building. This is unpretentious – a good example of a Victorian parish church, designed in 1880 by a local architect, Joseph Farmer. There is attractive stained glass in the south chancel window, and the communion table, ornate pulpit and reredos are evidence of local craftsmanship. At the west end is a wall hanging, with embroidery depicting local families and trades, created in 1989.

St. Chad, Kynnersley

The combination of a Georgian tower with medieval nave and chancel is here very attractive. The tower was built in 1722-23, and has a parapet with obelisks at the corners. The rest of the church is medieval, and, according to the reticulated tracery of the east window of the chancel, from the Decorated period (first half of the 14th century). The windows of the nave were all renewed in the 19th century. At the east end of the nave is a double bell-cote, which is probably medieval. Inside there is a west gallery, and a font which appears to consist of a plain Norman bowl on a Victorian stem. The nave is divided from the chancel by an arch resting on corbels.

St. Michael and All Angels, Lilleshall**

The name derives from Lill's hill, the eminence north of the village now crowned by an obelisk to the first duke of Sutherland. In Domesday Book *Linleshelle* was one of the manors held on behalf of St. Alkmund's church, Shrewsbury by the priest Godbold. (The same man held, and gave his name to, Preston Gubbals; he also held Uckington and Atcham.)

There presumably was a Saxon church here, but no trace of this remains. The present church was built in stages over four hundred years, and exhibits work of every style of later medieval architecture. The earliest part is the south doorway, which is late Norman (Transitional), *c*.1190. It has two orders of shafts, and above is decorated with chevron carving. Further east along the south wall of the nave another Norman doorway has been inserted; this again shows chevron carving in two planes, and the capitals of the shafts have some water-leaf adornment. The chancel is Early English, with a lancet window in the south wall; the east window of the chancel

Fig.18.12 St. Michael and All Angels, Lilleshall: the Perpendicular tower

was inserted later, probably in the 15th century. The plain low arcade (Fig.3.13) separating the north aisle from the nave is Decorated and the east window of this aisle shows reticulated tracery of the Decorated period. Lastly, the tower (Fig.18.12) is late Perpendicular, with battlements and pinnacles, and a frieze below the parapet. Two stone shields are set in the south wall of the tower, one of which has the crest of the Levesons of Lilleshall.[10]

There are a number of fine furnishings. Pride of place must go to the excellent Norman font, which is earlier than any other part of the church, and may date from *c*.1100 (Fig.10.6). The bowl stands on a 19th-century stem, and there are medieval encaustic tiles from the chancel around it. At the west end of the nave is mounted a fine Royal Coat of Arms with the initials CR; there is some dispute over whether this refers to Charles I or II. The roofs are interesting: above the north aisle is a trussed-rafter roof, and over the nave are tie- and collar-beams; both are thought to be late medieval.

In the north wall of the chancel is one of the finest monuments in Shropshire (Fig.11.30), to Sir Richard Leveson (d.1661) and his wife (d.1674). It was thought to be the work of Edward Marshall and his son Joshua, who created monuments elsewhere to two daughters of Alice, Duchess Dudley; Lady Leveson was a third daughter.[11] More recently it has been attributed to Thomas Burman.[12] The large monument shows two reclining figures, with an imposing architectural surround, columns on each side, putti beside them and a pediment above.

Talbot chapel, Longford*

This chapel is in the care of the Churches Conservation Trust and is all that remains of the medieval church in Longford. Originally it was the south chancel chapel, built around 1300 (the overlap between Early English and Decorated). It is notable for two monuments: in the floor is a 14th-century tomb slab bearing an incised cross with a young man's head; and a very fine standing wall-monument to Thomas and Anne Talbot, d.1686 and 1706 respectively. There is an inscription panel, flanked by Corinthian columns, and above a pediment, drapery, cherubim etc.

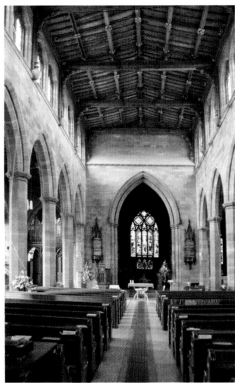

Fig.18.13 St. Nicholas, Newport: the nave looking east

St. John the Evangelist, Muxton

This is a brand-new church, built in 1997 to replace a mission church of the 1890s provided by the duke of Sutherland. The building provides a rather featureless worship area, with a small sanctuary screened off on one side, thus maximising flexibility of use. There are good facilities for community services.

St. Nicholas, Newport**

The church dates back to the 12th century – but virtually nothing of that age survives. The later medieval church comprised a western tower, which does survive, nave and north and south aisles, and chancel. In 1432 Thomas Draper obtained a licence to found a chantry with two priests, and ten years later a college was established, with a master and four chaplains.[13] The college was dissolved in 1547. In the 1720s a ghastly incongruous north aisle with a semicircular apse and chancel were built, and are depicted in the Williams painting of 1791. This was taken down during the extensive rebuilding in the following century: the chancel was rebuilt in 1866 by E. Haycock jun; John Norton rebuilt the nave and south aisle in 1883-85, the north aisle in 1890-91, and the south porch in 1904. So one sees today externally the medieval west tower and a Victorian church.

The building, as a whole, is however attractive, and of red sandstone. The western tower is fairly squat, with a late Decorated west window and a late Perpendicular west doorway. The tower opens into the nave by a tall arch, and the reconstructed arcades of the nave are also tall (Fig.18.13). Over the nave is an original Perpendicular roof, low-pitched and embossed (Fig.8.12). In the north wall of the north aisle are two medieval tomb-recesses transferred from the east wall of the aisle.

In the chancel is an alabaster tomb-chest of c.1520; there are recumbent effigies, small figures and angels round the sides and engaged columns at the corners — a sign of Renaissance influence. There is also the memorial to Elizabeth Blakemore (d.1828), with a large seated angel. There is some excellent Victorian stained glass: especially good is the south window in the chancel – Burne-Jones designed the figures in the upper panels, and Ford Madox Brown the lower panels. There is glass by Kempe in the windows of the south chapel. Elsewhere there are several windows with modern glass, of varying quality. In the north aisle is a Crucifixion by Christopher Whall, dated 1920. The plain octagonal font is dated 1660. In the base of the tower is a collection of 18th-century benefaction boards.

All Hallows, Rowton

The manor of Rowton is of great antiquity. At the time of Domesday it was held by Edith from Earl Roger, and the presence of a priest was recorded. All Hallows church consists of a nave built of large blocks of red sandstone and a shallow brick chancel, dating from 1881. It is uncertain how much of the nave is really medieval – the lancets in the nave are very wide, and clearly do not date from the 13th century.

St. Andrew, Ryton*

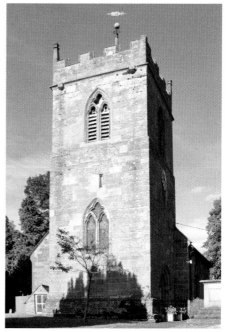

Ryton church has a lovely situation, on an eminence overlooking the Worfe valley. From the exterior, the nave and chancel appear to be entirely Victorian, and it is chastening to learn that the chancel was built in 1720. All the windows now are Gothic, and were so when Sir Stephen Glynne visited in 1849. Were they originally thus, or had they been altered before Glynne's visit? The north aisle was added in 1886. The tower (Fig.18.14) was built in 1710; Cranage commented that the window tracery is Decorated, and if original this is a remarkably late example of Gothic survival. There is an excellent 14th-century octagonal font, carved with quatrefoils (Fig.10.18).

Fig.18.14 St. Andrew, Ryton: the tower (1710)

St. Luke, Sambrook*

Although the parish of Sambrook was formed only in 1856, the place-name is old, being recorded in Domesday Book as *Semebre*, meaning 'sandy stream'.[14] The village is pleasant, and St. Luke's church, an early Victorian building, is set in a spacious and well-tended churchyard, the very epitome, one might think, of prosperous, rural England.

St. Luke's was built in 1856 of red sandstone; the architect was Benjamin Ferrey (see p.35). The church consists of nave and chancel, with a north aisle and vestry, south porch, and a western timbered belfry with wooden spirelet. It is a pretty building (Pevsner described it as 'wilful'), set in a neatly maintained churchyard. The church (Fig.18.15) is executed in the then fashionable Decorated style, as enjoined by *The Ecclesiologist*; most of the windows show rather complex Decorated tracery, though others are single or paired cusped lancets. High in the west wall is a rose window. There are alternating rows of grey and brown slates in the roof. The interior (Fig.18.16) is comfortable and restrained; the font has pillars of marble and the pulpit is of stone. The piers of the north arcade have plain circular moulded capitals. There is some good Victorian stained glass by Charles Gibbs.

St. Mary, Sheriffhales

The church consists of a western tower, with nave, chancel and north aisle. There is a Norman window in the north wall of the nave. The nave was built in 1661 and has a double hammer-beam roof. The north aisle is said to be the original church; the arcade dividing it from the nave may have come from Lilleshall Abbey. The chancel and the western tower are Georgian. The chancel is spacious and has some attractive original panelling.

Fig.18.15 St. Luke, Sambrook (1856) by Benjamin Ferrey

Fig.18.16 Sambrook: the chancel

170

St. Andrew, Shifnal***

The magnificence of St. Andrew's church undoubtedly dates from Shifnal's importance as an ecclesiastical centre in Saxon times. It was the minster of an extensive Saxon parish which included Kemberton, Ryton, Dawley and Sheriffhales. In the Domesday Book it was known as *Iteshale* (later becoming *Idshall*). The name Shifnal came into use in the 14th century and gradually replaced the former name. In the 12th century the church was acquired by Shrewsbury Abbey.

Fig.18.17 St. Andrew, Shifnal

St. Andrew's (Fig.18.17) is a cruciform church, with nave, porch, and north and south aisles, north and south transepts, a crossing tower, and a chancel with a south chapel. Although the main part of the church (nave, porch, aisles, transepts and tower) is Early English (13th century), there are remains of the earlier Norman church. The chancel and south chapel were built during the Decorated era, and most of the windows of the aisles are Perpendicular insertions.

The visitor enters the church through the south porch (Fig.7.5); this is a fine, two-storeyed structure, the upper storey extending internally above the south aisle. The outer doorway has a trefoiled arch above, the inner doorway is plain. The porch is vaulted with ribs resting on shafts, and at the apex is a stiff-leaf boss. The window of the room above, formerly a school-room, has plate tracery.

The nave has Early English arcades (Fig.18.18), with the arches supported by octagonal columns. The west wall has a plain pointed doorway, with a three-light window above with cinquefoil tracery in the apex. At the crossing, the tower is supported by four tall multishafted arches. Beyond, the chancel arch is Norman and round-headed; on the west side of the arch is some dogtooth decoration. Cranage pointed out that above the dogtooth, there is unusual Norman carving: 'It appears to be a fruit-bearing twisted branch coming out of the mouth of a human head. There

Fig.18.18 Shifnal: the south arcade

Fig.18.19 Shifnal: carving on the Norman arch of the crossing

is a large finial above' (Fig.18.19). There is a further Norman arch leading from the south transept into the chapel. Beyond this there was originally an apse, traces of the roof of which can be seen inside the chapel. There is a late Norman doorway in the south wall of the south transept, and a Norman window in this transept now looks into the south aisle.

In the Decorated period (14th century) the chancel was extended; the Norman chancel ended where the communion rails now are, and two deeply-splayed round-headed windows remain in the north wall. The other chancel windows are Decorated: especially notable is the lovely five-light east window, with complex reticulated tracery above, recently restored (Fig.18.17). The south chapel was also built in the Decorated era and has a less elaborate reticulated east window. Outside, this chapel has a tomb-recess with an ogee-headed canopy. Perpendicular windows were inserted in the next century in the north transept and the south aisle, and battlements were added to the tower, south transept and aisle.

The fine hammer-beam roofs of the nave and chancel probably date from the end of the 16th century after damage from an extensive fire in Shifnal in 1591. There are some notable monuments. Earliest is the 13th-century coffin-lid inscribed with a floriated cross in the chapel. Also in the chapel are the memorials to Olive Brigges (d.1596), an alabaster effigy on a tomb-chest; and to Humphry Brigges (d.1626) and his wife, again showing recumbent effigies on a tomb-chest. In the north side of the chancel is the effigy of a priest (Thomas Forster, d.1526) in a tomb-recess; and on the south side, a bust of Magdalen Briggs (d.1598). There is some good Victorian stained glass in the west window of the nave and the east window of the chancel. The pulpit is Jacobean, altered later. The font is Victorian.

St. Chad, Stockton

The church is situated on a knoll, with extensive views westwards towards the Wrekin. The lower part of the tower is Perpendicular, the upper storey dating from the early 17th century. The rest of the church was radically renewed in 1857-58. The old walls of the nave and chancel were refaced internally and externally – the sandstone of the exterior has now a rather strident appearance – but a Norman window, now opening only internally was preserved in the north wall of the chancel. The octagonal font is Perpendicular, with blind arcades and quatrefoiled circles containing flowers on the stem and bowl. There is some good woodwork in the Jacobean pulpit and reading desk. The roofs are interesting: a wagon-roof in the nave (which may include some Jacobean timbers), and a panelled oak ceiling in the chancel.

St. Mary, Sutton Maddock

At the time of the Domesday Book, the settlement was called *Sudtone* (south town), being the southern part of the Saxon parish of *Iteshale* (Shifnal). Sir Stephen Glynne visited Sutton Maddock in 1840 when he found the church rebuilt 'in the course of the last century in the wretched style so often adopted in Shropshire'. This Georgian church was probably built in 1766 by Richard Colley[15] and, unusually, it terminated in an apse. I suspect Glynne would have approved of the present building which dates from 1888, designed by Thomas Nicholson and Son of Hereford. The church (Fig.18.20) is pleasantly situated adjacent to the hall, a little isolated from the village. The tower bears the date 1579 and is late Perpendicular (see the square-headed 'Tudor' windows in the belfry); over the south belfry window is the figure of a grotesque animal (? a lion). There is some attractive Victorian glass in the east window.

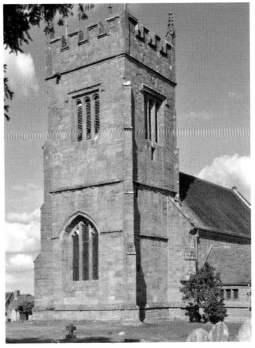

Fig.18.20 St. Mary, Sutton Maddock (1888) by Nicholson and Son

All Saints, Tibberton

This church, built of red sandstone, was designed by J. Baddeley in 1842. It is in the Early English style, the windows being lancets with Y-tracery. There was a previous church, painted by Williams in 1790.

St. Mary and St. Bartholomew, Tong***

Tong church is one of the great treasures of Shropshire: a noble example of Perpendicular architecture, accurately dated because of the circumstances of its foundation, and containing an outstanding assembly of late medieval monuments the equal of any parish church in the country.

In the Domesday survey, the manor of *Tuange* was held by Earl Morcar on behalf of Earl Roger. The place-name is said to mean 'tongs, fork of a river,[16] and the church guide points out that two streams do indeed meet at the western end of the site of Tong castle.

Cranage stated that the earliest record of the church is in the late 11th century, for Earl Roger endowed it and gave it to Shrewsbury Abbey before 1094. There is no trace now of any Norman church, but Cranage (and Pevsner) believed that part of the south arcade

Fig.18.21 St. Mary and St. Bartholomew, Tong

is Early English, and that the present south aisle was probably the nave of the original Norman church. The remainder of the building is Perpendicular, built by Lady Isabella de Pembrugge in 1410 when she founded a chantry college in memory of her husband; the Vernon chapel was added one hundred years later.

The church (Fig.18.21) stands proudly, just north of the M54, and is built of red sandstone. It is a cruciform building (rare in the Perpendicular era) with a central square tower, becoming octagonal and supporting a short spire. Tower, nave and chancel are adorned with battlements and pinnacles in the finest Perpendicular manner. The octagonal stage of the tower has windows only on the four cardinal sides, but the spire above has lights on all eight faces, an exceptional arrangement.[17]

The interior is so dominated by the tombs that it is easy to ignore the architecture – which is a pity, for there is much to admire. The nave is divided from the aisles by arcades of five bays; the piers are octagonal, the capitals plainly moulded. As already indicated the arcades are different: the north is loftier, but slight differences to the mouldings and the bases of the piers of the south arcade betray to the expert that this arcade is earlier.[18] The roof of the nave is of low pitch with arched braces, and panelled with bosses at the intersections.

The chancel is divided from the nave by the Perpendicular rood screen, with much fine carving of leaves and tendrils, and there are parclose screens at the east ends of both north and south aisles. The chancel has a fine early Perpendicular east window of five lights, and the stained glass is mostly by Kempe – though he is said to have re-used fragments of medieval glass executed in the manner of the celebrated York glazier John de Thornton.[19] The chancel is furnished with an excellent range of 15th-century choir-stalls with misericords (Fig.14.11); the finest of these shows an Annunciation, with the Archangel and the Virgin framing a representation of the Crucifixion.[20] The stalls have tall backs with exquisitely rich tracery, and there are poppy-heads at the ends of the benches. Opening from the chancel to the south is the Vernon chapel, built in 1510 in the latest Perpendicular fashion, with fan-vaulting and pendants. In the floor are some medieval encaustic tiles.

The octagonal font is Perpendicular, adorned with shields, and the pulpit is Jacobean. In the vestry, not normally open, is an embroidered vestment ornamented with cherubs, flowers, etc. Its date is uncertain: Cranage said medieval, Pevsner *c.*1600.

But good as the architecture and other artefacts are, it is of course the monuments that bring visitors from far and wide to Tong. For the sake of clarity, I will describe first the unique series of monuments relating to the founder, Dame Isabella de Pembrugge, the Vernons and Stanleys; these are in the crossing before the chancel steps, and in the chantry chapel. There then follows brief notes on the other monuments which are displayed around the church.

1) Sir Fulke de Pembrugge (d.1409) and Dame Isabella (d.1446) (Fig.11.5). Recumbent, alabaster effigies on a tomb-chest, the sides of which are decorated with arches; angels are present on the east side only. Lady Isabella's head rests on a pillow with angel supporters.

2) Sir Richard Vernon (d.1451) and Benedicta of Ludlow (Fig.11.6). Sir Richard was great-nephew to Sir Fulke and inherited Tong Castle. This is the finest of the monuments, exhibiting very high standards of workmanship. Sir Richard is depicted in full armour, his head resting on a helm, his feet on a lion. He wears the SS collar of the House of Lancaster (instituted by John of Gaunt in the late 14th century), and bears the figure of St. James with two rods strapped to his staff, perhaps in token of pilgrimage to Santiago de Compostela. His wife is elegantly clad in a long cloak with richly carved brooches, her head resting on pillows. Her hair is bound by a bejewelled net bunched over the ears. Around the sides of the chest are canopied niches in which stand a notable series of saints[21] and angels bearing plain shields.

3) Sir William Vernon (d.1467), son of Sir Richard, and his wife Margaret. The altar tomb is of Purbeck marble, inlaid with a superb brass. Sir William is in chain and plate armour, his wife with a hood and wimple and clad in a mantle. At her feet there appears to be an elephant, but it may really be a dragon, the traditional symbol of St. Margaret.[22]

4) Sir Henry Vernon (d.1515), son of Sir William, and his wife Anne (Fig.11.9). He endowed the chantry chapel in 1510. The monument is under a panelled elliptical arch – a big superstructure with four brackets and crocketed canopies for images, with vaulting typical of the late Perpendicular era. Around the sides of the chest are narrow bays with angels and wider ones with shields.

5) Humphrey Vernon (d.1542), son of Sir Henry, and his wife Alice. An altar tomb, with an incised slab of alabaster. Humphrey is depicted as a soldier, at his feet a dog. At the side of Alice's head is a lion rampant.

6) Richard Vernon (d.1517), son of Sir Henry, and his wife Margaret. This tomb near the pulpit shows alabaster figures of Richard in plate armour, wearing the SS collar, with sword, dagger and gauntlets lying at his side.

7) Sir Thomas Stanley (d.1576), his wife Margaret, and their son Sir Edward Stanley (d.1632) (Fig.11.9). Richard Vernon's son, Sir George Vernon, is buried at Bakewell, Derbyshire, and left two daughters, Margaret marrying Sir Thomas Stanley. With the Stanley tomb we have moved from the late medieval to the Elizabethan era. This is an elaborate monument, with the effigies of Sir Thomas and Lady Margaret above, and Sir Edward beneath (irreverently dubbed 'the bunk bed' by a group of visiting schoolboys!).

8) Arthur Vernon (d.1516), youngest son of Sir Henry, has two memorials: in the floor of the chantry chapel is an excellent brass depicting him in academic robes, and on the west wall of the chapel is a bust (Fig.11.10).

Other monuments include a brass of Sir Randulph Elcock (d.1510), a priest of the college, in the wall of the south aisle, and an imposing memorial to George Durant (d.1780) on the pillar by the stairs to the belfry (just visible in Fig.14.11).

St. Michael, Waters Upton

Built in 1864, this is one of Street's lesser churches in Shropshire; but it is neverthe-less lifted above the run-of-the-mill level of mid-Victorian churches by the quality of the window tracery. At the east end there is intersecting tracery combined with cusping; and at the west, three cusped lancets and a rose window above. Moreover, many of the windows are filled with 19th- and early 20th-century glass of above-average quality. So the overall effect of the building is pleasing. It consists of nave and chancel undivided, and a western bell-turret.

Woodcote chapel*

Woodcote (meaning 'wood cottages') manor is recorded in Domesday Book and is an ancient chapelry of Sheriffhales. The chapel is in the grounds of Woodcote Hall, now a nursing home. It is a small and simple building, with an impressive array of monuments to the Cotes family who lived in the hall for several hundred years.

The chapel consists of an undivided nave and chancel, and is built of red sandstone. The south doorway is late Norman, with two orders of shafts with rings fairly low down. The capitals are carved with rather primitive foliage. The windows are square-headed, double lights, probably 16th-century. There has been some rebuilding of the west wall, with later windows. The humble interior is distinguished by the superb incised alabaster slab to Humphry Cotes, slain at the Battle of Bosworth Field (1485), and his wife. He is clad in armour and she wears the pedimental head-dress. The slab is said to be the work of Henry Harpur and William Moorcock, alabasterers of Burton upon Trent.[23] There are several further wall-monuments to the Cotes family extending to the 19th century.

Woodcote chapel has recently closed, but the key is available for visitors at the office of the nursing home.

Shrewsbury

Fig.19.1 St. Eata, Atcham, by the river Severn

St. Eata, Atcham**

St. Eata's has a lovely situation on the east bank of the Severn (Fig.19.1), close to the old Georgian bridge which used to carry the A5 over the river. This strategic site was well known to the Romans, for there was a ford over the river at Atcham,[1] and Roman stones are embedded in the walls of Atcham church. The Anglo-Saxons also were active in the area, for aerial photographs have revealed a substantial set of early Saxon buildings at Frog Hall.

Atcham (or Attingham) means 'the ham or homestead of Eata's

people',[2] and the dedication of the church to St. Eata is unique. Eata was a friend of St. Cuthbert and was in turn abbot of Old Melrose and of Lindisfarne (664). The Saxon church at Atcham was mentioned in Domesday Book, and it is likely that some of this survives (see below). In 1075 the Anglo-Norman historian Ordericus Vitalis was baptised here; he lived at the abbey of St. Evroul in Normandy and wrote the history of Normandy and England (*Historia Ecclesiastica*) between 1123 and 1141.

The church (Fig.19.2) consists of undivided nave and chancel, with a south porch and a west tower. The oldest part is the nave, and stones with a scale-leaf pattern built into the wall have been traced to the roof of a Roman mausoleum at the confluence of the rivers Tern and Severn about a mile away.[3] High up in the north wall is a small, round-headed, apparently Norman, window; internally, this has a triangular head formed by two sloping stones passing through the full thickness of the wall except for the round-headed outer facing. Triangular-headed windows are typical of Anglo-Saxon building, and are well seen at the Saxon church at Deerhurst in Gloucestershire. The Atcham window was thought by Taylor and Taylor[4] on balance to indicate a pre-Conquest (i.e. Anglo-Saxon) date for the main fabric of the nave. Further hints of Anglo-Saxon work are side-alternate quoins and plinths of square section.[5] Other windows in the nave are Perpendicular insertions. The chancel is Early English, the east window showing three lancets under one arch; the north and south windows in the chancel show Y-tracery. The priest's doorway is also Early English as is the main south doorway within the porch. The lower two storeys of the tower (Fig.6.1) are Early English with lancet windows, and here also is some Roman masonry. The west portal has been renewed, but is very complex, with five orders of shafts. The upper storey of the tower is Perpendicular, with a quatrefoil frieze and a parapet above. The porch is timber-framed and dated 1685. Tie-beams span the chancel, while collar-beams and arched braces roof the nave.

The octagonal font (described by Glynne as 'bad') is dated 1675, and is carved with two pairs of initials, probably of churchwardens.[6] There is an incised slab which was formerly in old St. Chad's, Shrewsbury. This is to Edward Burton (d.1524) and his wife Joyce; Greenhill thought that the male figure and the lady's head have probably been re-cut.[7] The stained glass is notable: in the east window is some 15th-century glass brought here in 1811 from Bacton in Herefordshire; it shows the family of Miles ap Harry (Parry). In the north window is some more glass from Bacton, commemorating Blanche Parry, maid of honour to Elizabeth I. An inscription records that the glass 'being much broken and neglected' was removed from Bacton and brought to Atcham by Mrs. Mary Burton, a descendant of the Parry family.

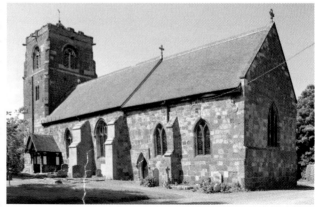

Fig.19.2 Atcham: the tower, nave and chancel

178

St. Mary Magdalene, Battlefield***

Battlefield is unusual among medieval churches because it can be precisely dated, the body of the church having been built in 1406-08. The battle of Shrewsbury was fought on 21 July 1403 between the rebel forces of Henry Percy (Hotspur) in alliance with the Welsh leader Owain Glyndwr and those of the king, Henry IV; it ended with the defeat of the rebels and the death of Hotspur, immortalised by Shakespeare in *Henry IV Part One*. Casualties were high, and 1,600 bodies were buried at the site of the battle.

The local rector, Roger Ive, obtained a licence from the king for land for the foundation of a chapel where prayers could be said for the dead and mass celebrated daily. The king granted a foundation charter which created a perpetual chantry, with a college consisting of a Master and six chaplains. This lasted until the Reformation, when chantries were suppressed and the college was dissolved in 1548. The church then became a parish church, but suffered severe neglect in the 18th century when the roof of the nave collapsed. The Williams painting of 1790 shows the nave roofless! When Sir Stephen Glynne visited Battlefield in 1831, he found the western part of the nave still unroofed, though the eastern portion was 'neatly fitted up for divine service'. The church was extensively restored by the Shrewsbury architect S. Pountney Smith in 1861-62. In 1982 it was declared redundant and has since been cared for by the Churches Conservation Trust. The key to the church may be obtained from the Visitor Centre about a quarter of a mile away.

The church (Fig.19.3) is quite isolated at the end of a lane, in peaceful surroundings shielded from the outside world by the Shrewsbury-Crewe railway embankment – though recent industrial development is coming perilously close. The nave and chancel were built in the first decade of the 15th century; it is striking and very unusual to see adjacent windows built at the same time in the Decorated and Perpendicular styles (Fig.3.16) – a classic example of the overlapping of medieval styles and a warning against the too rigid separation of building periods. The fine Perpendicular tower was built at the end of the 15th or early in the 16th century. In the gable at the east end of the chancel is a statue of Henry IV.

Internally, the church is spacious and dignified, consisting of a nave and chancel without aisles. The hammer-beam roof (Fig.8.16) is fine, and dates from the Victorian restoration, as does the screen

Fig.19.3 St. Mary Magdalene, Battlefield (1406-08)

179

Fig.19.4 Battlefield: the screen and roof

(Fig.19.4) and the font. There are Perpendicular sedilia in the south wall of the chancel, and opposite is a Gothic monument to John Corbet, (d.1817). Also on the north wall of the chancel is a marvellous wooden Pieta dating from the 15th century – unfortunately it is not easy to see the fine features of the carving because it is placed so high. In the vestry is some medieval glass from Normandy – in the north window is a 14th-century lady; in the east window are three lights showing a 16th-century king, a 15th-century monk and an unidentified figure (Fig.12.3). There are also some interesting exhibits relating to the battle of Shrewsbury.

Christ Church, Bayston Hill

The church built by Edward Haycock sen. in 1843 is now a private dwelling. It has been replaced by a new Christ Church, built in 1983 to cater for the increased population of the area which is now an outer suburb of Shrewsbury. The new church has an excellent set of premises, including a large 'worship area', hall, offices, kitchen etc, much used for community activities.

Built of yellow brick, the new church is not architec-

Fig.19.5 Christ Church, Bayston Hill (1982-83) by P. Scarisbrick

turally distinguished, but it displays considerable flexibility of use and it is good to see such a thriving church. The rather featureless interior (Fig.19.5) could be improved by some fittings – at present there is no pulpit, no lectern, no font. The altar is raised on two steps, and there is a plain cross on the wall behind it. To the right of the sanctuary is an impressive array of electronic aids for modern music; to the left, a rather more traditional organ.

Holy Trinity, Bicton*

At the time of the Domesday Book, Bicton was part of the holding of St. Chad's church, Shrewsbury, and the original church here was a chapel of ease to St. Chad's. This church was built of brick in the 17th or early 18th century, but was replaced in 1885 by the present building on a new site.

It is a substantial church by Lloyd-Oswell, and although rather conservative for its date, is the best of his Shropshire churches. It is built of local stone, and consists of a nave with south aisle, chancel, and an impressive tower which occupies the angle between the chancel and the east end of the south aisle (Fig.19.6). The

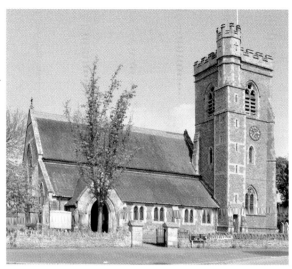

Fig.19.6 Holy Trinity, Bicton, (1885) by Arthur Lloyd-Oswell

windows are paired lancets in the south aisle, but elsewhere exhibit Decorated tracery. The arcade of three bays divides the nave and chancel, the piers and capitals being round, the arches double-chamfered. From the chancel, arches open into the base of the tower on the south side, and into the vestry on the north. Here the arches rest on floriated capitals more typical of the 1860s than the 1880s. The corbels supporting the chancel arch are plainer. The font is made of plain marble and is rather good. There is excellent Kempe glass in the east window and in the windows of the south aisle.

St. Mary, Eaton Constantine

The name 'Eaton' means 'settlement by a river', and this is appropriate here, for Eaton Constantine stands on rising ground within a mile of the river Severn. 'Constantine' refers to Thomas de Costentin who held the manor in 1242.[8] The village is best known as the home of Richard Baxter, the Puritan divine, whose house may still be seen.

The Reverend Williams painted the old church in 1786, showing a building with a west wooden bell-turret, a wooden south porch and dormer windows in the nave. This church was replaced in 1841 by the present building in the Early English style. The sole survival from the old church is the Norman font – a plain tub with a band of cable moulding around the lower part of the bowl. There are some box-pews.

St. Thomas, Hanwood

Cranage recorded that a new church was finished here in 1701, but no trace of this remains. The present church is built of brick, with stone dressings, and was erected in 1856. It consists of a nave and chancel, and weather-boarded belfry. There is a polygonal apse, and at the west end a gallery. The rather garish glass in the east window is by David and Charles Evans. The font is Norman, with fluting at the sides, and this presumably came from the medieval church.

Little Berwick chapel**

This is an extra-parochial church in the grounds of Berwick House. Berwick is mentioned in Domesday Book, the manor being valued in 1087 at £9. Cranage stated that Berwick was mentioned in the 13th century as a chapel of St. Mary's, Shrewsbury, and said that a quarter of a mile south of the present building is a barn which may well include part of the north wall of the medieval chapel.

The present chapel (Fig.19.7) shows three well-marked building stages. Earliest is the nave, which was erected in 1672, with plain straight-headed windows

Fig.19.7 Little Berwick chapel

on the north and south walls. The western tower dates from 1731 and has an arched western doorway, and a series of arched windows above rising to a parapet with urns. Also of this date is the south porch and one window with a prominent keystone. The eastern end of the church is the work of Mr. Walker, 1892-94.

The interior is a delight (Fig.19.8). There are a set of box-pews, with a squire's pew, and a plain panelled pulpit, all probably dating from the late 17th century. It is recorded that John Wesley preached from this pulpit in 1769. In the chancel are two most unusual choir-stalls with misericords; these appear to be Jacobean and are intricately carved. The wrought-iron communion-rail is 18th-century. On the south side of the nave is a memorial to two young girls of the Powys family, by Chantrey. Also in the nave is a standing figure of a young girl reading; the provenance of this is not known; it appears to date from the mid-19th century. There is a western gallery, with several hatchments of the Powys family.

Fig.19.8 Little Berwick: the interior, looking west

Access: Services are held every Sunday at 11am, and visitors are welcome then. At other times, application should be made to Mr. and Mrs. Angell-James of Berwick House, Shrewsbury.

Holy Trinity, Meole Brace***

Meole Brace church is one of Shropshire's best-kept secrets. Ignored by most books on English parish churches, even by John Betjeman and Simon Jenkins, it is a distinguished Victorian church and it houses one of the best sets of stained glass by Morris and Co. anywhere in the country.[9] Furthermore it does not court publicity: though a Grade 2* listed building, there is no guide book. And although the key is readily available from the parish office next to the church on weekday mornings,

Fig.19.9 Holy Trinity, Meole Brace (1867-68) by Edward Haycock jun.

the number of visitors appears relatively few.

Originally a separate village, Meole Brace is now an attractive and leafy outer suburb of Shrewsbury. The manor of Meole is recorded in Domesday Book, with the bishop of Chester, St. Mary's church, Shrewsbury, and one Edith (apparently not Queen Edith, wife of Edward the Confessor) holding land there. Meole is a river name, while Brace is derived from Aldolf de Bracy who held the manor in 1206.[10] The medieval church began to give serious problems in the 18th century: the Reverend Edward Williams painted this building in 1787 showing a lovely old church with a half-timbered upper storey of the tower. This was replaced in 1799 by a cruciform brick church, with a short west tower.[11]

The present building was erected in 1867-68, the architect being Edward Haycock junior. He was responsible for six other churches in Shropshire, but this is by far the best. It is a large well-proportioned building, set in a spacious churchyard surrounded with trees. It is built of red sandstone, mainly in the Decorated style. It consists of a north-west tower (Fig.19.9), a nave with north and south aisles, and an apsidal polygonal chancel with an organ chamber and vestry on the north, and a short transept on the south. The interior (Fig.19.10) is enlivened by a free use of contrasting red and buff stone. The arcades, the north of four bays and the south of five, have cylindrical piers, the capitals alternating with plain mouldings and luxuriant foliage. The transepts open into the chancel by one bay, and

Fig.19.10 Meole Brace: the north arcade and chancel

again the capitals are florid. The roof timbers are supported by a stone corbel-table with carvings. There is an imposing pulpit, complete with sounding-board, and an octagonal font, with alternate faces carved and inlaid with marble.

But the chief glory of Meole Brace is the marvellous assembly of stained glass of the Pre-Raphaelite School (Figs.12.8 and 12.9). The central window in the apse depicts the Crucifixion, with the Virgin Mary below, the work of Sir Edward Burne-Jones. On either side of the Crucifixion scene are representations of apostles, kings and martyrs. To the left are Old Testament scenes by Burne-Jones and Ford Madox Brown, and to the right New Testament scenes by Burne-Jones and William Morris. A further window in the centre of the south aisle is also by Ford Madox Brown and Burne-Jones. Elsewhere is later glass from the Morris firm and also two windows in quite different style by Kempe.

St. Chad, Montford

Montford church is situated prominently on a knoll above the river Severn; there was a medieval church here, but this was replaced in 1737-38 by the present building, designed

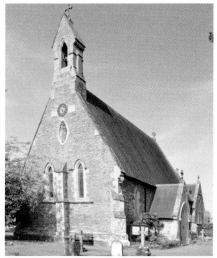

by William Cooper of Shrewsbury. Built of red sandstone, it is a pleasant, plain Georgian church, with a west tower, nave and chancel. The windows are arched, with pilasters on either side and a keystone at the apex. The Y-tracery was probably inserted during a restoration of 1884. Inside, there is a west gallery resting on cast iron columns and a font which is probably medieval. There is an attractive reredos, showing a Nativity scene, and some good stained glass by Burlison and Grylls.

Christ Church, Shelton and Oxon

The church (Fig.19.11) was built in 1854 to serve a new parish carved from St. Chad's Shrewsbury. The architect was Edward Haycock jun., and although the building is entirely in the lancet style, it is quite a lively design.

Fig.19.11 Christ Church, Shelton and Oxon (1854) by Edward Haycock jun.

St. Mary the Virgin, Shrawardine*

The place-name is said to mean 'enclosure by a hollow',[12] the hollow being thought to be Shrawardine Pool. The manor stood near to a ford over the river Severn, its importance being attested by a substantial Norman castle whose ruins stand about 100 yards from the church. Most of the medieval church was destroyed by Royalist troops in 1645 to prevent the opposition from using the church as a cover for attacking the castle; so Shrawardine church today, like Stokesay, largely dates from the Commonwealth period. The nave was rebuilt in 1649, but the chancel remained a ruin until 1722.

The church (Fig.19.12) is built of red sandstone, and at least part of the north wall is probably medieval for there is a cusped lancet window which looks original. The other north window, like the high west window, is a very broad lancet, which is surely 17th-century. On the south side, both the main doorway and the priest's doorway in the chancel are round-headed, but probably not medieval. The best artefact is the fine Norman font – a circular bowl, with scalloped carving on the underside. The pulpit and the lower part of the screen are Jacobean, or possibly earlier. The communion rails, reredos and west gallery date from the 17th century.

Fig.19.12 St. Mary, Shrawardine

Shrewsbury Abbey*** (the parish church of the Holy Cross)

There can be few parish churches in England which have been twice considered for elevation to the status of a cathedral, but this has happened to Shrewsbury Abbey – the first was immediately after the Dissolution of the Monasteries in 1540, and the second was in the 1920s – and on each occasion the proposal was rejected. Nevertheless the abbey remains an impressive monument, of almost cathedral-like proportions, and full of interest.

It stands on low ground, just to the east of English Bridge, occupying a site of great convenience, immediately by the side of the main road from London to north Wales (the later A5). The town of Shrewsbury developed in the 10th and 11th centuries, and

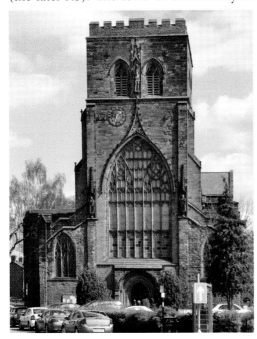

*Fig.19.13 Shrewsbury Abbey:
the tower and west façade*

there was a small apsidal Saxon church on the site of the present abbey. Shortly after the Norman Conquest, Roger de Montgomerie, one of William I's relatives, was made earl of Shrewsbury; he built castles at Quatford, Shrewsbury and Montgomery, and in 1083 he founded the Benedictine Abbey of St. Peter and St. Paul; originally it was a daughter house of Séez, Normandy. After the Dissolution in 1540, the eastern part of the church was taken down, and the nave continued as a parish church; the existing east end of the abbey dates from the rebuilding in 1887.

There are three distinct phases of building at the abbey, and these are easy to identify. The oldest is the original Norman building instituted by Earl Roger. Then came the Perpendicular building of the last half of the 14th century at the west end. And finally the whole eastern end of the church was built by J.L. Pearson in 1886-87.

It is best to begin the tour of the abbey by inspecting the noble west façade (Fig.19.13). The base of the west tower is Norman and the original Norman west doorway (*c*.1100) survives. This doorway has a round arch, with three outer roll-mouldings. Round the corner, the south doorway is almost a hundred years later – it is no longer pure Norman, but Transitional (between Norman and Early English). The capitals here have upright leaves – a sign of Early English building. Above the west doorway is the marvellous early Perpendicular window – the finest such window in Shropshire. It consists of seven lights, with above an ogee crocketed canopy, typical of the Decorated style, here persisting into the Perpendicular era. The upper part of the tower is Perpendicular; dendrochronological tests of the roof-timbers of the tower and bell-chamber have given dates of 1365-95.[13] Round the corner on the north side is the fine three-storeyed Perpendicular porch. The entry to the porch is via an arch with a square compartment, springing from columns on each side. The interior of the porch is vaulted, and the inner door opening into the nave is a Norman arch with mouldings upon shafts.

Then walk through the outer west doorway and note that the inner doorway is older than the outer one. This dates from the first building, some time between 1083 and 1100. There are two orders of shafts with scalloped capitals. Step inside into the nave, and immediately the contrast between the Norman and Perpendicular arcades becomes apparent. At the western end of the nave, the tall tower arch is Perpendicular; the two western bays are also Perpendicular – they are surmounted by a clerestory but no triforium. Then the character of the nave changes abruptly: the three eastern bays of the nave are early Norman (Fig.19.14), with big round piers supporting semicircular arches; above them is the triforium, originally Norman, but modified in the 14th century; and above this the clerestory which dates from Pearson's reconstruction.

Fig.19.14 Shrewsbury Abbey: Norman arcade and triforium, Victorian chancel

J.L. Pearson (see p.36) used the Early English style to build the eastern end of the church, so the chancel is furnished with tall lancet windows. The architect was a specialist in vaulting, and he used his expertise to the full in roofing the choir. Pearson was also responsible for the reredos, which is a large triptych with a great deal of gilding.

In the nave is the font, a large moulded capital, said to be made from a Roman capital. Also in the nave is a 14th-century sculpture of the seated Virgin. The 19th-century pulpit is modelled on the refectory pulpit (Fig.14.1) outside the abbey, and contains a statue of St. Winifred. In the north aisle are a Norman pillar piscina and the remains of the shrine of St. Winifred – part of a 14th-century reredos. On one of the piers of the crossing is a painting by Bridges, 'Angels at the Sepulchre'.

The abbey has an extensive collection of monuments, most of which have come from other churches. They include, in the north aisle:

1) William Charlton and wife, d.1544. An alabaster Gothic memorial from All Saints, Wellington.
2) Speaker Richard Onslow, d.1571. A tomb-chest from old St. Chad's, Shrewsbury.
3) William Jones, d.1612. Another tomb-chest from St. Alkmund's, Shrewsbury.
4) John Loyd. A wall-plaque, with a half-figure.
5) A lawyer, *c.*1300, from old St. Chad's.
   In the south aisle:
6) A late-13th-century headless knight.
7) A priest, *c.*1300. An excellent coffin-lid, with foliated cross, chalice, bell, book and candle.
8) Two bearded men from St. Alkmund's; originally on one slab: late 14th century.
9) A knight, late 13th century, with his hand on his sword; from Wombridge.
10) Mary Anne Burd, d.1859, by P. Hollins; Faith on a pedestal.
11) Edwards Jenkins, d.1820, a Gothic reredos without figures.
    In the nave:
12) Nathaniel Betton and relatives, an early-19th-century relief.

All Saints, Shrewsbury*

The Anglo-Catholic tradition in Shrewsbury is maintained at All Saints, North Street, a good Victorian church built in 1875-76 by Edward Haycock jun. The exterior is undistinguished, and lacks a tower. Internally, the church is seen to be on a substantial scale, with nave and chancel, and north and south aisles. There is attractive polychromy in the arcades, and the piers are alternately round and octagonal. This rhythm is reflected in the clerestory windows, which are alternately pointed and circular. The best feature is the stained glass: in the north aisle are two windows by Kempe, and in the south aisle a 1918 window in the Morris style.

Cathedral: Our Lady Help of Christians and St. Peter of Alcantara**

The Roman Catholic Cathedral occupies a prominent site on Town Walls, commanding an extensive view to the south. It was built in 1853-56, the architect being Edward Pugin, son of Augustus W.N. Pugin (see p.31). It was originally intended that the building should have a tall spire, but this was abandoned because of the conditions of the site. So the cathedral, which is not large, consists of a nave with lean-to aisles and clerestory above, a chancel, a south-east chapel added in 1901 and a porch added in 1906. The arcades are of five bays, with octagonal piers and

*Fig.19.15 Shrewsbury Cathedral:
the nave and chancel*

florid capitals (Fig.19.15). The clerestory windows are unusual, being composed of spheric triangles. The chancel is not very deep, the east window of seven lights with complicated flowing tracery.

The greatest treasures of the cathedral are the stained glass windows. Many of them, including the east window, are by Hardman. Especially attractive are the series of windows by Margaret Rope (1882-1953; Figs.12.16-12.18), erected between 1906 and 1921.

Emmanuel Church, Harlescott, Shrewsbury*

This is an Anglican/Methodist church built at the very beginning of the 21st century, serving newly built-up areas to the north of Shrewsbury. The architect was Robert Netherwood.

Built of red brick, with areas of contrasting blue brick above the entrance, Emmanuel church is modern, without being aggressively so (Fig.19.16). The visitor is welcomed into an anteroom through which one passes into the church proper; the two areas are separated by a removable birch-framed and glazed screen. The roof is supported on scissored trusses and purlins in softwood; these are fully visible and create a sense of height. The interior (Fig.19.17) is dominated by a hanging behind the altar worked by members of the congregation in Indian silks, to the design of Sarah Netherwood. It measures 12 x 16 feet, and shows the dove of the Holy Spirit in the rays of the sun (or the flames of Pentecost). This hanging imparts an impressive devotional atmosphere. The altar and other chancel furnishings are made of beech to the design of the architect.

Fig.19.16 Shrewsbury, Emmanuel, Harlescott (2001) by Robert Netherwood

Fig.19.17 Shrewsbury Emmanuel: the interior

The Holy Spirit, Roseway, Harlescott, Shrewsbury

This church was built in 1936 to the design of Herbert North. It was praised by Harbison as 'one of the best churches of the 1930s'.[14] It has a saddleback tower, with twin gables below. The church was closed in 1963 because it had become inadequate for the growing population; the building remains, but has been somewhat mutilated since it became a private club.

The Holy Spirit, Meadow Farm Drive, Harlescott, Shrewsbury**

The above church was replaced by the present building in Meadow Farm Drive, and it is probably the best church of the 20th century in Shropshire. Built in 1961, the new church of the Holy Spirit has an exciting façade: from the exterior it is immediately obvious that this is no ordinary post-war church. The unusual tower and bold lozenge pattern of the west front (Fig.19.18) immediately suggest the possibility of good things inside, and the visitor is not disappointed. The auditorium (Fig.1.7) is large, divided into seven bays, with ample space at the west end for social activities. The sanctuary and altar are a feast of colour; and behind the altar a large cross and a framework of vertical patterns divide the sanctuary from the small polygonal Lady chapel beyond (Fig.19.19). The modern font is noteworthy.

Fig.19.18 Shrewsbury, The Holy Spirit, Harlescott (1961) by Bernard Miller

Fig.19.19 Shrewsbury, The Holy Spirit: the Lady chapel

Holy Trinity, Belle Vue, Shrewsbury

A chapel of ease within the bounds of the parish of St. Julian was consecrated in 1837, and a large chancel was added to this in 1860. In 1886 the chapel (but not the chancel) was demolished and replaced by the present building, to the design of Lloyd-Oswell.

The 1860 chancel (at the west end) is the best feature of the church; it is light and airy, and has an arcade of two bays on either side, the piers with florid Corinthian capitals typical of the age. The rest of the church is spacious, with rather heavy wide arcades of three bays each; some of the piers are round, some octagonal, and the capitals are now much plainer. Clearly the excesses of the 1860s are lessening 20 years later – but not, alas, in the alabaster font, which is over-ornate.

Old St. Chad, Shrewsbury

St. Chad's church may well have been the earliest church in Shrewsbury, perhaps origi-nating in the 7th century,[15] and in Anglo-Saxon times, and again in the 12th century, it was a collegiate church, with a dean and ten canons. The cruciform medieval church was substantial, but its central tower collapsed in 1788 and all that remains of old St. Chad is the south chancel chapel. This can be visited by asking for the key by e-mail from: sytmaggie@yahoo.com.

The surviving remnant has Decorated windows on its east and south walls. On the north wall externally are the sedilia from the former chancel, and above them a blocked lancet window. At the north-west corner is the crossing pier which formerly supported the tower and at the south-west corner is the stair-turret of the former transept. Inside is a monument to Thomas Edwards (d.1634) and his wife: a kneeling couple depicted on each side of a prayer-desk. There are also a dilapidated Norman font with a lozenge pattern and 17 hatchments to the Corbet, Hill and Mytton families.

St. Alkmund, Shrewsbury**

If Shrewsbury did not possess the abbey and the churches of St. Chad and St. Mary, St. Alkmund's would be regarded much more highly. For this church of very ancient founda-tion is not appreciated as much as it deserves.

St. Alkmund was the younger son of Alhred, king of Northumbria; he died *c.*802 (or 822) at Lilleshall, Shropshire, and his relics were removed to the collegiate church dedi-cated to him in Derby. St. Alkmund's church in Shrewsbury (also originally a collegiate foundation) was founded *c.*912 by the formidable Aethelflaed, daughter of Alfred the Great and wife of Ethelred, king of Mercia. Other churches dedicated to St. Alkmund are at Whitchurch (p.139), Aymestrey in Herefordshire, and Blyborough in Lincolnshire.

From its foundation, the collegiate church of St. Alkmund boasted a community of a Dean and 12 canons; by the time of the Domesday survey, it was substantially endowed, with about 14 manors in Shropshire. In 1148 Lilleshall Abbey was founded, and gradu-ally the prebendal stalls at St. Alkmund's were suppressed and their property transferred to Lilleshall, leaving St. Alkmund's an impoverished vicarage.

The medieval church of St. Alkmund's was very fine, almost as great as St.Mary's, but after the collapse of Old St. Chad's in 1788 there was general alarm about the safety of both St. Alkmund's and St. Mary's. Some 'questionable advice' was received about the safety of the structure, and finally an Act of Parliament decreed the demo-lition of the church and the rebuilding of all but the tower and spire. St. Mary's was saved

Fig.19.20 Shrewsbury, St. Alkmund: the nave looking west

from a similar fate by one vote.[16] It seems to be generally agreed now that such drastic action was unnecessary.

As a result, St. Alkmund's now consists of a fine Perpendicular tower and spire, similar to that of St. Mary's, and a late Georgian nave and chancel. There is a good four-light west window, and the tower arch opening into the nave is remarkably tall (Fig.19.20). The tower has battlements and pinnacles, and the spire (Fig.5.3) has three sets of dormer windows. The architect of the new church was John Carline senior (1761-1835), and he designed it in a Gothic style; the building was chiefly remarkable for the cast-iron tracery of the windows made at Coalbrookdale.[17] Most of the tracery of the windows was replaced by stone in the 19th century, but three windows remain with iron tracery, two at the west end and one at the north-east corner. The interior is a large hall, without aisles, and with just a shallow chancel at the east end. It is the earliest example of a Gothic revival church in Shropshire, with window tracery in the Decorated style. There is a wall-monument to Sir Thomas Jones (d.1702) by James Paget, consisting of an urn flanked by putti, and a pediment above.

The greatest treasure of St. Alkmund's is the splendid east window of painted glass by Francis Eginton (1773-1834). He used stains and enamels on clear glass with the aim of imitating oil-painting (Fig.12.4). The design purports to be an emblematic figure of Faith but is, in fact, a copy of the Madonna in Guido Reni's Assumption of the Virgin in Munich. When seen on a sunny morning, the effect is stunning. Eginton's work may also be seen at Brockhampton-by-Bromyard church in Herefordshire.

St. Chad, Shrewsbury***

St. Chad was the first bishop of Mercia, making his episcopal seat at Lichfield; he died in 672 and was canonised in 779. After the collapse of the tower of Old St. Chad in 1788, the new church was built in 1790-92 to the design of George Steuart. The result is the finest 18th-century church in Shropshire; and the church enjoys a beautiful situation overlooking the park known as the Quarry and the broad sweep of the river Severn.

George Steuart (c.1730-1806) had previously designed the fine house at Attingham Park near Shrewsbury, and the church of All Saints', Wellington (q.v.). St. Chad's is, however, on a much grander scale and is much more innovative, the most striking feature being the circular nave. Steuart may well have derived this from a design by James Gibbs for St. Martin-in-the-Fields, London.[18] Gibbs envisaged a circular nave with a circular arcade supporting a partly domed ceiling. Although the design was rejected, Gibbs thought it worthy of inclusion in his highly influential work *A Book of Architecture* (1728).

St. Chad's appears to be built of Grinshill stone, and it is surprising to learn that the church is basically

Fig.19.21 Shrewsbury, St. Chad

brick, and merely faced with stone.[19] The entrance is via an imposing portico (Fig.19.21) with four Tuscan columns with a pediment above. Beyond rises the tower, square below, then a tall octagonal stage with paired Ionic pilasters; above this is a circular stage with free-standing Corinthian columns surmounted by a dome and cross. The emphasis so far is all on verticality, but beyond the plan consists of two intersecting circles, the larger forming the nave and the smaller the entrance lobby.[20] Seen from the Quarry, the emphasis changes from vertical to horizontal. The lower stage of the nave is rusticated with rectangular windows and above is a series of tall round-arched windows divided by paired Ionic pilasters as in the tower. Above is a cornice and parapet with balustrading.[21]

Internally, the visitor passes from the entrance hall under the tower to an anteroom from which two arms of a graceful staircase sweep upwards to the gallery. Then one passes onwards to the auditorium, a wonderful circular space, with galleries above and a shallow chancel ahead. The chancel (Fig.19.22) is flanked by paired Corinthian columns on either side of a large Venetian window. Short Ionic columns support the gallery, and very tall Corinthian columns rise to the flat ceiling; the columns have a core of cast-iron – probably due to the influence of John Simpson, the engineer of the Caledonian Canal, who supervised the building of the church, and William Hazeldine, a local iron-master who provided ironwork for the church.[22] Box-pews in concentric circles are not now as high as they were originally; but in 18th-century churches it was important that every worshipper could see and hear the preacher – and St. Chad's provided seating for over 2,000 people. The ceiling exhibits delicate plasterwork and a central gilded sunburst.

Originally, the chancel window was filled by glass by Francis Eginton (as at nearby St. Alkmund's; q.v.); this was replaced in 1853 by David Evans' remarkable work. This is a sombre but brilliantly coloured rendering of the Deposition, after the painting by Rubens in Antwerp Cathedral. There are four further windows by Evans illustrating biblical subjects, also derived from paintings. Two busts by Chantrey are placed one on either side of the chancel – these are in memory of John Simpson and William Hazeldine who both died in 1815. The ornamental surrounds are by J. and J. Carline. The font is an oval bowl. The elegant pulpit was made in 1892 of copper and brass in the Arts and Crafts style. As at old St. Chad's, there are a large number of hatchments on the walls of the gallery and in the vestibule. On the way out, the visitor passes on the left St. Aidan's chapel; this is dominated by an impressive modern rood beam. The chapel has been

Fig.19.22 Shrewsbury, St. Chad: the sanctuary

recently refurbished as the memorial chapel for the Shropshire Light Infantry and the Hereford Regiment. Morning and evening prayer are said here daily.

St. George, Frankwell, Shrewsbury

St. George's was built in 1832 by Edward Haycock sen. The exterior is a grim reminder of the style of the Church Commissioners. The interior is more attractive – a cruciform church with large lancet windows. It is made memorable by the stained glass. The very striking east window is by David Evans, a representation of three apostles in glowing bright colours. In two windows of the nave is later Victorian glass.

Linked with St. George's is Greenfields United Church, a joint Anglican/Methodist church.

St. Giles, Shrewsbury*

The church of St. Giles was first recorded in 1136,[23] and the associated hospital for lepers, probably situated to the west of the church, in 1155. Although the present church is largely Victorian, the work of Pountney Smith in 1860-63, there are some remains from the preceding Norman church. The church consists of a nave and chancel, with a north aisle and north chancel chapel, a vestry and a south transept. The south wall of the nave and the south doorway is Norman, and the south window of the south transept is round-headed, though with later Decorated tracery below. The north arcade is 14th-century; and the former chancel arch from the same period is now placed between the north aisle and chancel, immediately adjacent to a Victorian arch, giving a very odd effect. The Norman font is very good: there is zigzag around the rim and on the stem, and around the bowl a series of blank Norman arcades enclosing figures of uncertain meaning. According to Cranage, the font originally came from High Ercall. There is stained glass by David Evans (?) and by Kempe.

Fig.19.23 Shrewsbury, St. John Sutton (Greek Orthodox)

St. John, Sutton, Shrewsbury*
(now the Greek Orthodox Church of the Holy Fathers of Nicea)

At the time of the Domesday survey, the manor of Sutton near Shrewsbury was held by Wenlock Priory. St. John's church (Fig.19.23) was largely built of sandstone in the 13th century, for there are typical lancet windows in the north, east and south walls. It is uncertain whether the surviving building is nearly the whole of the medieval church, or whether it is just the chancel – the former is more likely to be true. At any rate the west end of the church became ruinous and

Fig.19.24 Shrewsbury, St. John Sutton: the iconostasis

was replaced early in the 18th century by an ugly brick wall containing a large three-light window. During the 19th century the church gradually fell into disuse, and by 1948 it had become a farmer's store. In 1991 the Greek Orthodox Church purchased the building for £50, and with much hard work from the congregation and help from English Heritage and the Historic Churches Preservation Trust restored it for public worship.

The interior has been beautifully and sensitively restored. A western gallery has been erected and this hides steel girders which hold the north and south walls together. At the east end of the church is the modern icon screen, made mostly of old oak, with an iconostasis (Fig.19.24) of scenes from the New Testament, with saints and patriarchs. To the left of the door is a plain ancient font – this was present in the old church and is probably Norman, though it is possible that it came from the nearby Roman settlement of Wroxeter. There are vestigial medieval paintings on the north and south walls: on the north wall is a realistic representation of the murder of St. Thomas à Becket, and on the south some floral patterns.

Access is not easy: the building is a short distance along a tiny lane about 200 yards east of the Percy Thrower Garden Centre on Oteley Road, on the north side of the road. Walk along the lane for 50 yards, and then through a gate into a field. Visitors are welcome at the Sunday services at 10.30am, but at other times the church is locked.

St. Julian, Shrewsbury**

The dedication was originally to St. Juliana, as the Domesday Book states: 'St. Juliana's church holds a half hide, the value was and is 8s.' This is a modest holding compared with other Shrewsbury churches – St. Mary's, St. Chad's and St. Alkmund's. St. Juliana was a virgin of Nicomedia who was martyred early in the 4th century.[24] The church is one of the earliest foundations in Shrewsbury, but of the medieval church only the west tower remains. This is a noble structure (Fig.5.3) of two components: the lower part is Early English, *c.*1200, built of Keele red sandstone, opening into the church on the north, south and east with acute arches. There is a wide lancet window on the west wall. Above the second string-course the tower is Perpendicular and of yellow Grinshill sandstone;[25] the belfry windows are each of three lights. Above are a quatrefoil frieze, battlements and eight pinnacles. Pritchard rebuilt the top, replacing the battlements with a balustrade and urns; these in turn were replaced with pinnacles in the 19th century.

Fig.19.25 Shrewsbury, St. Julian: the interior looking east, Tuscan columns ascend to the ceiling

In 1749 the roofs, walls and pillars of the old church were found to be much decayed, so the body of the church was demolished and the rebuilding assigned to Thomas Farnolls Pritchard, then a young man of 25.[26] Pritchard's church was plainer than it appears at present, since the south elevation was 'beautified' in 1846 by the addition of pilasters, cornice and balustrade. The north elevation was not altered, so the visitor can readily contrast the work of the 18th and 19th centuries. On each side are two tiers of windows, round-headed above and square below.

Pritchard's interior originally had galleries against the north, west and south walls, supported by Tuscan columns (Fig.19.25); the columns remain, but the galleries were taken down, probably in 1883. The very acute tower arch opening into the nave is by Pritchard; from the east end, it beautifully frames the lancet in the west wall of the tower. There is a shallow chancel, with a large Venetian east window.

There is excellent stained glass in St. Julian's. In the south window of the chancel is the figure of St. James; this is early 16th-century glass from Rouen and was bought in London for £30 during the French Revolution.[27] Even more striking, and dominating the church, is the glass in the east window by David Evans, one of his finest works; it dates from 1861. The central section depicts above the Transfiguration of Christ, with the three sleeping disciples bathed in light; and below the scene of the other disciples failing to heal an epileptic boy. On the left is the Baptism of Christ, and below a Nativity scene; on the right, the Last Supper, and the Deposition of Christ from the Cross. The whole assembly is one of the finest stained glass windows in Shropshire (Fig.12.5) In the side windows of the nave are the arms of various Shropshire families, probably dating from the 18th century.

St. Julian's was closed for worship in 1976 and is now privately owned. For 20 years it was a craft centre, but it is pleasing to record that the handsome interior has recently been re-ordered and the building opened for Evangelical services on Sunday mornings and evenings. There is no public access to the church except at the times of the Sunday services (11am and 6.30pm).

St. Mary the Virgin, Shrewsbury***

That the finest parish church in Shrewsbury should no longer be used for regular worship must strike the visitor as sad, perverse, astonishing. Yet it is so, St. Mary's having been declared redundant in 1987, and its care is now vested in the Churches Conservation Trust. It had fallen victim to the same problem that has afflicted the churches in the City of London – many parishioners had moved to the outer suburbs of Shrewsbury, leaving too few people to support the churches in the centre. The hope must be that one day it will be restored for worship – it is too great a building to remain indefinitely a museum of art. Yet what art! – for St. Mary's is outstanding architecturally, and it houses an internationally important collection of English and continental stained glass.

St. Mary's dominates Shrewsbury, being built at its highest point, and the spire, attaining a height of 222 feet, is one of the tallest in the country (Fig.19.26). The church was originally a Saxon foundation and later became a collegiate church consisting of a dean, seven prebendaries and a parish priest. The foundations of the Saxon church were found under the present nave during excavations in the 19th century; the building was 76 feet long and terminated in an apse. This church must have been demolished around 1140 when a cruciform Norman church was built. This consisted of a nave and chancel, with a crossing probably supporting a low central tower, and north and south transepts. The arches separating the transepts from the north and south aisles, and from the chapels

Fig.19.26 (left) Shrewsbury, St. Mary: the spire
Fig.19.27 (above) Shrewsbury, St. Mary: the Transitional north
arcade, showing semi-circular arches with slender multishafted piers;
stiff-leaf foliage on the capitals

to the east of the transepts, are low, round-headed arches, typical of the mid-12th century. Around 1170 the lower storeys of the west tower were built in red sandstone; the tower arch opening into the nave is pointed, in odd contrast to the arcades of the aisles. Above the tower arch in the west wall of the nave is a Norman window, now opening into the ringers' chamber, and above this, and partly obscured by the Perpendicular roof, are two further blocked Norman windows opposite the belfry.

Towards the end of the 12th century St. Mary's was largely transformed into its present state. At this period, Norman (Transitional) architecture was giving way to Early English, and the result was the highly unusual arcades (Fig.19.27) which now divide the nave from the north and south aisles. Note that the arcades are still semicircular (Gothic has not yet quite taken over); yet the piers are certainly not the solid round ones typical of earlier Norman building (cf Holy Cross, Shrewsbury) but instead are slim, finely subdivided and crowned by stiff leaf foliage (Fig.9.18) typical of the Early English style of the 13th century. The carving on the capitals of the north arcade is more accomplished and sophisticated than on the south, indicating that the north arcade is later by, perhaps, 20 years.

The earlier Norman chancel was lengthened, heightened and vaulted in the early 13th century.[28] The pointed chancel arch is taller than the arcades and above it two two-light windows were inserted in 1894. The other arches from the crossing into the transepts are of similar style. Externally, the south porch was also built c.1200, and shows a round-headed doorway with three orders of shafts and a tall arch with zigzag and other motifs.

In the mid-14th century the south or Trinity chapel was built with early Perpendicular windows, and at about the same time the windows in the north chapel, partly Decorated and partly Perpendicular, were inserted. In the 15th century, a clerestory was built above the nave, and the fine nave roof (Fig.1.1) was constructed c.1500. This is a panelled roof of low pitch, richly adorned with delicately carved bosses at the intersections and cusped quatrefoils in the panels. The top stage of the western tower was also added, surmounted by the spire. Also in the Perpendicular era the south aisle received its three fine windows.

St. Mary's has one of the finest collections of stained glass in the country, mostly brought from elsewhere. The great east window of the chancel dates only from the Victorian restoration of 1858, but it contains the Jesse window comprising English glass from the 14th century, made at the time when medieval English stained glass was at its peak. Where was it made? It is believed that the glass was originally given to the Franciscan church in Shrewsbury, being later transferred to old St. Chad's, and then in 1792, after the collapse of that church, to St. Mary's. It represents the Tree of Jesse, tracing the genealogy of Jesus back to David's father Jesse. The figure of Jesse is seen lying horizontally in a deep sleep across the three centre lights; from him arises a vine which connects above with the kings and prophets of Israel, and the figures of Mary and Joseph with the infant Jesus, St. Matthew and St. Luke; above this are scenes depicting the Nativity, Baptism and Crucifixion. Under the figure of Jesse is a row of figures including Sir John de Charlton, donor of the window, Edward III, and a Virgin and Child. The glass in the tracery part of the window is Victorian, and it has been estimated that about 60% of the rest is medieval.

Continental glass from Germany, Belgium and the Netherlands was collected by the Reverend William Rowland; he was vicar of St. Mary's from 1828-52. Three lancet windows in the north wall of the chancel contain scenes from the life of St. Bernard of Clairvaux.

This is early 16th-century German glass, and it came from Altenberg Abbey, near Cologne. In windows at the eastern end of the north aisle and at the eastern and western ends of the south aisle is 15th-century glass from Trier Cathedral; the windows depict donors of the glass, with saints behind. In the south wall of the Trinity chapel and the western window of the south aisle is glass from the church of St. Jacques in Liege; further glass from the Low Countries may be seen in the north aisle and in the north transept chapels of St. Catherine and St. Nicholas. Glass by David Evans may be seen in the Trinity chapel.

At the west end of the church is the octagonal Perpendicular font, with quatrefoils and flowers carved on the panels, and hollow arcading on the stem. In the sedilia of the Trinity chapel are three rather battered 15th-century alabaster panels, with the kneeling donor below and above representations of the Trinity and the Virgin and Child;[29] these are of unknown provenance, but were probably made in Nottingham.

St. Mary's is not a particularly good church for monuments, but the following may be noted (in chronological order):
1) In the north wall of the vestry, an Anglo-Saxon tomb-slab, *c*.1000.
2) The early 14th-century tomb-chest of Simon de Leybourne (d.1315) in the Trinity chapel; the knight reclines with crossed legs, a dog at his feet. Around the tomb-chest is blind cusped arcading.
3) A rococo tablet to Mary Morhall, d.1765, by T.F. Pritchard, in the north wall of the chancel.
4) In the north chapel, the 1840 memorial to Admiral Benbow, d.1702.
5) Under the tower, the reclining effigy of Col. Cureton, d.1848, by Sir Richard Westmacott.

St. Michael, Shrewsbury
This is a plain classical building (Fig.19.28) dating from 1829-30, the architect being John Carline junior. An incongruous Gothic chancel with lancet windows was added in 1873. The church was closed for worship and is now a masonic hall. The iron columns supporting the gallery are still there, but David Evans' stained glass has gone.

St. Peter, Monkmoor, Shrewsbury
This is an unpretentious brick church, now whitewashed, consisting simply of nave and shallow chancel, built in 1939.

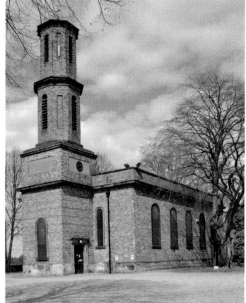

Fig.19.28 Shrewsbury St. Michael (1829-30) by John Carline junior

Holy Trinity, Uffington
This is a church built in 1856 by S. Pountney Smith in the Early English style. The south doorway is good, with shafts on either side and stiff-leaf capitals. The north aisle is divided

from the nave by an arcade with fairly restrained dogtooth ornament. The church is notable mainly for the six small panels of late 17th-century German glass in the windows of the south side of the nave; on the north side are small roundels and panels of Flemish glass.

Holy Trinity, Uppington*

The church appears now to be mainly Victorian, the work of J.P. Pritchett in 1885. He built the western tower and restored the rest of the church. Although the keystone of the south porch bears the date 1678, the rest of the porch appears to be Victorian. The plain south doorway is Norman, as is the chancel arch which was heightened in 1885. There is Norman carving carried from the imposts on either side.

The most interesting features of Uppington are outside the church. The best is the blocked north Norman doorway (which can also be seen inside), the 11th-century tympanum (Fig.9.10) is crudely carved with a dragon, either late Saxon or early Norman. Unfortunately, it is now showing signs of weathering. On the south side of the church is a remarkably ancient yew, and also a Roman altar found near the church in 1927; Uppington is very close to the Roman town of Wroxeter.

St. Lucy, Upton Magna*

This is the only dedication in Shropshire to St. Lucy. The nave and chancel are originally Norman – there are two small Norman windows in both the north and south walls of the chancel, the eastern pair being at a higher level than the western. The plain south doorway of the nave is also Norman. The Decorated windows in the south wall of the nave are later insertions. The tower is Perpendicular (Fig.19.29), with diagonal buttresses, battlements and a quatrefoil frieze below them. The tower arch is tall, and the west window Perpendicular, of three lights.

The Williams painting, dated 1786, shows a large dormer window adjacent to the tower on the south side, and a half-timbered porch. The church was subjected to a drastic restoration in 1856 by G.E. Street; the dormer

Fig.19.29 St. Lucy, Upton Magna: the tower

Fig.19.30 Upton Magna: the remodelled chancel by G.E. Street

Fig.19.31 Upton Magna: monument to Walter Barker (d.1644)

window was taken down, and a new porch built. Street added a north aisle, and rebuilt the east wall. The chancel was extensively remodelled: as often in Street's churches, a low stone screen, with marble inlays and surmounted by wrought-ironwork, now divides the nave and chancel (Fig.19.30). The chancel arch was rebuilt, and a marble reredos added.

Under the tower is the imposing monument to Walter Barker, d.1644; but the monument may well be later, for it was funded by the will of Barker's daughter Anne. The deceased is shown semi-reclining against a background of Corinthian pilasters rising to an open pediment (Fig.19.31).

St. John the Baptist, Withington*

According to Cranage, the former church had a medieval stone chancel and a brick nave dating probably from the 18th century. The building was demolished and replaced by the present structure in 1874, the architect being G.E. Street. Although not one of his finest designs, it is a satisfying building in red sandstone, with a tall western tower and a steep broach spire reminiscent of Street's church of St. James the Less, Westminster. The best part of the interior is the chancel, divided from the aisleless nave by a low stone screen. The reredos, built into the east wall, is a striking representation of the Crucifixion, with figures on either side. Screen, stone pulpit, reredos and font were all designed by the architect.

Today, the church is distinguished mainly because of its 16th-century brasses. These are now mounted on Iroko boards and are displayed in the nave and chancel. In the south wall of the nave is the brass to John Onley and his wife (*c.*1525), he in armour, she with contemporary costume, together with small figures of seven sons; a group of three or four daughters has been lost. In the north wall of the chancel is the brass to Adam Grafton (d.1530), priest, rector of Albright Hussey, Upton Magna and Withington, and Master of Battlefield College. He is wearing his cope, almuce, surplice and cassock. The quality of these late medieval brasses is high, and they are much sought after by brass-rubbers.

St. Andrew, Wroxeter***

The church of St. Andrew is more anciently steeped in history than any other in Shropshire. This of course derives from its proximity to the Roman fort of *Viroconium*, and masonry from there was plundered in the construction of the church about 1300 years ago. Cranage substantially deduced the complex building history of the church at the end of the 19th century, and a hundred years later his conclusions have been largely confirmed by recent archaeological excavations.[30]

White and Barker speculate on the possible presence of a Christian basilica in late Roman Wroxeter, and wonder about the possibility of the early Saxon church being a monastic foundation. By the time of the Domesday survey, the church there was well established, the presence of the church and no fewer than four priests being mentioned. At the time of the Conquest, the manor was held by Thored, but it then passed to the Sheriff Reginald, who held it under Earl Roger of Montgomery. The church was given to Haughmond Abbey by Richard FitzAlan in 1155. The college of priests was replaced by a vicar appointed by the Abbot of Haughmond in 1347.

The gateway to the church is marked by two Roman columns with capitals (Fig.2.1); these were erected on the square-cut bases of Roman columns in 1855. The church now consists of chancel, nave and west tower, with a small vestry to the south-west of the chancel; previously there existed a south aisle, separated from the nave by an arcade. The history is best understood by walking round the exterior of the church, beginning with the north side. The earliest part of the building is the eastern two-thirds of the north wall of the nave (Fig.3.1). This is built of Roman masonry, and dates from the 7th or 8th centuries[31] and to the 8th or 9th centuries.[32] There is evidence of a small blocked square window high up in the wall; to the east of this is a triple lancet window which is a 13th-century insertion, and to the west of it is a later Perpendicular window. A string-course can be seen at the top of the wall; the boundary between the Saxon work and the rest of the nave can clearly be discerned five feet to the west of the Perpendicular window; there is a hint of Saxon long-and-short work at the margin. The fact that the string-course continues for two inches beyond the west face of the quoining has been adduced as evidence that it continued round the corner along the original west wall of the Saxon building.

In the late 12th century, the chancel was added; two round-headed windows remain in both the north and south walls (those in the south wall are now blind), and there is also a blocked priest's doorway in the south wall. On the outside, this doorway exhibits a double row of zigzag, and the capital shows stiff-leaf foliage. Internally the arch has a double row of dogtooth. A string-course runs below the windows and is also carved with dogtooth. The present east window of the chancel is a Perpendicular insertion, but above it is a small original Norman window. In the 13th century, three-light lancet windows were inserted in the north walls of the chancel and nave, and the nave was extended westwards towards the tower. (The most westerly two-light window in the north wall is a Victorian insertion.) Probably also early in the 13th

Fig.19.32 St. Andrew, Wroxeter: the tower

century a south aisle was built. The base of the tower (Fig.19.32) is late Norman like the chancel, while the upper storeys are late Perpendicular (16th century). Set in the masonry of the upper storeys of the tower are fragments which may have come from Haughmond Abbey after its dissolution in 1539; some are figures said to represent St. John the Baptist, St. Peter and other saints. In 1763 the 13th-century south aisle was demolished and the present narrow aisle and vestry were built. Part of the shaft of a 9th-century Saxon cross was set into the top of the south wall; the carving is intricate, and a dragon, foliage scrolls and interlace may be discerned (Fig.9.1). This shaft can be identified in an 18th-century drawing of the churchyard cross.[33]

The interior (Fig.19.33) is equally exciting. The church has old brick floors, and the oaken box pews are plain but good. Both the tower arch and the chancel arch are Transitional, pointed, but with both Norman and Early English features, such as stiff-leaf and trumpet-scallop capitals; built into the base of the south jamb of the chancel arch is a further carved stone of Saxon origin, with birds pecking at snakes. In the north wall of the chancel is a trefoiled arch with ball-flower adornment;

Fig.19.33 Wroxeter: the interior, looking west

Cranage suggested that this may be an Easter sepulchre. The roof is late Perpendicular, with collar-beams and tie-beams. The enormous plain font is thought to be the inverted base of a Roman column (Fig.10.1); the rough beadings around the rim may be Anglo-Saxon. Beyond the font is an impressive iron-bound chest from the 14th century. There is some fine woodwork from the 17th and 18th centuries – notably the Jacobean pulpit and communion-rails. There is a little late medieval stained glass in one of the nave windows, but most of the rest of the glass is 19th-century, some by David Evans of Shrewsbury.

There are some excellent monuments in the chancel. The earliest and finest is the tomb-chest of Sir Thomas Bromley (d.1555), Chief Justice of England, and his wife, probably by Richard Parker of Burton upon Trent.[34] There are alabaster effigies (Fig.11.14), and around the sides panels with shields with scrolls and the figure of a young woman. Next is that of Sir Richard Newport (d.1570) and his wife, daughter of Sir Thomas Bromley; this memorial is still largely medieval in style, though there are hints of Renaissance influence in the twisted colonettes at the corners (Fig.11.15). On the north wall of the chancel is the tomb of John Berker (d.1618) and his wife Margaret, grand-daughter of Sir Richard. This is fully Renaissance, with Tuscan columns and strapwork surrounds in the panels. All these tombs retain much of the original colouring. Finally on the south wall of the chancel is the marble monument to Francis Newport, first earl of Bradford, (d.1708). This is almost identical to Grinling Gibbons' monument to Admiral Churchill (d.1710) in Westminster Abbey;[35] the flaming urn is particularly admired.

20
Telford

Brookside
Buildwas
Coalbrookdale*
Dawley*
Donnington Wood*
Eyton-upon-the-Weald Moors
Hadley
Ironbridge
Jackfield*
Ketley
Lawley*
Leighton*
Little Wenlock
Longdon on Tern

Madeley*
Malinslee*
Oakengates
Preston-upon-the-Weald Moors
Priorslee
Rodington
St. George's**
Stirchley, All Saints
Stirchley, St. James***
Wellington, All Saints**
Wellington, Christ Church
Wombridge
Wrockwardine**
Wrockwardine Wood

Brookside Pastoral Centre
This is a combined Methodist/Anglican church, built in 1967 to care for the rapidly growing population of Telford new town.

Holy Trinity, Buildwas
The place-name has occasioned some comment: Gelling believes that the latter part of the name, derived from OE *waesse* and usually translated as 'swamp' or 'marsh', really means 'land by a meandering river which floods and drains quickly',[1] and Buildwas, of course, is on the river Severn. The manor was held by the bishop of Chester at the time of the Domesday survey. The abbey was started in 1135 as a Savigniac foundation, and later became Cistercian (see p.22). There was in addition a much humbler medieval parish church, but nothing is known of this.

The present church dates from 1720, the chancel being rebuilt in 1864. The Williams painting of 1790 shows a short western turret, with a much flatter pyramid top, quite different from the present timber-framed belfry which probably dates from 1864. The windows of the nave are round-headed and the date 1720 is recorded above the porch. The modest interior has a western gallery and a good Jacobean pulpit.

Holy Trinity, Coalbrookdale*

In contrast to St. Luke's, Ironbridge, built in 1837 on a shoestring, Holy Trinity followed 14 years later and was munificently endowed by Abraham Darby IV. But there is more than an economic difference between the two churches: for in the intervening years, the High-Church revival initiated by Pugin, Newman and others had taken root; Early English was out of fashion and *The Ecclesiologist* had decreed that Decorated was the favoured Gothic style; and the shallow chancels of the 18th and early 19th centuries had been replaced by the deep, elevated chancels then in vogue.

So while St. Luke's is precariously placed on a hillside, hemmed in by other buildings, Holy Trinity (Fig.20.1) occupies a prominent site and has a spacious churchyard, with a well-tended avenue bordered by flowerbeds leading to the west front. It is a large church, consisting of a nave with eight bays, aisles,

Fig.20.1 Holy Trinity, Coalbrookdale (1851) by Reeves and Voysey

chancel and western tower, and built of stone to a design of Messrs. Reeves and Voysey. It is in the Decorated style, with the windows displaying different patterns of tracery. The corbels supporting the wall-posts of the roof of the nave are carved with heads representing members of the Darby family, with the eastern two depicting Queen Victoria and the then bishop of Hereford. The altar is mounted on fine marble steps, and the excellent decoration of the chancel is by H.S. Goodhart-Rendel in 1931. The finest artefact in the church is the Flemish glass in one of the south windows; this is 16th-century work, depicting the

Last Supper, with some of the heads of the disciples portrayed as Flemish peasants worthy of Brueghel. The glass came from a Bavarian monastery and was a wedding-gift to Mrs. Henry Whitmore (née Darby), who presented it to the church.

Holy Trinity, Dawley

The medieval church of Dawley was badly afflicted by mining subsidence from the end of the 18th century and it was replaced by the present building (Fig.20.2) on a new site in 1845.

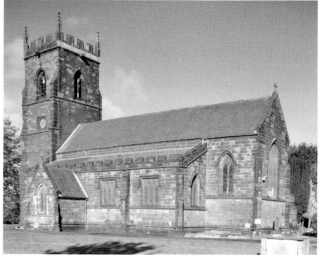

Fig.20.2 Holy Trinity, Dawley (1845) by Harvey Eginton

The architect was Harvey Eginton, who also built Broseley at about the same time. It is a less ambitious church than Broseley, and the windows of the aisles are straight-headed, compared with the arched Perpendicular windows at Broseley. An excellent late Norman font survives from the old church. This has arcades around the sides, chevron decoration below, and a Tree of Life on one side. (Fig.10.16)

St. Matthew, Donnington Wood*

Fig.20.3 St. Matthew, Donnington Wood (1842), by Sir George Gilbert Scott

St. Matthew's was originally a chapel of ease in the parish of Lilleshall, intended to serve the surrounding colliery district.[2] It is not easy now to envisage the area in 1843 when Sir George Gilbert Scott was invited to build a new church, for it is now engulfed with new building as part of the expansion of Telford. Yet St. Matthew's undoubtedly imparts much-needed grace to its environment (Fig.20.3), and the building is in fact a lovely church, especially inside.

It consists of a nave, transepts and chancel, a tall building in the Early English style, but given by Scott many touches which distinguish it from run-of-the-mill Shropshire churches of the 1840s. At the crossing are three tall arches, north, east and south, which rest on shafts standing on floriated corbels. The south transept has been later modified to form a Lady chapel, and in the east window of this is some excellent glass by Kempe, complete with his 'wheatsheaf' signature. The glass in the east window of the chancel may also be his. There is a west gallery.

St. Catherine, Eyton-upon-the-Weald Moors

The Weald Moors is a flat area north of Wellington, drained by streams flowing into the river Tern. 'Weald' means 'wild, waste moor', and Eyton is from OE *Eg-tun*, meaning 'settlement on an island or in land by a river'[3] – an apt description of the parish.

The church (Fig.6.11) stands almost alone beside a farm, and was built in 1743. It is a pleasing red-brick building, with stone quoins, and wide round-headed Georgian windows. A polygonal apse was added in 1850 and fortunately the same type of window was used (*cf* Preston-upon-the-Weald Moors nearby). There is a west gallery, and some nice fragments of old glass in one of the north windows, including an early 16th-century depiction of St. Catherine. Unfortunately, the interior is disturbed by the garish glass in the east window.

Holy Trinity, Hadley

Hadley was a township in the parish of Wellington and because of the rising population, a church was built in 1856 on a site given by Miss Ellen Thorneycroft.[4] The architect was T.E. Owen of Southsea. The church (Fig.20.4) consists of a nave and chancel, with a north-western bell-turret. It is built of red and yellow brick, with dressings of Grinshill stone. There is a western gallery. A parochial centre was added at the west end in 1981.

St. Luke, Ironbridge

St. Luke's church occupies a commanding position above the Iron Bridge, halfway up the hill overlooking the Severn gorge. It was a Commissioners' Church of the 1830s, built of yellow brick and, of course, in the Early English style. The architect was Thomas Smith of Madeley.

Because of the difficult site, the normal orientation of the church is reversed, with the tower (Fig.20.5) at the eastern end and the shallow chancel at the western end. There are galleries round three sides, supported by cast-iron columns which rise above the galleries to the ceiling. The striking stained glass in the chancel window is by David Evans of Shrewsbury, and depicts SS Peter, James and John. Originally, the church seated 1,062 people, but the number of seats has been drastically reduced.

St. Mary, Jackfield

The first church at Jackfield was built in 1759 as a chapel of ease to Broseley, but it was replaced by the present church in 1863, the parish of Jackfield having been formed out of Broseley parish in the preceding year. Old St. Mary's gradually became ruinous and was demolished in 1961.

The church of 1863 (Fig.5.7) was designed by Sir Arthur Blomfield (1829-99), and it is the best of the architect's four churches in Shropshire. Pevsner remarks that it was built when Blomfield was under the influence of Butterfield,[5] and, one might add, of Street

Fig.20.4 Holy Trinity, Hadley (1856) by T.E. Owen: the interior

Fig.20.5 St. Luke, Ironbridge (1835-36) by Thomas Smith: the tower

also. The style might be described as French Gothic, a vogue of the 1860s. There is much use of polychromatic brickwork and the capitals of the piers are very florid. The church is small, nave and chancel only, with an unusual bell-turret between nave and chancel. It is notable mainly for its distinguished tiles – appropriately enough, for it is next door to the Jackfield Tile Museum. A reredos of hand-painted tiles by Craven Dunnill was inserted in 1961,[6] and there are tiles by Maws elsewhere in the sanctuary. There is excellent stained glass by Heaton, Butler and Bayne in the apse.

St. Mary the Virgin, Red Lake, Ketley

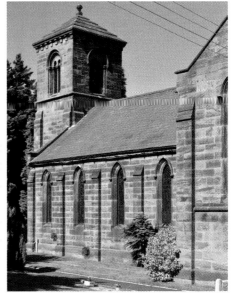

Fig.20.6 St. Mary the Virgin, Ketley (1838) by Thomas Trubshaw

The place-name means 'cat-grove', and the area was originally a township in the parish of Wellington. During the 18th century coal-mining was developed, and Red Lake was a colliers' settlement.[7] The church was built by James Trubshaw in 1838 mainly in the Early English style (Fig.20.6), at the expense of the second duke of Sutherland. It is built of dressed sandstone, and consists of a nave, shallow chancel, transepts, and a western tower. The west doorway is neo-Norman, with one shaft on each side, the capital being carved with scallop, and the hood-mould adorned with heads. The windows are lancets, also with hood-moulds. Inside there is a western gallery. The plain octagonal font has a crown carved on one face.

St. John the Evangelist, Lawley*

Fig.20.7 St. John the Evangelist, Lawley (1865) by John Ladds

Lawley is recorded in Domesday Book, but was said to be of little value; its worth had declined to 20s. from 12s. in 1066. Later the township became part of the parish of Wellington. Following the development of the coalfield the population rose and the need for a parish church increased. St. John's church was built in 1865, largely due to the efforts of Benjamin Yates of Lawley. Originally it was a chapel of ease, erected on a site given by the Coalbrookdale Co. and Lord Forester;[8] the architect was John Ladds.

The church (Fig.20.7) is built of red and yellow brick, with stone dressings. The use of poly-chromatic brick was probably due to the influence of G.E. Street, whose well-known church of St. James the Less, Pimlico, had been completed in 1861. Like St. James', St. John's tower has a steep pyramidal roof, though here the tower is situated unusually in the angle between the nave and chancel. The church also consists of a south porch, nave and chancel, with a polygonal apse (Fig.20.8); a vestry to the

Fig.20.8 *Lawley: the interior looking east*

north of the chancel is divided from it by an arcade with one pier. The windows are lancets. There is an excellent marble font comprising a plain bowl based on a purple octagonal stem.

St. Mary, Leighton**
A priest at Leighton is mentioned in Domesday Book, so presumably there must have been a church here in the 11th century. Nothing is known about the medieval church; the present building is pleasantly situated in the grounds of Leighton Hall and dates from 1714. It consists of a brick nave and chancel, and a western timbered belfry (Fig.20.9). It is in classical style, with arched windows in both north and south walls, in one of which Gothic tracery has been inserted later. There is a west gallery.

Fig.20.9 *St. Mary, Leighton (1714)*

The church is notable for an impressive array of monu-ments. Earliest is a very fine effigy of a knight in full armour dating from the late 13th century. Considerable traces of

Fig.20.10 *Leighton: stone effigy of a knight in full armour, late 13th century*

colour remain, especially on the shield which displays the Leighton arms.[9] The knight's head rests on two pillows and there is a lion at his feet (Fig.20.10). Next is an incised slab to William Leighton (d.1520) and his wife; unfortunately the figures are rather worn and not easily discerned. A cast-iron slab in the floor of the nave commemorates William Brown (d.1696). There are a good number of later memorials to members of the Leighton and Kynnersley families, the most notable of which is that to Thomas Kynnersley (d.1843) by J. Evan Thomas, showing a large pedestal and urn (Fig.20.11).

St. Lawrence, Little Wenlock

Little Wenlock is a pretty village nestling at the foot of the Wrekin, and perhaps it deserves a finer church than St. Lawrence's. The church is indeed a strange amalgam – medieval north aisle, 17th-century west tower, and Victorian nave and chancel. The north aisle was the nave of the original church, though the Decorated-style windows are probably Victorian insertions. The tower was rebuilt in 1667 in the Perpendicular style. In 1822, a south aisle of brick was added to the medieval nave. In 1875-76 a brick chancel was built at the east end so that

Fig.20.11 Leighton: memorial to Thomas Kynnersley (d.1843) by J. Evan Thomas

the south aisle became the nave and the old medieval nave became a north aisle – separated from the Victorian nave by an arcade of four bays.[10]

St. Bartholomew, Longdon on Tern

Domesday Book records that Longdon on Tern was held by St. Alkmund's church, Shrewsbury, but there is no record of any ancient church here. St. Bartholomew's church was built of red brick in 1742, but the present church looks entirely Victorian and dates from 1854. All the windows are Gothic, not Georgian – tall lancets in the shallow chancel, and Decorated in the nave.

St. Michael, Madeley*

If Telford's church at Bridgnorth was built on a fairly lavish scale, his later church at Madeley was by comparison a budget job. Yet it is not a mean building, and the church history of Madeley is of considerable interest.

There was a church here from Norman times, and it was appropriated to Wenlock Priory *c.*1330. Like St. Mary Magdalene, Bridgnorth, Madeley church was painted by Edward Williams in 1789. By 1794 the church had become unsafe and was demolished. Telford employed an unusual design for the new church – an octagonal building on classical lines, but without the portico, columns, pilasters and large windows which give such distinction to Bridgnorth. The plain, square tower (Fig.20.12) projects forwards from the octagonal nave, and the windows of the nave are displayed in two tiers. The interior is not octagonal, the corners being cut off by vestries. The chancel is an addition of 1910. There are galleries on three sides, supported by Tuscan columns below. Very weathered monuments of the Brooks family may be seen externally over the north-east and south-east faces. The extensive churchyard is remarkable for its cast-iron tombs, one of which is to 'Fletcher of Madeley'.

It is this remarkable man who gave distinction to his parish in the mid-18th century. He was a Swiss, Jean Guillaume de la Fléchere, anglicised to John William Fletcher, and rector of Madeley from 1760-1785. In 1755 he came under the influence of John Wesley, and later achieved national prominence because of the Methodist revival then taking place within the Church of England. He founded Methodist societies throughout the coalfield, and concentrated on the conversion of the poor.[11] Like Wesley, he was anti-Calvinist, believing that all may be saved; and he became embroiled in theological controversy with Quakers and Roman

Fig.20.12 St. Michael, Madeley, by Thomas Telford (1796)

Catholics. John Wesley preached from the pulpit in Madeley church in 1764, and regarded Fletcher very highly: 'So unblameable a character, in every respect, I have not found, and I scarce expect to find another on this side of eternity.'[12] Fletcher died, worn out by his

labours, in 1785, but for a further 30 years his ministry was continued by his widow Mary. Throughout this period, the Methodists in Madeley continued within the parish church, long after they had seceded from the Church of England elsewhere; there was no independent Methodist society in Madeley until 1833.

St. Leonard, Malinslee*

Malinslee had a 12th-century chapel, presumably then in the parish of Shifnal. This became ruinous in the 19th century and was demolished in 1971. A new church was required to accommodate the rapidly growing population of the area during the early Industrial Revolution, so the old chapel

Fig.20.13 St. Leonard, Malinslee, by Thomas Telford (1805)

was succeeded by the third and last (1805) of Thomas Telford's three Shropshire churches; it is less stylish than Bridgnorth, and smaller and plainer than Madeley. It is not certain that Telford was directly involved in scaling down his Madeley design for Malinslee.[13] Standing in a spacious churchyard, the dignity and grace of the new church are impressive. Like Madeley, the church externally is octagonal and built of ashlar (Fig.20.13). There is a western tower, with rustication around the doorway. The windows are arranged in two tiers.

Inside there are galleries on the north, west and south sides, resting on plain Tuscan columns, with further columns rising to the ceiling. The galleries have recently been screened off from the nave by glass partitions. Below, the old pews have been removed, yielding a flexible space for worship and for social activities. The chancel is shallow. There is some striking stained glass, perhaps the most impressive being the Good Samaritan window on the south side (1910), in the style of Morris and Co.

Holy Trinity, Oakengates
This church dates from 1855 to a design by Ewan Christian, a well-known Victorian architect. It is built in banded red and blue brick, and consists of a nave with short north and south aisles, a central tower and a chancel. The windows are lancets, except for the east window. Behind the altar there are some excellent locally-made tiles.

St. Laurence, Preston-upon-the-Weald Moors
This is a plain red-brick Georgian church, completed in 1742; a chancel with lancet windows was added in 1853. Some original 18th-century panelling survives, and there is an elegant font – a scalloped bowl standing on a slender stem adorned with foliage (Fig.10.20), which is said to date from 1905.[14]

St. Peter, Priorslee
Priorslee was anciently a chapelry of Shifnal. There was a medieval church, recorded by the Rev. Williams in 1790, but this was replaced by the present building in 1836.

This unassuming church did not gain Cranage's approval, and its external appearance has probably not improved since then. The interior, however, is pleasing: there is a west gallery, and an enormous gilt reredos imported from another church lends a surprising dignity to the sanctuary (14.17).

St. George, Rodington
The manor took its name from the river Roden, a pre-English river name,[15] and it is surprising to find that the Domesday Book mentions the presence here of both church and priest. The medieval church has long since disappeared, but there is a painting of a Georgian church built in 1751 with wide round-headed windows. This in turn was replaced in 1851 with the present building, constructed of brick, with stone dressings. It consists of nave and chancel, with a north aisle, and an engaging wooden bell-turret with spirelet which projects from the west wall. The windows are mainly late 13th-century in style (Early English verging on Decorated). Towards the west end of the interior, a section of the wall of the medieval church is revealed; this was discovered in 1929. There are some nice Victorian tiles in the sanctuary. The church is now an Anglican/Methodist ecumenical partnership.

Fig.20.14 St. George, St. George's (1862) by G.E. Street: the north arcade

Fig.20.15 St. George's: the chancel

St. George, St. George's**

This fine church by G.E. Street is not nearly so well known as it merits. St. George's started life as a chapel of ease in the parish of Lilleshall in 1806, and the first church was a plain brick building in the form of an equal-armed cross.[16] This was replaced in 1862 by Street's church, which is his best in Shropshire.

It stands on high ground to the north of Telford, and its tower is a considerable local landmark. The church is built of rough grey stone, and its distinction is immediately apparent. It consists of a nave with north and south aisles, a chancel, and a south porch under the tower.

Cranage described the church before the completion of the tower, and he mentioned 'an unfinished tower forming a south porch'. The tower was completed in 1929 by Bertram Butler. Street had intended a stone spire, but Butler changed this to an upper storey complete with battlements and pinnacles. Even so, the tower is by no means conventional, and is unusually light in style.

The interior (Fig.20.14) is impressive indeed, and shows well Street's love of structural polychromy. The arcades, chancel arch, and half-arches in the aisles are outlined by red brick, as is a cross high above the chancel arch. The low chancel (Fig.20.15) is tunnel-vaulted, with transverse arches, and the east window is a complex arrangement of lancets, trefoils and quatrefoils. The piers of the arcades are varied – some octagonal, others cylindrical, and all the lush capitals are different. Further carving is present in roundels above the piers. The nave is much higher than the chancel, and the clerestory windows are alternately lancets and paired lancets with plate tracery.

There is some good stained glass, especially the more subdued tones evident in the windows of the south aisle. The pulpit is of stone, and the square font rests on four pillars with a central stem.

All Saints, Stirchley

This is a combined Anglican/Roman Catholic church built in 1976. From the exterior, it appears rather drab and depressing, the only distinguishing mark being four reinforced concrete girders which project upwards through a central lantern to an apex, in the form of an imitation spire. The interior, however, is more appealing. The central worship area is lit from the lantern above and is demarcated by the base of the girders, which unify the design. All the furniture – communion-table, lectern, font – is movable, making the space very flexible. The worship area is encompassed by a suite of rooms for community activities which would be the envy of many an urban church.

The church of Christ the King, Hollinswood is an ecumenical chapel in Meeting Point House in the town centre.

Fig.20.16 St. James, Stirchley: the Norman chancel; beyond is the Georgian nave

St. James, Stirchley***

St. James' is a fascinating building, and it has some excellent furnishings. The church is first recorded in 1238, when it was given by Osbert, lord of Stirchley, to Wenlock Priory.[17] But the church is older than that, for the chancel is Norman; here are two small, round-headed windows on the north, one on the south, and two on the east wall, one high above the other (Fig.20.16). Between the two is a blind arch, visible both internally and externally. On the south wall of the chancel is a two-light window with a quatrefoil in the apex (*c*.1300). The chief glory of St. James is the magnificent chancel arch, one of the two finest chancel arches in Shropshire (*cf* Upton Cressett). The arch (Fig.9.6) is set in the filling of a larger arch.[18] There are two orders of shafts and three concentric arches. The inner displays chain-links, and the outer two chevron, one at right-angles to the wall. One of the north capitals is scalloped and the others are carved with varying foliage.

The nave was encased in brick around 1740, and a brick-built north aisle was added in 1838. The windows of the nave and aisle are wide, round-headed and Georgian. Internally there are north and west galleries, some 18th-century box-pews, and a splendidly austere 18th-century pulpit, complete with sounding-board. There is some good Victorian stained glass. The church became redundant in 1978 and was sold to Telford Development Corporation.

It is pleasing to record that recently the church has been cleaned and restored, and access is now easy, the key being held at the adjoining guest house. A visit is strongly recommended!

All Saints, Wellington**

It is a pity that All Saints', Wellington suffers by comparison with St. Chad's, Shrewsbury – both are by the same architect, George Steuart, Wellington being a little earlier, but clearly built on a less ambitious scale than St. Chad's.

The earliest church in Wellington was presumably a Saxon building, for the existence of a priest is mentioned in the Domesday survey. Later there was a medieval church, the outlines of which are known from old engravings. This building was demolished in 1787 and replaced by the present church in 1788-90. The exterior badly needs cleaning, which would transform its appearance. Even so, All Saints' is distinguished. The west front (Fig.20.17) is of three bays, separated by tall Tuscan pilasters; above is a pediment and then a rather plain square tower. Along the sides are two tiers of windows with ornamentation between the tiers.

The interior was unfortunately altered in 1898. Originally the north, south and west galleries were supported by cast-iron columns, and further columns ascended from the galleries to the ceiling. The cast-iron columns were appropriate in an area celebrated for its ironworks. These columns were banded, and quatrefoil in cross-section in the Gothic manner. By the 1890s they offended Victorian taste and were then concealed by scagliola, an imitation stone of cement and chips giving a marble appearance. Is it too much to hope that one day their original appearance may be restored? The columns are now Tuscan below the galleries and Corinthian above. There is a shallow apse at the east end (Fig.20.18). Some good Victorian glass fills the windows above the galleries and elsewhere. In the south-eastern vestry are two early Victorian monuments, one by Peter Hollins.

All Saints' is a thriving church – exterior cleaning and interior restoration to the original would bring it to the first rank of Shropshire churches.

Fig.20.17 All Saints, Wellington (1788-90) by George Steuart

Fig.20.18 Wellington: the chancel

Christ Church, Wellington

A chapel of ease called Christ Church was consecrated in 1839.[19] The building was designed by Thomas Smith of Madeley and closely resembles his earlier church at Ironbridge (q.v.). It is built of yellow brick in the Early English style, with lancet windows throughout. The west tower carries large corner pinnacles. The interior is spacious; originally there were north, south and west galleries, but now only the west remains.

St. Mary and St. Leonard, Wombridge

An Augustinian priory was founded at Wombridge c.1130-35, and was dissolved in 1536. The Lady chapel of the priory survived as the parish church until 1756 when it collapsed and was replaced by a brick church consisting of a nave and a small west tower.[20] In 1824 this church was enlarged by the addition of transepts, galleries and an eastern apse. In 1960 the brick nave was encased with stone and the church was rebuilt. It now consists of a nave with short aisles, chancel and western gabled tower. There is a transverse arch across each aisle giving the effect of north and south transepts. The general style is early Decorated.

St. Peter, Wrockwardine**

Wrockwardine is a pretty village clustered around St. Peter's church, a precious enclave so close to Telford. The second element in the place-name usually means 'enclosure' or 'settlement', so the name means 'enclosure by the Wrekin'. Wrekin is the British name for Wroxeter, transferred to the hill.[21] Gelling believes that 'Wrockwardine, with its partly pre-English name and dominant situation on a raised shelf of land, was a pre-English settlement of more than average size and importance'.[22] As at Alberbury, there was apparently a group of hamlets around a central village. Wrockwardine has an impressive entry in the Domesday Book. The manor was held by Earl Roger; the church was held by St. Peter's church, Shrewsbury; and the presence of a priest was also recorded.

So Wrockwardine church certainly dates back to Anglo-Saxon times, even though there is no trace of Saxon work in the present building. It is a cruciform building, with nave, chancel, north and south transepts, a central tower, and north and south chapels on each side of the chancel. The complexity of the building is matched by equal complexity in its history, which is not easy to unravel.

Fig.20.19 St. Peter, Wrockwardine: the columns of the crossing

From the exterior, the eastern half of the nave is Norman – note the blocked Norman doorways in the north and south walls; there is also a blocked round-headed doorway in the south wall of the south transept. In the north wall of the north transept is a Norman doorway with one order of shafts; the eastern capital has scalloping, the western some leaf carving. The western half of the nave probably dates from the 14th century. The central tower (Fig.6.2) is supported by huge buttresses which are based on the walls of the nave, transepts and chancel. The tower itself is Early English below, with lancet windows, and Decorated above, with an embattled top and pyramid roof.

On entering the church, the nave is seen to be long, without aisles. Most of the nave windows, Decorated in character, have been renewed. The west window is Perpendicular in character but dates from 1854; it replaced the true Perpendicular window described by Glynne after his visit in 1850. At the crossing are four massive multishafted piers; these are late Norman, but they have suffered much later adaptation and strengthening. The carving of many of the capitals has been lost, but one of the north-western capitals exhibits fine narrow fluting (Fig.20.19), and the corresponding capital on the south shows volute. The other south-western capitals display some primitive foliage. The piers support four pointed arches, dating from the late 12th century.

In the west walls of both transepts are blocked half-arches; it is believed that these were constructed in the expectation that aisles would be added to the nave, but these were never built. There are Perpendicular windows at the ends of each transept. The chancel was originally Early English, and one tall lancet window survives in the south wall. The east window of the chancel is a fine Decorated insertion. Chapels fill in the corners between the chancel and the transepts on each side; the north is earlier, and has a late Decorated east window, the south is Perpendicular and does not extend as far east as the north. There is a blocked doorway in the east wall of the south chapel. Each chapel is entered from the chancel by a low arch.

There are some excellent furnishings. The elaborate pulpit is Jacobean. The communion rails show much fine carving and are dated 1685; they were reinstated in 1931 having been found in Wrockwardine Hall.[23] Near the crossing is a small ancient but weathered font, of uncertain date, but possibly Norman. There is very good stained glass by Kempe in the east window of the chancel and in the end windows of both transepts. Some other windows also display good Victorian glass. In the north chapel is a fine rococo monument to William Cludde (d.1765); this shows an urn above, and below the tablet are heads of cherubs (Fig.20.20), said to be stylistically very similar to the Cressett monument at Cound (Fig.11.34). Both may be the work of T.F. Pritchard.[24]

Fig.20.20 Wrockwardine: monument to William Cludde (d.1765)

Holy Trinity, Wrockwardine Wood

This church was built in 1833; the architects are usually stated to be Samuel and Thomas Smith of Madeley (father and son). Unlike Thomas Smith's later Gothic churches at Ironbridge and Wellington, this building is in Classical style, and it is more likely to be the work of Samuel. It is one of the last such churches in the county. It was originally a plain preaching box, built of brick, with round-headed windows and a western tower. An apse was added later in the 19th century. In 1902, four stone balls surmounting the tower were replaced by pinnacles.[25]

West Shropshire – Pontesbury

Alberbury**	Marton
Annscroft	Middleton-in-Chirbury*
Cardeston*	Minsterley**
Chirbury*	Pontesbury**
Ford*	Shelve*
Great Wollaston	Wattlesborough
Habberley	Westbury**
Hope	Worthen**
Lea Cross	Yockleton*
Longden	

St. Michael, Alberbury**

Alberbury, now a small village very close to the Welsh border, has a distinguished and complicated ecclesiastical history, and a fine church. The place-name means 'the fort of Aluberg or Ealhburg', both of which are known to be OE feminine names.[1] Before the Conquest, Alberbury was a minster church. At the time of Domesday the manor was held by Earl Roger, and the parish was extensive, containing 12 townships. In the 12th and 13th centuries Alberbury had four portioners. The church was given to Shrewsbury Abbey in the mid-12th century, but later it was assigned to Alberbury Priory, which gradually acquired the patronage of all four portions.[2]

The priory was one of three English dependencies of the French abbey of Grandmont and was founded in 1228, the site of the priory being within a bend of the river Severn, about one and a quarter miles from the village. It had a troubled history,[3] and as an alien priory it was vulnerable to royal predators; it was finally suppressed by Henry VI in 1441, the estate passing to All Souls' College, Oxford.

St. Michael's church stands close to the remains of the castle and consists of a nave and chancel, with a northern tower and a south aisle, known as the Loton chapel. The architecture is very uneven in quality – the medieval sections are good or excellent, the Victorian (1845) mediocre. The substantial tower is Early English with lancet windows and flat buttresses; it has a saddleback roof, the only example in Shropshire, with gables to the east and west (Fig.6.4). The eastern half of the nave is originally Norman, with a round-headed window in the south wall, but the west end is wholly Victorian. The roof of the nave (Fig.21.1) is one of the finest in the county, consisting of collar-beams on arched braces, and five tiers of wind-braces with quatrefoil cusping. The chancel is Victorian, with neo-Norman windows in the east wall.

The elegant south aisle is by far the best part of the church. Built *c*.1320-30 in the Decorated style, it is divided from the nave by an arcade of three bays, with clustered piers of four shafts. The east window, originally very wide, is blocked. In the west wall high up is a window described as a spheric triangle, similar to the one at Moreton Corbet. The south windows are of three lights. In the south wall is a

Fig.21.1 St. Michael, Alberbury: roof over the nave

piscina, and a fine tomb-recess with cusping and a slab decorated with ball-flower. The unusually carved roof of the aisle (Fig.21.2) has tie-beams and queen-posts, with pendants added in the 19th century.

There are two good wall-monuments side by side in the north wall of the nave. That to Sir Richard Lyster (d.1691) was originally in old St. Chad's, Shrewsbury. On each side of the inscription are standing genii. The rococo monument to another Sir Richard Lyster (d.1766) is more complex. It is by T.F. Pritchard and comprises a central tablet with eulogy, flanked by scrolls. Above is an urn, and on either side of this are cherubs. The cherub on the left is standing, that on the right is seated and above his right shoulder is a hat on a pole. This refers to a scene in the House of Commons when Lyster protested against a decision of the House, and to make his point he kept his hat on in the chamber.[4]

*Fig.21.2 Alberbury:
roof over the south aisle*

Christ Church, Annscroft*

Annscroft was originally a squatter settlement and the parish was created in 1872 from the parishes of Condover, Meole Brace and St. Chad, Shrewsbury, following the building of Christ Church three years previously. The architect was J.L. Randall of Shrewsbury, and his design is lively. The church is built of sandstone, with dressings of paler stone. Perched on a bank above the road, it comprises a nave and chancel, divided by a low stone screen, and a north aisle separated from the nave by a two-bay arcade. The capitals of the piers are very florid. The aisle has a long series of small lancet windows; above is a rose window set as a dormer. The east window has three lancets, and above is a slender oval window. The doorway has shafts with capitals on each side, and above is a slender spirelet. The design owes much to the French Gothic tradition, which enjoyed a vogue in England in the 1860s.

St. Michael, Cardeston*

Cardeston church is first mentioned in 1276,[5] and one window in the chancel survives from before that date. By the 18th century the medieval church was 'much decayed' and it was replaced by a new building in 1749. This building was drastically remodelled in 1844, as shown below, so that today the appearances are more Victorian than Georgian.

The church consists of a nave and chancel, with a thin western tower (Fig.21.3). The south wall of the chancel contains one 12th-century window with a round rear-arch, discovered during restoration in 1905. The chancel arch possibly survives from the Georgian church, but all the Perpendicular-style windows in the nave date from the 1844 restoration, as does the tower. The latter is unusual in that the square lower stage becomes octagonal above angle broaches.

There is a west gallery, supported by a beam dated 1678. The plain octagonal font is late medieval. In the chancel is a barrel-organ acquired in 1850; it has a range of some 20 tunes. There is good glass in the east window in the Morris tradition, dated 1909. Of much the same date is a fresco which occupies much of the windowless north wall of the nave. Entitled Behold the Lamb of God, it is by an unknown artist.

Fig.21.3 St. Michael, Cardeston, showing the church as it was in 1840 and again in 1848

St. Michael the Archangel, Chirbury*

Chirbury means 'fortified place with a church'; and the name is apt, for there was a fort here during the Danish wars in 915[6] and Domesday Book mentions the presence of two churches and a priest. The fort may have been sited at a rectangular enclosure to the north-west of the village, but excavation has not confirmed this. The manor had been held by Edward the Confessor, but after the Norman Conquest it was held by Earl Roger. No trace of the churches mentioned in the Domesday survey remains.

An Augustinian priory was founded at Snead in the late 12th century and moved to Chirbury c.1220. Chirbury church as we see it today is just the nave of the former priory, the original crossing, transepts and choir having been demolished. Surviving from the former priory is the base of a 13th-century column, probably from the former chapter-house. It is in the churchyard wall opposite the north-east corner of the church. The present chancel is a mean brick structure added to the nave in 1733; it has three wide lancet windows on the east side, and one each to the north and south. The existing nave

Fig.21.4 St. Michael the Archangel, Chirbury: the nave and chancel

Fig.21.5 Chirbury: the tower

(Fig.21.4) is probably the original nave of the church before the arrival of the monks, but the arcades and aisles were added later in the 13th century (the Early English period). The arcades lean outwards to a considerable degree. The chancel arch and the windows of both north and south aisles date from a Victorian restoration. There are no clerestory windows. The roof of the nave is Perpendicular, and consists of collar-beams on arched braces, with wind-braces laterally. The lower part of the tower was built *c*.1300, while the upper storey, battlements and pinnacles are Perpendicular (Fig.21.5).

The medieval font is circular, with angled projections; its age is unclear. In the base of the tower, which is the entry into the church, is a wall-monument to the Pritchard family and some hatchments. The best stained glass is in the north and south windows of the chancel, and is by Powell's; the figures are in blue, maroon and brown. There is also a window by Kempe in the south aisle. The stone mosaic reredos, an Annunciation scene flanked by panels of flowers, is also by Powell's. Also in the chancel is an 18th-century brass chandelier and nearby a memento mori to Richard Lloyd, d.1589.

St. Michael, Ford*

At the time of the Domesday survey, the manor of Ford was held by Earl Roger, and with an annual value of £34 it was one of the most prosperous in the county. It derives its name from its proximity to one or more fords across the Severn, to the north.[7] The church occupies the highest site in the village, and consists of a nave with north aisle, and chancel, with a western bellcote (Fig.21.6).

The nave and chancel originally date from *c*.1200, but very little of the medieval building remains. The south doorway of the nave is round-headed, with a round moulding. To the east of this is a lancet window, set in a splayed round-headed rear-arch (as at Cardeston nearby). The priest's doorway in the chancel is pointed. The rest of the church dates mainly from the restoration of 1875, when the north arcade and aisle were added and the windows in the nave and chancel were inserted.

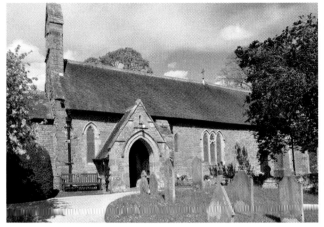

Fig.21.6 St. Michael, Ford

The finest artefact is the 15th-century roof of the nave, which consists of alternate hammer-beams and collar-beams with arched braces; at the sides are three tiers of cusped wind-braces. The screen is late Perpendicular and rustic, without fine tracery. The reredos appears to be a compound of Jacobean wood-work, with, in the centre, five panels with human figures said to be of 16th-century Flemish workmanship.

St. John, Great Wollaston

Great Wollaston was a chapelry in the parish of Alberbury, first recorded in 1289.[8] The present church is a very simple building of 1787-88, constructed of re-used rubble from the former chapel, which was said to be much decayed. It comprises an undifferentiated nave and chancel, with a western bellcote. There are no windows in the north wall; those in the south and east wall were rendered Gothic in 1885. From the former chapel is an 18th-century brass commemorating Thomas Parr, who died in 1635 at the alleged age of 152. In his one hundredth year he was required to stand in a white sheet in the church porch at Alberbury as a penance for fathering an illegitimate child.[9]

St. Mary, Habberley

Habberley is a pleasant small village at the foot of the Shropshire hills. The ancient church is a humble building, just nave and chancel, with a western bellcote. There are plain Norman doorways, both north and south, with scratch marks (?masons' marks) very evident on the south side. Most of the windows are lancets, but there is one square-headed 'Tudor' window on the south side. There is a plain ?Norman font, and attractive panelling around the walls of the nave.

Holy Trinity, Hope

If Shelve reminds one of upland Yorkshire, Hope, a short distance down the valley, is more like Devon. For here the church is prettily placed in woodland, and access to the church (Fig.21.7) is across a footbridge over an infant stream. The church was built by Edward Haycock sen. in 1843, and is in the Early English style

Fig.21.7 Holy Trinity, Hope

221

then prevailing. It consists of an undivided nave and chancel, with a western bell-turret. There is a west gallery, and a complex array of roof timbers – tie-beams and king- and queen-posts.

St. Anne, Lea Cross
This church was built in 1888 as a proprietary chapel (licensed, but unconsecrated by the bishop) and was originally the responsibility of the second portioner of Pontesbury parish (see p.224). The architect was J.L. Randal of Shrewsbury. It is a large and solid church, built of red brick with stone dressings, with a central tower and short spire, a north-west porch, and a rose window at the west end. At the west end of the church is a low baptistery, divided from the nave by an arcade. The font and pulpit are of marble. In the chancel is the large altar-tomb of Mrs. Anne Hawkes (d.1882), mother of the builder of the church. I have not been able to gain access to the church, which is now privately owned.

St. Ruthin, Longden
Longden is first recorded as a chapel of ease in the parish of Pontesbury in 1548. It is a small church, with a nave of sandstone probably dating from the late Middle Ages. Various brick excrescences were added later, including a small polygonal chancel. The interior is rather dull: the oak pulpit is plain, and may date from the later 17th-century.[10] The baluster font at the west end of the nave is probably 18th-century.

St. Mark, Marton
This is a simple church in the Early English style dating from 1855. It consists of a nave and chancel, with a north porch and a western bellcote. The triple lancets of the east window contain some good Victorian glass.

Holy Trinity, Middleton-in-Chirbury*
The 1840s were not a good time for church building in Shropshire on the whole, but this church is a pleasant exception. It is remote and lonely, situated in lovely hill-country not far from Mitchell's Fold stone circle, and in spring and summer the churchyard is a delight, with a great variety of wild flowers, including martagon lilies. The church was built in 1843, the architect being Edward Haycock sen.; it is one of his better buildings, with nave, transepts and polygonal apse. It is in the Early English style, with lancet windows; a pier divides the transepts from the nave.

But what gives this church its distinction is the transformation of the interior wrought by the Reverend Waldegrave Brewster, who was vicar from 1872-1901. He was responsible

Fig.21.8 Holy Trinity, Middleton-in-Chirbury: bench-ends carved by the Reverend W. Brewster

Fig.21.9 Middleton-in-Chirbury: a capital

for demolishing the chancel and replacing it with the apse. He undertook a long programme of carving the altar and the ends of the pews (Fig.21.8) with an astonishing variety of subjects – among these is an old lady in a mob-cap, a man with a long beard, a dog, and a sinister head with pointed ears. He also carved in stone the capitals of the piers, taking as his theme a story relating to Mitchell's Fold involving a fairy cow and a wicked witch (Fig.21.9). The cumulative effect of his work is enchanting. There are two stained glass windows by Kempe and Co.

Holy Trinity, Minsterley**

The place-name implies that here was a minster church in Saxon times (for it is recorded in Domesday Book as *Menistrelie*), but if so there is no documentary record of it. Indeed throughout the Middle Ages, Minsterley was a chapel of ease subordinate to Westbury, and this remained so until 1689. The present church was apparently built because the Thynnes from Longleat in Wiltshire needed a new church in Minsterley when they acquired Minsterley Hall nearby. The architect was William Taylor of London.[11]

This building was a sharp break with the past in Shropshire, for here at last was the first church built on Classical lines, an essay in rural Baroque. The few other 17th-century churches in the county had harked back to the Gothic past. Minsterley was also the first Shropshire church to be built in brick; the dressings are of Grinshill stone. The most striking aspect of the church is undoubtedly the west façade (Fig.21.10), a complex composition with a bewildering variety of subjects. One wonders what the parishioners felt about it when it was first built! At either side, giant rusticated columns run from the base to the arched pediment above the clock. On either side of the west portal are further rusticated columns, and above a segmental arch, with a frieze decorated with

Fig.21.10 Holy Trinity, Minsterley (1689) by William Taylor

skulls and bones. Between this and the clock is a wide-arched window, flanked by pilasters decked with garlands, and above yet more rustication. Four symmetrically-placed rectangular windows complete the façade. Above is a weather-boarded belfry, crowned by four little pedimented gables. The north and south elevations have large round-arched windows with cherubs' heads in the keystones; between the windows are tall sloping buttresses.

The interior is more sober in the Protestant tradition, with some fine original woodwork, notably the excellent pulpit with large sounding-board, the communion rails and the panelling of the chancel. There is a west gallery, above which is displayed a set of maidens' garlands. These 18th-century fancies were lovingly constructed in memory of young betrothed girls who died before their wedding-day, and Minsterley has a collection of seven.

St. George, Pontesbury**

Pontesberie means either 'fort on the river Pant' or 'Pant's fort' (Pant being a Saxon personal name).[12] In either event, the settlement is a very ancient one and was marked for pre-eminence by being the site of a Saxon minster. In the 12th century, a motte and bailey was erected close to the church. The church itself was first recorded in 1254, but it is apparent from the Williams painting that the tower at least was older than that, as it had unmistakable Norman features. An unusual feature of the tower was that it was built alongside the north wall of the nave; originally, it was detached from the nave (as probably was nearby Worthen).

During the Middle Ages, Pontesbury was a collegiate church from which a college of priests served an extensive surrounding area. It was also unusual in that it was staffed by three portioners, one of whom was styled dean. For hundreds of years the rector of the first portion was responsible for services for 26 weeks in the year, the rectors of the second and third portions being each responsible for 13 weeks.[13] This arrangement persisted until 1909 and in the 19th century caused a lot of friction worthy of the attention of Anthony Trollope.

In 1825 the tower collapsed and it became necessary to rebuild much of the nave and to build a new, western tower. The medieval chancel alone escaped undamaged. The church today therefore comprises a tower and nave built in the Early English style by John Turner of Whitchurch in 1829 (one of the first Gothic revival churches of Shropshire), and a chancel of about 1300. The latter contains two-light windows on the north and south with Y-tracery; the east window is of five lights, with uncusped intersecting tracery and a quatrefoil at the apex.

Fig.21.11 St. George, Pontesbury: font, nave and chancel

Fig.21.12 Pontesbury: the tower (1829) by John Turner

There is an aumbry in the north wall, and piscina and priest's doorway in the south. The nave (Fig.21.11) is wide and spacious, and has both north and south aisles; the arcades have probably been rebuilt using some of the medieval masonry. Medieval masonry also survives in part in the walls of the aisles, especially the north. The south-western tower also dates from 1829, and is built of buff-coloured Grinshill stone (Fig.21.12).

The Norman font consists of a circular bowl, on the underside of which is carved a series of scallops (Fig.21.11). Jacobean panelling has been relocated in the north and south walls of the chancel. The reredos is a striking representation of the Crucifixion by G.E. Street. There are several memorial tablets, the most entertaining being that to Thomas Davies, a London merchant who died in 1754. The monument shows two female figures, and below a ship in full sail; the carvings represent Faith, Hope and Charity. The marble monument to Richard Ward of Offley (d.1762) is by T.F. Pritchard; at the top is a broken scrolled pediment enclosing a coat of arms surrounded by a rococo cartouche.[14]

Within the past few years, the west end of the nave has been drastically revised to provide a kitchen, toilets and a new room for social and religious purposes. The adaptation has been skilfully executed, and the result greatly enhances the value of St. George's to both congregation and community.

All Saints, Shelve

The place-name is from OE *shelf*, and Shelve is indeed situated on an area of relatively flat ground, but high up among the Shropshire Hills, in the area much scarred by former lead-mining. Life here must have been hard and bleak in previous times, and the survival of the church is no mean achievement. At 1,150 feet above sea-level, the parish church is not the highest in the county – that distinction belongs to Bettws-y-Crwyn. The whole area east of the Stiperstones – and the church – remind one more of Yorkshire than Shropshire.

There was a medieval church here, recorded by Williams in 1790. The

Fig.21.13 All Saints, Shelve (1839)

present very simple building dates from 1839 (Fig.21.13) and is an attractive stone-built edifice consisting of an undivided nave and chancel, and a thin west tower. It is in the Early English style, and was built to the design of the Rev. T.F. More. Surviving from the former church are the ancient nine-sided font, plain with vertical strips, possibly Norman; the rood-beam above the sanctuary; and some 17th-century panelling in the chancel, together with the pulpit and reading-desk. The Creed, Lord's Prayer and Decalogue are on boards in the north and south sanctuary walls. The attractive glass in the east window is of Christ and the disciples at Emmaus.

St. Luke, Snailbeach

Snailbeach is a scattered community which developed to serve the local lead mine, which closed in 1913; barytes working on the old tip finished in 1955.[15] Three churches were built here during the 19th century – Baptist (1833), Methodist (1876) and St. Luke's parish church (1872). St. Luke's is a rather austere chapel with an apsidal chancel and lancet windows (Fig.21.14). The interior is attractive.

Fig.21.14 St. Luke, Snailbeach (1872)

Fig.21.15 St. Mary, Westbury

St. Margaret, Wattlesborough

A brick mission church built in 1936.

St. Mary, Westbury**

Domesday Book records the presence of two priests (but no church) in Westbury, and from then Westbury was served by two rectors knows as portioners. (Burford and Pontesbury each had three portioners, Alberbury four.) The two portions were served by separate incumbents until 1862, when the second portion was assigned to the newly created parish of Yockleton.[16]

St. Mary's (Fig.21.15) consists of a nave, chancel, spacious north aisle, and a western tower. The medieval tower fell in 1753 and was replaced by the present structure built in the Classical style. There is rustication around the west door, and above this is a large Venetian window. The next stage has circular windows on each face, and the belfry has round-headed windows, with a parapet

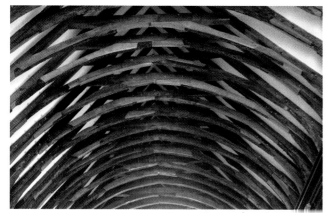

Fig.21.16 Westbury: the roof over the north aisle (1342), said to be the oldest roof of its kind in the country

above. The nave and north aisle are basically medieval, but all the windows of the north and south walls date from a Victorian restoration. The large east window of the north aisle has intersecting tracery, much restored; the west window of the aisle is the only original window remaining; it has two lights under a square head, and dates from *c.*1400. The arcade is a good Early English structure, with circular piers and plain capitals, a chamfer and a roll-moulding. The medieval chancel was pulled down in 1753 and rebuilt in the Classical style; this in turn was reconstructed in the Early English manner in 1887. The best features of the interior are the roofs of the aisle and the nave. The latter exhibits nine trusses with collar-beams on arched braces; laterally there are three tiers of wind-braces, the middle tier consisting of cusped quatrefoils. The roof of the aisle is much more unusual (Fig.21.16) having trussed rafters, with collar-beams on arched braces. Dendrochronology has given a date of 1342.[17] This is said to be the oldest roof of its kind in the country and has recently been restored with the aid of a substantial grant from English Heritage.

The best of the wall-monuments is that to John Topp (d.1736). There are also several hatchments.

All Saints, Worthen**

Worthen (from OE *Wordign*, meaning 'enclosure') has an extensive entry in the Domesday Book describing a manor worth £10 before 1066, but there is no mention of a church or a priest. There are several unusual features about Worthen church: the tower is to the north of the nave, the chancel is Georgian; and the varied assembly of ancient pews is the finest in Shropshire.

The tower (Fig.21.17) is massive, with walls five feet thick at ground level, and it is likely that it was a place of refuge in this troubled border area during the early Middle Ages. The lower part is Norman, the upper stages Perpendicular, with an 18th-century parapet. The porch (Fig.7.2) dates from the 17th century, with open woodwork on each

Fig.21.17 All Saints, Worthen: the tower

side. The south doorway is Early English, and the spacious nave itself is also probably 13th-century – though the tracery of the windows is Decorated, but restored. There are no aisles: but in view of the great width of the nave (33 feet), Mercer speculates that there may once have been one or two timber arcades.[18] The west window is Perpendicular, with a small cusped round window above. The roof of the nave has tie-beams, with collar-beams on arched braces. Between the medieval nave and the Georgian chancel is an odd chancel arch which may have been re-assembled. The chancel was built of brick in 1761; it is attractive, with wide arched windows.

The best feature is the assembly of old pews – Jacobean box-pews on each side, and a range of plain benches, possibly medieval, in the middle (Fig.14.13). There is further Jacobean woodwork in the chancel. The pulpit is plainer – probably late 18th- or early 19th-century. The font is a plain octagonal bowl on a cylindrical base. There is a rather dingy wall-memorial to Dr. Daniel Price (d.1631) in the chancel, with columns and strapwork.

Holy Trinity, Yockleton

A chapel at Yockleton, to which there is no reference before the early 17th century, was probably built by Shrewsbury Abbey;[19] apparently this had disappeared by 1763. The present attractive church (Fig.6.14) is set on a knoll at the west end of the village. It was built in 1861 to the design of Edward Haycock jun. and is a substantial building consisting of a south-west tower with broach spire (complete with dormer windows), nave and chancel, with a south aisle. The arcade dividing the aisle and nave has pointed arches with plain moulded capitals. The chancel arch rests on corbels with florid capitals. There is a clerestory above the south aisle. The east and west windows are more or less Decorated in style, the other windows being paired lancets, short on the south side and tall on the north. The chancel is raised three steps higher than the nave, and the sanctuary two steps higher still – an arrangement which *The Ecclesiologist* would doubtless have approved. The good glass in the east window is by Kempe and Co., and is a memorial to the fallen in the 1914-18 war.

Church Stretton and the Stretton Hills

Acton Burnell***	Dorrington*
Acton Scott*	Frodesley*
All Stretton	Hope Bowdler*
Dorrington	Kenley*
Betton Strange	Langley*
Cardington**	Leebotwood*
Church Preen*	Little Stretton
Church Pulverbatch	Longnor**
Church Stretton**	Pitchford***
Condover***	Ryton, near Condover
Cound**	Smethcott*
Cressage*	Stapleton*
Cwm Head	Woolstaston*

St. Mary, Acton Burnell***

'Acton' usually means 'settlement by the oaks', and there are five Actons in Shropshire, four of which are differentiated by family names (Burnell, Pigott, Reynald and Scott; Acton Round presumably means a round settlement). Acton Burnell is the most distinguished of these because of the legacy of Robert Burnell (d.1292), Lord Chancellor of England and bishop of Bath and Wells.

At the time of the Domesday Book (1086), *Actune* was held by Robert Fitz Corbet from Earl Roger; a hundred years later it was held by Thomas Burnell, and it remained in that family until 1316.[1] Robert Burnell was born in the village and rose to become chaplain and secretary to Prince Edward, who succeeded as Edward I in 1272. In 1283, following his campaign in north Wales, the king summoned a parliament at Shrewsbury and adjourned it to Acton Burnell, the Lords sitting in the hall of the castle, and the Commons in a nearby barn.[2] Next year, Robert Burnell began his castle at Acton Burnell, the attractive ruins of which stand just to the north of the church.

St. Mary's (Fig.22.1) is the finest Early English church in Shropshire, and unlike most English parish churches, the whole church was built in the same style. It is a highly sophisticated and expensive church, erected at the height of Robert Burnell's career (say 1270-90). It was built on a cruciform plan, with nave, chancel, and north and south transepts; a small tower in the angle between the north transept and the chancel was added in 1887-89. Around the nave and transepts is a corbel-table, with many grotesque carvings.

Fig.22.1 St. Mary, Acton Burnell, with the castle beyond

Building began at the west end and proceeded eastwards, for the west window, with its three stepped lancets, is noticeably plainer than the east, and the nave is plainer than the sumptuous chancel. The windows in the nave are trefoil-headed lancets, and the roof over both nave and chancel has collar-beams on arched braces. The octagonal font, at the west end of the nave, has eight shafts around the stem supporting a cusped arcade (Fig.10.17); it is the finest Early English font in Shropshire. The chancel arch rests on short marble shafts set on corbels with elegant stiff-leaf foliage; the arches from the nave to the transepts are similar. The chancel is adorned with arcades of trefoil-headed lancets, four on the south and three on the north, with rich mouldings, marble shafts and foliated capitals. The geometric tracery of the east window heralds the imminent arrival of the Decorated style: at the top is a circular window resting on two arches, each of which encloses a trefoil above a pair of lancets. In the south wall is a very fine double piscina.

The south transept is plain, and contains a Decorated tomb-recess with ogee arches and crockets. The north transept is paved with medieval encaustic tiles and is distinguished by five very fine monuments:

1) A tomb-chest with ogee niches to Sir Nicholas Burnell (d.1382). On it is the finest memorial brass in Shropshire, depicting an armoured knight under a canopy.
2) On the east wall is the enormous Elizabethan monument to Sir Richard Lee (d.1591) and his wife (Fig.11.17). Two alabaster effigies lie on a slab, and behind are their nine children shown frontally. Above is an arch and a rich architectural surround with an achievement at the top and a caryatid on each side.
3) High on the opposite wall is a typical Jacobean monument to Sir Humphrey Lee (d.1632) and his wife (Fig.11.21). Two figures kneel on each side of a prayer-desk, with six kneeling children shown in profile below. This accomplished monument is by Nicholas Stone (1586-1647).
4) The wall tablet of Lady Mary Smythe (d.1764), surmounted by a cross and two burning lamps. It has been postulated that this may be the work of T.F. Pritchard.[3]
5) A military tablet of 1794 to William Smythe, signed by King of Bath.

St. Margaret, Acton Scott*

Sir Stephen Glynne went to Acton Scott in 1855 and pronounced the church 'uninteresting' – a verdict which today's visitor might find harsh, for it is an appealing church (Fig.22.2), although it has suffered at the hands of 19th-century restorers and does not have outstanding treasures. The building consists of a western tower, south porch, nave, north chapel and chancel; much of the masonry is indeed medieval, but the windows were all renewed in the 19th century. The south porch was added in 1722, and the north chapel in 1820; it is likely that the chancel was rebuilt at that time.

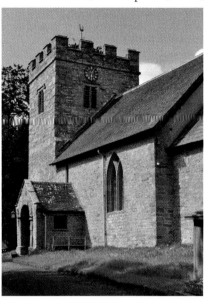

The atmosphere within is homely, with a domestic feel imparted by the west gallery and early 19th-century pews. There are three hatchments on display – two over the gallery and one over the pulpit. The font, reading-desk, pulpit and screen probably date from the early 19th century. In the chancel is an excellent late brass to Thomas Mytton, Elizabeth his wife (d.1571), and nine sons and two daughters. To the north of the altar is a large architectural monument to Edward Acton (d.1747); the sarcophagus has Tuscan columns on each side, a shield and pediment above (Fig.22.3). It was designed by William Baker.

Fig.22.2 St. Margaret, Acton Scott

St. Michael, All Stretton

All Stretton takes the first part of its name from an early owner, but Ekwall says that it is not clear whether the name was OE Aelfred (male) or Aelfgyr (female). All Stretton church is perched uncom-

Fig.22.4 St. Michael, All Stretton (1902)
by Arthur Lloyd-Oswell

Fig.22.3 Acton Scott: monument
to Edward Acton (d.1747),
by William Baker

Fig.22.5 All Stretton: the interior

Fig.22.6 All Saints, Berrington: the south arcade

fortably on a steep hillside next to the road through the village (Fig.22.4). It was built in 1902, the architect being Lloyd-Oswell. The building is of stone, and it consists of a nave and apsidal chancel (Fig.22.5), and a south-east tower with a half-timbered belfry.

All Saints, Berrington**

Berrington means 'homestead by a fort'[4] and in the Domesday Book it is called *Beritune*; Domesday also notes that St. Peter's in Shrewsbury held the church and priest of this manor. The Domesday entry strongly implies the presence here of a Saxon church, and certainly indicates the presence of a church in early Norman times (perhaps reflected in Berrington's remarkable font). There is no trace now of Saxon or Norman building.

All Saints consists of a western tower, nave with south aisle, and chancel. The nave is Early English, divided from the aisle by a low arcade (Fig.22.6), and there is an original lancet window in the north wall. The trussed-rafter roof over the aisle is late medieval in origin. The chancel may be later, for the east window has excellent Decorated tracery. The tower is later still, Perpendicular with a large Perpendicular west window, diagonal buttresses and battlements.

The interior is unfortunately dark, even on a sunny day; this is caused by the glass in the east window, and the organ blocking the window in the south of the chancel. To compound this, heavy curtains block light from the west window. It is a pity that this is so, for there is so much in Berrington church to admire. Pride of place must go to the oldest object in the church, the font (Fig.10.11). This remarkable structure is rudely carved with seven heads around the brim, together with a beast, a lighted candle and a cockerel. The carving probably dates from early Norman times, though White and Barker believe that the bowl itself is the base of a Roman column.[5] As so often in Norman sculpture, the significance of the carvings is quite unclear. The other outstanding treasure is the oaken effigy of a man (Fig.11.1) in a tomb recess in the south aisle. It depicts a knight in 13th-century armour, his head resting on cushions and his crossed legs resting on a lion. His identity is unknown.

At the west end of the nave, high up in the corners, are two remarkable sculptures of the late 12th or 13th centuries. These are demi-figures: the one at the south appears to have a devil on the left shoulder and be wielding a stick in the right hand; the other wears some sort of cape. The significance of these figures is unknown – it has been suggested that they represent the damned (south) and the blessed (north).

There are several monuments, the best being that to Mrs. Greaves (d.1628), a kneeling Jacobean figure almost hidden high up to the east of the organ; and to Rebekkah Williams (d.1827) by John Bacon the Younger (1777-1859), showing a woman kneeling, with her arm on a sarcophagus and an obelisk behind. There is an excellent Victorian pulpit standing on a stem. The stained glass is by David Evans and depicts St. John the Evangelist, St. John the Baptist and St. Peter. It dates from *c*.1820.

St. Margaret, Betton Strange
A small 'Early English' church built in 1858 in the grounds of Betton Hall.

St. James, Cardington**
Cardington is a pretty village in the attractive countryside north of Wenlock Edge. The church (Fig.22.7) consists of a nave without aisles, a chancel, a west tower and a south porch. The oldest part is the nave, and the remains of blocked Norman doorways can readily be discerned in both the north and south walls. It seems that the eastern half of the nave was built in the early 12th century (there is some vestigial herringbone masonry in the north wall) entered by the now blocked door-ways, and that later in the same century the nave was extended westwards. In the south wall there still remains a transverse piece of masonry and a little carving from the doorway. To the west of the blocked south doorway is the good timbered porch, dated 1639 (Fig.7.4), and through this is the main south doorway – a round-headed late Norman structure, with one order of shafts and leaf carving on the eastern capital; the western capital is badly eroded. The door itself is dated 1648. Opposite this doorway on the north side is a further very plain blocked doorway, with the remains of the tympanum above. There is an inter-nally splayed Norman window in both the north and south walls of the nave; the other windows are Decorated insertions. The nave is roofed with tie-beams and collar-beams on arched braces. There is an unusual Jacobean pulpit, carved with a merman on each panel. The font is Victorian.

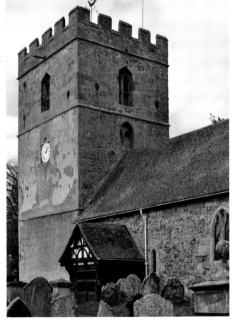

Fig.22.7 St. James, Cardington

The chancel is later than the nave, and externally the masonry is quite different. It is Early English, but the triple lancet in the east wall is not original. The Williams painting (1787) shows a window of two lights, with a round window above. Unusually, the priest's doorway in the chancel is in the north wall. In the south wall is an excellent double piscina, with cusped tracery above. To the east of this is the large monument to Chief Justice Leighton of Plaish (d.1607); this is an impressive Jacobean monument (Fig.11.26), with the deceased depicted lying on his left side on the tomb-chest; the family kneel around the chest, and above is an a broad arch with strapwork. This is the earliest monument in Shropshire where the deceased is shown lying on his side.

The tower is Early English below, with lancet windows, and a Perpendicular upper storey with battlements. It opens to the nave by an Early English tower arch.

St. John the Baptist, Church Preen*

'Preen' is thought to be derived from OE *preon* ('pin' or 'brooch') used to described the shape of the local hill.[6] The settlement is situated 750 feet above sea-level in a nook facing south-east. The churchyard is memorable because of the ancient yew, one of the largest and oldest in the country. At the time of Domesday, the manor of Preen was held by Helgot from Roger, earl of Shrewsbury, but by 1163 it had been granted to Wenlock Priory. A small monastic cell was established here in the 12th century, and survived as a priory until 1534.[7]

The priory ran at right angles from the south side of the church, and the building

survived into the 18th century.[8] It was later demolished and replaced by the present Preen Manor, designed by Norman Shaw in 1870. The result is that the south side of the church cannot be seen because it immediately adjoins the manor. The church is approached from the north-west. It is a very long, narrow church, Early English, with lancet windows throughout, probably built *c*.1200. The east window is composed of three separate lancets of equal height. One of the lancets in the north wall of the nave has a rectangular low-side window beneath. There is a good Jacobean pulpit and reading-desk. The west wall collapsed during restoration in 1866, and the bell-turret and roof of the church date from this time. In *c*.1925 a small battlemented chapel was added to the south of the chancel.

St. Edith, Church Pulverbatch*

Gelling conjectures that the name Pulverbatch, the site of a castle and manor, apparently means 'the valley of the river Pulre'.[9] The manor is recorded in Domesday Book as *Polrebec*. The castle is now represented by a motte and bailey situated half a mile to

Fig.22.8 St. Edith, Church Pulverbatch: the Georgian tower (1773)

234

the south-west of the church; and Morris believed that the church also occupies a mounded and possibly defensive site.[10]

It seems that the medieval church was destroyed by the Welsh before 1414, and the successor building was remodelled in Georgian style in 1773.[11] The 18th-century tower survives (Fig.22.8), and it is the best part of the present church. The architect is unknown, but some believe it may have been T.F. Pritchard.[12] The tower has three stages, with rusticated quoins and similar stonework around the doors and windows. The west doorway was blocked in 1828, but above is an arched west window, and a circular window above that. The bell-openings are arched with Y-tracery, and at the top is a parapet with vases at the corners. An external staircase gives access to the ringers' chamber.

In 1854 the nave, north aisle and chancel were built by Edward Haycock sen. The style is Decorated (the dominant style of the 1850s). The capitals of the arcade are surprisingly restrained. The plain font is Perpendicular in style, but looks Victorian. There is a west gallery and a set of box-pews, the rear ones labelled 'Free'.

St. Laurence, Church Stretton**

The Roman road from Wroxeter to Leintwardine used the pass in the hills, and from this road the name Stretton is derived. Both a church and priest are mentioned in the Domesday Book, so there must have been a Saxon building here, but no trace of this remains.

St. Laurence's is an imposing cruciform church (Fig.6.10) with a complex building history.[13] It consists of a nave and chancel, with a crossing and central tower, and north and south transepts, each with a westward extension, and an organ chamber projecting northwards from the chancel. The nave is Norman and flat Norman buttresses can be seen at the corners. Norman doorways are present in both the north and south walls. The blocked north doorway is external and has been modified; the western jamb is original, but the masonry on the eastern side has been re-set. Above the doorway are a carved stone and a sheila-na-gig. The south doorway now opens into the western extension of the transept and has one order of shafts with volutes on the western capital.

Late in the 12th century the church became cruciform, with the erection of four great piers to support the central tower (Fig.22.9); transepts were added and the chancel rebuilt. The abaci of the capitals are Norman (some of the carving of the capitals has been renewed), but the arches are pointed, indicating Transitional architecture (see p.14). The capitals exhibit stiff-leaf foliage and a series of heads. In the north transept there is an Early English doorway (now opening into the west extension), and a recessed lancet window in the east wall. The extensions to the transepts were built by Pountney Smith in 1866-68; the north extension is now enclosed by a glass partition to form an Emmaus chapel; the south extension is divided from the transept by a Victorian arcade and to the west is a vestry.

The chancel is Early English, though some of the windows are later insertions. There are Early English doorways on both north and south walls: that on the north may originally have led to the tower. On the sill of a square window in the south wall of the chancel, 11 feet above the floor, is a piscina; this indicates that there was an altar on the rood loft which formerly was above the screen dividing the nave and chancel. Some of the windows in both chancel and transepts are later medieval insertions, and the tracery may have been modified in the 17th and 19th centuries.

The roofs of the nave, chancel and north transept are of trussed rafters, without longitudinal purlins or ridge-pieces;[14] some of this may be as early as the 13th century, as at nearby Wistanstow. The roof of the south transept is later, perhaps *c*.1500; there are collar-beams with arched braces, and a single tier of wind-braces. The extensive reredos behind the altar is composed of Jacobean panelling, and further panelling from the former pulpit may be seen at the western end of the nave where the font was previ-

Fig.22.9 St. Laurence, Church Stretton: the interior, with the memorial to three brothers over the crossing

ously sited. The octagonal font is now in the south transept – a rather inappropriate site; it is Perpendicular, and three of the eight faces of the bowl have carvings: shields and geometric patterns with flowers. There is some good stained glass in the chancel: in the east window are figures of Christ flanked by St. Peter and St. John by David Evans of Shrewsbury (?*c*.1819); other windows contain Flemish roundels from the 16th and 17th centuries. Below the ceiling in the crossing (Fig.22.9) hangs a gridiron (St. Laurence's emblem) with twisted pieces of copper to represent flames; this was made by John Skelton in 1971 in memory of three brothers who lost their lives in a fire.

Finally, there is the tower; the lower part is Early English, with lancet windows clearly seen. But when was the upper storey added? It is certainly in the Perpendicular style and most authorities have accepted that it dates from the 15th century. But the Perpendicular style persisted well into the 17th century, and I am uncertain whether this tower is pre- or post-Reformation. The top of the tower is embattled, and there are corner pinnacles and rather decayed gargoyles. On the south-east corner of the tower is a statue of St. Laurence.

St. Andrew and St. Mary, Condover***

The place-name appears to mean 'bank (OE *ufer*) by the river Cound'. In Anglo-Saxon times, Condover was the centre of a very extensive parish, being a minster church served by a college of priests; later there were chapelries in Frodesley, Leebotwood, Longnor and Stapleton, all of which subsequently achieved parochial status. Before the Norman Conquest the manor was held by Edward the Confessor, but afterwards it was part of the extensive holding of Earl Roger. Domesday Book mentions the presence of a priest, so presumably there was a church here at that time. All trace of that building has disappeared, but the north transept of the present church does indeed date from later Norman times. White and Barker believe that masonry from the public buildings of Roman Wroxeter may be incorporated in the fabric of the church.[15]

The later medieval church was substantially destroyed in November 1660 when the tower collapsed, sparing only the Norman north transept, the Early English chancel and perhaps the south transept. The whole of the rest of the church, the nave and the tower, were rebuilt in sandstone in 1662-64 (Fig.22.10); and even at that late date there is no trace of classical influences, the style chosen being late Perpendicular (so-called 'debased'). Thus the aisle windows are straight-headed 'Tudor' windows, and the tower looks late medieval. An engaging and unusual feature of the exterior is the half-timbered gable in the south transept, which may have been built in *c*.1607 by Edward Scriven. The north transept has round-headed Norman windows with nook-shafts.

The interior impresses by its generous width, spanned by a superb hammer-beam roof (Fig.8.15). Apart from the 17th-century western truss, the roof was constructed in 1878.[16] There are no arcades. The font, at the north-east corner of the nave, was carved by Landucci of Shrewsbury, with sculpture of the Baptism of Christ. The chancel was rebuilt in 1867-68 by Reginald Cholmondeley, who was Lord of the Manor, and at the same time the north chancel chapel was added as a mortuary chapel. The chancel has a Decorated style east window, with lancets in the north and south walls.

Fig.22.10 St. Andrew and St. Mary, Condover

The chancel and chapel house a notable collection of monuments, spanning the centuries from Elizabeth to Victoria. In chronological order they are as follows:

1) In the south wall of the chancel, the fine alabaster monument to Thomas Scriven (d.1587) and his wife (Fig.11.16). On the sides of the tomb-chest are seven children.

2) Next to the above, over the vestry door, a bust of Martha Owen (d.1641), with her baby in front. This monument was brought from old St. Chad's church, Shrewsbury.

3) In the north wall of the chapel, a fine two-tiered monument erected by Jane Norton, who died in 1640 (Fig.11.23) Above are depicted Jane Norton and her husband Bonham; below is her eldest brother Sir Roger Owen, shown in armour, and her father Judge Owen, in legal attire. Each couple is kneeling, facing each other across a prayer-desk.

4) Below the east window of the chapel is another excellent monument to Roger Owen and his daughter Catherine (Fig.11.35), usually attributed to the French sculptor Roubiliac (though at least one authority believes that it may be by Sir Henry Cheere).[17] Roger Owen is depicted semi-reclining, with his wife seated at his feet.

5) The kneeling figure which dominates the chapel is Sir Thomas Cholmondeley, cousin of Reginald, who died on his honeymoon in Italy in 1864. The sculptor was George Frederick Watts, whose work was said by Esdaile to be 'not unworthy of the masterpiece of Roubiliac hard by'.

6) To the west is the sad monument to Alice Cholmondeley and her infant daughter. Mrs. Cholmondeley died in childbirth in 1868, and the monument is the work of her husband Reginald.

St. Peter, Cound**

The village takes its name from the Cound Brook, the name being said by Ekwall to be identical with the British names of Kent and Kennet.[18] In Domesday Book, the manor is recorded as *Cuneet*.

The splendid church of St. Peter consists of a western tower, nave with north and south aisles, and chancel, built at various times in the past six hundred years. The rather stumpy tower has a good Decorated west window in the lower stage, but above is clearly Perpendicular, with battlements, pinnacles and gargoyles. The nave, chancel arch and south aisle are Early English, with a south arcade of circular piers and simple moulded capitals (Fig.22.11). The south doorway is of the same period, with a good stone porch and wooden roof. The fine door is late medieval, and has a remarkable knocker, a rare survival.

The north aisle is rather poor Victorian work, but the chancel, also Victorian, is spacious and impressive. It was rebuilt by S. Pountney Smith in 1862. The east window is Decorated in character, and is filled with some excellent stained glass, the work of C.E. Kempe. There are some medieval floor-tiles in front of the altar. There is are several monuments, the best being in the north wall of the chancel. The finest is to a former rector, Edward Cressett, late bishop of Llandaff (d.1755). It is probably by T.F. Pritchard of Shrewsbury.[19] The inscription is placed between a decorative panel below, of red marble edged in white, with three winged heads of cherubs in white marble; above is a concave-sided plate with rococo foliage and adorned with the bishop's mitre, crozier etc. (Fig.11.34).[20] Another remarkable monument is that to Robert Cressett (d.1728): this features a skull flanked by bats' wings. Other monuments are in the north and south aisles.

There is a fine Jacobean pulpit dated 1633, with an unusual backboard, and some panelling of the same era is displayed around the chancel; some of this may have come originally from Cound Hall. Above the chancel arch are the remnants of a medieval wall-painting showing part of a Doom, including a crucifixion scene, with Christ in Majesty above. In the south aisle is a medieval chest, a piscina in the south wall, a carved head in the wall which probably was originally a corbel, and some fragments of medieval stained glass in the east window. At the west end is an excellent Norman font, c.1150, with a series of rosettes

Fig.22.11 St. Peter, Cound: the arcade and chancel; note the remains of the Doom over the chancel arch

around the bowl and a rim of foliage above (Fig.10.9). Beneath the tower arch is part of the old screen, rather crude work with solid panels, not open tracery, later painted with the Ten Commandments, Lord's Prayer and Creed. The roofs of the nave and south aisle are of the trussed-rafter type, and, though restored, largely date from the later Middle Ages.

Christ Church, Cressage*

The place-name possibly reflects a very early Christian site, for it means 'Christ's oak'; Ekwall comments that this may indicate an oak at which the gospel was preached by missionaries. Another intriguing fact indicating a very early Christian site is the dedication of the medieval church to the Celtic St. Samson (c.485-565). The VCH comments[21] that it is very unlikely that a dedication to a Celtic saint would have been made after the end of the 7th century. (In 664 the Synod of Whitby determined that henceforth the Roman form of Christianity rather than the Celtic would prevail in England.)

The medieval church of St. Samson, painted by Williams in 1785 (Fig.2.2), was subject to repeated flooding by the nearby river Severn and in 1841 a new church was built on higher land. The architect was Edward Haycock sen., and the church was erected in the rather starved Early English style prevalent in the 1840s. Externally the church is unpromising: it is rather austere, with a monotonous series of lancet windows and a thin west tower. The interior, however, is a delight: there is a nave, a very shallow chancel (*The Ecclesiologist* would not have been impressed) and a west gallery on cast-iron piers. The greatest treasure is the stained glass in the east window, the work of David Evans and paid for by the Reverend Richard Scott in 1843 (*cf* Harley, p.255). Here Evans eschewed the garish colours he used elsewhere and incorporates in the windows roundels of stained glass in the Flemish style, which repay close study. Evans' signature may be found in the lower right-hand corner. The other fine artefact is the octagonal pulpit (Fig.14.4) reassembled from panelling from St. Samson's, bearing the date 1635.

St. Michael, Cwm Head

Situated at the head of a tributary valley of the Onny, Cwm Head church must have been inaccessible when it was built in 1845, and is still remote, with only a few cottages nearby. It was built in the neo-Norman style, an idiom which achieved a limited popularity in the 1840s (*cf* Llanymynech), and consists of a nave, an apsidal chancel, and a thin north-east tower. The architect was H.J. Whitling.

St. Edward, Dorrington

Dorrington was constituted an ecclesiastical parish in 1845, having previously been part of Condover. The church was built at his own expense by J.T. Hope of Netley Hall.[22] The architect was Edward Haycock sen., who did a competent job. In the 1840s the Early English style was dominant in Shropshire, and Dorrington was built in conformity with this. It is a handsome church, built of ashlar. Lancet windows are used throughout, and the sole exception to the Early English style is the attractive tower, which bears an arcaded parapet, pinnacles at the corners, and a recessed spire (Fig.6.15). Inside there is a west gallery, a stone reredos depicting the Adoration of the Magi, a hammer-beam roof, and one hatchment.

St. Mark, Frodesley*

Frodesley, an attractive village off the old Roman road Watling Street West, was originally a chapelry of Condover, later becoming an independent parish. The medieval church was demolished in 1809 because the building had become unsafe, and in its place was built a Georgian church of sandstone, with wide arched windows, pilasters at the angles and an endearing western bell-turret. Unfortunately, the effect was spoiled by the addition in 1859 of an incongruous north aisle, with lancet windows.

The interior is notable for its box-pews, panelled chancel, and west gallery. The pulpit and reading-desk incorporate some 17th- and 18th-century panelling. There is a hatchment in the north wall of the chancel. The rough stone font appears to be medieval; there is also a pedestal font installed in 1829.

St. Andrew, Hope Bowdler*

In Domesday Book, the manor is recorded as Fordritishope, 'hope' meaning valley. Bowdler is derived from a Norman family, de Bulers (*cf* Ashford Bowdler). The medieval church was replaced in 1863 by the present building, which was designed by the Shrewsbury architect S. Pountney Smith (see p.36) and built of Soudley banded sandstone.[22] It is rather austere for its time, built mainly in the Early English style with lancet windows throughout (Fig.22.12). The

Fig.22.12 St. Andrew, Hope Bowdler (1863) by S. Pountney Smith

pyramid roof of the tower and the roof of the nave and chancel are enlivened with bands of alternating red and grey slates. Inside, both the chancel arch and the tower arch have rounded piers, with plain capitals and scallop carving. There is a good Jacobean pulpit, dated 1639, and some interesting glass including a few medieval and Flemish components in a window opposite the south door. There are also some windows by Kempe.

St. John the Baptist, Kenley*

Kenley church has not had a good press: Sir Stephen Glynne dismissed it as 'very poor', and Cranage concurred – 'a poor medieval structure' – but proceeded to extol the fine views to the north and west. And indeed both authors commented favourably on the roof and the pulpit.

And that just about sums up Kenley. It is a plain medieval church, of uncertain date, consisting of an undivided nave and chancel and a western tower. The tower is low, with just a few slit-like openings. The nave and chancel probably date from the late 12th century – there is a blocked round-headed doorway in the north wall of the nave, and on the north wall of the chancel the jambs of a further blocked doorway are visible. The east window, of two lights, is a Decorated insertion, and other windows date from the restoration of the church in 1854. There is an excellent chancel roof, consisting of collar-beams on arched braces, with wind-braces laterally; the nave roof is simpler. The best feature is the pulpit – a fine Jacobean structure complete with its tester.

Langley chapel**

Langley chapel (of no known dedication) stands alone in a field; disused and neglected for many years, it was the first church to come under the care of the Ministry of Works in 1915, and it is now administered by English Heritage. The parish of Ruckley and Langley apparently had two chapels in the Middle Ages,[24] but from Elizabethan times we hear only of Langley. Two dates are recorded – 1564 on the outside of the building, and 1601 on a roof beam – so it appears that Langley is that great rarity, a church built in Elizabethan times.

The chapel consists of a combined nave and chancel, with a weather-boarded bell-turret above the west gable. The west window is a rather wide lancet, the east has three stepped lancets with Y-tracery at the top. The bell-turret is supported by a timber construction at the western end of the nave. The division between nave and chancel is marked by a tie-beam, with roofs of different construction on either side – trussed rafters in the chancel, and collar-beams on arched braces and wind-braces in the nave. On the south side, a plaster frieze with Tudor ornamentation connects the roof with the wall of the nave.

It is, of course, the interior furnishings that gives Langley its distinction, for they provide an almost unique record of the arrangements favoured in Puritan circles at the beginning of the 17th century. There are medieval tiles on the floor of the sanctuary, with tracery designs and shields. The communion table, now, alas, a modern replica since the original was stolen, is surrounded on three sides (north, east and south) with a communion rail – a plain top with book-rest and boards for kneeling. (The very strictest Puritans would have had a bench on the west side also.) All the other furnishings are original (Fig.22.13) and include rough benches with poppy-heads, a movable pulpit, a musicians' pew and a large, square reader's desk.

At Langley, the 17th century comes to life; it is a very moving interior, comparable only to some of the early Quaker meeting-houses. But here, extreme Puritanism was still comprehended within the Elizabethan settlement – the Church of England was meant to include all shades of religious opinion, from Laudian Anglo-Catholics to Puritans. It is a shame that it did not continue thus!

Fig.22.13 Langley chapel: the interior furnishings

241

St. Mary, Leebotwood*

According to Gelling,[25] Leebotwood means a place in Botwood where Haughmond Abbey was making woodland clearings in the second half of the 12th century. This would fit in with the fact that the manor in the Domesday Book was known simply as *Botewde*, *leah* (a forest clearing) being added later.

The church is built on glacial moraine, which probably provided a more secure foundation than the alluvial soil of the village centre along the Shrewsbury Road.[26] It is a simple rectangular building, with undivided nave and chancel, and a plain western tower completed in 1829. Presumably most of the masonry of nave and chancel is medieval (it is conjectured that the church was built *c*.1200),[27] but the windows – all lancets – have been renewed. The south doorway, probably Early English, was blocked and converted into a wide window when the tower was added. The interior (Fig.22.14) is rendered homely by the profusion of 18th-century furnishings and fittings. A set of box-pews, panelled pulpit and west gallery are all of this period. The roof is a mixture of collar-beams on arched braces and collar-beams supported by queen-posts. On the west side of one of the trusses are carvings in low relief of winged dragons, with a head at each end.[28] An extensive medieval wall-painting of the Nativity was uncovered in 1976. There are several monuments to the Corbetts in the chancel, the best being to Uvedale Corbett (d.1701). The stained glass in the east window is probably by David Evans, *c*.1854.

Fig.22.14 St. Mary, Leebotwood: view from the chancel – box-pews, west gallery, wall-painting

All Saints, Little Stretton

This is a picturesque church built in 1903 (Fig.22.15), painted to look half-timbered.[29] The whole interior is wooden.

Fig.22.15 All Saints, Little Stretton (1903)

St. Mary, Longnor**

Longnor (meaning 'long alder copse') derives its name from an alder copse on the banks of the river Cound near the church.[30] St. Mary's is that rarity among English parish churches – a building entirely of one medieval style, in this case, Early English. It was originally a chapel in the parish of Condover, and in the Middle Ages it was adjacent to the manor house, the original site of which can be seen as a mound under the trees near the south end of the church. The ubiquitous Corbets took over the manor in the 13th century, and in the 17th century the surrounding village was cleared to provide a suitable setting for their new hall which was built in 1670. The Corbets destroyed or moved other villages for parks at Acton Reynald, Moreton Corbet and Adderley.

Thanks to this clearance, St. Mary's is now attractively situated overlooking the grounds of Longnor Hall. It is a very simple sandstone building, just an undivided nave and chancel, with a 19th-century western bell-turret. It was

Fig.22.16 St. Mary, Longnor: the west façade

built *c*.1280 and has been scarcely altered since. Both east and west windows (Fig.22.16) consist of three lancets, with uncusped circles above (*cf* Acton Burnell) – a feature of building seen towards the end of the Early English period and an indication that Early English would soon give way to Decorated. The tracery of the east window is original, that of the west window was renewed in wood in 1840. The windows in the north and south walls are all groups of lancets, six on the south and eight on the north; each group is surmounted by a continuous hood-moulding externally, and there are fine cylindrical mouldings within. The roof (Fig.8.3) is of trussed rafters, plain and original.

The interior (Fig.22.17) is notable for the wooden furnishings. The communion rail and oak reredos date from the 17th century, and the set of box-pews is dated 1723. There is a squire's and a vicar's pew, and a plain pulpit and reader's desk, all

Fig.22.17 Longnor: box-pews, pulpit and chancel

dating from about this period. There is a large late-18th-century west gallery, which is entered by an external flight of stone steps. When this gallery was enlarged in 1840, the north and south doors were blocked and a new western doorway added. There is a piscina in the usual position in the chancel, but remarkably a second piscina was discovered in the south wall of the nave, just to the west of the junction with the chancel, indicating that there was a second altar here. Both the piscinae were uncovered in 1980 when plaster was stripped from the walls of the church. Several hatchments of the Corbet family hang in the nave.

St. Michael and All Angels, Pitchford***

The manor takes its name from the presence here of mineral pitch, and a bituminous well was in existence until recent times. Architecturally, Pitchford church is a simple building; St. Michael's earns its stars because of its monuments and for its lovely setting beside Pitchford Hall and its lake.

It is known that a chapel was present at Little Eton, Pitchford in the early 12th century[31] and the Norman remains found in Pitchford church make it likely that this was the site of that chapel; for in the north wall of Pitchford church is a small round-headed Norman window, and beneath it and to the west of it is herring-bone masonry – a style of building which had disappeared by about 1120-30. There is also a round-headed door in the north wall of the chancel. The rest of the church is basically Early English, with lancet windows throughout. Decorated windows were inserted in the south wall of the nave and chancel early in the 14th century. The east end of the church was rebuilt in 1719 – note the classical columns outside – and the present east windows date from a later modification in 1819. There is a short western bell-turret.

Fig.22.18 St. Michael, Pitchford: the interior, looking east

The interior (Fig.22.18) shows the nave and chancel undivided, without aisles, the walls being lined by a series of hatchments relating to the Ottley family. At the west end is a plain tub-shaped font of uncertain age, probably 12th- or 13th-century. The organ is a notable instrument, from the early 19th century. There is a fine Jacobean reading-desk and pulpit, with tester above. Just west of the pulpit is some medieval glass representing the head of Christ. In the chancel are some medieval encaustic tiles, and the communion rail dates from the 17th century. Behind the altar, part of the Perpendicular rood screen has been fashioned into a reredos – note the delicate tracery along the upper margin and the vertical linen-fold panelling below.

The finest monument is the oaken effigy of a knight dating from the late 13th century (Fig.11.2). The effigy, 7 feet long and carved from a single piece of oak, is thought to be of Sir John de Pitchford. He is shown in full armour, in the act of pulling the sword-blade from the scabbard. His feet rest on a lion. The effigy lies on an arcaded tomb-chest carved with shields of arms.

The other excellent monuments in Pitchford are the four 16th-century incised alabaster slabs (Fig.11.11) now displayed vertically around the chancel, dating from 1529, 1534, 1578 and 1586. They vividly portray the changes in costume of the period – the early ladies have a pedimental head-dress, the later ones a full Elizabethan ruff. The quality of all four is good – the earlier pair appear to be the work of the Burton on Trent alabasterers Richard and Gilbert Royley, the later ones are signed or initialled by John Tarbrook of Bewdley.[32]

St. Thomas, Ryton, near Condover
A small church built in 1896 in the parish of Condover.

St. Michael, Smethcott*
Smethcott (meaning 'the smith's cottage') is basically a medieval church substantially rebuilt in 1850. It stands on a knoll, apart from other habitations, and consists of just nave and chancel, with a south porch and a western bell-turret (Fig.22.19). From the Norman period survive a blocked north doorway with plain tympanum and a similar priest's doorway in the south wall of the chancel. On either side of the priest's door two short strips of Norman masonry displaying nail-head ornament

Fig.22.19 St. Michael, Smethcott

are embedded in the wall. A small round-headed window in the north wall of the chancel has also been preserved. But the most interesting ancient survival is the remarkable oblong font – a plain elongated bowl of quite indeterminate date – it could be Norman, or much earlier. The nave roof, with hammer-beams and collar-beams on arched braces, was partly constructed from old timbers by William Hill.[33]

St. John the Baptist, Stapleton*
Stapleton is an ancient manor, recorded in Domesday Book as *Hundeslit*. The church was probably built around 1200;[34] its most remarkable, if not unique, feature is that it was a two-storeyed building, for reasons unknown. 'A piscina high on the south wall of the chancel confirms that the church was originally on the upper floor, the ground floor presumably forming an undercroft'.[35] The date when the two storeys were transformed into one is not known. The western tower was added in 1832.

The result of these changes is a very tall church (Fig.22.20), with two tiers of windows. Below are narrow straight-headed vertical slits, widely splayed within, four on the north side and one on the south. The walls in the lower storey are four feet thick. Above, the walls are only three feet thick, and there are lancet and Decorated windows, the latter dating only from the 19th century. There is a priest's door in the lower storey, now half-buried, and a blocked doorway on the north side. The altar (Fig.14.18) is very wide, and is composed of handsome Jacobean panelling, as is the reredos. On either

Fig.22.20 St. John the Baptist, Stapleton

side stand two tall wooden German candlesticks brought from Nuremberg, dated *c*.1500.

St. Michael, Woolstaston*

The place-name means 'Wulfstan's settlement', and it is recorded in Domesday Book as being held by Robert Fitz Corbet, from Earl Roger. It is a pretty village, 800 feet above sea level on the north-eastern slopes of the Long Mynd, and St. Michael's stands graciously back from the village lane surrounded by attractive gardens.

The church is a simple Early English building, of the late 12th and early 13th centuries; this explains the juxtaposition of round-headed and pointed arches which are a feature of the building. It consists of nave and chancel only, with an attractive Victorian bell-turret and spirelet (Fig.22.21). All the windows are lancets; but the priest's doorway in the south wall of the chancel has a rounded arch, with chamfered jambs. The main south doorway has a pointed arch. The finest treasure is the font – a very curious example with two bowls, one set upon the other (Fig.10.2). The upper bowl is plain and probably Norman; some have speculated that the lower one may be Roman in origin from nearby Wroxeter.

In the chancel is a piscina with a pointed arch in the south wall, and an aumbry with a round-headed arch in the north. The nave roof is of the trussed-rafter type, and is probably medieval; the roof of the chancel is of the hammer-beam type, dating from the restoration of 1864-66. From this time also comes the excellent woodwork of the pulpit, lectern, reading-desk and communion rails by William Hill.

Fig.22.21 St. Michael, Woolstaston

246

23

Corvedale and Wenlock Edge

Barrow**
Benthall**
Bourton*
Broadstone
Broseley*
Culmington*
Diddlebury**
Easthope*
Eaton-under-Heywood***
Harley*
Holdgate***

Hughley***
Linley**
Much Wenlock***
Munslow**
Rushbury*
Sheinton*
Shipton*
Stanton Long*
Tugford**
Willey*

St. Giles, Barrow**

Barrow is one of the few churches in the county which is partly of Anglo-Saxon origin. The name is OE for 'grove'. Curiously enough, Barrow is not mentioned in Domesday Book – but it is well known that many churches in existence in Saxon times are not recorded there. Throughout the Middle Ages, Barrow was subject to Wenlock Priory, which had been founded in the 7th century.

St. Giles is situated on a lonely windswept hillside, with just a farm and a cottage for company, and little evidence of other habitation. Its survival for over a thousand years seems little short of miraculous. It would be difficult to say that the church is beautiful, but it impresses because of its very great antiquity, its plainness and simplicity, and perhaps above all because it is still a place of Christian worship.

The church (Fig.23.1) consists of chancel, nave and tower, and building was in that order. The chancel is clearly the oldest part; externally, on the north wall of the chancel, are the remains of a strip pilaster, and to the east of this a Saxon window, splayed both internally and externally (Fig.23.2).

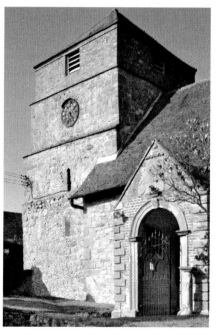

Fig.23.1 St. Giles, Barrow

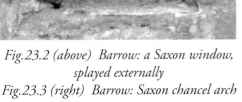

Fig.23.2 (above) Barrow: a Saxon window,
splayed externally
Fig.23.3 (right) Barrow: Saxon chancel arch

The east wall of the chancel was rebuilt three times in the 19th century. The south wall of the chancel is Saxon, but inserted into it is an early Norman window and just below this a late Norman priest's door which just cuts into the earlier window above. Internally, the very plain chancel arch is Saxon, with what Pevsner calls 'the characteristic square hood mould' (Fig.23.3); the openings on either side of the arch are Victorian. Cranage thought that the chancel might date from the 8th century; but Taylor and Taylor[1] felt that in view of the doubly-splayed north window and the pilaster strip, a 10th-century date is more likely; while the Victoria County History opted for the early or mid-11th century.[2]

Next is the nave, probably constructed in the late 11th century, with round-headed windows in the north and south walls, and a Norman south doorway, with a plain tympanum above. (It is known that this was previously carved.) There is also a blocked Norman doorway in the north wall of the nave. The tower arch at the west end of the nave was the original west doorway of the church, and if one goes into the present ground floor of the tower, one sees above the doorway an 11th-century Norman tympanum, with rows of simple geometrical patterns (Fig.9.11). The tower came last, probably about 1100. The font is a plain Norman tub, and in the north wall of the nave is a hatchment. In the later Middle Ages a north chapel or transept was added; this was rebuilt in brick in 1688 and in stone in 1894. The attractive south porch was built in 1705. Outside the porch is a curious stone pedestal-like structure of unknown significance. It has been suggested that this may be part of a pre-Saxon British cromlech.[3]

Fig.23.4 St. Bartholomew, Benthall (c.1667), next to Benthall Hall

St. Bartholomew, Benthall**

The place-name appears to mean 'nook' or valley where bent-grass grows.[4] At the time of the Domesday survey it was probably part of the manor of Much Wenlock,[5] and during the Middle Ages the chapel at Benthall, dedicated to St. Brice, was dependent on Wenlock Priory. This chapel was destroyed in 1645 during the Civil War and the present church was built *c.*1667.

It is thus a simple 17th-century church (Fig.23.4), plain and unpretentious, consisting of a nave and chancel undivided, and a western bell-turret. It stands next to Benthall Hall (now owned by the National Trust), a short distance from the rather scattered commu-

nity. The almost square nave windows have flattened arches outside; the east window was 'gothicised' in 1884. Later a western apse was added. There is a west gallery and a hammer-beam roof (Fig.23.5). The pulpit and reading-desk are Jacobean. The font is probably also 17th-century. In the chancel is a monument to Ralph Brown (d.1707), with scrolls and an open segmental pediment (Fig.11.31). There are some cast-iron slabs in the churchyard.

Fig.23.5 Benthall: the interior from the chancel

Holy Trinity, Bourton*

Bourton means 'settlement by a burg or fortified manor'. Domesday Book stated that the manor was held by Wenlock Priory, and 'Edric from it. Aelfric, his father, held it', and added enigmatically, 'he could not withdraw from the Church'.

The church consists of a nave and chancel, with a Victorian north aisle, and a timber-framed belfry. The south doorway is Norman, but much of the rest of the fabric dates from the 1844 alterations. There is a west gallery. The handsome hatchment in the north aisle is of Sir Robert Lawley, Baron Wenlock (d.1834). There is an excellent Jacobean pulpit (Fig.14.3), richly carved, and similar work may be seen on the lectern and reading-desk.

Broadstone chapel

If you love the remote and obscure, then Broadstone chapel is for you. It is a chapel of ease in the parish of Munslow in Corvedale. At the time of Domesday, Broadstone was part of the manor of Stanway in the parish of Rushbury, but at some time later it was transferred to Munslow.[6] The chapel stands alone in a field, approached by a track from the lane leading from Broadstone Farm on the Corvedale Road to Holdgate and then by a public footpath. It is of uncertain antiquity – all the windows are now lancets, but they were not shown thus in the Williams painting of 1790, and they must have been inserted during the restoration of 1842-4. Cranage stated that before this time the chapel was used as a farm building, with services only twice a year. The eastern bell-turret and the south doorway are also probably Victorian. The roof is composed of tie-beams and queen-posts, and there is a rude Jacobean pulpit and communion-table.

All Saints, Broseley*

The wooded parish of Broseley was transformed by the development of coal-mining in the late 16th and early 17th centuries, and again in the 18th century when John Wilkinson developed the first steam engine in his ironworks. The Williams painting of 1791 shows the parish church of St. Leonard with a medieval tower with battlements, and a nave and chancel of 1710-16, built presumably to cater for the expanding population. This church in turn became inadequate and it was replaced by the present building in 1843-45, the architect being Harvey Eginton.

All Saints is the finest early Victorian church in the county, a stately building constructed throughout in an authentic Perpendicular style (Fig.23.6). The only unhappy feature is the upper stage of the tower, which

Fig.23.6 All Saints, Broseley (1843-5) by Harvey Eginton

appears top-heavy. The church consists of a west tower, two-storey porch, nave with aisles and chancel. There are five bays in the arcades, the piers multishafted with rather plain capitals. The style is restrained (Fig.23.7), without the excesses common 20 years later. The stained glass in the west window by Kempe is unfortunately hidden by the organ.

All Saints, Culmington*

In Domesday Book, Culmington (recorded as *Comintone*) was held by wild Edric from Earl Roger. The meaning of the place-name is uncertain: it seems most likely that 'Culm' means 'winding river' (from the Welsh *cwlwm*). Culmington is indeed on the winding river Corve (which may have been called Culm), so the name may mean 'the settlement of dwellers on the Culm'.[7]

All Saints' church (Fig.23.8) consists of an undivided nave and chancel, and a west tower with a truncated stone broach spire surmounted by a structure in aluminium erected in 1969. The

Fig.23.7 Broseley: 'Perpendicular' arcade and clerestory in this Victorian church

tower has narrow lancet windows and is clearly 13th-century, the lower part of the spire being added about a century later. However, the spire was never completed – a painting by Williams in 1790 shows the small spire covered with oak shingles. Between 1790 and 1796 the spire was covered with lead sheet, but by the 1960s the lead had become crystalline and water was wreaking havoc with the masonry; so the present structure was fabricated, being put in place by helicopter.

The nave is unusual in that in both north and south walls there is herring-bone masonry (Fig.3.5). This is usually taken to indicate a date between *c*.1050 and 1125 (i.e. late Saxon or early Norman). In the north wall at Culmington there is a small round-headed window, deeply splayed internally, which confirms an early Norman date for this work. It is strange that neither Cranage nor Pevsner (1958) comment on the herring-bone masonry; indeed Cranage asserted that he could

Fig.23.8 All Saints, Culmington

find no evidence of 12th-century work here. The rest of the nave and chancel are Early English like the tower, with tall narrow lancet windows, and two Decorated windows inserted later.

Internally, the church is remarkably light. The roof of the nave is good, with collar-beams and wind-braces. Between the nave and chancel is the screen, part of which is original late Perpendicular (the bressumer and some of the tracery on the north side) and the rest restored in the 19th century. Just to the west of the screen is a piscina, indicating that in the Middle Ages there was an altar nearby. Above may be seen the stairs leading to the former rood loft; this was lit by a small rectangular window. Externally, a projection corresponding to these stairs may be seen in Fig.23.8, where it looks like a buttress (*cf* Munslow).

In the south wall of the chancel is a double piscina, and to the west of this is a fine 14th-century tomb-recess, with two rows of ball-flower ornament, and then a square opening (a low-side window) which has been walled up until recently – its significance is uncertain. There are a number of monuments in the chancel, but none is of any great merit.

St. Peter, Diddlebury**

The name denotes its Saxon origin, being the burgh (or settlement) of Duddela, an Old English personal name. Diddlebury is one of the handful of Shropshire churches which is indisputably of Saxon origin; and it is therefore not surprising that the church is recorded in the Domesday book under the manor of Corfham – one of only about 20 churches mentioned in the county.

The church (Fig.23.9) consists of a heavily buttressed west tower, a nave with south aisle and south porch, and a chancel with north transept now forming a vestry and organ-chamber. The Saxon work is in the north wall of the nave and part of the base of the tower. Externally note the masonry of the north wall of the nave: here are well-dressed stones ascending to a height of 15 feet; the masonry above this is later. Along the base of the north wall is a triple plinth, which continues westward under the adjoining part of the north wall of the tower. In the wall is a blocked round-headed doorway (Fig.3.4), with big blocks forming the imposts and a raised moulding which frames the doorway and its arch. To the west of this, note the Saxon window, which is a small round-headed window splayed both internally and externally. This may be compared with a true Norman window a few feet further east, which is splayed internally only. Internally, the most striking feature is the herring-bone masonry (Fig.3.2) which may be seen in the north wall of the nave and extending into the west wall of the tower. In a window

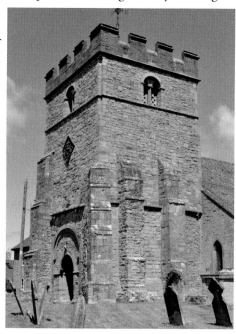

Fig.23.9 St. Peter, Diddlebury

in the nave are fragments of a Saxon cross, with interlace and other carving. The nave was extended eastwards later in the Norman era.

In the west wall of the early Norman tower is a very large partially blocked arch set above a Transitional west doorway (Fig.23.10). The significance of the blocked Norman arch is unknown, but it probably led to some sort of fore-building which was later demolished.[8] Newman has recently suggested that there was probably a Saxon porch at the west end and that this was grandly enlarged in the early 12th century, and heightened into a full-blown tower later in the century.[9] The top stage of the tower is Perpendicular. The tower arch is Transitional, and the arcade separating the nave from the south aisle is Early English. The south wall itself is 19th-century. The octagonal font is Perpendicular.

The chancel is 12th-century, with Norman windows in both north and south walls. The east window is Victorian Decorated, but genuine early Decorated windows may be seen in the

Fig.23.10 Diddlebury: the Transitional west doorway; what was the purpose of the huge blocked arch above?

north and south walls of the chancel; in the north window may be seen some medieval glass representing the Crucifixion. Also in the chancel are two Decorated recesses with ball-flower ornament.

St. Peter, Easthope*

Along Wenlock Edge there are seven settlements whose name includes the Saxon *hop* (meaning 'secluded valley'); these are from east to west Presthope, Easthope, Wilderhope, Millichope, Middlehope, Westhope and Dinchope.[10] Easthope has a lovely situation, with a raised circular churchyard, which may indicate a pre-Christian site of worship.

The small church is very attractive from the outside, with its half-timbered western bell-turret (Fig.23.11). The nave and chancel are undivided. The church was nearly destroyed by fire in 1928; parts of the walls survived and the building was reconstructed and reopened the next year. A narrow splayed window in the north wall may originally have been Norman; the east window is Decorated,

Fig.23.11 St. Peter, Easthope, rebuilt after a fire in 1928

and there is an Elizabethan or Tudor straight-headed window in the south wall. The 18th-century communion-rails survived the fire. There is an attractive screen. The most impressive artefact is the very rare hour-glass attached to the pulpit, and dated 1662. It consists of a wrought-iron bracket with a preaching-glass within (Fig.14.8). Hour-glasses were introduced in the 17th century in many churches to measure the duration of the parson's sermons, but few survive. There are two stained glass windows by Kempe and Co.

St. Edith, Eaton-under-Heywood***

The place-name is rather surprising, for Eaton means 'settlement by a river', and this Eaton is merely on a small tributary of the river Onny. But Eaton-under-Heywood is set in glorious countryside at the foot of Wenlock Edge and the church of St. Edith is a little-known treasure. St. Edith is said to have been the daughter of King Egbert of Wessex (reigned 802-839). He founded a Benedictine nunnery in the Forest of Arden which was moved to Polesworth in Warwickshire and dedicated to St. Edith.

Domesday Book does not mention Eaton, but it does include the manor of Ticklerton, one mile from Eaton.

Fig.23.12 St. Edith, Eaton-under-Heywood

Ticklerton was originally fairly central to Wenlock Priory's large manor, but the priory's acquisition of Upper Millichope (*c.*1115) perhaps made Eaton more central to those estates, and so it became the most eligible location for the church of a parish of widely separated hamlets.[11]

The nave and tower of the church are Norman, the chancel Early English. The tower (Fig.23.12) is unusually sited at the south-east corner of the nave, and the bell-openings are of two round-arched lights separated by a dividing shaft and under a larger rounded arch. The tower opens into the nave by an arch, and also has a south doorway with a pointed arch. The upper part of the tower has Perpendicular battlements and short pinnacles.

There are two Norman windows in the north wall of the nave and one in the south; other windows are insertions of the 14th and 15th centuries, renewed in 1869; the two-light west window looks original. The roof of the nave shows tie-beams, with collar-beams on arched braces. Between this and the lower roof of the chancel is a tympanum painted in the 1860s with the arms of local landowners. Along the feet of the rafters are a series of carved wooden faces, some of them 'green men' of uncertain antiquity. There is an excellent pulpit with a sounding-board, dated 1670. The lower part of the pulpit is earlier, with linenfold, and possibly dates from the late 16th century. There is a plain tub font, probably Norman.

Fig.23.13 *Eaton-under-Heywood: life-size oaken effigy in a Decorated recess, with ball-flower adornment*

In the Early English chancel are three widely spaced plain lancet windows of equal height – a most unusual arrangement. These windows were restored in 1869, and it is not certain that this represents the original design. The excellent roof of the chancel is of low pitch, panelled and embossed (Fig.8.10). In the north wall of the chancel is a 14th-century recess with ball-flower decoration (Fig.23.13); this contains a life-size oaken effigy. The deceased is clad in hood and overcoat, and wears pointed shoes.

St. Mary, Harley*

Harley (meaning 'hares' wood') at the time of the Domesday Book was part of the extensive holding of Helgot, who gave his name to Holdgate (qv). The medieval church was demolished in 1845, leaving only the tower, the rest of the building being by S. Pountney Smith (see p.36).

The tower is mainly Perpendicular and the body of the church is a rather conventional building, with lancet windows in the chancel and Perpendicular windows in the nave. There are, however, several interesting features. The oldest by far is the large, plain, presumably Norman font retrieved from the previous church. Also from the previous church, and the finest artefact in the present building, is an excellent late 15th-century brass to the Lacon family. This is now set into the floor of the chancel, just to the right of the altar. It depicts a man in armour and his lady in costume of the day, and below their eight sons and five daughters. On either side of the chancel arch are two hatchments of the Harnage family. Finally, in the east window is some excellent stained glass by David Evans; it contains roundels executed in the Flemish style very similar to that in nearby Cressage, and like the glass at Cressage it was the gift of the Reverend Richard Scott, dated 1846.

Holy Trinity, Holdgate***

This wonderful church has been under threat: the parish has but 32 residents and clearly the task of caring for the building is daunting. Fortunately, grants from English Heritage and the Shropshire Historic Churches Trust have come to the rescue.

At the time of the Domesday Book, Holdgate and the neighbouring manor of Stanton Long were both known as *Stantune*; Holdgate was one of the small number of manors in Shropshire mentioned as possessing both a church and a priest, so presumably there was a Saxon church here. The name *Stantune* was later given to Stanton Long. Holdgate took its name from Helgot, a Norman who held the manor and later built a castle; the latter also is mentioned in Domesday Book. During the Middle Ages, the parish was served by three portionists (priest, deacon and sub-deacon) who formed a secular college,[12] an arrangement which survived the Reformation – the sub-deacon's portion lasted until the 1630s, the deacon's until 1888.

Both castle and church were built on the highest point of a ridge over-looking Corvedale.[13] The oldest part of the present church is the nave, dating from the 12th century; for high on the west wall is a Norman window which now looks into the tower. The ornate south doorway (Fig.9.2) is outstanding: the capitals of the shafts are carved with volutes, scallop and foliage, and

Fig.23.14 Holy Trinity, Holdgate: the tower

there is also slight ornamentation of the bases. The arch is complex: the inner moulding has a variety of large beak-heads, next comes a frieze of arches and other patterns, then zigzag, then an outer hood-mould of pellet on the right and curious 'arrow' shapes on the left. The lower part of the rather squat tower (Fig.23.14) is 13th-century, the upper part

Fig.23.15 Holdgate: the interior looking west

Perpendicular, with battlements and gargoyles. The chancel also probably dates from the 13th century, with two Early English lancets in the east wall. Other windows in both nave and chancel are later Decorated insertions. High on the outer south wall of the chancel is a sheila-na-gig (Fig.9.15), a pagan fertility symbol (*cf* Church Stretton and Tugford).

The outstanding font (Fig.10.12) bears some resemblance to the work of the Herefordshire School of carvers, particularly the font at Chaddesley Corbett (Worcestershire) which also shows serpents. The upper moulding is the cable ornament, and around the bowl are complex carvings of interlace and serpents, below which is some foliage. Around the stem is upright zigzag, and at the base are four rather curious heads.

There is some notable woodwork: some of the benches in the nave are medieval (Fig.23.15), and there is a carved Jacobean family pew, somewhat damaged (*cf* Cleobury North).

St. John the Baptist, Hughley***

Hughley is not mentioned in Domesday Book, but the settlement has been identified as almost certainly the half-hide held by Wenlock Priory in the hundred of Condover. This manor (known as 'Legh' or 'Leye') was perhaps held by Edric the Wild;[14] 'Hugh' comes from Sir Hugh de Lega, first mentioned *c*.1170. The church is situated at the foot of Wenlock Edge, and is rather spuriously mentioned by Housman in *A Shropshire Lad*: 'The vane on Hughley steeple / Veers bright, a far known sign' – an example of poetic licence since there has never been a steeple at Hughley church!

The church is, in fact, well-known and justly admired not for its non-existent steeple but for the quality of its screen, the finest in Shropshire; but there is also a good deal else to appreciate. The aspect of the church from the exterior (Fig.23.16) is marred by the surrounding yew trees, which are densely set. The earliest part of the church is the Early English 13th-century north wall of the nave, with its lancet windows. The rest of the church was built towards the end of the Decorated period, *c*.1360. In the chancel, the east window shows curvilinear, almost Flamboyant, tracery,[15] and there are fragments of medieval stained glass here and in the north window. To the right of the altar is a corbel projecting in the form of a lady's head, and in the south wall a rare pillar piscina. There are medieval tiles on the floor of the chancel, and an excellent boarded trussed-rafter roof, with bosses; the boarding was the work of Norman Shaw in the 1870s. There is a good Jacobean pulpit. The western bell-turret is half-timbered, with brick nogging, and dates from 1701. The south porch is a little earlier.

Fig.23.16 St. John the Baptist, Hughley

The screen probably dates from the end of the 15th century (Figs.13.3 & 13.4). It has three lights on each side of the central section, and the tracery under the arches is extremely varied. Above is a coved cornice, with carvings of birds, grapes and flowers and below a band of wavy quatrefoils.[16] The disposition of the ribs in the vaulting produces a stellar plan. The upper part of the dado (the lower part of the screen) is also delicately carved.

St. Leonard, Linley**

Linley ('meadow where flax is grown') is not mentioned in Domesday Book, the earliest reference to the name being in 1166.[17] In the Middle Ages Linley was subject to Wenlock Priory, and later it was linked with Broseley. The little church stands alone, along a rough drive leading to Linley Hall. The church has recently been closed for worship and it is hoped that the Churches Conservation Trust will take it over and re-open it. The building consists of a Norman tower, nave and chancel, dating from the second half of the 12th century; it has never been enlarged, though a good deal restored.

The belfry of the late Norman tower has paired round-headed windows on the north, west and south aspects, set slightly recessed; above is a corbel-table with carved heads in the Kilpeck manner (Fig.6.3). The tympana of both north and south doorways are worth noting (Figs.9.12 & 9.16). Above the blocked north doorway is carved a pagan fertility figure, a 'green man' with sprays of foliage issuing from his mouth. Similar figures may be seen at Church Stretton, Holdgate (Fig.9.15) and Tugford, but this is easily the biggest. Above the green man is a semicircle of stars. The tympanum of the south doorway is carved with zigzags.

Internally the chancel arch and the tower arch are Norman: the former is plain, but the half-columns supporting the tower arch have capitals elaborately carved with scrolls and nail-heads (Fig.9.8). There are Norman windows in the north and south walls of the chancel; the neo-Norman windows in the east wall are due to Sir Arthur Blomfield's restoration in 1858. The windows in the nave are insertions of the 14th or 15th century. The Norman font (Fig.10.14) is finely carved with cable ornament, foliage and grotesque heads. In the blocked north doorway is an unusual memorial slab to two Roman Catholic monks who died at Linley: Francis Anderton (d.1779) and George Johnson (d.1803); above the inscription are carved rustic scenes and rural implements. These monks worked from Linley Hall, which was then the seat of the Lacons, a notable Catholic family. The hatchment of Richard Lacon (d.1803) hangs in the nave.

Holy Trinity, Much Wenlock***

The parish church of Much Wenlock has recently been transformed by extensive changes at the base of the tower, which have revealed the very impressive west portal. As a result, the church has now been propelled into the first rank of Shropshire churches.

Wenlock's name is derived from Welsh *gwyn-loc* – 'white monastery' – according to Ekwall. As we have seen, Wenlock Priory (Fig.2.4) is the oldest Christian foundation in Shropshire (*c*.680), and was originally a convent for monks and nuns, the king's daughter, Mildburga, being the first abbess. It is thought that Holy Trinity church was originally built for worship by the nuns, and St. Mildburga was first buried in the Lady chapel of this Saxon church; her remains were transferred to the Priory church in 1101. Roger, earl of Montgomery re-founded Wenlock Priory *c.*1080, and possibly this may have necessitated the rebuilding of the parish church early in the 12th century.

Holy Trinity (Fig.23.17) consists of a nave with south aisle, chancel with a south chapel, west tower and south porch, and displays building in every style of medieval architecture. The nave and the western part of the chancel are Norman, the most impressive feature being the wide chancel arch. Remains of blocked-up Norman windows may be seen high in the south wall of the chancel and above the arcade, and there is a blocked north doorway in the nave. The west window of the nave is Norman, with nook shafts on each side. The west tower came later in the 12th century (the Transitional period). It has flat Norman buttresses, with pointed arches to the north and south, providing a passage through the tower. The belfry has paired round-headed windows under a common arch. The battle-

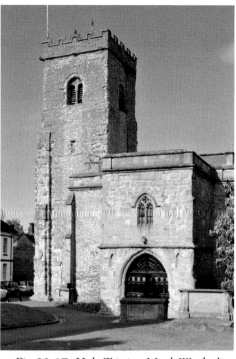

Fig.23.17 Holy Trinity, Much Wenlock

ments were added in the Perpendicular period, together with a spire, demolished in 1930. The addition of the tower to the earlier nave resulted in obscuring the finest west front in Shropshire.[18] But recent alterations have resulted in the opening up of the ground floor of the tower, which has now become the main entrance to the church. So the very impressive west doorway can now be seen (Fig.23.18); it has two orders of shafts with block capitals,

Fig.23.18 Much Wenlock: the recently revealed Norman west doorway

and in the arch chevron decoration and several roll mouldings. If it is possible to climb up the tower, the visitor may see above a large window flanked by two nook-shafts, and above this three tiers of blind arcading, with much chevron decoration.

In the early 13th century the church was extended by the addition of a south aisle; it is separated from the nave by an arcade of still substantial piers, though the arches are pointed (Fig.23.19). The eastern extension of the south aisle forms a Lady chapel, now opening into

Fig.23.19 Much Wenlock: the south arcade and chancel

the chancel by a 14th-century arch. The chapel has a piscina in the south wall. All the windows in the south aisle and chapel are Victorian: the east window has intersecting tracery, and the south windows complex reticulated tracery. Also in the Early English period was added the fine two-storey porch. The inner doorway is Early English, but the door itself may be Norman, with original 12th-century ironwork. In the 14th century the chancel was extended eastwards.

There are vaulted sedilia on the south wall and to the east of these a piscina. On the north side is an aumbry. The east window is early Perpendicular, though still with an ogee-shaped gable above it. On either side of this window is a niche with a canopy above. Corbels against the north and south walls of the chancel are carved with heads.

The fine pulpit is Jacobean, and has some carvings of mermen (*cf* Cardington). The font in the nave is Victorian, and is made of Caen stone carved with symbols of the Passion and the symbols of the four evangelists. In the Lady chapel is the original Norman font which was re-discovered in the 20th century. There are several memorial brasses in the chancel: the best is to Richard Ridley (d.1592) and his wife, kneeling figures in Elizabethan costume.

At the west end of the nave is a memorial to William Penny Brooks, a surgeon in the town, who made a major contribution to the rebirth of the modern Olympic Games.

St. Michael, Munslow**

The name of the parish has aroused much interest: it combines a Saxon personal name (Mundel) with OE *hlaw* (a 'tumulus or burial mound'). Gelling discussed the seven Shropshire settlements with this combination,[19] noting that two of them, Munslow and Purslow, were medieval hundreds. In the Domesday Book the manor was recorded as *Estune* (Aston), and the presence of a priest was noted. The parish now contains two small villages, Munslow and Aston Munslow, the church being sited at Munslow.

St. Michael's church (Fig.23.20) is attractive, situated well away from the main road.

Fig.23.20 St. Michael, Munslow

Fig.23.21 Munslow: unusual tracery in this Decorated window

From the exterior, note first the splendid 14th-century wooden porch, with delicate tracery at the sides (Fig.7.1). To the east of the Decorated window in the south wall of the nave there is a projection which appears to be a buttress: in fact this was to accommodate the stairway to the former rood loft, the doorway to which can be seen inside; a similar feature is seen at Culmington.[20] The lower stages of the tower are Norman (see the small round-headed windows), the upper storey is Perpendicular, and the parapet was added in the 18th century. Before entering the church, it is worth negotiating the nettles and walking round to the north aisle to see the unusual and fine Decorated tracery of some of the windows: the tracery shows arches on the apices of other arches (Fig.23.21).

Internally, the tower opens into the nave by a Norman round-headed arch, with a hood-mould decorated with ?flowers (*cf* Halford). The Decorated north aisle is separated from the nave by a plain Perpendicular arcade, though the easternmost arch is Victorian (as is the chancel arch). The chancel is Early English, with lancet windows in both north and south walls; the east window is of the 'Herefordshire' type, with three lights, the middle one rising to the apex of the window without tracery. There is a piscina in the south wall of the chancel, and a corbel bearing an angel in the south wall of the nave near the chancel arch; this probably supported the former rood loft. Doorways to this loft can still be seen.

There is an excellent Perpendicular octagonal font, with blank arches on the stem and quatrefoils with flowers around the bowl. Some of the 15th-century bench-ends are carved with patterns; especially notable is the westernmost pew on the south side. In the chancel is an incised slab depicting a priest, dating from the early 16th century. In the north aisle are two tablets by Thomas Carline of Shrewsbury: a rather conventional Gothic monument to Thomas Pemberton (d.1832), and a more accomplished Greek one, with cherub, urn and obelisk, to the Reverend Richard Powell (d.1845). There is also an unusual slate monument to William Churchman (d.1602), showing a skull, an hourglass, a scroll and a recumbent figure wrapped in a shroud; and a further shrouded figure on a wooden panel, dated 1674.[21] The medieval chest is enriched with carving.[22]

Some of the stained glass is rewarding: the best is a medieval ensemble in the westernmost window of the south aisle, showing a kneeling family of five figures with two Madonnas above. Also notable is the easternmost window of the north wall of the north aisle, with glass, probably 16th-century German, commemorating the Reverend John Lloyd (d.1528). The Victorian glass is less interesting.

Fig.23.22 St. Peter, Rushbury

St. Peter, Rushbury*

Rushbury is pleasantly situated in Apedale, at the foot of Wenlock Edge, and the church is a good example of Transitional and Early English building, with some evidence of older work. The latter is evidenced by the herring-bone masonry which exists low down in both north and south walls of the nave. In the north wall, the masonry is interrupted by a blocked Norman doorway, with a plain tympanum above. Herring-bone masonry is seen in both Anglo-Saxon and early Norman building, and both Cranage and Taylor and Taylor[23] thought that on balance this was late Saxon rather than Norman. The lancet windows in the nave (Fig.23.22) were inserted in the 19th century and are not recorded in Williams' painting of 1789. The south doorway is Transitional – a pointed arch, with capitals showing early leaf formation. The south porch is of timber on a stone base; much of the woodwork is old, possibly Perpendicular.

Both the chancel and tower were built *c*.1200, and here the lancet windows are original. The tower is short and squat, with paired lancet windows in the belfry; the top storey with battlements is Perpendicular. The tower arch opening into the nave is wide, and Transitional in character. The nave was probably extended eastwards of the herring-bone masonry later in the 12th century. The chancel is a good example of Early English building, and the lancets here are genuine. Especially impressive are the three tall lancets in the east wall; internally, these have slender nook shafts with waterleaf capitals. The priest's doorway in the south wall now leads into the Victorian vestry. The stalls in the chancel are largely made of carved 17th-century panels.

The finest features are the roofs; both chancel and nave have collar-beams, arched braces and wind-braces laterally; in addition, there are hammer-beams over the chancel, and tie-beams over the nave. The font is a plain tub, probably Norman, on a modern base.

St. Peter and St. Paul, Sheinton

Sheinton means 'beautiful place' according to Ekwall.[24] The church stands on a bank beside the road, and externally is remarkable for the half-timbered belfry which juts out above the west wall. Nearly the whole church was rebuilt in 1854 when the north aisle was added. The interior is rather dark. The best feature is the woodwork: there is a Jacobean pulpit and some at least of the box-pews are old. In the south wall of the chancel is a small effigy of a woman of unknown date, and in the north wall is a low-side window. There is a double hammerbeam roof (Fig.8.17). At the west end of the nave, the supporting timbers of the belfry are visible – two main posts, with arched braces and struts.

St. James, Shipton*

At the time of the Domesday survey, Shipton (meaning 'sheep farm') was held by St. Milburga's Priory, Wenlock. The church is remarkable nowadays for its Elizabethan chancel (Fig.5.1), a great rarity for hardly any churches were built during the reign of Elizabeth I. The nave and lower part of the tower are much older, and date from the late 12th century.

The church (Fig.23.23) is finely situated next to the Elizabethan hall. Externally, the nave and tower are buff-coated, the upper part of the tower weather-boarded with a pyramidal roof. The interior is simple and serene, the Norman nave contrasting well with the Elizabethan chancel. There is a blocked Norman window in the south wall of the nave and a north doorway of the same period. The other windows in the nave are later insertions of the 13th or 14th centuries. The font is a

Fig.23.23 St. James, Shipton

plain Norman bowl. The tower arch is pointed, and therefore Transitional (c.1200); the chancel arch is Norman and round. On either side of the latter are large squints, which may or may not be of the 12th century.

By 1553 the chancel (Fig.5.1) was 'in great ruin'. A notice records that: 'This chancel was reedified and builded of newe from the foundacion, and glased at the charges of John Lutwich, youngest sonne of Richard Lutwich of Lutwiche; in the xxxi yeare of the gracious reigne of Queene Elizabeth. 1589.' The east window, with intersecting tracery, is constructed in the Decorated style of 250 years earlier, and the lower part of the window contains some Elizabethan stained glass. Also original are the iron stanchions of the windows and the trussed-rafter roof. In the chancel is a painted panel commemorating Mary Mytton (d.1640), and some ancient pews with poppy-heads. There is a plain Jacobean pulpit and reading-desk, and a communion-rail with twisted balusters.

A modern tablet records the departure from Shipton of four children of Samuel More in the *Mayflower* in 1620. Three of the children perished during the voyage or shortly afterwards, but one survived to an old age in Massachusetts. Their interesting story is told in a booklet available in the church.

St. Michael, Stanton Long*

Stanton Long appears to have been separated from the neighbouring parish of Holdgate at some time in the 12th century (p.255). The small church of St. Michael is nicely situated, with fine views across Corvedale towards Wenlock Edge (Fig.23.24). It consists just of nave and chancel, with a western timber-framed belfry; the attractive south porch has some ancient timbers at the entrance, though the side-walls are Victorian. Even older, however, is the south door, which is dated *c*.1200, and which has some good ironwork. The doorway itself is plain late Norman (Transitional, as the arch is pointed). The chancel arch is Victorian. In the south wall of the chancel is an early Decorated tomb-recess. There are two piscinae, one in the chancel, and another in the east end of the south wall of the nave,

Fig.23.24 St. Michael, Stanton Long

indicating that once there was a further altar here. The unusual stone reredos was designed by F.R. Kempson of Hereford and constructed in 1888. The roofs are good – in the nave the wind-braces form quatrefoils, and in the chancel the collar-beams have carved bosses.

St. Catherine, Tugford**

Tugford has a fine situation in Corvedale, at the foot of Brown Clee Hill, and St. Catherine's church is a delight. The manor (*Dodefort* in Domesday Book) was given to St. Peter's church, Shrewsbury, and it belonged to Shrewsbury Abbey until the Dissolution. It is a single-cell church, mostly Norman, the nave older than the chancel, and the tower is Early English (Fig.6.6). There is an original deeply splayed Norman window in the north wall of the nave, and the south doorway is round-headed, with one order of shafts on each side. The east capital has trumpet carving, and the west has stiff-leaf. The arch above has a keeled moulding with lozenge decoration. The priest's door in the south wall of the chancel has an excellent and very unusual floriated tympanum, which may be 11th-century and re-used.[25] At the east end of the north and south walls of the chancel are tomb-recesses, each with an arch supported by columns on either side, with foliage akin to water-leaf below the capitals. On the north side of the chancel are two further tomb-recesses from the Decorated period, with ogee-arches and cusping.

The interior is beautifully light. Internal to the south doorway, and high up, are two small sheila-na-gigs (medieval fertility symbols). Nave and chancel are covered by a barrelled plaster ceiling. There is a west gallery, the front of which is panelled with tracery probably from the former rood screen. The font is 13th-century, with a fourteen-sided bowl divided from the stem by broad cable-moulding. The parish bier is dated 1617, and has some defaced lettering of that period. In the chancel are some rude 17th-century communion rails, and behind the altar a wrought-iron candelabrum and candle-sticks. There are a few fragments of medieval glass in the east window. There is an original deeply-splayed Early English lancet window in the north wall of the chancel; the other windows are paired cusped lancets with a trefoil above. The east window has reticulated tracery of the Decorated period.

St. John the Baptist, Willey**

Willey (meaning 'meadow with willow trees')[26] is mentioned in Domesday Book, and the parish church does indeed date from Norman times. The manor was part of the holding of Earl Roger, and during the Middle Ages it was held by various families. In 1618 it was bought by John Weld, merchant and town clerk of London. His descendant George Weld (d.1748) left the manor and estate in trust for his grandson George Forester, son of his daughter Elizabeth who had married Brooke Forester of Dothill.[27] At George Forester's death in 1811 the estate passed to his cousin Cecil, who took the name Weld-Forester, and in 1821 was created the first Baron Forester. The estate is presently owned and managed by the Trustees of the Forester family Trusts.

Fig.23.25 St. John the Baptist, Willey

The church is situated near the old hall and is no longer used for regular services, being maintained by the Willey Estate. It is an attractive building, with work from the 12th, 18th and 19th centuries. The nave and chancel are basically Norman, and small Norman windows remain in the south wall of the chancel and the north wall of the nave. In the jambs and splay of one of the Norman windows, decorative painting, said to be from the 12th century, was formerly visible.[28] The west tower (Fig.23.25) was rebuilt in 1712 and displays wide round-headed windows with a keystone above. The windows of the north wall of the nave probably also date from this time, as does the now blocked window at the west end of the south wall of the nave. The rest of the church – the arcades and all the south aisle and the Gothic windows in the chancel, north aisle and tower – were built by Sir Arthur Blomfield in 1880. The capitals of the arcade are not, perhaps, Sir Arthur's happiest design, but in other respects the Victorian work is good.

The font at the west end of the nave is a plain Norman tub, and opposite it, now in the sill of the blocked window, is a further basin. There is a Jacobean reading-desk and pulpit, and some panelling from the same period in the chancel. There are two Weld monuments in the chancel, one signed by R. Eykin of Wolverhampton. At the east end of the south aisle is an accomplished reredos depicting the Resurrection by Sir John Boehm; it is in memory of the second Lord Forester (d.1874). At the west end of this aisle is the raised Forester pew, where some hatchments are displayed. At the west end of the nave are the Arms of Queen Victoria carved in wood. The stained glass in the east window is by Morris and Co., made in 1933.

There is no public access to the church except by special arrangement with the Willey Estate Office. The gardens are sometimes open to the public in the summer under the National Gardens Scheme, and on these days the church is open.

24

The lower Severn Valley – Bridgnorth

Acton Round**
Alveley**
Astley Abbots*
Aston Eyre***
Billingsley**
Bridgnorth, St. Leonard*
Bridgnorth, St. Mary Magdalene**
Chelmarsh**
Chetton
Claverley***
Glazeley*
Highley*

Middleton Scriven
Monkhopton
Morville**
Oldbury
Quatford**
Quatt***
Sidbury*
Tasley
Tuckhill*
Upton Cressett**
Worfield**

Acton Round church**

This church, of no known dedication, is a delight. Set amidst the rolling south Shropshire countryside, and near to a distinguished Queen Anne manor house, the building itself is not particularly fine, but it houses three fine treasures. Acton Round was formerly a chapelry of Much Wenlock. Cranage speculates that the eastern end of the church may have been round or apsidal – perhaps the work of the Knights Templars – quoting from a register by Sir Thomas Butler, who was the abbot of Shrewsbury at the time of the dissolution.

The church (Fig.24.1) consists of nave and chancel, and a western timber-framed belfry. The nave is almost certainly Norman – there is no direct evidence for this, but the south door with its ironwork has been dated to c.1200. The chancel is later than the nave, and was rebuilt in 1714. The chancel arch between the nave and chancel is late Victorian. About the middle of the 18th century a north mortuary chapel was added to the west end of the nave for the Actons of Aldenham. Probably at the same time the priest's door in the south wall of the chancel received its unusual ogee heading

Fig.24.1 Acton Round church

(reminiscent of Shobdon, Herefordshire). The octagonal font is ancient, but of uncertain date. Near to it is an antiquated stove, which almost ranks as one of the treasures of the little church.

On the north wall of the chancel is an excellent monument to Richard Acton (d.1703) and his wife (Fig.11.32); the two demi-figures are depicted holding hands in a horizontally oval frame.[1] The monument is signed Stanton: this is Edward Stanton (1681-1734); both he and his father William were accomplished sculptors with an extensive national practice.[2] It is a pity that this fine work has been overshadowed by the much larger memorial in the chapel. This is to Sir Whitmore Acton (d.1731) and his wife (d.1760), by T.F. Pritchard.[3] It is celebrated for combining rococo motifs of the mid-18th century with unmistakable Gothick features[4] – one of the earliest works of the Gothic Revival, a little later than the church at Shobdon. The monument (Fig.11.33) consists of a sarcophagus in an architectural frame; the side-columns have Corinthian capitals and there are garlands and lamps; but in addition the frieze has pseudo-Perpendicular lozenges, with foliage surmounted by a row of cinquefoiled Gothic arches.

It is good to record that the final treasure at Acton Round is wholly modern, and was installed in the millennial year 2000. Above the south door internally is mounted a remarkable carving of the Annunciation by Andrew Pearson. The work is shaped like a Norman tympanum, and the figures of Gabriel and the Virgin are carved in the style of the 14th century.

St. Mary the Virgin, Alveley***

The place-name is derived from Ælfgyp (a woman's personal name) and *leah* (a 'meadow'). At the time of the Domesday Book Alveley was reckoned to be in Staffordshire and was among the lands held by Earl Roger. After 1086 it was considered to be part of Kingsnordley and given by Henry II to Guy Lestrange.

The church (Fig.24.2) stands on a knoll above the village and has many attractions. The lower parts of the western tower are Norman, the upper storey being added in 1779. The west window of the tower is a much later Perpendicular insertion. The tower arch is rounded, and so are both arcades, the north being a little earlier than the south (Fig.24.3). The south capital of the tower arch displays Norman carving, which Thurlby believes to derive from the Herefordshire School of Romanesque sculpture.[5] At the angle of the capital is a head, and issuing from the mouth on each side are stems ending in trilobed leaves. The north arcade (*c*.1180) consists of rounded columns with square capitals carved with leaf patterns; the columns of the south arcade are similar, but the capitals are circular and their carving is more advanced, showing more Early

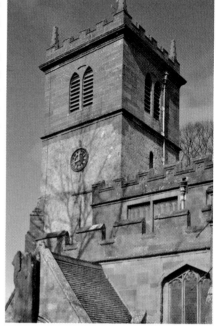

Fig.24.2 St. Mary, Alveley

English character – and the responds on the east and west ends show fully-developed stiff-leaf carving. The south chapel is Decorated, with some ball-flower on the opening into the aisle. The clerestory is Perpendicular, with pairs of straight-headed windows over each arch. The roof of the nave is of low pitch, with arched braces.

The chancel was originally Early English, but was almost completely rebuilt at the restoration by Sir Arthur Blomfield in 1878-79. The east window, sedilia and piscina have all been renewed. The chancel arch springs from clustered columns with moulded capitals.

Fig.24.3 Alveley: the Norman south arcade; note the stiff-leaf on the east respond

The greatest treasure at Alveley is the embroidered altar frontal discovered in an old chest in *c*.1865; an excellent replica is shown in the south aisle and is used at festival services. It dates from the 15th century and depicts figures of the faithful departed surrounded by cherubim, the whole decorated with lilies and pomegranates. The original was shown at the Exhibition of late Gothic Art at the Victoria and Albert Museum 2003-04.[6]

Next to the tower arch, and currently hidden by a bench, is a fine brass to John Grove (d.1616). There is stained glass by Kempe in the east window and the same artist was responsible for the reredos in the south aisle, which is painted on zinc.

Near to the church, in a private house not open to the public, are some remarkable carvings from the Herefordshire School, analysed by Thurlby.[7] These include a panel showing a trousered warrior very similar to the work at Kilpeck, Herefordshire and Billesley, Warwickshire, and a figure of Samson and the lion similar to the tympanum at Stretton Sugwas, Herefordshire. The provenance of this work is quite unknown.

St. Calixtus, Astley Abbots**

The Book of Saints lists several SS Calixtus (or Callistus) but it is not known why one of these is venerated at Astley Abbotts. Astley means 'east meadow', and in the Middle Ages it belonged to Shrewsbury Abbey; before that it was part of the parish of Morville. The church is pleasantly sited, and has some unusual and interesting features.

The tower and west front (Fig.24.4), described by Cranage as 'elaborately ugly' were

Fig.24.4 St. Calixtus, Astley Abbots

built in 1857. In contrast, the north wall of the nave is Norman and retains two Norman windows; inside, a blocked Norman doorway may be seen. The south wall of the nave is Victorian. The chancel is, most exceptionally, dated 1633, the date being on the east gable. It is notable that the window tracery is Decorated, not Perpendicular (*cf* Shipton). Over the chancel is a hammer-beam roof resting

Fig.24.5 Astley Abbots: the nave and chancel

on corbels carved with a lion, a unicorn, a phoenix and a Pegasus. All round the chancel and nave is panelling dating from the 17th century (Fig.24.5). The pulpit is also panelled and is dated 1633.

There are two treasures which are easy to overlook. In the east window is a small panel of stained glass from the early 13th century. It shows a figure of Christ under a canopy, the drapery much restored. Marks comments that this is comparable to a figure of Noah in Canterbury Cathedral – these two being the earliest appearances of a canopy in stained glass.[8] In the blocked north doorway is a maiden's garland, like those seen at Minsterley (q.v.), commemorating a young woman who was drowned in the river Severn while on her way to her wedding.

Aston Eyre church***

The motorist driving along the Corvedale road from Craven Arms to Bridgnorth goes through the village of Aston Eyre in a few seconds, and is probably unaware of the gem he/she has missed. For the unobtrusive church situated just above the road possesses one of Shropshire's outstanding treasures, and the church does not have to be open for the visitor to see it – for it is above the doorway, the main entrance into the church. It is the Norman tympanum (Fig.1.4) described on p.56.

The church itself (of no known dedication) consists only of nave and chancel with a western bellcote; it was a chapelry to Morville (a Benedictine priory in the 12th century). Both nave and chancel are Norman (12th-century), the nave probably around 1150, and

Fig.24.6 Aston Eyre church: the chancel arch

the chancel later. Between is the chancel arch, which is pointed, thus Transitional in style, built probably after 1160 (Fig.24.6). The east window, of three spaced round-headed lights is Victorian: a painting of 1844 shows a wide lancet with Y-tracery. The exterior of all the Norman windows has been renewed. The Norman south doorway has one order of shafts; the capitals display some foliage, probably renewed.

St. Mary, Billingsley**

Billingsley was included among the possessions of Morville church which Earl Roger gave to Shrewsbury Abbey; later (*c*.1147) it appears to have been transferred to the Abbey of Séez.

The church consists of a nave and chancel, with a western bellcote and a south porch. It is built of attractive multicoloured sandstone, and all except the west wall was rebuilt in 1875. The porch is an excellent example of medieval woodwork.

To the east of the porch is a blocked Norman doorway of unusual appearance (Fig.9.13); instead of shafts there are recessed vertical columns of masonry on either side, topped with capitals, the western hatched and the eastern scalloped. Below the capitals is a narrow band of cable moulding. The tympanum is ornamented with plain hatched triangles, and above is a roll moulding. Over the outer arch are three grotesque heads, presumably corbels. It seems that the whole doorway was reassembled when the south wall was rebuilt in 1875; for when Sir Stephen Glynne visited Billingsley in 1846, he makes no mention of a blocked south doorway, though he does describe three corbel-heads on the exterior of the south side of the nave; and he also mentions a blocked north door. Instead he describes the south doorway, within the porch, as 'Norman but plain and rude, with two orders stopped by impost mouldings'. It is strange that Glynne did not mention the blocked south doorway: the Williams painting of 1790 shows the arch of the doorway, with the three corbel-heads in their present position. It does not show the tympanum nor the capitals nor the columns of masonry beneath the capitals – presumably all these were put in place during the rebuilding of 1875. Where, I wonder, did the tympanum and the capitals come from?

All the windows of nave and chancel have been renewed, and the chancel arch is a neo-Norman 19th-century construction. The font has a plain Norman bowl and base, with a 19th-century stem. There is a Jacobean pulpit and reading-desk. In the north wall of the chancel is a fine, 14th-century Easter sepulchre (Fig.24.7), built to house the consecrated host between Maundy Thursday and Easter Day. Below the ledge is an arcade of four cusped arches, and above a Decorated structure with cusping, ogee arches, and a trefoil space below a crocketed arch set between upright columns.

Fig.24.7 St. Mary, Billingsley: 14th-century Easter sepulchre

St. Leonard, Bridgnorth**

The earliest reference to Bridgnorth appears to be the foundation there by Aethelflaed, daughter of King Alfred, of a fort in 912. This may well be related to the report in the Anglo-Saxon Chronicle of 896-7 of the Danes building a fort on the Severn at a crossing-place on the river at *Cwatbrycge*; today, there is a settlement between Bridgnorth and Quatford known as Danesford. During the Anglo-Saxon and Norman periods, Bridgnorth was part of the extensive parish of Morville, and it really only became important when Robert de Bellesme moved his castle from Quatford to the strongly defensible site which was available at Bridgnorth. A medieval church evolved to serve the community which gathered around the castle, and later in the Middle Ages this church contained a number of chantry chapels. By the early 19th century, the church was said to be in a deplorable condition, and the Rector, the Reverend George Bellett, instigated the task of rebuilding.

Crowning the Bridgnorth skyline today is the warm sandstone of the tower of St. Leonard's church complementing Telford's church near the castle. St. Leonard's consists of a south tower, a nave with aisles, a chancel, and an octagonal library at the east end of the north aisle. The church is almost entirely Victorian, the work of William Slater (1819-72), and very little of the medieval fabric remains. Work began with the chancel in 1846, proceeding to the nave and aisles in 1860-62, and finally the tower in the 1870s.

St. Leonard's is a church on a grand scale, and it is unfortunate that it is no longer used for regular worship; it was declared redundant in 1976 and is now in the care of the Churches Conservation Trust. Entry to the church is through the south doorway of the tower; this rises above to three stages and is crowned by battlements and by a short spirelet at the top of the stair turret (Fig.24.8). The nave and aisles together compose a very wide church. Over the nave is a hammer-beam roof of the 1660s (*cf* Condover). The chancel is spacious, with tiled floors, and a restored medieval roof supported by carved stone corbels retrieved from the earlier church. To the north of the chancel is the octagonal vestry and library, which formerly housed the extensive library of the Reverend Hugh Stackhouse given to the church in 1742; the books are now in Shrewsbury.

There is Victorian stained glass in the east window of the chancel by Clayton and Bell, and in the south window by William Wailes. The octagonal font is made of alabaster, the work of T. Earp (1894). On the altar at the east end of the south aisle are a cross and candlesticks designed by Bainbridge Reynolds (1898) in the Arts and Crafts style.

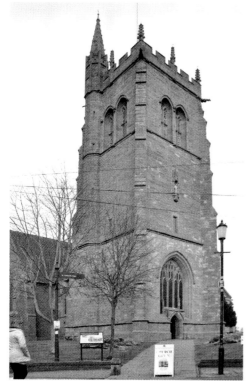

Fig.24.8 Bridgnorth, St. Leonard: the tower

St. Mary Magdalene, Bridgnorth**

Thomas Telford (1757-1834) was of course primarily an engineer, building bridges, canals, roads and harbours. In 1787 he became surveyor of public works for Shropshire, then at the height of its industrial revolution, and after 1790 he designed three churches in the county: St. Mary Magdalene, Bridgnorth (1792), Madeley (1796), and Malinslee (1805).

But the history of St. Mary Magdalene's church begins a long time before Telford. A collegiate church was founded at Quatford by Roger de Montgomery in 1086 and was transferred to Bridgnorth in 1101 following the rebellion of Robert de Bellesme against Henry I. Robert built a castle on this defensible site, and the first church of St. Mary Magdalene was the chapel of the castle. A later medieval church followed, but by the late 18th century this was showing signs of dilapidation. The Williams painting of 1789 shows a Perpendicular west tower and a Decorated chancel, both of stone, with a stuccoed nave with wide windows. Two years later, Telford (who had correctly predicted the collapse of St. Chad's church in Shrewsbury in 1788) examined the church and advised that it be completely rebuilt. He

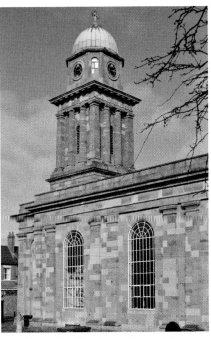

Fig.24.9 Bridgnorth, St. Mary Magdalene (1792) by Thomas Telford – the 'south' elevation

was commissioned to design the new building on the same site – but whereas the medieval church was conventionally orientated east-west, Telford's church was orientated north-south, providing a fine vista along East Castle Street.

The exterior view from the north presents a noble façade, with a portico of four Tuscan columns with a pediment above and rustication above the doorway. Above is the square tower with further rustication around the base, then a belfry with Tuscan columns carrying a cornice, an octagonal clock-stage and a lead dome. The sides of the nave are also impressive, with very tall round-arched windows separated by pairs of Doric pilasters (Fig.24.9). The apsidal south end was added by Sir Arthur Blomfield in 1875. The interior (Fig.24.10) is beautifully light, with Ionic arcades and a west gallery. The ceiling is flat. Blomfield's apse adds dignity, enhanced by a high baldacchino over the altar.

Fig.24.10 Bridgnorth, St. Mary Magdalene: the Ionic arcade

St. Peter, Chelmarsh**

The place-name is thought to derive from OE *cegel*, meaning 'pole', and it has been postulated that this and other marshes may have been marked out by posts.[9] Chelmarsh has a distinguished church with a late Norman north aisle, a Decorated nave and chancel (unusual in Shropshire) and a Georgian tower.

An unusual aspect of Chelmarsh is that the Decorated work here can be accurately dated. A branch of the Mortimers of Wigmore was established in Chelmarsh,[10] and it is known that Hugh de Mortimer endowed a chantry in 1345. Cranage persuasively argued that this is the approximate date for the Decorated architecture. But before this there was a Norman church, and evidence remains in the north aisle. Here is a blocked Norman doorway, with scalloped capitals and a prominent roll-moulding in the arch. The Decorated character of the rest of the building is best appreciated from the south (Fig.24.11), where there are three tall two-light windows, with a quatrefoil in the apex; and from the east, where there is a fine Decorated window of five lights with much intersecting tracery, very similar to the east windows of Kinlet and Stottesdon (q.v.). Much of the masonry of these windows has been renewed. The priest's door in the south of the chancel has a hood-mould over it continuous with the string-course.

Entry into the church is through a modern porch where three old fragments of carving have been inserted, including a defaced representation of the Crucifixion. These may have come from a churchyard cross. Internally, the nave is divided from the north aisle by a Decorated arcade of four bays, and some of the capitals display that characteristic feature of the Decorated era, the ball-flower (Fig.9.20). At the east end of the aisle is a piscina, which means that there was an altar there, probably the altar of Hugh de Mortimer's chantry chapel. The doorway to the former rood loft may be seen high up on the north wall over the screen. In the north of the chancel is part of an altar tomb of *c.*1475. The excellent stained glass in the east window is by Kempe. The screen (Fig.8.2) and the panelling in the chancel and north aisle are mostly the work of the Reverend R.T. Seddon, vicar here from 1887-1906. The roof of the nave and chancel is the original trussed-rafter roof of 1345. The pulpit is partly Jacobean. The font is a Norman tub on a modern base.

The brick tower with stone quoins dates from the early 18th century (Fig.24.11), but in it has been inserted a fine Decorated window which presumably was the original west window of the nave. At the top is a balustrade with corner pinnacles. There is a rather poor west door.

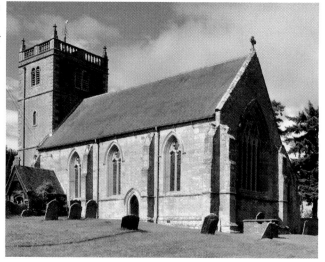

Fig.24.11 St. Peter, Chelmarsh

St. Giles, Chetton

The village of Chetton stands at the end of a lane off the road from Ludlow to Bridgnorth. Before the Norman Conquest the manor was held by Lady Godiva, and the presence of a priest was mentioned in the Domesday Book. The church consists of a medieval chancel and south doorway, a nave rebuilt in 1788, and a western tower dating from 1829. The chancel is Early English, with lancet windows in the north and south walls; the lancet windows of the east wall have been reconstructed because Glynne in 1854 described a Perpendicular window there! The fine south doorway into the nave is also Early English, and consists of two orders of shafts with moulded capitals. The rest of the nave is Georgian, but all the windows were 'gothicised' in the 19th century. There is a reredos of Jacobean woodwork and a plain octagonal font of uncertain date.

All Saints, Claverley***

The quality of the medieval wall-paintings uncovered in 1902, the variety of the architecture, the late medieval memorials, and not least the attractiveness of the village place Claverley in the front rank of Shropshire churches.

Claverley is 'clover meadow', and was mentioned in the Staffordshire section of Domesday Book as *Claverlege*. There was probably a Saxon church here, though it is not mentioned in Domesday. Earl Roger held the manor, and the church was connected with the collegiate foundation which he endowed at Quatford.

The earliest part of the present church is the west wall and parts of the north wall of the nave; these are Norman, probably of the first half of the 12th century; they are followed by the impressive north arcade of solid round piers supporting semicircular arches (Fig.24.12). The north aisle contains sundry hatchments, memorials, Commandment boards, likened

Fig.24.12 All Saints, Claverley: the Norman north arcade with spectacular wall-painting

by Jenkins to 'an ecclesiastical antique shop'.[11] After the north arcade, but still in the Norman period, came the lower part of the tower on the south side of the church (Fig.24.13). The tower originally had three external walls, on the east, south and west; the addition of the aisle in the 13th century and the chapel in the 15th necessitated the building of two further arches to communicate with these. In the north wall of the tower can be seen evidence of the original Norman base uncovered during restoration in 1902 (Fig.24.14). The piers of the south aisle are octagonal, the arches of course pointed. The capitals are adorned with heads, beasts and upright leaves. The west window of the nave shows intersecting tracery, indicating that it was inserted into the Norman wall *c*.1300. A niche in one of the piers supporting the tower is said to have been originally either a confessional or a seat of penance. In the Decorated period (mid-14th century), the fine chancel was rebuilt, the east window being an excellent example of Decorated tracery. On the south

Fig.24.13 Claverley: the tower

wall of the chancel are ogee-arched sedilia. The clerestory, the north and south chapels, the fine porch with chamber above (Fig.7.3) and the upper storeys of the tower are Perpendicular. The south aisle was also rebuilt and crenellated. The roof of the nave is of low pitch, panelled and boarded, with extra decoration over the easternmost bay forming a ceilure above the former rood 'heavily ornamented with square flowers and leaves'.[12] The roof of the chancel is of the hammerbeam type, with arched braces and collar-beams.

There are two fonts: the earlier plain one may be Saxon or early Norman; the later is certainly Norman. It is of the beaker type (Fig.10.7), with simple arcading, the shafts showing greatly varied decoration; around the foot is a band of beading. The spandrels are filled with inverted fleur-de-lis.[13] The 'Jacobean' pulpit is dated 1715.

In the north aisle is an incised slab to Richard Spycer, merchant (d.1448) and his wife Alice. He wears a long coat with a low fur-edged collar; Alice has a horned head-dress.[14] In the south chapel (the Gatacre chapel) is the splendid tomb of Sir Robert Broke, Speaker of the House of Commons

Fig.24.14 Claverley: the original Norman base of the tower, uncovered during restoration in 1902

(d.1558) and his two wives, the second of these being born Dorothy Gatacre. The effigies are of alabaster. This is still a medieval memorial, with just a hint of Renaissance influence in the twisted colonettes which separate the many children standing against the walls of the tomb-chest. On the east wall of this chapel are two large incised alabaster slabs commemorating Sir William Gatacre (d.1577) and his wife Helen, and Francis Gatacre (d.1599) and his wife Elizabeth. Sir William is shown in armour, while Helen has a striped veil with a high ruff; this slab is a late work of the firm of Royleys of Burton upon Trent (Fig.11.12).[15] Francis has a gown with false sleeves decorated with a vertical row of buttons.

But of course the greatest treasure is the medieval wall-painting above the Norman north arcade. This has been dated to *c.*1200, and at first was thought to portray the Battle of Hastings because of a supposed resemblance to the Bayeux tapestry (Fig.24.12). Expert opinion[16] later concluded that the series is a representation of the conflict between seven Christian virtues and seven pagan vices, depicted as a battle between equestrian knights. The paintings are lively (three of the knights are shown falling from their horses) and are in a remarkably good state of preservation. Between the windows of the clerestory and in the spandrels of the arches may be seen other painting of a much later date – 15th century. Over the chancel arch is part of a Doom (representing the Last Judgment), also probably of 15th-century origin.

St. Bartholomew, Glazeley*

Glazeley's entry in Domesday Book mentions the presence of a priest, so presumably there was a Saxon church here. If so, that has disappeared without trace, and so has its medieval successor recorded by Williams in 1790. The present church was built in 1875, the architect being Sir Arthur Blomfield; its design is attractive without being outstanding, and the church is built mainly in the Decorated style. It consists of a nave and chancel, with a western bellcote. The Victorian font has nail-head around the lower rim of the bowl; outside the church is a rather battered Norman tub-shaped font and the remains of a medieval stone coffin. Between nave and chancel is a very high wooden structure, scarcely functioning as a screen, with Gothic arches ascending to the roof.

To the north of the altar is a distinguished brass commemorating Thomas Wylde (d.1599) and his wife in Elizabethan attire; above are heraldic arms, and below are depicted four sons and two daughters. There is excellent stained glass in the east window – a Nativity scene by C.E. Kempe.

St. Mary, Highley*

Highley (*Hugelei* in Domesday Book) does not mean 'high meadow', but 'Hugga's meadow'.[17] Later Highley became a colliery village of brick houses, but St. Mary's church at the southern end of the village imparts much-needed grace to its environment.

St. Mary's consists of a nave and chancel, with a west tower and south porch. Both nave and chancel were originally Norman, and Norman windows remain high up on each. There is a blocked Early English doorway in the north wall of the nave, and the south doorway is also Early English. There is good ironwork on the door dating from the same period. High up in the south wall of the nave are two square-headed late Perpendicular windows, and the tower also is Perpendicular, with battlements and pinnacles. Both tower arch and chancel arch are pointed, and probably Perpendicular. The roof of the nave is of low pitch, panelled and embossed. There is a late medieval cross in the churchyard.

St. John the Baptist, Middleton Scriven

A scrivener is an old-fashioned term for a scribe, but here Scriven is probably a family name.[18] There was a medieval church here, painted by Williams in 1791. This was replaced by the present building in 1843-48, constructed in a rather starved Early English style. It consists of a nave, chancel, western bellcote and a south porch with some barge-boarding. There is a blocked Early English doorway at the west end of the north wall which looks original. The exotic font is a medley of medieval motifs dating from the 19th century, including the Adoration of the Magi and St. George and the dragon. There is stained glass by David Evans and William Wailes.

St. Peter, Monkhopton

As in other examples, 'hopton' refers to a settlement in a valley, in this case an escarpment valley south of Much Wenlock,[19] the prefix denoting that the manor belonged to Wenlock Priory.

The church's antiquity is effectively disguised by the rendering in ochre of the whole exterior (Fig.3.12). Nevertheless, the building is basically Norman, and there are Norman windows in the chancel. The sole remarkable feature of the interior is the internal ornamentation of the south chancel window: this shows three orders of moulding, a chain between two rows of chevron (Fig.9.3).

St. Gregory, Morville***

The place-name appears to mean 'open country by the Mor Brook';[20] the earliest written reference to it is in the Domesday Book, where it is called *Membrefelde*. The importance of Morville church in the 11th century is reflected in the length and detail of the entry in

Fig.24.15 St. Gregory, Morville: the church with Morville Hall

Domesday Book: 'This manor's church is in honour of St. Gregory and before 1066 it had 8 hides of this land; 8 canons served there. St. Peter's Church [Shrewsbury Abbey] holds this land from the Earl [Roger] ... 9 villagers, 1 smallholder and 3 priests with 9 ploughs.' This was clearly an impressive establishment, for Morville was the centre of an extensive Saxon parish which included Bridgnorth and extended as far as Billingsley, Astley Abbots and Cold Weston. Domesday Book points out that the whole of the hundred of Alnothstree belonged to the manor of Morville. A further unusual feature of the entry is the specification of the dedication to St. Gregory, a dedication which has lasted to the present day. There is now no trace of the Anglo-Saxon minster church. After the Conquest, Earl Roger gave it to Shrewsbury Abbey (St. Peter's church); in 1138 Morville became a Benedictine priory, a daughter cell of Shrewsbury, and so it remained until the Reformation. At the Reformation, the priory was disbanded and on its site an Elizabethan hall was built. This was refaced in the 18th century, and is now owned by the National Trust.

The church is one of the few Norman buildings of which there is documentary evidence of the date of construction, for a statement in the Chronicle of Florence of Worcester says, 'In 1118, Geoffrey de Clive, bishop of Hereford consecrated a new church at Morville which had been built by the monks of Shrewsbury'; he goes on to relate that after the consecration, two women and five horses were struck by lightning and killed.[21]

St. Gregory's is a spacious and dignified Norman church now set in parkland next to Morville Hall (Fig.24.15). The church was built in phases during the 12th century, beginning with the nave and chancel in 1118; this was followed by the tower, and lastly by the aisles. High on the west wall of the nave is a Norman window, now looking into the tower; this proves that the nave was built before the tower. The lower stages of the tower are Norman, the upper much later. The chancel arch is decorated with the 'billet' pattern – short, raised rectangles repeated at regular intervals (Fig.24.16). The capitals of the chancel arch are carved, on the north with scrolls and on the south with a human figure. The round-headed arcades are supported by square piers with shafts of the late-12th century; most of the capitals have upright leaves. Square-headed windows in the nave and chancel are

Fig.24.16 Morville: the Norman nave and chancel arch

later insertions. The clerestory was added in the 19th century, replacing a series of dormer windows.

Above the piers of the arcades hang four wooden carvings dating from the middle of the 17th century; these represent the four Evangelists, each accompanied by his symbol – St. Matthew with a man or angel, St. Mark with a lion, St. Luke with an ox and St. John with an eagle. The font (Fig.10.13) is a Norman tub, carved with medallions and human faces, and with cable ornament around the rim and base of the bowl. Note the excellent ironwork on the door, some of which is 800 years old. In the north chancel window is some medieval stained glass, depicting the Crucifixion.

St. Nicholas, Oldbury

Oldbury is, in effect, an outer suburb of Bridgnorth. The church, originally in the parish of Morville, was apparently founded in the 12th century, but little of the fabric of the present building is medieval. So today it looks Victorian, and comprises a nave, north aisle, south porch, chancel, and a western bell-turret. The windows are lancets, except for the west window, which has plate tracery. There are some older monuments: two tablets of the early 18th century, and a draped-urn monument of *c.*1830. There is some good Jacobean panelling at the west end of the church.

St. Mary Magdalene, Quatford**

Domesday Book records that the manor of Eardington (on the west bank of the Severn) was held by Earl Roger, and that he also held the 'borough' of Quatford (on the east bank) 'which paid nothing'. In addition to building a motte-and-bailey castle at Quatford, he also founded (in 1083/6) a college of priests. But within 15 years, Roger's son Robert had rebelled, and realising that the fortified site at Quatford was vulnerable, he removed both castle and college to Bridgnorth. And so it was Bridgnorth, not Quatford, that later prospered and became a Norman new town – even though Robert was forced to surrender to Henry I in 1102.

But Quatford church, of course, remained (Fig.2.5), and it was totally rebuilt at some time in the later 12th century. The most remarkable feature of the church is that it was apparently built entirely of tufa – a type of limestone in which the rocks have been formed by spring-water laden with calcium carbonate bubbling through sphagnum moss. The calcium carbonate was deposited in the form of a precipitate and gradually hardened. When the rock dries out, it develops a characteristic pitted appearance, like a petrified sponge (Fig.3.6). The use of tufa is often taken as a sign of relatively early Norman building, and the stone was not much used after *c.*1150 – but perhaps Quatford is an exception, for most authorities date the work here to *c.*1180. Today the chancel and the entire north wall of the nave consist of tufa, and even more remarkably, the chancel arch is also built of this material. Windows with Decorated tracery were inserted into the tufa walls of the chancel and nave in the 14th century. The south wall of the nave was taken down in 1857, and a south aisle and porch constructed of sandstone, but

Fig.24.17 St. Mary Magdalene, Quatford: the font, probably Norman, with some later carving

the Victorians re-used blocks of tufa in the porch and also in blocking the low-side window in the south wall of the chancel. The tower was rebuilt in 1714, but it looks anything but Georgian, being apparently Perpendicular with battlements and pinnacles.

Inside, the most notable feature is the tufaceous chancel arch. Unfortunately the details of the carving are now rather worn, but it remains an impressive and very rare structure. In the north wall of the chancel is a deeply-splayed Norman window, and in the south wall a Decorated piscina and the blocked low-side window mentioned above. There are some medieval tiles. There is a good Victorian pulpit.

The tower arch is Norman, but the arcade and south aisle are Victorian. In the north wall of the nave are the Royal Arms of George III. The font is unusual: it appears at first sight to be Norman, and indeed there is geometrical patterning around the lower part of the bowl which could be Norman. But the upper part of the bowl is carved with very un-Norman quatrefoils, which could have been done at any time from the 14th century onwards (Fig.24.17). In the porch are two coffin-lids from the 13th century, with incised crosses.

St. Andrew, Quatt***

The derivation of Quatt and Quatford has given etymologists a deal of trouble. Quatt appears to be a shortening of Quatton, and one theory is that the two names are the tun (homestead) and ford of Cwatt (a personal name); alternatively, the first component may be OE *Cwead* – a muddy place. At the time of the Domesday Book, Quatt was among the possessions of Earl Roger, and for some reason was included among the Warwickshire folios. After forfeiture by Earl Roger's son, it came into the hands of Henry I and was divided among the sons of Helgot, the lords of Castle Holdgate.

Fig.24.18 St. Andrew, Quatt:
Georgian tower and nave, with medieval chancel

At first sight, St. Andrew's church, attractively situated opposite the magnificent 18th-century dower house, appears to be Georgian (Fig.24.18), and indeed the tower, nave and the wall of the north aisle were built of brick in 1763. The architect for the Georgian building is usually stated to be Richard Colley, who also built Sutton Maddock; but Ionides makes a case for considering T.F. Pritchard to be responsible.[22] The chancel, north chapel and arcade are medieval of varying periods.

Earliest is part of the chancel, for the priest's doorway in the south wall is Norman, with a round-headed arch. The chapel to the north of the chancel is a fine example of Decorated building. The arcade is of uncertain date: it appears to be Perpendicular, with octagonal piers and concave sides, yet Pevsner thought that the quadrant-mouldings of the arches were more typical of the 14th century. The east end of the arcade is not bonded into the wall by a corbel or respond, but terminates in a free-standing column. Of the same era as the chapel is the wide round-headed arch between the chancel and the chapel; it is very unusual to find a round-headed arch dating from the 14th century. The tall windows in the chancel are Perpendicular, as is the fine roof (Fig.24.19). The chancel arch is Georgian, and the windows of the nave and north aisle are typical wide round-headed Georgian windows, with a keystone at the apex externally.

The font is a plain Norman structure, with a cable moulding between the bowl and the stem. The fine pulpit and reading-desk are dated 1629. The reredos (Fig.24.19) has probably been fashioned from the Perpendicular rood screen, and is richly carved. There is stained glass by Henry Holiday for Powell's and by Kempe in the chancel.

Fig.24.19 Quatt: the sanctuary

Quatt contains a notable series of monuments. These include:

1) Francis Wolryche (d.1614) and his wife. Two effigies on a tomb-chest, with children around the sides, and a baby at the base, below the heads (Fig.24.20).
2) Sir Thomas Wolryche (d.1668). A large tomb-chest with marble top and no effigy.
3) Sir Francis Wolryche (d.1689). Similar to the above.
4) Lady Mary Wolryche (d.1678), wife of John Wolryche, son of Sir Thomas. A remarkable monument in white marble, showing the deceased loosely robed, semi-reclining, and holding a lute (Fig.11.30). On either side are baroque twisted columns, and above is an open segmental pediment containing a vase. Mrs. Esdaile writes, 'The architec-

Fig.24.20 Quatt: the tomb-chest of Francis Wolryche (d.1614); two effigies on a tomb-chest

tural setting is inferior to the figure, which is unfortunately unsigned, but is certainly London work by a very notable master' – praise indeed for a monument in a little-known Shropshire church.

Fig.24.21 Holy Trinity, Sidbury: herring-bone masonry in the south wall of the nave

Holy Trinity, Sidbury*

Sidbury is a very ancient church, as evidenced by the herring-bone masonry in the west and south walls of the nave. It is basically, therefore, an early Norman church, but this was heavily disguised by the Victorian restorers of 1878-81. The church (Fig.24.21) consists of a western timber-framed belfry, nave, chancel, and an 18th-century vestry to the north of the chancel which was probably originally a mortuary chapel. There is a blocked Norman west doorway, and above this are courses of herring-bone masonry.

There was an original Norman font with a lead lining, but this was destroyed during a fire in 1911. It had intersecting arcading, and above tendrils and foliage.[24] There is a sketch of this font in the vestry, dated 1909. The present font is a rather poor replica. In the vestry are two very similar monuments of the reign of Queen Anne: these are to Anne Cresswell, d.1705, and Richard Cresswell, d.1708 aged 88. A Latin inscription records the faithfulness of Richard Cresswell to Charles I during the Civil War.

St. Peter and St. Paul, Tasley*

Tasley, on the western outskirts of Bridgnorth, was in medieval times a chapelry of Morville. There used to be a thatched timber church here, but this was pulled down in 1840 when the present building was erected. It is a typical Commissioners' Church, built in the Early English style. It is hard to dissent from Pevsner's judgment that it is 'a depressing building of only too well preserved yellow brick'. Yet there are several redeeming features inside. The stone octagonal font is Perpendicular, with quatrefoils on three faces, and a half-quatrefoil on a fourth. The screen is rather primitive, but dates from the late 15th or early 16th century. There is a Jacobean pulpit.

Holy Innocents, Tuckhill*

Tuckhill church evidently does not wish to advertise its presence, for it is entirely concealed within a wood, and no notice-board advises visitors of its whereabouts. This is a shame, for the church is a good example of the architecture of the 1860s. The architect was J.P. St. Aubyn, who restored Clunbury. The church (Fig.24.22) consists of a nave and south aisle, chancel and a western bellcote and short spire; the style is mainly Decorated. There is a good reredos, with a Crucifixion scene; and some Kempe glass in two windows. There is a modern lectern, with a carving of an angel.

Fig.24.22 Holy Innocents, Tuckhill (1865), by J.P. St. Aubyn

St. Michael, Upton Cressett**

The Upton family dates from Saxon times, and was joined in marriage to the Cressetts in the 14th century. The church (Fig.24.23) consists of a nave and chancel, with weather-boarded belfry and short lead spire, and a south chapel. The body of the church dates from the second half of the 12th century, and the Norman arches are exceeded in quality in Shropshire only by those of Edstaston. The most remarkable is the chancel arch (Fig.24.24), which has four orders of zigzag and other mouldings; originally it was surrounded by a hood-mould, a fragment of which can be seen at the south end of the arch. The south doorway of the nave also has a fine Norman arch, with two orders ornamented with different kinds of chevron; there is also chevron on the abaci. Above the arch is a zigzag hood. The capitals are sculpted with scrolls, volutes and a pattern resembling ears of corn. The doorway is partly hidden by the 14th-century timber-framed porch. The font (Fig.10.5) is Norman, with cable moulding at top and bottom, and carved arches around the bowl, which is lined with lead. There are Norman round-headed windows in the west and south walls of the nave, and the north wall of

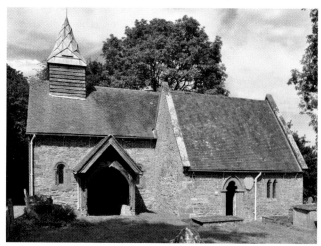

Fig.24.23 St. Michael, Upton Cressett

Fig.24.24 Upton Cressett: the chancel arch

the chancel. Some of these windows show nook-shafts, but the exterior of these has been renewed. The east window in the chancel is a very unusual single lancet; it may have been originally round-headed and converted into a lancet in the Early English era.

Also in the 13th century a north aisle was built (later demolished) and the arcade is now bonded in the north wall of the nave. The capital of the east respond has two large billet motifs, and between them a Tau cross (T-shaped) upside down. In the same century a chapel was built to the south of the chancel, joined to the chancel by an Early English arch; to the east of this arch may be seen the remains of a further arch of uncertain significance. In the west wall of the chapel is a medieval wall-painting depicting an angel and possibly two other figures. In the north wall of the chapel is a rubbing of a brass formerly housed in Upton Cressett and now transferred to Monkhopton; it shows effigies of Richard Cressett and his wife Jane, with two sons and three daughters, dated 1640. The church was closed for worship in 1959 and is now in the care of the Churches Conservation Trust.

St. Peter, Worfield**
Worfield takes its name from the river Worfe, a name possibly meaning 'wandering' or 'tired'.[25] It is an exceptionally pretty village, best seen in summer when the cottage gardens leading to the church are most colourful. St. Peter's is a large and distinguished church; at first glance it appears to be uniformly Decorated in style (though somewhat restored), with a notable tower and spire, the latter being the finest in Shropshire. Closer inspection, however, reveals certain obscure hints of an earlier building – features which neither Glynne, Cranage nor Pevsner were able satisfactorily to explain.

The church consists of the south-western tower and spire (Fig.6.7), nave with north and south aisles (the base of the tower occupying the westernmost bay of the south aisle), and chancel. The interior is rather dark, due to the stained glass in every window. The arcades are Decorated, dating from the 14th century, with octagonal piers and head-stops on the hood-moulds. On each side, the easternmost bay is narrower than the others, indicating to Cranage that there must have originally been north and south transepts. Below the eastern respond of the south arcade is a nook-shaft which Pevsner describes as 'decidedly Norman'. The chancel is Decorated, and the chancel arch has a little ball-flower decoration; the screen between nave and chancel is partly original Perpendicular.

At the west end of the church are further anomalies. In the north wall of the tower, facing into the nave, is what Pevsner described as a 'double piscina' without a drain – but what an unusual place for a piscina; above is a large lancet window now functionless and opening internally. Externally, between the Victorian porch and the tower, is a small pointed window of two lights. It may well be that all these

Fig.24.25 St. Peter, Worfield: monument to Sir George Bromley (d.1588) and his wife; alabaster effigies on a tomb-chest

unexplained features are relics from an earlier church which were re-set when the present building was erected.

In the north aisle are two fine monuments and three hatchments. The earlier tomb is to Sir George Bromley (d.1588) and his wife (d.1622) (Fig.24.25). These are alabaster effigies, the lady placed behind and a little above her husband. The effigies are placed in a good architectural setting, complete with Renaissance details. Nearby is the imposing Jacobean monument to Sir Edward Bromley (d.1626) and his wife; again there are recumbent alabaster effigies in a heavy six-post edifice.

Perhaps the finest feature of Worfield is the tower and spire. The tower, like the rest of the church is of red sandstone, but the recessed spire is of grey stone.

25

Bishop's Castle and Clun Forest

Bedstone*   Llanfair Waterdine
Bettws-y-Crwyn**   Lydbury North**
Bishop's Castle*   Lydham*
Bucknell*   Mainstone*
Chapel Lawn   Mindtown*
Clun**   More*
Clunbury**   Newcastle on Clun
Clungunford*   Norbury*
Clunton   Ratlinghope
Edgton*   Stowe*
Hopesay**   Wentnor*
Hopton Castle

St. Mary, Bedstone*

Bedstone church is a very strange amalgam of Norman and neo-Norman parts, cobbled together by F.R. Kempson of Hereford in 1879 – a late date for neo-Norman work. The original 12th-century features are as follows: a plain round-headed chancel arch; the remains of a priest's doorway visible externally on the south wall of the chancel; and two small round-headed windows, deeply splayed internally, one in the south wall of the nave and the other in the north wall of the chancel. To this Kempson added a round-headed west doorway with chevron carving above, and one order of shafts with capitals etc.; and an extraordinary row of round-headed windows in both north and south walls of the nave. These are splayed inside, with the corresponding areas externally filled with further round-headed blind windows – giving a row of seven on the outside. The windows on the north side are filled with very good Kempe glass, which earns the church its star; they depict a king, a prophet, St. John the Evangelist and the Virgin and Child. There is a plain Norman font, with a simple moulding around the middle of the bowl. Above the west doorway is a timber-framed belfry with a shingled broach spire.

St. Mary, Bettws-y-Crwyn**

At 1,253 feet above sea-level, St. Mary's church is the highest parish church in Shropshire, possibly the highest in England. Why was the church built in such a remote and inaccessible situation? The question is discussed in *The Gale of Life*.[1] No village has ever developed in the thinly-populated parish, which remains a scattered collection of farm-houses. With its Welsh name of partly uncertain meaning (though *bettws* is Welsh for chapel from OE

287

bed-hus – 'oratory'), and its situation west of Offa's Dyke, it would seem to be much more Welsh than English, yet it has always been in Shropshire, and in the diocese of Hereford.

The origin of St. Mary's is lost in antiquity, but at some stage it was appropriated to Abbey Cwmhir, a Cistercian monastery in mid-Wales founded in 1143. By 1276 the chapel belonged at least in part to the Prior of Chirbury. By 1331 it was recognised as a dependency of Clun and therefore belonged to the Prior of Wenlock. After the Reformation, the Visitation-book of Bishop Westfaling mentions that Bettws is in the diocese of Hereford, and ranked as a united curacy with Llanfair Waterdine.

Today the church is seen as basically medieval, but so thorough was the restoration of 1860 that little remains to help in dating the building. All the windows are Victorian lancets, and the bell-turret dates from the restoration. It is a small church, just nave and chancel, and its great attraction lies in the furniture and fittings (Fig.1.8). The late Perpendicular screen of Spanish chestnut is outstanding, one of the finest in Shropshire (Fig.13.1); it has round arches, mullions running up into their apices, and small and intricate panel tracery. There is a frieze of heavy pierced quatrefoils above the dado. The roof is also good (Fig.8.7), and may be late-medieval; it has collar-beams on arched braces, and two lateral tiers of wind-braces carved into quatrefoils. The communion rail is simple and rustic, and may be Jacobean. The benches (Fig.14.13) are of rude craftsmanship – an unusual feature is that they are inscribed with the names of farms in the parish which can still be identified today, though all the names of the farmers' families have changed.

St. John the Baptist, Bishop's Castle*

Sir Stephen Glynne visited Bishop's Castle in 1852 and was not favourably impressed: 'A poor church much altered and vilely arranged ... the whole church miserably dark and encumbered by pues and galleries.' His opinion must have been generally shared, for eight years later the church (with the exception of the tower) was radically altered to the design of Thomas Nicholson of Hereford: the chancel and aisles were totally rebuilt, and the nave heightened to allow a clerestory. Removed from the old church was a fine Early English doorway; this can now be seen in the wall of the vicarage garden. The old church had suffered much damage in 1645 during the Civil War; a few days after a Royalist force was defeated just outside the town, the church was partly burnt by the Royalist commander as it had been used 'for the preaching of sedition'. There was such severe damage that the church had to be rebuilt in 1648.[2]

The building is on a substantial scale, with western tower, north porch, nave with north and south aisles, north and south transepts, and chancel with north and south chapels. The tower (Fig.25.1) is low and sturdy, apparently Norman, but both Glynne and

Fig.25.1 St John the Baptist, Bishop's Castle: the tower

Cranage thought otherwise. Glynne wrote: 'The tower seems of late character', implying a post-Reformation date, and Cranage concurred, attributing it to the post-Civil War period. The arcade of the nave is perhaps the best feature of the Victorian church: tall, stately, multishafted columns, with plainly moulded capitals, give a chaste appearance not typical of 1860. Above is a clerestory with circular windows. In the chancel, unfortunately, the architect succumbed to the fashions of the day, the capitals of the arcade being floridly adorned.

Surviving from the old church are two artefacts in the south transept: a plain Norman tub font; and the most interesting object, a demi-figure of an Elizabethan divine, now upright in the south-west corner. At the time of Glynne's visit, this figure was described as 'an effigy of a priest carrying a bible, the figure intercepted across the middle by plain stone work, below which are seen the feet'; the lower part of this figure has evidently since been lost. There is some excellent Victorian stained glass by Powell's, O'Connor and Henry Holiday.

St. Mary, Bucknell*
Bucknell earns its star purely because of the font, the building itself being undistinguished. The church is largely the product of the extensive restoration of 1870; the only signal reminders of the previous building are the blocked priest's door in the south wall of the chancel, dating from the 13th or 14th century, and what Glynne described as a sepulchral arch in the north wall of the chancel. There is an attractive shingled broach spire on a wooden bell-turret at the west end. Internally, the nave is separated from the north aisle by an arcade with very florid capitals; the chancel arch is similar.

The font (Fig.10.10) is 11th-century, though whether Anglo-Saxon or early Norman is hard to say. There is a human head on the east aspect of the bowl, surrounded by intricate interlacing patterns; the head is reminiscent of the 11th-century tympanum at Stottesdon.

St. Mary, Chapel Lawn
St. Mary's is a typical church of the 1840s, built in the Early English style by Edward Haycock sen. A shallow polygonal apse appears to have been a later addition.

St. George, Clun**
The churchyard is circular, which may well indicate a pre-Christian site. There was almost certainly a Saxon church here, but no trace remains, and it is not mentioned in the Domesday Book. It appears, however, that Clun was then a minster church, serving a very wide area. St. George's has a complex building history which is difficult to unravel. The damage sustained in the Civil War and the extent of the restoration in 1877 have caused much uncertainty. Fortunately, Sir Stephen Glynne visited Clun in 1850 and left a valuable description of the church before the restoration.

The oldest part of the present fabric is the round-headed arch at the eastern end of the north arcade; this is a plain Norman arch, built before 1150, but it is probably not in its original situation. It may have originally led to a north transept, or may even have been a chancel arch – but there is no evidence for either suggestion. The rest of the arcades date from the second half of the 12th century – the Transitional period – for here are sturdy Norman pillars supporting pointed arches, signifying the arrival of Gothic (Fig.3.9). There are prominent square abaci over the columns, and deeply scalloped capitals. There is a clerestory only on the south side, with the windows directly above the piers.

The massive Norman tower (Fig.2.6) came a little later, for a Norman window high in the west wall of the nave now looks into the tower. The tower was almost certainly a place of refuge for the populace in the troubled years of the 13th century. It is distinguished by a double-pyramid roof – a feature which is also seen in Hopesay and More. There is a fine west doorway at the base of the tower, with three plain orders.

The excellent roof of the nave and chancel was revealed by the restoration in 1877 by the distinguished architect, G.E. Street; there are collar-beams on arched braces, with three tiers of wind-braces laterally. The eastern part of the roof is probably Victorian, but the western half is mostly older, probably Perpendicular. The roof over the wide north aisle is even finer.

The chancel was almost completely rebuilt in 1877, and the sedilia, east window, screen and choir-stalls all date from this time. Here the lancet windows have nook-shafts of Purbeck marble. There is some good woodwork: the pulpit is Jacobean (Fig.14.5), and so is the reredos at the eastern end of the north aisle. High over the altar of the north aisle is a carved wooden canopy which is panelled, with bosses at the intersection of the ribs, and probably dates from the early 16th century. Altar canopies were a feature of some medieval churches and they were designed to give greater dignity to the altar (like a ceilure in the roof); very few survived the Reformation.

The font is an octagonal bowl resting on a shaft surrounded by eight columns; its date is uncertain. On its west face is an incised geometrical rosette. The north porch provides an imposing entrance, and above it is a chamber which was previously a school-room. Remains of the stair to this room can still be discerned on the east side externally. There are benefaction boards in the porch. The main doorway is late Norman, with very worn capitals. Outside the church is a tomb-recess with ball-flower decoration on the north side of the nave; to the west of this is a further late Norman doorway with dogtooth decoration, much of which has been renewed.

St. Swithin, Clunbury**

Clunbury is an ancient village. The Bronze Age (*c*.2000 BC) Clun to Clee ridgeway passed through the parish, and Bronze Age implements have been found here.[3] The Saxon name means a fortified site or manor house on the river Clun. The Domesday survey records that before 1066 the manor was held by Sweyn, a substantial landowner. In 1086 the manor was held by Robert de Say, lord of Clun, who also owned Kempton, Purslow, Obley and Coston, all in the present parish of Clunbury. Clunbury church and St. George's, Clun were given by Isabella de Say to Wenlock Abbey in 1190. By 1340 Clunbury was a separate parish.

The church (Fig.25.2) is basically Norman, as evidenced by the south doorway (two capitals with plain Norman carvings), and by small round-headed windows with deep internal splays in the north and south walls of the nave and the north wall of the chancel. To the east of the present Victorian porch are the remains of the lower part of the west jamb of a further south doorway. The base of the tower is Norman, but later than the nave for the window above the Norman tower arch opens into the tower. The upper parts of the tower were probably rebuilt in the 17th century. The other windows in the nave are Decorated (*c*.1300-50). The north-west window of the nave is Victorian. The chancel was largely rebuilt in the 19th century.

Fig.25.2 St. Swithin, Clunbury

In the south wall of the nave, near the reading-desk, is a piscina indicating the earlier presence of an altar. This corresponds externally with a 13th-century tomb-recess, which probably originally housed the donor of the altar. The font is a plain Norman bowl, standing on a modern base and steps. By the font stands a Jacobean chest, and the back of the Jacobean pulpit. In the north wall of the nave are two monuments by Samuel Stead of Ludlow to members of the Edwards family; they consist of urns above a plain tablet. The roof (Fig.8.9) is the finest artefact in the church – collar-beams on arched braces, with one tier of quatrefoiled wind-braces, dated dendrochronologically to 1495-96.[4] There is some excellent stained glass, including one window in the south of the nave by Kempe and Co.

St. Cuthbert, Clungunford*

St. Cuthbert's church (Fig.25.3), standing attractively next to the meadows flanking the Clun river, was so over-restored in the 19th century that it almost appears a Victorian church. Yet in fact only the north tower and porch are Victorian (by E. Turner, 1895), the rest of the church dating from *c*.1300. The church consists of tower, nave, chancel and north chancel chapel, and Cranage thought that the nave and north chapel were Early English (late 13th century), and the chancel Decorated (early 14th century). The roofs over the chancel and the nave have recently been dated by dendrochronology to 1329 and 1338-39, respectively,[5] largely confirming Cranage's opinion. Unfortunately, the roofs are hidden by ceilings. The organ is a fine work of Binns.[6]

Fig.25.3 St. Cuthbert, Clungunford

St. Mary, Clunton
A small stone-built church dating from 1870-71.

St. Michael, Edgton*
Edgton is recorded in Domesday Book as *Egedune* ('hill with an edge or brow').[7] St. Michael's is a small medieval church, largely rebuilt in 1895. It consists of nave and chancel, with a small bellcote. There are two original narrow lancets of the 13th century, one above the west door and one in the south wall of the nave. The other wider lancets, and the east window, date from the rebuilding. The plain west doorway is probably late Norman, though it may well not be in its original position.

There are some interesting furnishings: some box-pews with carving and texts, dated 1631; two recently restored hatchments; and a plain round font, possibly 12th-century, on a modern stem.

St. Mary, Hopesay**
The name of the village derives from the Anglo-Saxon 'hope' meaning an enclosed valley and affixed to this is the surname of Picot de Say, who was given lands in south Shropshire and elsewhere by William the Conqueror; his name is also commemorated in Stokesay nearby, and at Moreton Say, near Market Drayton. At the time of the Domesday survey (1087), the village was recorded as 'Hope', the manor being held by Picot from Roger, earl of Montgomery.

The present church (Fig.25.4) dates from the second half of the 12th century, the period when Norman and Early English features commonly appear side by side. The south doorway is Norman, with a round arch and a bold roll moulding over a plain tympanum; the columns at the side have capitals with rather worn carving – the western capital has a volute and primitive leaves, the eastern is scalloped. The priest's doorway in the south wall of the chancel is also round, but plain. Internally (Fig.25.5), the chancel arch between the nave and the chancel is pointed (i.e. Early English), and probably dates from *c*.1200.

There are narrow lancet windows in the north and south walls of the chancel, and a broader lancet in the north wall of the nave near to the pulpit. On the outside of this window are iron hooks for the shutters which preceded glass, and on the inside some irregularity of the sill indicates the remains of steps which previously led to a rood loft.

The east window is Victorian, but the window in the south-western corner of the chancel is a two-light Decorated window; although Mercer argues that this window replaced an Early English lancet, and was not an insertion.[8] From the exterior, it can be seen that below the western half of this

Fig.25.4 St. Mary, Hopesay

Fig.25.5 Hopesay: the nave and chancel

window is a rectangular opening, now blocked, indicating a previous 'low-side' window; the purpose of low-side windows is unknown. Further 'Decorated' windows in the south wall of the nave are probably 19th-century, but to the west of the porch is another 14th-century window of two lights; in the quatrefoil above the sub-arches is a fragment of stained glass consisting of a coat-of-arms dating from the end of the 14th century celebrating the marriage of Richard Fitzalan, earl of Arundel, with Philippa Mortimer.

There is some Jacobean carving at the back of the choir seats. There is a western gallery, which is probably 19th-century, replacing an earlier one erected in 1631. The recently restored Royal Arms of George III (1776) are placed against the west wall. There are two fonts: at the west end stands an ornate Victorian font of 1856; and just to the west of the doorway is the original plain Norman font. When Glynne visited in 1871 it was in a farm-yard; later it was moved to the new church at Bryn; and when that church closed in 2008 it was returned to Hopesay.

The best feature of the church is the nave roof, dating from the 15th century (Fig.8.8). This consists of seven trusses; four of these have collar-braces, with open quatrefoils and trefoils above. The central truss and those against the end walls also have tie-beams. On each side are two purlins between three fine rows of wind-braces in quatrefoil patterns. An unusual feature is the fine ornamented panelling on both the north and south walls, showing blank arcading like the dado of a screen.

The tower is difficult to date accurately. It must be later than the nave, for there is no tower arch communicating with the nave, but it cannot be very much later – it is squat, with rectangular slits for windows, and is probably early 13th-century. There are diagonal buttresses at the south-west and north-east corners, probably added in the 14th century. A flat two-stage buttress at the north-west corner is really an extension northwards of the west wall; a similar structure may be seen at the south-east corner. Two other fairly hideous buttresses are much later and support the north and south walls.

The upper storey of the tower shows a truncated pyramid, with a low upright storey and then a smaller pyramid roof. Hopesay shares this 'double-pyramid' form with the churches at nearby Clun and More, and in Wales at Knighton and Kerry; Glynne called it the 'Montgomeryshire dovecote type'.

St. Edward, Hopton Castle

Hopton Castle is a very pretty village, with half-timbered houses and the impressive ruins of the castle keep; this sustained a siege in the Civil War, resulting in the notorious massacre of the Parliamentary defenders. The church is not, perhaps, quite worthy of its situation, being a conventional building designed by Thomas Nicholson of Hereford in 1871. The windows are cusped lancets, and the east window has in addition sexfoil tracery above. The church consists of an undivided nave and chancel. The ornate stone pulpit features a series of pillars, heavily encrusted with foliage. The bowl of the font is plain, with thick cable moulding around the stem. The Victorian stained glass is attractive.

St. Mary, Llanfair Waterdine

The church of 'St. Mary by the water' (the translation of the place-name) is situated close to the river Teme, where it forms the boundary between Shropshire and Wales. There used to exist here a medieval church (Fig.25.6), allegedly 11th-century, with oak pillars, beautifully carved, and a fantastic array of box-pews and roof timbers. All was wantonly swept away in 1853 in what Cranage described as 'one of the most wicked cases of vandalism I have ever come across'; instead arose the present aseptic building, a plain edifice in the Decorated style, by Thomas Nicholson.

Fig.25.6 Llanfair Waterdine: the medieval church painted by the Rev. Edward Williams in 1791

Though the building is mean, there are a few redeeming features: the pine pews, each bearing the name of a farm in the parish (as at nearby Bettws-y-Crwyn); the timbered roof of trussed rafters; and best of all the communion rail composed of timbers from the late Perpendicular rood screen, containing a remarkable inscription which has defied interpretation.[9]

St. Michael and All Angels, Lydbury North**

The manor of Lydbury North was held in the reign of King Offa (757-796) by Egwin Shakehead; later it passed into the hands of the bishops of Hereford who held it at the time of the Domesday survey. The church was clearly important then, for it was mentioned specifically in the Domesday Book.

The massive, heavily buttressed western tower probably dates from the early 13th century, at least as far up as the corbel-table (Fig.25.7); the battlements are Perpendicular. The buttresses probably date from 1624.[10] On the south, the belfry windows are late Norman, those on the other faces being pairs of lancets. The fine south porch is wooden, probably late Perpendicular, with barge-boarding. Proceed through the ancient studded south door, and to the left is the late Norman font – a round basin cut out of a square block, the lower sides of which are deeply scalloped. The tower opens into the nave by the tower arch, which is Transitional, being pointed with late Norman scalloping.

Fig.25.7 St. Michael and All Angels, Lydbury North

The long nave (Fig.25.8), without aisles, is basically Norman, with one small round-headed window in both north and south walls. The roof is very fine, consisting of tie-beams, collar-beams on arched braces, and one tier of wind-braces on each side. There is a wonderfully complete set of Jacobean box-pews (Fig.14.16) and also a Jacobean pulpit.

On the left of the nave, a plain Norman arch opens into the north transept, the Plowden chapel. This probably dates from the early 14th century; it is plainly furnished with an altar and piscina, and in the angle between the chapel and the chancel are the stairs to the former rood loft. The rude screen separating the nave from the chapel is late Perpendicular.

Fig.25.8 Lydbury North: the nave, roof, screen and chancel

Directly opposite the Plowden chapel is the south transept, the Walcot chapel. The arch into this chapel was built in 1901-02 by J.T. Micklethwaite as part of his conservative restoration; on either side of the arch are heads of Queen Victoria and King Edward VII. The chapel itself was built by the Walcot family in the mid-17th century, probably after the Restoration of Charles II (1660). This was a rare date for church-building; the chapel has an upper floor, which was previously used as a schoolroom.

From the south transept, turn right into the nave and here, between the nave and chancel, and dominating the entire church, is the greatest treasure of Lydbury North, the Perpendicular (but much restored) rood screen, surmounted by a fantastic and very rare tympanum (Fig.25.8). This is inscribed with the Creed, Ten Commandments and Lord's Prayer, and is dated 1615. The screen has wide divisions separated by vertical columns with fine tracery above; the upper part of the dado is pierced by quatrefoils.

Pass through the screen into the Norman chancel; the round-headed windows here (three in the north wall, one in the south) are larger than those in the nave, and probably date from a little later in the 12th century. In the south wall of the chancel is the priest's door – a Norman doorway; externally this has chevron decoration in the arch and one order of shafts on each side. The east window of the chancel is Perpendicular; on the north is a square recess, an aumbry, and on the south an arched piscina and a two-light Decorated window.

Holy Trinity, Lydham*

Lydham church (Fig.25.9) has two delights to offer the visitor – a notable churchyard, with 35 yews all beautifully shaped by a skilled topiarist, and an excellent roof. The church itself is unremarkable – a small building, with nave and chancel, and a western bellcote. A priest was mentioned at *Lidum* in the Domesday Book, so there was probably a Saxon church here. There is now no trace of this but the church is clearly of medieval

Fig.25.9 Holy Trinity, Lydham

origin, being built probably around 1200; it was, however, substantially rebuilt in 1642 – hence the deceptive tracery of most of the windows, which appear to date from the early 14th century. There is a plain, panelled Jacobean pulpit, and a set of box-pews. There are Victorian tiles in the sanctuary, and also a number of Oakeley family memorial tablets and one hatchment. There is a plain octagonal font.

The roof of the chancel consists of trussed rafters, and is said to be 13th-century;[11] over the nave there are collar-beams on arched braces, one tie-beam and one tier of quatrefoiled wind-braces on each side.

St. John the Baptist, Mainstone*

The name of the village, which is traversed by Offa's Dyke, comes from OE *maeganstan* – a 'big rock'.[12] This refers to a stone now in front of the pulpit which was used as a test of strength by the young men of the parish, and possibly also as a measure for a bag of wheat (200lb. plus 4.5lb. for the bag!). The Dyke passes just to the west of the churchyard (is Mainstone the only church on the Dyke?). The state of the former church, recorded by a watercolour of the Rev. Williams in 1791, was causing increasing concern in Victorian times and the building was replaced in 1887 by a new edifice in the Decorated style. The building itself is conventional and not of great interest, but the visitor is pleasantly surprised by the treasures contained therein.

Outstanding is the Perpendicular roof retained from the previous church. It has no less than three tiers of quatrefoiled wind-braces laterally, with collar-beams on arched braces; even more remarkable is the antique carved panelling between the wall-plate and the roof timbers which continues in both nave and chancel on each side (cf Hopesay). There is a plain tub font, probably Norman, and a large medieval chest. The glass in the east window by Powell's is excellent: a representation of the risen Christ, adored by the Virgin and by Saints John the Baptist and John the Evangelist.

St. John the Baptist, Mindtown*

Fig.25.10 St. John the Baptist, Mindtown

This remote little church (Fig.25.10) is perched on a knoll just to the west of the Long Mynd, commanding extensive views. Its appeal rests on its quaintness and its situation rather than its architecture, which is non-specific and ambiguous. It probably does date from Norman times, even though that begs the question, why should the Normans (or indeed anyone else) bother to build a church here?

There are hints of 12th-century work in the church: Cranage pointed to the rounded arch of the north window and a possible Norman string-course at the east end of the nave. There appears to be part of a medieval consecration cross mostly hidden behind the plaster of the north wall of the nave. And the plain rough bowl of the font looks Norman, though the base is later. The communion rail is crude but appealing 17th-century work, and a Jacobean pew has been reassembled to form a screen at the west end of the church. The nave is covered by a trussed-rafter roof, and the chancel has purlins with ornamental purlin-braces. One truss has both tie- and collar-beams, the other a collar only.

St. Peter, More*

More church is closely bound up with the More family of Linley Hall, who have owned much of the land in the parish since the 12th century. But the history of More goes back much further: for the Romans organised extensive lead mining at Linley, and relics of their works can be seen today at Linley Hall.[13]

The church consists of a medieval tower (Fig.25.11), distinguished by the double pyramid roof similar to Clun and Hopesay (q.v.), a 17th-century north transept and an early Victorian nave and chancel. Under the top pyramid of the tower there is a space all round the tower, with vertical strips of wood; below is another opening with horizontal strips; and below this the second truncated pyramid rests on the walls of the tower.[14] The nave and chancel were rebuilt by the Rev. T.F. More in 1845 – Cranage describes the architecture as 'dull in the extreme' – the long series of lancet windows in the south wall of the nave and chancel exemplify this. The interior (Fig.25.12) is more pleasing – there is a good set of Victorian box-pews and a hammer-beam roof. The west gallery is supported by cast-iron pillars. On the floor near the font is a Roman mosaic; it is thought that this probably did not come from the Roman settlements nearby, but from Europe, being brought back to England by a gentleman on the Grand Tour. Projecting from the north wall of the nave is a 17th-century transept, which was built as the More

Fig.25.11 St. Peter, More

family mortuary chapel; here are some hatchments and a memorial by Field to Harriott More, wife of the architect (d.1851); this depicts a woman standing on a pedestal with an urn. The church formerly housed an important library of early theological books given to the parish by Richard More in 1680 'to teach the minister sound doctrine'; the books are still available to the parishioners, but are now safely housed in Linley Hall.

Fig.25.12 More: the nave, roof and chancel

St. John the Evangelist, Newcastle on Clun

This is a plain stone church designed in 1848 by Edward Haycock sen. There are lancet windows and a hammer-beam roof. The garish glass in the east window is by David Evans.

All Saints, Norbury*

Norbury is a small parish in lovely countryside to the west of the Long Mynd. The attractive village clusters round All Saints church, which until 1894 was a chapelry in the parish of Lydbury North. Sir Stephen Glynne visited Norbury in 1852 and was not impressed. 'A mean church, with only chancel and nave and a rude square tower at the west end ... the interior has a gloomy appearance entirely pewed.' Twenty-seven years later the nave was rebuilt and a porch and spire added; rebuilding of the chancel followed in 1892, the architect being Henry Curzon.

So today the tower alone is medieval, an unbuttressed structure dating from the 14th century, and surmounted by a shingled broach spire (Fig.6.14). The tower is built of a local calcareous sandstone of the Pentamerus beds.[15] Madge Moran comments that 'some of the stones appear to be very porous and spongelike, but the durability seems to be unaffected'. The nave and chancel are plain and undistinguished, the most appealing feature being the late Victorian painted ceiling which was uncovered only after the end of the Second World War. The south door survives from the old church; it is of studded oak with some simple iron work. Also from the old church is the 14th-century octagonal font. There is a massive ancient yew in the churchyard.

St. Margaret, Ratlinghope

Visit St. Margaret's church for its setting in some of the finest scenery in the county, and for the churchyard, outstanding in its profusion of wild flowers in the spring; but the church, perhaps, is not quite of the same standard. For such a wild place, it is a very ancient community: the Domesday Book records that it was held by Robert Fitz Corbet, and in both 1066 and 1087 it was waste. The place-name has caused a lot of discussion, but appears to mean 'the valley (hope) of Rotel's people'.[16] By the end of the 12th century prosperity had returned to the area, for here in about 1209 was founded an Augustinian priory as a daughter-cell of Wigmore Abbey. This priory survived until the Dissolution in 1536, and no traces of the priory buildings remain.

The church consists of a nave and chancel, with a weather-boarded belfry. It is uncertain how much, if any, of the priory church survives in the masonry of St. Margaret's; Cranage thought that none of the architectural detail was likely to be medieval, and Pevsner concurred. It is probable, therefore, that most of the building dates from the 17th century and this is confirmed by the inscription on the door saying that the door was made and given by the churchwardens in the year 1625. Cranage thought that the tie-beam roof probably also dated from that period. The communion rails date from the 18th century, and are made of wrought iron.

St. Michael, Stowe*

When Sir Stephen Glynne visited Stowe in 1864, he found the church in the process of an almost entire reconstruction; apart from the roof, scarcely any of the original work was retained. Today, this beautifully situated church (Fig.25.13) high above the Teme valley, looks mostly Victorian; the masonry of the nave may be original, but it has been drastically restored; and the chancel looks all Victorian.

Fig.25.13 St. Michael, Stowe

The interior has a good roof, which Cranage thought probably dated from the 17th century; there are tie-beams with queen-posts, alternating with collar-beams and laterally there are two tiers of wind-braces. Otherwise, the interest, and the appeal, lies in the unusual Victorian and Edwardian ornamentation of the chancel. The reredos is dated 1901 and is a mosaic depicting on the left St. Michael weighing souls, and on the right St. George slaying the dragon. A further mosaic of 1911 depicting Faith is on the north wall of the chancel. Pevsner accurately described these as in the Arts and Crafts mould, with the ornamentation rather Art Nouveau. Stained glass depicting the Ascension is in the east window, and Hope and Charity are depicted in the south windows of the chancel; these are memorial windows from 1878 to 1895.

St. Michael and All Angels, Wentnor*

In the Domesday Book, Wentnor is *Wantenovre*; the second element derives from OE *ofer* – Gelling regarded Wentnor as the best site supporting her hypothesis that *ofer* is used for a site on the tip of a flat-topped hill spur.[17] And this perfectly describes Wentnor's situation – on a knoll to the west of the Long Mynd, with extensive views over the steeply falling ground. The first element of the place-name may be a Saxon personal name.

Fig.25.14 St. Michael and All Angels, Wentnor

At the time of the Domesday survey the manor was held by Roger Fitz Corbet from Earl Roger; the advowson was given to Shrewsbury Abbey in 1095. The church (Fig.25.14) was partially rebuilt in 1885 by Henry Curzon, but surviving from the Norman church are the blocked doorway in the north wall and a small round-headed window, deeply splayed in the Norman manner. The imposts of the blocked doorway are carved, the east with early dogtooth, the west with horizontal fluting. The south doorway is a little later, with a pointed arch and plain imposts. The rest of the nave and chancel are the work of Curzon. The roof of the nave is late Perpendicular, and shows tie-beams, collar-beams and arched braces, with one tier of lateral wind-braces. The chancel roof is Victorian. The handsome pulpit is Jacobean, with panelling behind arranged at right-angles. One notable tombstone at the west end of the church commemorates a hurricane and snow-storm which claimed the lives of seven villagers. Also at the west end is a wooden bell-turret, supported inside the church by a complex array of ancient and more recent beams.

The Clee Hills

Abdon*

Aston Botterell**

Clcchill

Clee St. Margaret*

Cleeton St. Mary*

Cleobury Mortimer**

Cleobury North**

Cold Weston

Coreley

Ditton Priors*

Doddington*

Farlow

Heath***

Hope Bagot**

Hopton Wafers*

Kinlet***

Knowbury

Loughton

Milson*

Nash*

Neen Savage**

Neen Sollars*

Neenton

Silvington*

Stoke St. Milborough*

Stottesdon***

Wheathill*

Whitton**

St. Margaret, Abdon*

Abdon, on the western side of Brown Clee Hill, is the site of a deserted medieval village;[1] mounds and undulations around the church remain as evidence of the former community which apparently left the area in the 14th century. The place-name is recorded in Domesday Book as *Abetune* (meaning 'Abba's tun or settlement'). The churchyard is circular, suggesting a pre-Christian site.[2] The church is small, consisting only of nave and chancel, with a western bellcote. The medieval church had become very ruinous by the late 18th century, when it was substantially rebuilt (Fig.26.1). The sole original window is the Decorated window in the south wall of the chancel, and comparison with the Williams painting of 1790 shows that even that has been re-pointed. Inside, there is an unusual timber construction between nave and chancel, consisting of two upright posts against the walls and independent posts, and above a tie-beam with king-post and diagonal queen-posts. The font is a plain 12th- or 13th-century tub.

Fig.26.1 St. Margaret, Abdon

St. Michael, Aston Botterell**

In Domesday Book, the manor is simply *Estone* (eastern settlement), but by 1203 it was held by William Botterell and by 1263 the manor had become Estin Boterel.[3]

The church (Fig.3.11) consists of a western tower, south porch, nave with south aisle and chancel. It is attractively situated next to a farmyard, and is notable for its two monuments. The tower was rebuilt, partly from old masonry, in 1884. The nave and chancel date from the late 12th and early

Fig.26.2 St. Michael, Aston Botterell: the south arcade and chancel

13th centuries. There is a small Norman window in the north wall of the chancel, and an Early English priest's door in the south wall. The low arcade (Fig.26.2) is Early English, with circular piers, capitals and abaci. The porch was built in 1639. In the east window is some stained glass which is possibly medieval. The font is Norman, and displays a single band of nail-head carving.

In the north wall of the chancel is a large, upright incised slab to John Botterell (d.1479) and his wife. Much of the details of John Botterell have unfortunately been lost. His wife's representation is less damaged, and she is shown wearing a pedimental head-dress. It is thought that this slab came from the same workshop as the one at Beckbury.[4]

At the east end of the south aisle is the impressive Elizabethan monument to another John Botterell (d.1588) and his wife (Fig.11.18). Two effigies lie on a tomb-chest, the gentleman in armour, with the children kneeling round the sides. A canopy above is supported by columns with classical mouldings.

St. Peter, Cleehill

A brick-built church, dated 1881, on the main road in Cleehill village.

St. Margaret, Clee St. Margaret*

Situated high on the western slopes of Brown Clee Hill, the settlement of Clee St. Margaret survived the later Middle Ages when its near neighbours Abdon, Cold Weston and Heath succumbed; as a result, the parish church now stands in an attractive village. The building is clearly of great antiquity. There was probably a Saxon church here, but no incontrovertible evidence of this remains. The most striking feature of the present building is the extensive herring-bone masonry (pp.11-13) in the walls of the chancel (Fig.26.3). The priest's door in the south wall of the chancel is very rude and plain – almost like the Saxon doorway at Diddlebury – but it too is probably early Norman rather than Saxon.

The church is small – just nave and chancel, with a western belfry, the chancel a little earlier than the nave. The south doorway is plain Norman and round-headed, but the chancel arch is pointed, though with plain Norman imposts; it is therefore Transitional, and must be later than the external walls. On either side of the arch is a hagioscope. There is a great variety of windows: a small Norman one in the north wall of the chancel, a two-light Decorated window in the south wall of the chancel, a wide, probably 17th-century window in the south wall of the nave, and lancet windows in the east and west walls, the former being restored. The font is a plain Norman tub on a modern stem.

Fig.26.3 St. Margaret, Clee St. Margaret: herring-bone masonry in the chancel walls

Within the chancel arch is a pair of handsome low Jacobean doors, and the pulpit is also Jacobean. The roof of both chancel and nave has timbers from the 14th or 15th centuries.

St. Mary, Cleeton St. Mary*

This is an attractive late Victorian church, with a fine situation on Titterstone Clee Hill, 1,000 feet above sea-level. The parish was formed out of the parishes of Farlow, Bitterley and Doddington, and the church was built in 1878 by Thomas Nicholson of Hereford. It is in the Early English style throughout, built at a time when this had passed out of fashion; yet it is much more impressive than similar churches built in Shropshire 30 or 40 years previously.

The church consists of nave and chancel, with a shingled broach spire resting on the west wall and three internal arches. Below the eaves of the spire is a row of recessed quatrefoils. A string course decorated with nail-head above and below runs all round the exterior. The windows are lancets, with the addition of a small vesica above paired lancets on each side of the nave. There are three very tall lancets at the east end, and one at the west end of the church. There is some very good Victorian stained glass by Hardman.

St. Mary, Cleobury Mortimer**

The elegant church and spire of St. Mary's dominates the high street of this attractive south Shropshire town, which takes the second part of its name from one of the great Marcher families. Domesday Book records that in Saxon times, Cleobury was in the possession of Queen Edith, wife of Edward the Confessor, and it passed to Ralph de Mortimer after the Norman Conquest. The book also records the presence of a priest, implying the existence of a Saxon church. The Mortimers took their family name from Mortemer in Normandy, and they were based at Wigmore Castle in Herefordshire, which was also in the hands of Ralph. Later in the Middle Ages, they became one of the most powerful families in the realm:[5] a descendant Roger Mortimer gained possession of Ludlow Castle and became enamoured of Queen Isabella, wife of Edward II. Together they overthrew the king, who was murdered in Berkeley Castle in 1327. They governed the country for a short time during Edward III's minority, but once the young king took power, Mortimer's days were numbered, and he was put to death in 1330; he probably founded the north chapel in Cleobury Mortimer's church.

The church consists of a nave with aisles and a south porch, a chancel with north chapel, and a west tower with spire. The base of the tower is late Norman, and the tower arch at the west end of the nave is round-headed and somewhat flattened (Fig.26.4) because of the weight of the tower above; the inner order of shafts has a capital with leaf

Fig.26.4 St. Mary, Cleobury Mortimer: the tower arch

decoration on the south side, the other orders being added in 1874 to give extra strength. The belfry windows have two lights divided by a shaft; the windows are pointed except on the east face where they are round-headed. At the top of the tower is a corbel-table. The tower (Fig.26.5) is surmounted by a lovely shingled spire, of the splayed-foot type (see p.44). The spire is not quite symmetrical when seen from certain viewpoints, though not nearly so twisted as the famous spire at Chesterfield.

The rest of the church is mostly Early English or early Decorated. The fine south porch has a holy-water stoup, one of fewer than ten remaining in Shropshire. Both the outer and inner doorways have pointed arches, with stiff-leaf foliage and heads on the capitals. In the first half of the 13th century the south aisle and chancel were built; the aisle has wide lancet windows which are not original, (though an original 13th-century lancet can be seen in the west window of the south aisle). The arcade of five bays has circular piers and capitals. The north arcade (Fig.3.10) and north chapel are a little later, perhaps 1300. The chancel arch is very fine, and has three orders of shafts with stiff-leaf and heads on the capitals. The arcades can be seen to lean outwards; they were stabilised by Thomas Telford in the 1790s, and later by the addition of buttresses. The east window of the chancel consists of three stepped and cusped lancets under a common arch; it

Fig.26.5 Cleobury Mortimer: the tower and spire

commemorates William Langland, the author of *The Vision of Piers Plowman*, believed to have been born here in 1332. The window was designed by Harry Burrow and made by Powell's in 1875. To the north of the chancel is a vestry, now an organ chamber. The roofs are medieval: collar-beams and trussed rafters in the chancel, and a rather more elaborate structure with collar-beams and wind braces in the nave. The font is Victorian.

St. Peter and St. Paul, Cleobury North*

The rather depressing external appearance of this church is deceptive, for there is much of interest inside. There is a south-western tower with a brick upper storey, nave, chancel and south aisle; the windows are mostly much renewed. The nave is divided from the aisle

Fig.26.6 St. Peter and St. Paul, Cleobury North: the parclose screen

by a low Early English arcade, and the chancel arch is of the same period. The chancel was rebuilt in 1890-91. The octagonal font is Early English, with a band of dogtooth around the base. In the east window is good German stained glass of 1892, and in the north and south windows of the chancel glass by D. and C. Evans of Shrewsbury, dated 1861. The roofs of nave, chancel and aisle are all old, but somewhat repaired.

The woodwork is excellent. Best is the three-sided parclose screen (Fig.26.6) which occupies nearly all the south aisle, dating from *c*.1500. It is well-preserved, but some of the tracery has been renewed in cast-iron. It is believed that this may originally have enclosed a chantry chapel of the Mytton family.[6] The pulpit is dated 1628, and has a tier of blank arches with caryatids between; below is further panelling and small arches, and a lozenge ornament up the sides. On the north side of the nave is a 17th-century family pew with a high back and pedimented top, decorated with vine leaves, fruit and other motifs (Fig.14.15). The pew is similar to that in Holdgate but in better condition. The communion rails are dated 1666.

St. Mary, Cold Weston

When I first visited Cold Weston in 1991, high on the western slopes of Brown Clee Hill, the church was deserted and dilapidated (Fig.26.7), standing alone in a field with just one cottage nearby. At that time it was intended to convert the building (which had closed for worship in 1981) into a private dwelling, and I expressed the hope that restoration

Fig.26.7 Cold Weston in 1991

could take place before irreversible decay had set in.[7] It is a pleasure to record that this is a tale with a happy ending: St. Mary's has been most lovingly rescued and is now a private residence (Fig.26.8). It is an evocative place, of which the present owners are well aware: standing alone in a circular churchyard (possibly a pre-Christian site), the church consisted of a nave and chancel, with a western bell-cote. There is a plain Norman north doorway, and one Norman

Fig.26.8 St. Mary, Cold Weston in 2012

window in the south wall of the chancel. The ancient tie-beam still marks the division between the former nave and chancel, and the plain octagonal font still graces the garden.

Adjacent to the church is a holloway, an ancient drovers' track, and to the north are extensive remains of the former medieval village, for Cold Weston, like Abdon and Heath, is a settlement that largely expired in the later Middle Ages. 'Platforms represent the sites of former houses. Elsewhere scarps and terraces define paddocks and small enclosures, while surrounding the whole complex are the remains of an extensive ridge-and-furrow field system.'[8] The views are extensive, including Brown Clee Hill, the Wrekin, Wenlock Edge and the Long Mynd. There is no public access to the church, but the deserted village can be explored by footpaths.

St. Peter, Coreley

Coreley is situated on the lower slopes of Titterstone Clee Hill; it is recorded in Domesday Book as *Cornelie*, the place-name meaning 'slope frequented by cranes'.[9] The church is an incongruous amalgam of a 13th-century tower with lancet windows, and a brick 18th-century nave and chancel. Above the tower is a shingled broach spire. The tower opens into the nave by an asymmetric tower arch co-eval with the tower. The nave and chancel were built in 1757; originally the windows were round-headed, but these were converted into unimaginative lancets in Victorian times. The chancel arch is of brick. The panelled pulpit is at least partly Jacobean.

St. John the Baptist, Ditton Priors*

The manor was described as *Dodentone* in Domesday Book, and was granted to Wenlock Priory in the 12th century. The church dates mainly from the 13th century and consists of a western tower with chamfered or splayed-foot weather-boarded spire (Fig.26.9), nave, south aisle and chancel. There are lancet windows in the tower, chancel and south aisle; other windows were probably inserted in the 15th and early 16th centuries. Especially good is the late 'Tudor' window in the south aisle. The arcade consists of four bays, with round piers and capitals; the two western arches are round, the others slightly pointed. There is no chancel arch, but a handsome screen divides the nave and chancel. The lower part of the screen is late Perpendicular, the upper part is mostly Victorian, and some of the tracery is cast-iron, as in nearby Cleobury North. At the west end of the south aisle are two pews, resembling those seen in Cleobury North and Holdgate; these are dated 1714 and came from the former church at Burwarton. The trussed-rafter roof over the nave and aisle is Victorian. In the nave are four commandment boards dating from the 18th or 19th centuries, and hatchments of Viscount Boyne (d.1855) and his wife.

St. John the Baptist, Doddington*

Built of ashlar in 1849 on an exposed site high on Titterstone Clee Hill, Doddington church has several unusual features. The windows of the western tower are round-headed, neo-Norman; those of the nave are wide lancets; whilst the east window is neo-Perpendicular (Fig.13.5). Internally there is a west gallery, nave and chancel. An attractive screen inter-

Fig.26.9 St. John the Baptist, Ditton Priors

poses between nave and chancel, and the communion rails are of wrought-iron. Some good tiling covers the lower part of the east wall. The octagonal font is panelled with quatrefoils and cusped arches in a Perpendicular fashion.

St. Giles, Farlow

Domesday Book refers to Farlow (*Fernelau*) as being in Herefordshire, and indeed it was an outlying parish in that county until 1844, being a dependency of Leominster. The name means 'fern-clad hill' – the church is situated high up a steep hill which must make access difficult in winter. There was a medieval church here, painted by Williams in 1791 and demolished in 1857; it was replaced by the rather dull building erected in the following year, the architect being R. Griffiths. Built in the Early English style, the main feature of interest is the south doorway which retains some fragments of the Norman doorway of the previous church. There is a good deal of zigzag, and an arch of intersecting arcading above. The well-carved capitals are Victorian. Inside, there is a plain Norman font, and a Victorian stone pulpit carved with figures of three apostles.

Heath chapel***

Heath is an ancient chapelry of the parish of Stoke St. Milborough, and the chapel is the sole relic of the medieval village. The uplands around Brown Clee Hill were always marginal land, and as the climate worsened in the Middle Ages the population declined and several villages withered away. So the chapel stands quite alone in a field (Fig.1.3),

Fig.26.10 (above) Heath chapel: the humble interior
Fig.26.11 (right) Heath: the south doorway

its modest and somewhat unprepossessing appearance belying the fact that it is possibly the most famous church in Shropshire.

The reason why it is so justly celebrated is because the building has been left virtually unaltered for 850 years – the single change being enlargement of the window in the north wall about 300 years ago. The church consists of just a nave and chancel, and was built *c*.1140. The windows are small, round-headed and deeply splayed, and one of them is in the central flat buttress of the west wall. There is a prominent string-course. The chancel arch (Fig.26.10) is simple and plain, though the flanking shafts have capitals with scallops and volutes. The south doorway (Fig.26.11) shows much chevron decoration, now rather worn, and the door retains some 12th-century wrought-iron-work. The font is a Norman tub, with a frieze of incised arcading around the top. The pulpit and box-pews date from the 17th century. Medieval wall-paintings survive, and were apparently discovered only in 1911 having been previously hidden by plaster; these paintings await conservation.

St. John the Baptist, Hope Bagot**

Hope Bagot nestles in a small cleft on the southern slopes of Titterstone Clee Hill, and its site is reflected in the place-name, 'hope' meaning 'enclosed place' or 'valley', while Bagot is a corruption of Robert Bagard who held the manor in 1242.[10] It is an enchanting spot, graced with a very fine small Norman church. Equally good is the churchyard, carefully managed for its abundance of wild flowers.

The nave and chancel are 12th-century Norman, the west tower probably 13th-century (Fig.26.12). The south doorway is round-arched, with hatching on the top of the capitals and abaci; the tympanum is plain. The doorway is protected by an attractive porch which may date from the 14th century. Inside the church, the eye is immediately arrested by the chancel arch (Fig.26.13) – a sturdy Norman construction, with carving of saltire crosses on the capitals and abaci, and continued laterally along the string-courses to the north and south walls. There are deeply-splayed Norman windows (Fig.3.8) in the north wall of both nave and chancel; the chancel window has hatching on the head-stone externally. The east window of the chancel, and the south windows of nave and chancel were inserted in the 13th and 14th centuries. There is a plain circular font, probably Norman. The excellent pulpit, communion rails and tie-beam roof of the nave all date from the 17th century.

Fig.26.12 St. John the Baptist, Hope Bagot

The tower is surmounted by a shingled pyramidal roof. The tower arch opening into the nave is a primitive pointed affair, with no distinguishing features.

St. Michael, Hopton Wafers*

Hopton means 'settlement in a valley', and Wafer is a family name. The manor was mentioned in Domesday Book, and like Cleobury North it was claimed as Worcester church land that had been alienated by Earl Swein. Later it descended to

Fig.26.13 Hope Bagot: the chancel arch

the Honour of Brecknock, and the church went to Brecon Priory. The second element in Hopton Cangeford, a nearby settlement, is also a family name. The attractive village nestles in a valley on the eastern slopes of Titterstone Clee Hill.

The church has a long history, being first mentioned in 1236. The medieval church was recorded by Williams in 1791, and at that time it possessed four dormer windows on the south side. This church was demolished in 1825 and entirely rebuilt in ashlar in the classical style two years later. It consists of a western tower, with nave and chancel. It is likely that originally the new church had wide arched windows, but at some later date the windows in the tower were made neo-Norman, whilst the nave windows were incongruously 'gothicised'. The interior is plain, with a west gallery and a Victorian screen dividing nave and chancel. From the gallery hang the Royal Arms of Queen Victoria. To the north of the altar is a large monument to Thomas Botfield (d.1843) by Edward Hodges Baily; the deceased lies semi-recumbent, with his wife kneeling at his side (Fig.11.37). Baily had previously worked on the reliefs at Marble Arch.[11]

Fig.26.14 St. John the Baptist, Kinlet

St. John the Baptist, Kinlet***

Kinlet is recorded in the Domesday Book as *Chinlete*, which perhaps means 'royal share or portion';[12] the manor had been held at the Conquest by Queen Edith, wife of Edward the Confessor.

Kinlet is the finest imparked church in Shropshire (Fig.26.14), standing alone next to Kinlet Hall. This is the result of the creation of Kinlet Park in the early 18th century, when the village was extinguished and the road diverted.[13] The church dates back to Norman times and consists of a nave with porch and chancel, transepts and a western tower. There are very fine semicircular Norman arcades separating the nave from the aisles, the north being a little earlier than the south (Fig.3.7). The tower arch is Early English, with capitals showing stiff-leaf decoration and heads. The south doorway has part of a Norman tympanum displaying a sunken star pattern.

The chancel arch is a very fine example of Early English, with three orders of shafts with plain capitals. The chancel and transepts were built in the Decorated period; Mercer points out that the transepts are oddly sited, being east of the chancel arch.[14] The east window to the chancel shows excellent Decorated tracery (Fig.3.14), similar to those at Chelmarsh and Stottesdon (q.v.). The roof of the chancel has trussed rafters. The transepts have three-light windows with intersecting and cusped tracery. In the south transept, there is evidence (according to Cranage) of a medieval chantry chapel, with a large double aumbry to the left of the altar, a piscina to the right, and a tomb-recess with ball-flower decoration in the south wall. West of the tomb-recess is a original doorway with ball-flower in the external hood-mould. In the Perpendicular period an attractive half-timbered clerestory was added to the nave; the roof was carried by crucks, functioning as arched braces rising from the top of the nave wall to a collar.[15] The tower is Early English below, with a Perpendicular top, previously adorned with battlements and pinnacles.

Kinlet has an impressive array of medieval monuments. The earliest is probably the alabaster figure of the Trinity in the east window of the south transept, showing God the Father cradling the crucified Christ in His lap.[16] This sculpture rests on a moulded corbel, probably its original site. Also in the south transept is the early 15th-century alabaster effigy of a lady with a baby at her side; this is probably Isabel Cornewall.

Then come the three magnificent monuments commemorating successive generations of the Blount family. These form a most instructive study, for the earliest is fully medieval, the second early Renaissance, and the third Elizabethan. The tomb-chest of Sir Humphry Blount (d.1477) in the chancel has recumbent alabaster effigies; at the sides under ogee-headed Gothic arches is a series of rather static weepers (Fig.11.7). Sir Humphry wears the Yorkist collar, prudently showing the sun of Edward IV and the white rose of York. The second tomb, of Sir John Blount, also in the chancel, clearly shows Renaissance influence (Fig.11.13): around the sides are weepers in groups of two or three, under arches with scrolls resting on colonnettes. Sir John, (d.1531), grandson of Sir Humphry, also prudently, wears the SS collar denoting allegiance to the House of Lancaster, who had by his time gained the crown in the person of Henry VII. The third Blount monument is the gigantic Elizabethan memorial in the north transept to Sir George Blount (d.1584) and his wife (Fig.11.19). The deceased are showing kneeling frontally above a single recumbent cadaver. Between and on either side of the figures are Ionic columns supporting a cornice with heraldic figures above. This is one of the finest monuments of its age in the country.

Lastly there are two less imposing monuments to the Childe family. The memorial to Thomas Childe (d.1708) has a frame without a pediment, with twisted side-columns rising to an entablature supporting flaming urns and a shield of arms. Two hundred years later, Capt. Charles Childe was killed in the Boer War, and his memorial tablet carries above a helmet and regimental sword.

There is some medieval stained glass in the east window of the chancel, with the figure of St. John the Baptist bearing a cup, a female saint with a palm branch and a bird and a knight bearing the Cornewall arms. Much of this glass was renewed in 1814 by Betton and Evans. The organ came from Millichope Hall and was installed here in 1894. It is inscribed by appointment to King William IV, 1830.

St. Paul, Knowbury

Standing on elevated ground to the south of Clee Hill, St. Paul's church is a pleasing sandstone edifice: the nave and west tower were built by John Grosvenor in 1838-9, and Edward Turner in 1883-4 added the chancel, stair-turret and porch.[17] Cranage described the 1839 church as a barn-like structure, without architectural pretensions; this was radically altered in 1884, producing a building mainly in the Decorated style, with a chancel two steps higher than the nave, and the sanctuary a further four steps higher, in accordance with late Victorian ecclesiological fashion. The pulpit is of stone, and there is a low wrought-iron screen between the nave and chancel. There is a rather heavy triptych behind the altar, German in character, and German also is the stained glass in the east window. The font is unusual, and not particularly attractive. Cranage thought it was of Renaissance character; Pevsner said it was like a large Norman capital turned upside-down.

Loughton church

There was a medieval church here, a chapelry attached to the parish of Chetton. This church has disappeared and the present building dates from 1622 – a rare date for a new church. The reason for the replacement church is unknown, but an inscription records that it was built at the expense of Bonham Norton Esq.; he was the husband of Jane Norton, and is commem- orated with her in the memorial at Condover (q.v.) but is buried in St. Faith's, London.[18]

Fig.26.15 Loughton church

The church is a humble building, plain and unpretentious (Fig.26.15). It consists merely of a nave and chancel, undivided, and a western bellcote. The windows are paired lights with straight tops. Both the south doorway and chancel arch probably incorporate part of the masonry from the earlier church. The pulpit and reading-desk are 17th-century, and probably the font is also.

St. George, Milson*

Domesday Book records that the manor of Milson was attached as an outlier to the manor of Neen Sollars, and for centuries the church remained a chapelry of that parish. The place-name in Domesday is given as *Mulstone*, said by Ekwall to mean 'Myndel's tun' (or homestead).

The small church is attractively situated, and has several features of interest. The nave and chancel are Norman, the tower (Fig.26.16) dating from a century later, with a tall narrow lancet window in the west wall. There is a very fine timber-framed porch (*cf* Munslow) which probably dates from the 14th century. The roof of the porch has tie-beams and

arched braces, and the gable has wavy barge-boards. The south doorway is Norman, with the capitals of the shafts carved with water-leaf on the left and scallop on the right.

The interior is spoilt by the absence of a chancel arch: instead there is an unattractive wooden lintel on supports. There are Norman windows on the north and south walls of the nave; the east window of the chancel is Victorian. The finest artefact is

Fig.26.16 St. George, Milson

the pulpit; this is not Elizabethan, as was once thought, but the work of the wife of an incumbent in the early 20th century; it displays much delicate carving. The octagonal font has just a plain round moulding, probably late medieval.

Fig.26.17 St. John the Baptist, Nash: the screen, roof and chancel

St. John the Baptist, Nash*

This is a plain church of the early 14th century, to which a north aisle was added in 1865. The west tower is surmounted by a weather-boarded broach spire. The nave (Fig.26.17) is divided from the north aisle by an arcade with very ornate foliage in the capitals, typical of the 1860s. Between nave and chancel is an unEnglish-looking screen, which was carved at Louvain and given to Nash church by the Hon. Georgina Rushout. In the nave are two hatchments of the 18th century, to Andrew Hill and his son, and a 19th-century one to Thomas Hodges. On the north wall of the chancel is a monument with a draped urn to Lucy Hill (d.1855). There is good Victorian glass in the chancel, especially the restrained tones evident in the south window.

St. Mary, Neen Savage**

Neenton, Neen Savage and Neen Sollars are all situated on the river Rea, and Neen was the former (British) name for the river (*cf* Nene in Northamptonshire).[19] Savage and Solariis were the surnames of the respective feudal owners in the 12th and 13th centuries.

St. Mary's is attractively situated. It is a late Norman building (Fig.26.18), consisting of nave, chancel and west tower. There are Norman round-headed windows in the chancel and nave and a blocked Norman north doorway. The priest's door in the south wall of the chancel is Norman, with 'Transitional trefoil decoration on the dripstone' (Fig.26.19),[20] similar to the 'crocus' motif at Halford (Fig.27.7). Other windows are Early English lancets (one with plate tracery), and late Perpendicular insertions. The fine timbered south porch is also late Perpendicular. The tower is late Norman, except for the top storey which was rebuilt

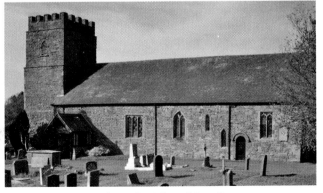

Fig.26.18 St. Mary, Neen Savage

after it was struck by lightning in 1825; originally it carried a timber spire. The south doorway is probably Early English.

Internally, there is no architectural division between nave and chancel. The tower arch is plain. The font appears to be Norman, but is 19th-century. There are two aumbries in the north wall of the chancel, and two piscinae – one in the south wall of the chancel and the other in the south wall of the east end of the nave. The latter must have

Fig.26.19 Neen Savage: the 'crocus' motif above the south doorway

served an altar placed before the rood screen. The screen itself is excellent (Fig.13.2), partly late Perpendicular but much restored after damage by fire following the lightning strike. The coving to support the rood loft is not original, but nearly all the cornice is old and very fine. Some of the tracery in the lights of the screen is old. The stained glass in the east windows contain tiers of small figures; Pevsner thought that this might well be of c.1825-30. Another excellent feature is the continuous roof of nave and chancel; this consists of trussed rafters, reinforced by tie-beams. Some of the latter are carved with the Tudor rose. The tie-beam resting on the west wall is carved with dogtooth, and Cranage thought that this might date from the 13th century; dendrochronology might confirm this. Along the north and south walls is a wooden cornice, carved with billet ornament.

Fig.26.20 All Saints, Neen Sollars

All Saints, Neen Sollars*

Neen Sollars was held by Roger de Solariis c.1195.[21] The village is attractively situated between the river Rea and the Mill Brook. Sir Stephen Glynne visited in 1846 and commented favourably on the scenery; he found the church had 'rather a solemn impressive appearance, though rude and the interior dirty and full of high pues'. Fortunately, change here has been for the better!

All Saints' is cruciform in shape (Fig.26.20), unusual in Shropshire village churches, and dates mainly from the Early English and Decorated periods. Thus the windows are single or paired cusped lancets, and the east window of the chancel has reticulated tracery (Fig.26.21)

Fig.26.21 Neen Sollars:
the crossing and chancel

– though the chancel was rebuilt in 1859. The tower has a shingled spire of the splayed-foot variety, and it rests on four acutely pointed arches with what Glynne described as 'octagonal half-columns in the piers'. The roofs are of trussed rafters, the best being in the north transept. The font is a plain tub, probably Norman.

In the south transept is a distinguished monument to Humfrey Coningsby (Fig.11.28); he was a great traveller and disappeared while travelling in Europe in 1610 and was never seen again. His sister erected the alabaster monument in 1624, and the accompanying legend should be read in full. The deceased is depicted in armour, lying on his right elbow on a tomb-chest; behind is an arch, with figures in the spandrels. The whole is enclosed in an architectural framework of considerable complexity.

All Saints, Neenton

This is a Victorian church, built by Sir Arthur Blomfield in 1871. It is a simple church in the Early English style, a conservative choice of style for its date. It consists of a nave and chancel, with a western bellcote. The most attractive feature is the Crucifixion in stained glass by Morris and Co. still in the Pre-Raphaelite style as late as 1922. There is a plain Norman font, and a late medieval chest carved with lozenges and quatrefoils. The churchyard is carefully maintained and has an abundance of wild flowers.

St. Nicholas, Silvington*

An aura of departed glory seems to surround this little church, set in wooded country on the northern slopes of Titterstone Clee Hill. I guessed (wrongly) that the village name was derived from the woodland; but Ekwall informs us that it means 'settlement on a slope'.[22] The church is all but hidden by the surrounding yews, and it seems that now there are few people to tend it – services are held only twice each month. Yet St. Nicholas has something to offer the discerning visitor, and the tranquillity of its environs is a great bonus.

The porch greets you with the notice that 'This porch was built by John Hil Gent and Ursula Hil Widdow 1662', and the excellent ironwork on the door is dated 1679. The south doorway itself is Norman, with single shafts with scalloped capitals, a plain tympanum, and a bold roll-moulding in the arch above. There is also a blocked Norman doorway in the north wall of the nave and an internally splayed Norman window in the tower. Other windows in the nave are mostly refashioned lancets of the 13th century. The tower is Norman, at least in the lower stages, and the tower arch opening into the nave (Fig.26.22) is slightly pointed (i.e. Transitional), with unusual leaf-carving especially on the north capital. The font is a plain Norman tub, with one roll-moulding around the stem. In the 13th century a chancel was added to the Norman nave, and at some time between 1550 and 1700 new windows were provided for the chancel. At this time the Early English chancel arch was moved eastwards, thus extending the nave at the expense of the chancel.[23] In recompense, perhaps, some 17th-century panelling was installed in the chancel.

St. Milburgh, Stoke St. Milborough

Sir Stephen Glynne visited St. Milburgh's in 1854 and commented that the church inside had 'a gaunt, gloomy look'. He conceded, however, that the situation commands a pleasing and picturesque view of mountain (*sic*), wood and valley, and this is true still.

Fig.26.22 St. Nicholas, Silvington: the tower arch

As in Glynne's day, most of the interest is external (Fig.26.23). The corners of an earlier, narrower nave may be seen in the angles between the tower and the west wall of the nave.[24] The solid tower is 13th-century up to the level of the corbel-table; the upper storey is later, either Perpendicular or post-Reformation. There is an attractive timber-framed porch, with brick nogging, probably dating from the early 18th century. Most of the windows are Decorated, though the east window of the chancel, with glass by David Evans, was installed in 1859.

Fig.26.23 St. Milburgh, Stoke St. Milborough

The interior is plain: both the tower arch and the chancel arch are 13th-century. There is a good roof, with collar-beams on arched braces, and queen-posts. The plain font was probably originally 12-sided, but appears to have been pared on its eastern face to give a fluting effect.

St. Mary, Stottesdon***

This remarkable church possesses two outstanding treasures – an 11th-century tympanum, and a 12th-century font – which together place it in the first rank amongst Shropshire churches. Stottesdon – the 'hill of the herd of horses' – is now a rather out-of-the-way village, but, like Morville, in Saxon times it was the centre of a far-flung parish; and it is believed that the west wall of the nave does indeed date from before the Norman Conquest.[25] Stottesdon is one of the small group of Shropshire churches mentioned in Domesday Book, thus confirming its very early origin. At that time the church was held by St. Peter's church (i.e. Shrewsbury Abbey).

The church (Fig.26.24) consists of a western tower, nave with north and south aisles, chancel and a south porch. It appears that the west wall of the nave was originally the west end of the Saxon church, and above it, now facing into the tower, is the tympanum. When the lower part of the tower was built, in early Norman times, this wall and the tympanum thus became internal.

Entry to the church is through the south porch; the outer doorway is Norman (Pevsner says that it has been re-set), and the inner is Early English. The arcade separating the north aisle from the nave is late 12th century, with massive, circular columns supporting round arches; the south arcade was rebuilt in 1867. The pulpit is Jacobean. There is no chancel arch, the chancel being divided from the nave by a late Victorian screen. The chancel is Decorated, and has a beautiful geometric east window, very similar to those of Kinlet and Chelmarsh nearby. Both aisles were extended eastwards to flank the west end of the chancel.[26] Curvilinear tracery may be seen in the east window of the south aisle. Note the fine sedilia (seats for the priests) in the south wall of the chancel, and next to them a piscina placed unusually low down – originally the floor of the chancel was a good deal lower. In the south window are fragments of 14th-century stained glass depicting heads of knights.[27]

The tympanum (Fig.9.9) is of course of outstanding interest because of its antiquity, but it would be difficult to describe it as beautiful. Access to it is behind the organ, in a rather obscure site. It was carved in the 11th century, either late Saxon or early Norman. At the apex of the triangle is a grotesque bearded head, and the upper part of the tympanum below is ornamented with crude geometrical patterns. On the lintel are carved some strange beasts, two of which are upside down, possibly representing a chase.

In contrast to the tympanum, there are no qualms about the beauty of the Norman font, an outstanding work of the Herefordshire School of Romanesque carvers, thought to date from *c*.1140. The complexity of the design is astonishing (Fig.10.15): around the bowl is a band of three-strand interlace, and below this are eight medallions containing *inter alia* an Agnus Dei, a lion turning his head back to bite his tail, a griffin, a large bird pecking the head of a smaller bird etc. The medallions are linked by a motif said to be derived from the south doorway at Kilpeck;[28] this has become so stylised that it resembles a human face. Further interlace is present on the stem and around the base is a trail of foliage. The technical skill displayed is highly accomplished, and Zarnecki attributed this

Fig.26.24 St. Mary, Stottesdon

font to the sculptor of the tympanum at Aston, Herefordshire.[29] Thurlby points out various resemblances between the Stottesdon font and other work of the Herefordshire School at Aston, Shobdon, Rock and Alveley.[30]

Holy Trinity, Wheathill*

This is a small Norman church consisting of nave and chancel, with a western bellcote. The best features are the south doorway and the chancel arch, both dating from the 12th century. The round-headed doorway has capitals carved with volutes or scrolls, and above is a tympanum covered with hatching. There is cable ornament around the top. The chancel arch (Fig.26.25) is similar, again with scrolls in the capitals. There is a small round-headed Norman window in the north wall of the chancel. The roof of the nave has tie-beams and queen-posts. The west wall was rebuilt in the 19th century.

Fig.26.25 Holy Trinity, Wheathill: the chancel arch

St. Mary, Whitton**

Although a medieval church, St. Mary's is memorable now for the excellent stained glass in the east window, the work of Sir Edward Burne-Jones in 1893. Above are three standing figures, and below an Annunciation and two Nativity scenes (Fig.12.10) The colours are rich and satisfying – it is worth going to Whitton for this window alone. There is more glass by Morris and Co. in the south window of the chancel, dating from 1911 (Fig.12.11).

The church (Fig.26.26) consists of a 14th-century western tower, and an undivided nave and chancel, the chancel being extended eastwards in 1891 by Sir Aston Webb. There are deeply splayed Norman windows in both north and south walls of the nave, and the south doorway is Norman; the arch is carved with pyramids, said by Cranage to be intermediate between a true Norman pyramidal form and Early English dogtooth. In the chancel are sedilia in the south wall, dating from Webb's extension.

Fig.26.26 St. Mary, Whitton

The south – Ludlow

St. Andrew, Ashford Bowdler*

The twin parishes of Ashford Bowdler and Carbonell lie on opposite banks of the Teme, and between them a ford by a clump of ash trees led a drovers' trackway from Wales into the West Midlands. Place-names along the route are said to indicate that salt was a major commodity carried along this way. Bowdler and Carbonell are named after Norman knights who held these manors in the 11th and 12th centuries. In the Domesday Book, the settlement is known as *Esseford*.

St. Andrew's church (Fig.27.1) stands perilously close to the bank of the river Teme, so near that the chancel collapsed into the river during reconstruction in 1904-06. To prevent a recurrence of this, much recent work to stabilise the east end has been carried out. The present building dates from Norman times and it appears to have begun life as a dependent chapelry of Bromfield Priory. There are blocked Norman doorways in both the north and south of the nave, and Norman windows survive in the chancel. To the west of the blocked doorway in the south wall is the main entrance to the church, dating from late medieval times. At the west end is a shingled bell-turret and broach spire. There are a number of monu-

Fig.27.1 St. Andrew, Ashford Bowdler

ments, of which the most interesting is that to Jonathan Green (d.1792), consisting of two urns in front of an obelisk; it is the work of William Humphries Stephens of Worcester. Beneath the bell-turret are two benefactions boards.

St. Mary, Ashford Carbonell*

The church is situated on rising ground above the village, with splendid views eastward over Clee Hill. It is clearly of 12th-century origin, but did not become a separate parish until 1880; before then, it was a perpetual curacy of Little Hereford. The apparently simple church (Fig.27.2), consisting only of chancel, nave and western bell-tower, in fact conceals a complex building history. The earliest 12th-century Norman church was much smaller than the present building, the chancel being extended to the east, and the nave to the west, probably in the 13th century. This was revealed by excavations undertaken during the restoration of 1882-83 under the supervision of Ewan Christian; he found that the original 12th-century foundations reached only one foot below the surface, while those of the east and west extensions attained a depth of three feet; furthermore, when the plaster was removed from the walls, there was a distinct difference in the

Fig.27.2 St. Mary, Ashford Carbonell

masonry employed, with clearly defined vertical lines from the wall-plates to the floor, showing where the junctions had been made. One consequence of these findings was the realisation that the priest's door in the south wall of the chancel, clearly Norman, had been moved eastwards and re-inserted in the 13th-century extension of the chancel.

Today, the most striking feature of the church is the east end of the chancel, where there are two small round-headed windows, and above a vesica window of almond-shaped form. The *vesica piscis* (literally 'fish's bladder') had the same meaning for the early Church as the symbol of the fish, the Greek word for fish – *ichthus* – being composed of the initial letters of the Greek for 'Jesus Christ, Son of God, Saviour'. A vesica window is rare in English parish churches, though one can be seen in the south transept above the main entrance in Abbey Dore church, Herefordshire. Sir Stephen Glynne visited Ashford Carbonell in 1855 and did not record the window. The explanation is that the window as seen today dates only from the restoration of 1882-83. At that time the east wall was reconstructed and a square-headed Decorated window was removed (and transferred to the west end of the south wall of the chancel), revealing two Norman windows; above and between them were stones which were part of an ancient vesica window; very few additional stones were needed for the restoration of the vesica.[1]

The nave and chancel are divided by the plain Norman chancel arch. Both nave and chancel exhibit a variety of Norman and Decorated windows, and at the west end of the nave is an Early English window of the 13th century. There is a blocked Norman doorway in the north wall of the nave; externally this exhibits dogtooth decoration, dating it to the end of the 12th century. The south doorway is Norman, with a plain tympanum above; the arch has been cut away. The roof of the chancel is Victorian, but the roof of the nave is late medieval and unusual. There are two tie-beams and two hammer-beams, but the latter are largely functionless as they do not support struts and braces; above are collar-beams and arched braces. The bells are housed in a weather-boarded belfry with a pyramid roof; the belfry is supported internally by a massive wooden structure of tie-beams and arched braces. The font is a plain Norman tub on a Victorian base; when Sir Stephen Glynne visited, it was catching rain-water in the churchyard!

St. Mary, Bitterley**

St. Mary's church is attractively situated next to Bitterley Court, half a mile from the village, on the western slopes of Titterstone Clee Hill. In Domesday Book the manor is known as *Buterlie* ('butter pasture'),[2] and the presence both of a church and a priest is noted.

The church (Fig.27.3) dates mostly from the Transitional period, when the Norman style was giving way to Early English (*c.*1200). It consists of a nave without aisles, chancel and a western tower. There are several lancet windows, one of which is round-headed. Other windows were inserted in the Decorated era, and have been renewed. The tower arch has also been renewed, but the shafts bear fillets, with stiff-leaf capitals. In the north wall of the chancel is a tomb-recess. The upper part of the tower is timber-framed and supports a short broach spire. The timber-framing and spire are 19th-century additions, for they are not present in the Williams painting of 1791 which shows a plain battlemented upper storey to the tower.

Fig.27.3 St. Mary, Bitterley

The font is the oldest artefact in the church: it is Norman, with rounded arcades on the bowl, and a little foliage above. Next is the very fine iron-bound chest, dating from the 13th century. South of the altar is the Jacobean monument to Timothy Lucye (d.1616) who is depicted kneeling in armour with a ruff around his neck, flanked by columns on each side (Fig.11.20). There is an excellent Jacobean pulpit, lectern and reading-desk. Finally, the screen and rood loft extend across the whole width of the church; it almost entirely dates from 1924, and the workmanship is good.

In the churchyard is a fine cross with a graceful shaft bearing a Crucifixion. Cranage dated this to the 14th century.

Boraston church

Boraston was an ancient chapelry of Burford and is a church of no known dedication. The medieval church was rebuilt by Henry Curzon in 1884-87, but there are blocked Norman doorways in both north and south walls of the nave. The masonry is all Victorian, apart from most of the south wall. The interior is plain, the chancel having a polygonal east end. The font is unusually fluted in the lower part of the bowl. Cranage recorded that it originally came from Buildwas, and dated it from the 17th or early 18th century.

St. Mary the Virgin, Bromfield***

Bromfield today presents a picturesque appearance, with the gatehouse nearby and the ruins of the former priory. It is a very ancient site, remains of both a prehistoric cemetery and a Saxon cemetery having been found in the vicinity.[3] In Anglo-Saxon times Bromfield was an important collegiate church, with 12 canons. In c.1060 Edward the Confessor gave it a grant of liberties, and it was of royal free status.[4] In the Domesday Book Bromfield is described as a holding of St. Mary's, Shrewsbury, and the church is mentioned. During the early 12th century the canons were gradually replaced by monks; a Benedictine priory cell was established in 1155 and was subject to St. Peter's Abbey, Gloucester. The priory was dissolved in 1540 and the buildings were taken over by Charles Foxe. He incorporated the present chancel in his house, and the church was not restored for worship until 1658. Some ruins of Foxe's Tudor residence can be seen on the south side of the chancel.

The approach to Bromfield church is memorable, with the river Onny to the left, the Priory gatehouse to the right, and a long path leading to the tower (Fig.4.3). The church consists of a nave and chancel undifferentiated, with a north aisle and a north-west tower; entrance to the church is through the porch at the base of the tower. The oldest feature is the very wide early Norman chancel arch which is now an integral part of the <u>east</u> end of the present chancel. The arch has one order of shafts and carving on the capitals. A further Norman round-headed arch opens into the north transept of what was once a cruciform church; the south transept has disappeared. Remains of small round-headed Norman windows can be seen at the west end of the nave in both the north and south walls. The roof of the nave has arched braces and diagonal queen-posts, dated 1577. The west window of the nave is Decorated, and there is a fine Decorated tomb-recess in the south wall of the nave. All the windows of the south wall date from the restoration of 1890. The fine arcade dividing the north aisle from the nave is Early English. The tower is also Early English apart from the Perpendicular top; the inner doorway has excellent stiff-leaf foliage on the capitals. The outer doorway is probably a little earlier, the stiff-leaf not so well developed. The windows in the tower and in the north aisle are lancets. Note the extensive corbel-table of carved heads below the eaves on the exterior of the north aisle.

The most notable feature of the interior is the Baroque painted ceiling of the chancel (Fig.27.4), the work of a Cheshire artist, Thomas Francis (1672). It is not a great work of art, but the pattern of angels, putti, clouds and streamers bearing texts together with symbols of the Holy Trinity bear witness to folk religion of the age of Charles II. His Royal Coat of Arms adorns the south wall of the nave – one of the largest in existence. There is linenfold panelling, probably from the 16th century, on the north and south walls of the chancel. At the east end of the aisle is Jacobean panelling with arabesques and the figures of the four evangelists, with

Fig.27.4 St. Mary the Virgin, Bromfield: the Baroque painted ceiling

linenfold at each end. The pulpit is Jacobean, and the communion-rails date from *c.*1700. The triptych behind the altar was designed by Hodgson Fowler, who restored the church, and painted by Buckeridge (*cf* Richard's Castle) and Floyd. Most of the stained glass is by C.E. Kempe, but there are some Flemish roundels in the vestry. The fine organ is by Walker, and has been recently restored.

St. Mary, Burford***

Burford is at the extreme south of the county, where Shropshire marches with the counties of Hereford and Worcester. The OE name means 'ford by a fort'; exceptionally, the Domesday Book records the presence of a church with two priests. The present church is pleasantly situated next to Burford House Gardens, near to the river Teme. It consists of a western tower, with nave and chancel, and a Victorian north vestry. The exterior presents an amalgam of medieval and Victorian features which are not always easy to disentangle. The lower part of the tower (Fig.27.5) is Perpendicular, but the upper

Fig.27.5 St. Mary, Burford:
the tower

storey was added in 1889 and is largely the work of Sir Aston Webb.[5] Most of the masonry of the nave and chancel is medieval, but the windows were mostly renewed at the time of the restoration. The battlements of the nave and chancel were probably also renewed at this time; they display varied carvings, at least some of which appears to be medieval. There is a north vestry, with a rose window which Pevsner ascribes to *c.1860*.

Do not be put off by the rather dark interior, for there are many treasures to see, both medieval and Victorian. In the nave, the tower arch is late Perpendicular, the chancel arch Victorian. At the west end of the nave is the Perpendicular octagonal font, some faces of which are carved with various motifs. There is some good Victorian glass by Powell in some of the south windows of the nave. By the south door is a holy water stoup, and nearby is a large medieval chest. The chancel and nave are divided by the Victorian screen made at Louvain. Other good Victorian furnishings include the pulpit, lectern, chandeliers, the screen in front of the organ, and above all the intricate roof of the chancel, replete with angels. Most of these were designed by Sir Aston Webb, an early believer in the Arts and Crafts style, and made by Starkie Gardner.

Burford is outstanding for the number and quality of its medieval and later memorials, extending from the 14th to the 19th centuries. The Cornwall family were lords of Burford for 400 years from the middle of the 14th century; they resided at Burford Castle (on the site of the present Burford House), and were succeeded by the Rushout family. In chronological order, the monuments are as follows:

1) On the floor to the south of the altar is the fine brass to Dame Elizabeth de Cornewayle, *c.*1370, wearing costume typical of the period.

2) On the north wall of the chancel is a painted Decorated tomb recess, with ball-flower characteristic of the first half of the 14th century. In the recess is the painted alabaster effigy of the Princess Elizabeth, daughter of John of Gaunt, duke of Lancaster; she married Sir John Cornwall KG and died in 1426, so the effigy is about a century later than the recess. The head of the lady rests on a cushion supported by angels, and at her feet is a dog.

3) Opposite to this, in the south wall, is an unusual 'heart tomb' commemorating Edmond Cornwall who died at Cologne in 1436; he directed that his heart should be enclosed in lead and buried in Burford church. Below is a small tomb-chest enriched with four cusped and pointed blank arches typical of the late 13th century – i.e. 150 years before the death of Edmond Cornwall. At the end of the long inscription is the statement that Edmond's daughter Elenor had 'such increase of children that seventeen score and odd people were descended from her body before she died' – i.e. over 340 people!

4) In the centre of the chancel is a rare oaken effigy to another Edmond Cornwall, d.1508; there are two angels by the pillow and a large dog at the effigy's feet (Fig.11.3).

5) The unique triptych to the north of the altar is the most outstanding of Burford's monuments. It is a huge Elizabethan piece, flanked by fluted pilasters and surmounted by a pediment, but for all these Renaissance details it is still largely medieval in sentiment. It was painted by Melchior Salabuss and dated 1588, the year of the Armada. The centrepiece shows life-size portraits of Richard Cornwall, ninth baron of Burford, Janet his wife, and their eldest son Edmund, tenth baron. Below, a narrow pair of doors open to reveal the figure of the cadaver of Edmund in his shroud. The outer panels have heraldic designs on the inner face, and on the outer face pictures of the 12 apostles; at

some stage these panels have been transposed, for the apostles should be on the inner face and vice versa.

6 & 7) Two monuments are fixed high up on the south wall of the chancel, consisting of two couples kneeling at a prayer-desk, a typical late Elizabethan or Jacobean design, dated 1630. The earlier one commemorates the eleventh baron Thomas, brother of Edmund the tenth baron; and the later one his son, the twelfth baron Thomas.

8) On the south wall of the nave near the screen is a very different memorial, to Lady Caroline Rushout, d.1818. This is by Sir Richard Westmacott and depicts Lady Caroline reclining and being ministered to by a standing angel – a typical theme of the Greek revival then fashionable.

9) Further west on the south wall is a memorial to the Reverend George Rushout (d.1842). This depicts an angel blessing a kneeling clergyman, and is attributed to the Westmacott school by Newman and Pevsner (Fig.11.36).[6]

Fig.27.6 St. Mary, Caynham: the chancel arch

St. Mary, Caynham*

Caynham church is set in a churchyard full of wild flowers, and containing also the remains of a cross probably dating from the 14th century. Although the church today is overall Victorian, there are significant and interesting Norman remains. Most unusual is the chancel arch (Fig.27.6): this dates from the Transitional period (1160-1200), and consists of a wide, central, pointed arch, flanked by two narrower pointed arches. Between the arches are square, plain Norman piers with imposts. The south doorway is Norman, with scalloped capitals and chevron decoration, and the small Norman window in the south of the nave has a stone above carved with saltire crosses. The west tower is Early English, with lancet windows.

The rest of the church is Victorian, the work of James Brooks (1825-1901) in 1885. He was a noted architect, an Anglo-Catholic best known for several churches in the East End of London. Brooks added a north aisle, separated from the nave by a low arcade, the piers having capitals carved with scallop, and rebuilt the chancel with a vaulted roof. The resulting interior is dark due to an abundance of rather undistinguished stained glass. There is an unusual reredos and a marble pulpit. The glass in the east window is by Kempe and Co.

St. James, Greete*

St. James's church is a quaint little building, consisting of a stone nave and stuccoed chancel, originally from the 12th and 13th centuries, a western bell-gable and south porch. The latter is Victorian, and the south doorway, of Norman character, probably is also. The most engaging feature of the church is the Perpendicular window in the north wall of the nave: this has wooden tracery (a great rarity), and in the western jamb is a corbel, which probably supported an image. Most of the other windows are 13th-century lancets, though the west window is round-headed and is presumably late Norman. The plain panelled pulpit (Fig.14.2) is probably 18th-century. There is a rustic communion-rail and a plain octagonal font. The trussed-rafter roof in the nave is Victorian.

Halford church

The place name means 'hawkers' ford', the river being the Onny which runs very close to the church. The south doorway proclaims the Norman origin of the church: the arch is round-headed and the hood-mould bears what Pevsner rather fancifully described as 'a chain of crocus-blossom forms' (Fig.27.7). Mercer points out that the same motif may be seen above the tower arch at Munslow, and above doorways at Neen Savage (Fig.26.19), Edstaston, and St. Mary's, Shrewsbury.[7] To the west of the doorway is the only medieval window in the church: a small internally-splayed late Norman window. All the other nave windows belong to the restoration of 1848. The chancel was totally rebuilt in 1887. The font is a plain Norman tub on a 19th-century stem.

St. Giles, Ludford*

Ludford is a settlement older than Ludlow, for it is mentioned in Domesday Book as part of the hundred of Wolphey in Herefordshire.[8] In the Middle Ages Ludford was a chapelry of the Benedictine priory of Bromfield. In 1216 St. Giles' hospital for lepers was founded next to the church; a few years later the hospital of the Holy Trinity (later St. John the Baptist's Hospital) was founded on the opposite bank of the Teme.

St. Giles' church is nicely situated in the village just across the river Teme from Ludlow, but unfortunately the church is made dark by an excess of Victorian stained glass and by surrounding trees and buildings. The church consists of a nave with a north chapel, chancel and a western tower. The nave is basically Norman, as evidenced by a west window which now opens into the tower; and there are blocked round-headed doorways in the north wall of the tower and the west wall of the chapel. The south doorway and the

Fig.27.7 Halford church: the 'crocus' motif on the south doorway

Fig.27.8 St. Giles, Ludford: brass to William Foxe (d.1554) and his wife, with children below

chancel date from later in the Middle Ages and the south wall of the nave and the east wall of the chancel are largely Victorian. There used to be a convex-sided triangular window like the ones at Alberbury and Moreton Corbet in the east wall of the chancel.[9] The tower is Perpendicular, though the battlements date only from the 1820s.

At the dissolution of the monasteries, St. John's Hospital became the property of William Foxe, and St. Giles' Hospital was demolished and replaced by a mansion house. The north chapel was rebuilt (re-using a Norman doorway) as a burial place for his family. In this chapel is an excellent brass to William Foxe (d.1554) and his wife – two standing figures, he in armour, she with a pedimented head-dress and gown; kneeling below are nine sons and six daughters (Fig.27.8).

Other less distinguished monuments include: (1) Edward Foxe (d.1635, though the monument is earlier) – a tomb-chest with columns; (2) Dorothy Charlton (d.1650) – a good wall-monument, with a bust between columns; (3) Sir Job Charlton (d.1697) – a recumbent effigy on a tomb-chest – a very late date for such a monument; (4) Lettice Charlton (d.1685), a baroque tablet with an heraldic cartouche; and (5) Samuel Sprott (d.1760) – a plain wall-monument with an urn at the top, and below a rococo cartouche – this is by T.F. Pritchard whose name appears on one side.[10] There is also a hatchment of Sir Francis Charlton (d.1729).

Broad Street Methodist Church, Ludlow*

The Methodist church in Broad Street was built in 1878-79 by William Ranger. Although a classical late Victorian building, the interior has recently been transformed to provide modern facilities, including a café. The church is built of red brick with stone dressings; there are Tuscan pilasters between the central doors. Internally, the church is beautifully light, with galleries on three sides (Fig.27.9). The café is staffed by worshippers from the town's Methodist, Anglican and Roman Catholic

Fig.27.9 Ludlow, Broad Street Methodist: the interior

congregations, and is open Mondays to Saturdays 10am to 2pm. Strongly recommended!

St. John, Ludlow

St. John's is a suburban church in Ludlow, built by Sir Arthur Blomfield in 1881. It is a rather conventional Early English design, late in the Victorian era for such a style, and hence lacking in originality. It consists of a nave and chancel, with a lean-to south aisle. There is a good reredos – a mosaic with painted tiles; the subject is Christ in Majesty, attended by angels, with prophets and saints on each side. There is some attractive Victorian glass in the chancel.

St. Laurence, Ludlow***

At the time of the Domesday survey, Ludlow was part of the manor of Stanton Lacy, then the most prosperous estate in Shropshire. The town was founded shortly after the building of the castle in 1085 by Roger de Lacy, and it developed as a planned settlement adjoining the castle, the church and the market square.

St. Laurence's is one of the greatest parish churches in England, and welcomes about 45,000 visitors each year. On superficial inspection it appears to be a typical Perpendicular building; but there are significant Decorated parts, especially in the porch and the north aisle, and a few vestiges of earlier building. Nothing remains of the structure of the original late-11th-century church, but 100 years later a second church was built in a style transitional between Norman and Early English (see p.14). It is said that a barrow was removed in 1199 in order to enlarge the churchyard.[11] Later, in the 13th century, the western part of the chancel was built and the main doorway was constructed in the Early English style. Around 1320, in the Decorated era, the porch was erected and the north aisle was rebuilt; later the church was enlarged by the addition first of a south transept and later a north transept. Finally, and most impressively, there was a massive rebuilding between 1433 and 1471 which transformed St. Laurence's into the glorious Perpendicular building which we see today. Much of this rebuilding was due to the wealthy Palmers' Guild, which endowed a number of chantries in the church.

The church (Fig.1.2) consists of a nave with north and south aisles and a south porch, north and south transepts, and chancel, with flanking chapels to both north and south. It is therefore basically cruciform, and from the exterior there is a marked contrast between the Decorated windows of the north aisle (Fig.9.21), and the Perpendicular windows in the south and at the east and west ends. The noble 15th-century tower is a landmark for miles around – above the crossing is a lantern with tall four-light Perpendicular windows on each face and well above this are the shorter belfry windows. Around the top are battlements, angle-turrets with pinnacles, and intermediate pinnacles on each side.

The interior of St. Lawrence's is a treasure-house; the outstanding features are the misericords in the chancel and the medieval stained glass which is in the north aisle, St. John's chapel, the chancel and the Lady chapel. With so much to see I think it best to describe a clockwise tour of the church, beginning with the porch.

The porch. Enter the church through the early Decorated two-storeyed hexagonal porch. This remarkable structure is one of only three hexagonal porches in the country (see p.46). The porch is vaulted, with a large boss at the junction of the ribs, and there are windows with Decorated tracery on each side. Above is the parvis room, previously used as a library. The fine south doorway is ahead – it has one order of shafts and a finely moulded arch.

The nave. Go through this doorway and enter the west end of the nave. On the left is the large, round, probably Norman font – the oldest artefact in the church; unfortunately, it is plain and rough. The nave itself is a noble structure – one of the finest in England. The arcades are tall in the Perpendicular manner, the piers consisting of four shafts with wave-moulding between. Only the shafts have plain capitals. Above the arcades are the clerestory windows, and above this the low-pitched panelled timber roof, with carved bosses at the intersections. The roof is supported by tie-beams resting on arched braces; from the tie-beams, short king-posts rise to the ridge-piece. The pulpit dates from 1910 and is by J.O.

Fig.27.10 Ludlow: west window by Thomas Willement (1860)

Scott; it is of carved wood resting on a stone base. The window above the west door on the visitor's left is very tall and consists of seven lights; there is reticulated tracery at the top, indicating that the window is transitional between Decorated and Perpendicular – ?c.1380. The glass in this window is by Thomas Willement (1786-1871) (Fig.27.10).

The north aisle. Beyond the nave is the north aisle, and the west window here is definitely Decorated, with ball-flower enrichment characteristic of the Decorated style (Fig.9.21). In the west end of the north aisle are two tomb-chests, c.1500, with a Tudor rose, cusped quatrefoils and canopies above. There are no effigies and the original purpose of these monuments is unknown. Turn to the right and walk along the north aisle towards the north transept, passing the Royal Coat of Arms. Two half-arches rise from either side of the transept and probably assist in buttressing the tower. The oldest glass in the church is here in the heads of the three easternmost windows of the north aisle (c.1320): the central panel depicts the coat of arms of Theobald de Verdun (d.1316) and on either side the arms of his two wives, Maud Mortimer (d.1315) and Elizabeth Clare.

The north transept. This was originally the Fletchers' (i.e. arrowmakers') chapel;[12] now it contains the organ in its fine organ-case, and in front is an ancient screen. The organ is by Snetzler, Gray and Davidson, and was rebuilt 30 years ago by Nicholson.[13]

St. John's chapel. Walk past the organ and go through the much finer parclose screen into the chapel of St. John the Evangelist which was the original chapel of the Palmers' Guild. The screen is the best in the church and consists of two-light divisions with much delicate panel tracery; above is a lovely carved cornice. There are three windows of 15th-century glass in St. John's chapel. At the west end of the north wall is the Annunciation window, showing in the upper lights a figure of Christ holding the orb and sceptre, the Archangel Gabriel, and the Virgin Mary at the Annunciation; below is St. Catherine with her wheel, St. John the Baptist holding a lamb, and St. Christopher carrying the Christ child over a stream (Fig.12.1). The next window in the north wall is the Creed window, in which articles of the Creed are linked with the 12 Apostles. The apostles are set in an architectural interior spanning all three lights, and the style is characterised by rather heavy shading.[14] In the east wall of the chapel is the Palmers' window, detailing a legend of the Palmers and King Edward the Confessor visiting the Holy Land.

On the north wall of the chapel is extensive panelling from the late 16th and 17th centuries, with much linen-fold and above a vine trail with fruit. The panelling and reredos on the east wall were installed in 1904. High above the altar is a wonderful 15th-century canopy or baldacchino, carved with angels, Tudor roses and pomegranates – a rare survival, for most of these were destroyed at the Reformation. On the south wall of the chapel is the fine monument to Sir John Bridgeman (d.1637) and his wife. Although this is a rather conservative monument for the period – two effigies with ruffs, still recumbent on a tomb-chest – this early use of black and white marble for the effigies is a foretaste of changes to come. The monument is rather doubtfully attributed to Francisco Fanelli, an Italian who worked, mainly in brass, at the court of Charles I.[15]

The crossing. From the chapel proceed to the crossing under the tower, and look up at the intricate patterning of the vaulting above The tower is supported by four great diamond-shaped piers each with five attached shafts separated by wave-moulding. Above the arches is the lantern; and over this the wooden vaulting is exquisitely carved with trefoil-headed arches and ribs combining to produce a stellar effect.[16] To the east of the crossing is the rood screen, another fine late Perpendicular screen with coving, cresting and pendants above the entrance. Go through this to enter the chancel.

The chancel. The western end of the chancel is dominated by the choir-stalls displayed on either side (Fig.14.9). The stalls themselves are famous for the complete set of misericords, one of the finest in England. The lower part of the stalls is original, made in 1447, the upper part Victorian. The poppy-heads on the bench ends are much disfigured, except for three on the south side which show a pietà (Mary nursing the body of Christ) and various saints and bishops.[17]

The misericords were carved in two distinct phases.[18] A set of 16 were made in the early 15th century, and eight of these include a carver's mark in the form of an uprooted plant. The remainder were commissioned by the Palmers' Guild soon after 1447. Table IX shows the wide range of subjects – notable is the almost complete absence of religious themes. The stalls are numbered 1-16 from east to west on the north and south sides. Many are satirical representations of domestic life – e.g. S3, the man warming himself by a fire; and N5, a kitchen scene, with a stewpot on the fire (Fig.14.10). The low life of taverns (often equated with brothels) is also evident – e.g. N3, where a nude woman guilty of giving short measures of ale is slung over the devil's shoulder and welcomed to hell by a devil playing the bagpipes. The sole evidence of a religious theme is possibly S1, the interpretation of which has been much debated. It seems most likely that the central figure represents a well-heeled merchant; he stands next to a barrel, with pattens and bellows. The man on the left originally pointed to the scene on the right, which shows a tomb, with spade, shovel, bones and skulls, 'a warning even to the healthy and wealthy always to be prepared for sudden death'.[19] Emblems from the late medieval kings and the houses of York (N13, N15, S10, S15) and Lancaster (N6 and

North side, from the west end:
1) a scold who has been gagged
2) a wyvern with a woman's head
3) the dishonest alewife carted off to hell by the devil
4) a mermaid with mirror and comb, flanked by dolphins
5) a kitchen scene, with a stewpot on the fire
6) a chained antelope, emblem of Henry VI
7) a bishop
8) the Prince of Wales' feathers
9) a fox in bishop's clothing, preaching to geese
10) a hart, emblem of Richard II
11) a king (?Edward III)
12 an angel with a shawm
13) a falcon and fetterlock, badge of Richard, duke of York
14) plain
15) four roses, emblem of the House of York
16) plain

South side, from the east end:
1) a prosperous merchant and a warning of sudden death
2) leaves
3) a pedlar drawing on his boots
4) a saltire on women's head-dress
5) an owl
6) a swan, emblem of the Lancastrians
7) a man warming himself by a fire
8) a wrestling match
9) mutilated, remains of birds and animals
10) a griffin, emblem of Edward III
11) a drinker drawing ale from a barrel
12) kneeling figures on either side of a barrel
13) a scholar in cap and gown
14) plain
15) reconstituted—a rose and fetterlock, emblem of the Yorkists
16) plain

Table IX The Misericords at St. Laurence, Ludlow

331

S6) are evident – especially prominent are Yorkist symbols, denoting the local power of the Mortimers and their links with Richard, duke of York.

The carvings on the chancel roof reflect some of the themes of the misericords. Like that in the nave, the roof is of low pitch and panelled, with bosses at the intersections. These exhibit a variety of carvings, including angels, beasts' heads, women, a bishop, an old man, a bird with a woman's head, and a falcon on a fetterlock.[20]

Beyond the stalls, the eastern part of the chancel is dominated by the high altar and the stone reredos behind; the latter, with tiers of statues, is mainly Victorian, but some medieval parts remain. To the right of the altar is the piscina and sedilia. On the floor of the sanctuary is an excellent marble mosaic designed by Sir Arthur Blomfield.

Some of the glass in the windows of the chancel is original (15th century), but there was extensive restoration by David Evans of Shrewsbury and others in the mid-19th century, and a lot of the glass is Victorian. There are three windows on both the north and south sides, and in addition there is the great east window. The east window depicts in 27 lights the legend of St. Laurence. The east window on the south side illustrates some of the Ten Commandments, and other windows on both north and south sides show a rich variety of saints.

The chancel houses some excellent monuments. On the north wall is the fine monument to Edward Waties (d.1634) and his wife, two figures kneeling on either side of a prayer-desk (Fig.11.22). Next is the classical monument to Theophilus Salway (d.1760), a rococo assembly with a putto on a pedestal, books, skull and bones etc. In the sanctuary is the monument to Sir Robert Townshend (d.1581) and his wife – two recumbent effigies on a tomb-chest with fluted Ionic columns (Fig.27.11). This Renaissance monument is set in

Fig.27.11 Ludlow, St. Laurence: tomb-chest to
Sir Robert Townshend (d.1581) and his wife

a Perpendicular recess. On the south side is the tomb-chest to Ambrosia Sydney (d.1574) with panels above containing coats of arms etc. Next is Edmund Walter (d.1592) and his wife – two recumbent alabaster effigies on a tomb-chest with kneeling figures around the sides. Strapwork and ribbonwork provide some Renaissance motifs, but otherwise this is a conservative monument for the last decade of the 16th century. 'The arched central portion with entablature above is recessed between flanking columns which project forward supporting their own entablatures at right angles to the wall.'[22]

The Lady chapel. From the chancel, proceed to the Lady chapel, at the south-eastern end of the church. In the Lady chapel is the famous Jesse window, showing the recumbent figure of Jesse below, and figures from the Old Testament purporting to show the descent of Christ from Jesse, the father of King David, with the figure of Jesus above (see rear cover). The heads of the figures are characterised by 'solemn expressions, hollow cheeks, beady eyes and heavy modelling'[23] and the glass is attributed to the same workshop which created the Jesse windows in Tewkesbury, Bristol Cathedral and Madley (Herefordshire). The glass originally dates from c.1330, but was much restored by Hardman and Co. in 1890. This is especially apparent in the figures in the outer panels.

On the north wall of the Lady chapel are several benefactions boards, and a board displaying the Ten Commandments dated 1561. On either side of the altar are ancient stone plaques of uncertain significance. There are two piscinae to the right of the altar; the eastern one has a trefoil arch above and dates from the end of the Early English period (late 13th century); the larger western one is semicircular and dates from the Transitional church built in 1199.

The south transept. From the Lady chapel, turn left into the south transept (St. Catherine's chapel), where there is one notable alabaster monument, that to Dame Mary Eure (d.1612) and her husband. Dame Mary is shown uncomfortably leaning on her left elbow, with the left hand supporting her cheek (Fig.11.27). John Webster said that persons so represented looked as if they died of toothache.[24] There is also a mural tablet to Alice Burrard (d.1703). On the east wall of the transept are the remains of a medieval wall-painting.

Finally walk along the south aisle, past two medieval piscinae, back to the entrance. Then walk 200 yards south to Broad Street Methodist, and have a cup of coffee!

Middleton chapel, near Ludlow*

Sir Stephen Glynne visited this humble chapel, two miles north-east of Ludlow, in 1854, describing the building as mean indeed, but also noting with enthusiasm the rood loft which remains to this day. It is a simple Norman church, just nave, chancel and bellcote. Norman windows remain in both nave and chancel, and in the north wall of the latter is a blocked Norman doorway with a plain tympanum above. There is a plain Elizabethan pulpit. The sanctuary is floored with Victorian tiles, and there is quite good glass in both east and west windows. At the west end is a Crucifixion dating from the early 19th century; in the central light of the east window is a further Crucifixion by Kempe and Co.

But the church is worth visiting for the remarkable rood screen and loft (Fig.13.6). This is an amalgam of late Perpendicular and 19th-century work, and it was complete by the time of Glynne's visit. The original work consists of the horizontal bars above the dado, the mullions and most of the tracing in the lights on either side of the central opening. Above the lights is upward coving, then at the base of the loft are original cornice beams in three rows, with vine-leaf carving. Most of the loft itself is not original, but above is a further Perpendicular rood-beam.

St. Michael, Onibury**

Onibury lies in the valley of the Onny, downstream from Stokesay. It takes its name from the river; Onny was previously thought to be a British name, but Gelling thinks an English origin is more probable.[25] At the time of the Domesday survey the manor was part of the land of the bishop of Hereford, and was held from him by Roger de Lacy. The presence of a priest was recorded, so the presumption must be that there was a Saxon church here; no trace of this remains.

The church consists simply of nave and chancel with a porch and western tower. The earliest feature is the Norman chancel arch – a plain round-headed arch with slight adornment of chevron and pellet at the top of the shafts extending laterally to the sides of the church. The nave has a simple tie-beam roof, with queen-posts directed at an angle (Fig.8.6). Most of the windows are Early English lancets – three in the east wall of the chancel. There is a blocked priest's doorway in the chancel, and a blocked doorway in the north wall of the nave; these two, and the main south doorway, are all pointed and probably of 13th-century origin. There is a straight-headed Decorated window in the south wall of the nave. The rather featureless tower is probably 14th-century. There is a good wooden Perpendicular porch.

The chief interest resides in the furnishings and fittings. The font has a circular bowl standing on an octagonal stem. There are remains of wall-paintings in both north and south walls of the nave and over the chancel arch. On the south wall of the nave are two painted consecration crosses, possibly dating from the 12th century.[26] The pulpit is probably 16th-century, with linen-fold panelling, and possibly some Jacobean additions. The church was sensitively restored in 1902 by Detmar Blow, who added the west gallery and the attractive iron lamps; the gallery bears the Royal Arms of Edward VII. In the chancel is a piscina with a deep basin. On either side of the altar are cast-iron slabs with inscriptions dated 1666 and 1673. Also in the chancel is a memorial to Dorothy Pitt (d.1657) with a moving tribute to the deceased in verse. While none of these items is outstanding in isolation, the whole impression is very satisfying.

All Saints, Batchcott, Richard's Castle**

Richard's Castle is a large parish that straddles the border between Shropshire and Herefordshire. The medieval church of St. Bartholomew is in the latter county, but towards the end of the 19th century it required extensive restoration. At this time (1890) the widow of Mr. Johnston Foster of Moor Park wished to build a new church in memory of her husband and his eldest daughter, and she engaged the eminent architect Richard Norman Shaw. He had already built the church at Peplow (p.136) and the house at Adcote in Shropshire.

A new site was chosen for the church at Batchcott, just inside Shropshire – a site more convenient for the parishioners. It is built of local stone, supplemented by larger facing blocks from Grinshill. It stands on sloping ground, with the result that there is a big substructure under the chancel. The church (Fig.5.8) consists of a nave, south aisle and chancel, the massive crenellated south-western tower being joined to the aisle by a porch – making the tower almost detached from the church. (The tower at the old church in Richard's Castle is fully detached.) It is still recognisably a Gothic church, though Shaw did not slavishly follow any particular medieval period. Thus the east window is Perpendicular, with fanciful and intricate tracery. The windows in the north wall of the nave are Decorated, and so is the window at the west end of the south aisle, which is encrusted with ball-flower externally (cf Ludlow, Leominster and Ledbury). There is also exuberant ball-flower with rosettes and a leaf pattern on the north and south doors of the chancel internally, but in

general the church is notably more restrained than earlier Victorian churches. The interior is spacious and the acoustics are excellent. The nave is divided from the chancel by a wrought-iron screen on a stone base. There is a very good pulpit with tester. The chancel (Fig.27.12) is noteworthy for the reredos, which was designed by Shaw and painted by Charles Buckeridge, and for the organ case also designed by the architect. The octagonal font adorned with quatrefoils came from the old church.

Fig.27.12 All Saints, Batchcott, Richard's Castle (1890): the chancel

St. Michael, Sibdon Carwood

Sibdon is an ancient settlement, recorded in Domesday as *Sibetune*. Cranage recorded that Sibdon was given with Clun to Wenlock Priory in the 12th century. The settlement of Sibdon Carwood is now reduced to Sibdon Castle (perhaps dating from the 17th century), a farm, and the church, which is now designated a proprietory chapel. The medieval church has disappeared and the present building appears to date from 1741, a date inscribed on a stone. The architect is unknown, but in the 1740s William Baker (1705-71), an associate of T.F. Pritchard, is known to have worked at Sibdon Castle.[27]

Access to the church is from the B3468, one mile west from Craven Arms; go through some white gates and along a drive marked 'Private carriage drive'. After half a mile, the church is on the right, set in attractive countryside just beyond the castle. It is an austere building, consisting of a nave, polygonal apse (added in 1871), and a thin west tower. The windows are straight-headed, with Gothic tracery beneath. The interior is plain, the chancel arch resting on corbels decorated with kings' heads below and stiff-leaf foliage above.

St. Peter, Stanton Lacy**

Stantone in the Domesday Book has an impressive entry: as part of the land of Roger of Lacy, it was held by Siward. There was land for 50 ploughs. There were 67 villagers, two smiths, five smallholders and four cottagers: between them they had 23 ploughs. A church had one and a half hides; two priests with two villagers had three ploughs. There were two mills valued at 26 shillings. The value of the whole manor was £25. Klein claims that this area was the richest and most productive land in Shropshire.

Fig.27.13 St. Peter, Stanton Lacy

With such prosperity, it is perhaps not surprising that here was a Saxon church on a substantial scale, and clear evidence of Saxon work survives to the present day. The church is cruciform, with a central tower, nave with south aisle, chancel and north transept (Fig.27.13). The Saxon work is visible in the west and north walls of the nave, and in the north transept. Here may be seen a series of vertical strips or pilasters which 'start from boldly projecting square corbels near the ground, and run up the wall in a series of long-and-short sections'.[28] On the north and west walls of the nave the pilasters stop halfway up, while on the north transept they rise to the full height of the walls.[29] In the north wall is a blocked Saxon doorway (Fig.3.3), with square jambs and a round-headed arch; above is a large stone carved with a plain cross, and above this again is a row of pellets, a horizontal corbel and a short pilaster strip. On the west wall, to the right of the five pilaster strips may be seen quoins of long-and-short work marking the boundary between the Saxon and later medieval masonry.

The rest of the church dates from the late 13th and 14th centuries, with evidence of both Early English and Decorated work. The interior is spacious, with the nave separated from the south aisle by an arcade of two bays with an octagonal pier between. The central tower is supported by the chancel arch, the crossing arch, and the arches leading to the north and south transepts, the first two having capitals ornamented with ball-flower. Externally, there are two Decorated tomb-recesses on the south aisle. Reference to the Williams painting of 1790 shows that the south transept, at least, has been considerably modified, presumably at some time in the 19th century.

St. John the Baptist, Stokesay**

Situated next to Stokesay Castle, the church (now the parish church of Craven Arms) appears a typical English medieval church. And so, originally, it was; but skirmishes around the castle during the Civil War caused severe damage to the church, which had to be rebuilt in 1654 during the Commonwealth. This period saw the construction of very few churches, so Stokesay is quite an exceptional building. The damage was greatest to the tower and nave (which were substantially rebuilt, re-using as much of the old masonry as possible), and least to the chancel, which required repair and re-roofing.

The name derives from OE *stoc* (a 'place' or 'enclosure') and the Norman family name Say (Picot de Say held the Honour of Clun after the Norman conquest – *cf* Hopesay and Moreton Say). The only survival of the Norman church is the south doorway, a plain round-headed archway with two shafts and scalloped capitals. The tower (Fig.5.2) looks medieval, but in fact it dates from the rebuilding; it is a solid edifice of three stages separated by string-courses. The nave and chancel are plain; in the south wall of the nave are two pairs of straight-headed windows; in the chancel (least affected by the rebuilding), the east window consists of three lights within a pointed arch, the central light not arched (like so many in Herefordshire). The roof of the nave is largely hidden by a ceiling, but the chancel roof dates from the rebuilding.

The interior is attractive mainly because of the survival of the 17th-century fittings. At the west end of the nave is a gallery dating from the late 17th or early 18th century (Fig.27.14). On the walls of the nave are a series of paintings dated to 1683 – the Ten Commandments on the north wall, the Lord's Prayer in the north-east corner, and the Creed on the south wall. There is a fine array of oaken box-pews with moulded panels and doors and elaborate hinges. The pulpit, complete with sounding-board or tester and reading-pew, dates from the 17th century. Even more impressive is the canopied pew on the north side of the chancel – a fine specimen with two compartments, each with seats on three sides (Fig.14.14).

Fig.27.14 St. John the Baptist, Stokesay the nave and west gallery from the chancel

Holy Trinity, Wistanstow*

The place-name probably means 'the holy place (stow) of St. Wistan'. He was the grandson and heir of the king of Mercia, and tradition has it that he was murdered in Wistanstow by his cousin because he refused to accept the crown. The church of the Holy Trinity mostly dates from the end of the 12th century, and is unusual in that it is one of the small group of cruciform churches in Shropshire. The central tower imparts a sense of grandeur to this relatively small building; the original late 12th-century tower finished at belfry level, where there are lancet windows; above this a change of masonry indicates that the upper stage was added later. The most notable feature of the exterior is the south doorway of the chancel (Fig.9.17): this is a late Norman (Transitional) doorway – round-headed, with the hood-moulding decorated with the dogtooth motif – dating it to the late 12th century. There is one order of shafts, with the capitals enriched with the carving of a beast's head on the left, and with leaves on the right. It is thought that this doorway was originally sited at the west end of the church, and traces of this can be seen in the masonry of the west end.

The nave is entered by the south doorway which cuts into a lancet window above; opposite this is a blocked north doorway which exhibits the same feature. The font consists of a small round bowl with a little moulding round the middle, resting on an octagonal stem. It is difficult to date but could be as old as the church. The nave roof has collar-beams on arched braces, with four tiers of quatrefoiled wind-braces laterally; it is said to date from 1630. The four arches supporting the tower are pointed, and may date from the 14th century.

The north transept contains two windows which are square-headed externally, but internally are deeply splayed and round-headed – typical Norman features. The roof over the transept is of the trussed-rafter type (Fig.8.1) and was dated by Cranage to *c.*1200; dendrochronology now gives a date range from 1192-1226[30] – a triumph for Cranage! This is Shropshire's earliest dendrochronological date for any building. The walls of the south transept are painted with texts on decorative frames of the 17th century (*cf* Stokesay). The chancel is plain, with three widely spaced lancet windows in the east wall and a group of three lancets on the south wall. Two small windows in the nave contain excellent stained glass by Margaret Rope (*cf* Shrewsbury Cathedral) and her cousin (Fig.12.22).

Glossary

Abacus: a flat slab above a capital.

Acanthus: a prickly-leafed plant whose leaves are represented in Corinthian capitals.

Advowson: the right of presentation of a priest to a church.

Agnus Dei: a figure of a lamb, representing Christ, bearing the banner of the Cross.

Alabaster: a compact marble-like form of gypsum (calcium sulphate) long favoured for memorial effigies.

Ambulatory: an enclosed walkway.

Apse: the semicircular or rectangular end of the chancel.

Arabesque: decoration using fanciful combinations of flowing lines, foliage and intertwined tendrils etc.

Arcade: a range of arches supported by piers or columns.

Arched braces: see Roof.

Architrave: the lowest of the parts of the entablature above a column.

Ashlar: blocks of masonry fashioned to even faces and square edges.

Augustinian canons: members of an order whose rule is based on the teachings of St. Augustine.

Aumbry: a recess or cupboard to hold the vessels for Mass or Holy Communion.

Austin canons: see Augustinian.

Ball-flower: an ornament resembling a ball within a globular flower, a motif used in Decorated architecture c.1300–1350.

Baluster: a small pillar or column of artistic outline.

Balustrade: a series of short columns, usually supporting a railing.

Barge-boards: projecting boarding along the edge of a gable to cover the rafters and to keep out rain.

Baroque: a vigorous, exuberant style of architecture prevalent in the 17th century in Europe, and in a modified form from about 1700–1720 in England.

Bay: the space between the columns of an arcade.

Beakhead: a Norman ornamental motif consisting of a row of birds' or beasts' heads with beaks biting into a moulding.

Benedictine: a monk or nun of the order founded by St. Benedict.

Billet: a Norman ornamental motif consisting of raised rectangles or cylinders with spaces between.

Blind arcade: an arcade of piers or columns attached to a wall.

Boss: a projection at the intersection of the ribs of a vault or roof.

Box-pew: a pew with a tall wooden enclosure.

Breccia: a lithified sedimentary rock composed of angular fragments.

Bressummer: a transverse beam supporting the superstructure.

Broach spire: a spire at the base of which sloping half-pyramids of stone effect the transition from a square tower to an octagonal spire.

Buttress: a mass of masonry projecting from or built against a wall to give extra strength.

Buttress, flying: an arch, or half-arch, transmitting the thrust from the upper part of a wall to an outer support.

Cable: a Norman moulding imitating a twisted rope.

Campanile: an isolated bell-tower.

Capital: the top part of a pier or column.

Caryatid: a female figure supporting an entablature.

Ceilure: an embellished part of the roof above the rood, or occasionally over the altar.

Censer: a vessel for the burning of incense.

Centaur: a mythical monster, half man, half horse.

Chamfer: a bevel or slope made by paring the edge of a right-angled block of stone, seen at the lower corners of the chamfered or splayed-foot spire.

Chancel: the east end of the church containing the altar.

Chancel arch: an arch at the east end of the nave opening into the chancel.

Chantry chapel: a chapel endowed for the saying of Masses for the soul(s) of the founder(s) after death.

Chevron: Norman zigzag moulding on arches or windows.

Choir: the east end of the church where divine service is sung.

Cinquefoil: an ornament divided by cusps into five lobes.

Clerestory: an upper storey of the walls of the nave pierced by windows.

Coif: a covering for the head worn by women.

Collar-beam: see Roof.

Common rafter: see Roof.

Consecration cross: five crosses incised on a stone altar, symbolising the Five Wounds of Christ; a set of 12 crosses marked on the inside and outside walls during the consecration of a church.

Console: a projecting bracket, often S-shaped, to support a cornice or decorative objects (vases, urns etc.)

Corbel: a block of stone projecting from a wall, often supporting roof beams.

Corbel-table: a series of corbels below the eaves.

Corinthian columns: one of the order of classical architecture.

Cornice: the top section of the entablature.

Coving: a concave moulding on the under-surface of a ceiling or screen etc.

Credence: a shelf over a piscina; a table beside the altar on which the bread and wine are placed.

Crenellated: notched or embattled (as in a parapet).

Cresting: ornamentation along the top of a screen etc.

Crocket: decorative projections on the sloping sides of spires, pinnacles, etc.

Crossing: in a cruciform church, the space at the intersection of the nave, chancel and transepts.

Cupola: a domed or polygonal turret crowning a roof.

Curvilinear: see Tracery.

Cushion: in Norman architecture, the rounding-off of the lower angles of the square capital to the cylindrical pier below.

Cusp: a projecting point between the foils in a Gothic arch.

Dado: decorative covering of the lower part of a wall or screen.

Decorated: historical division of English Gothic architecture, from c.1300–1350.

Diaper: a low-relief pattern, often composed of square or lozenge shapes.

Dogtooth: Early English ornamental motif consisting of a series of raised pyramids.

Doom: a picture of the Last Judgment.

Doric: one of the orders of classical architecture.

Double-framed: see Roof.

Drip-stone: a projecting moulding over doorways or windows to throw off the rain, usually ending in a carved stop.

Dugout: a hollowed log made into a chest.

Early English: historical division of English Gothic architecture from *c*.1200 - 1300.

Easter sepulchre: a recess in the north wall of the chancel used to house the consecrated Host between Maundy Thursday and Easter Day.

Eaves: the underpart of a sloping roof overhanging a wall.

Entablature: all the horizontal members above a column (architrave, frieze and cornice).

Fan vault: see Vault.

Finial: the top of a canopy, gable or pinnacle.

Flamboyant: the last phase of French Gothic architecture, characterised by wavy or undulating window tracery.

Fleuron: a flower-like ornament.

Fluting: vertical channelling in the shaft of a column.

Foil: a lobe formed by cusping of a circle or arch; trefoil (3), quatrefoil (4), cinquefoil (5), sexfoil (6) etc. express the number of shapes so produced.

Foliated: decorated with leaf ornaments.

Frieze: the middle division of the entablature.

Gargoyle: a projecting spout from a roof-gutter, often grotesquely carved.

Geometrical: see Tracery.

Gothic: the style of architecture characterised by pointed arches, sub-divided into Early English, Decorated and Perpendicular; revived in the 19th century.

Gothick: a style of architecture of the second half of the 18th century, in which Gothic forms were imitated.

Green man: a human mask with foliage issuing from the mouth.

Griffin: a mythical beast with a lion's body and an eagle's beak and wings.

Grisaille: monochromatic patterns on clear glass, in grey, brown or yellow, used from the 13th century onwards.

Guilloche: an ornamental motif consisting of interlacing curved bands enclosing circles.

Hammer-beam: see Roof.

Head-stop: the stop of a drip-stone or hood-mould carved into a head.

Herefordshire window: a group of three stepped windows under a common arch, with the mullions flanking the middle light extending up to the arch above; frequently used in Herefordshire churches around 1200.

Herring-bone masonry: in which the stones are laid diagonally, sloping in different directions in alternate rows to make a zigzag pattern; used in Anglo-Saxon or early Norman work (up to *c*.1125).

Hood-mould: projecting moulding over doors or windows to throw off rain-water.

Impost: the slab, usually moulded, on which the ends of an arch rest.

Ionic columns: one of the orders of classical architecture.

Jamb: the straight side of an archway, doorway or window.

Jesse window: in which Christ's descent from Jesse, father of King David, is depicted in stained glass.

King-post: see Roof.

Label: a drip-stone or hood-mould.

Lancet window; the tall narrow pointed window of the Early English period.

Light: a vertical division of a window.

Linenfold: panelling in which there is vertical patterning resembling parallel folds of linen, used in the 16th century.

Lintel: a horizontal stone over a doorway.

Lozenge: diamond-shaped.

Lucarne: a small opening to admit light.

Mandorla: an almond-shaped or oval panel.

Metope: in the Doric order, the space in the frieze between the triglyphs.

Misericord: a bracket on the underside of a hinged choir-stall, affording some support when standing, often intricately carved.

Mullions: vertical stone bars dividing a window into lights.

Nail-head: Early English ornamental motif, consisting of small pyramids repeated at intervals.

Neo-Norman: the imitation of Norman architecture in the 19th century.

Nook-shaft: a shaft in the angle of the jamb of a window or doorway.

Norman architecture: the massive Romanesque style of building, from 1066–1200.

Ogee arch: a non-structural arch formed by two S-shaped curves, with the concave parts above coming to a point, typical of the 14th century.

Order: in Classical building, a column, with base, shaft, capital and entablature; in Norman building, one of the successively recessed arches of an archway, or at the sides of a doorway, all the parts of a column (base, shaft and capital).

Parclose screen: a screen separating a chapel from the rest of the church.

Pediment: a low-pitched gable placed as a decorative feature above doorways, windows, etc.
    broken pediment: the central portion of the pediment is open.
    segmental pediment: part of the sloping sides is omitted.

Pellet: a Norman ornamental motif consisting of small balls regularly repeated.

Perpendicular: a historical division of English Gothic architecture, c.1350 - 1550.

Pier: a column of free-standing masonry supporting arches.

Pilaster: a shallow pier attached to a wall.

Piscina: a basin with drain in the wall to the south of the altar for washing the vessels used during Mass.

Plate tracery: see Tracery.

Plinth: the projecting base of a wall or column.

Poppy-head: a finial in wood at the end of a pew or bench, often carved.

Porphyry: a very hard rock, purple and white, used in sculpture.

Portico: a roof supported by columns at the entrance to a building.

Portland stone: an oolitic building-stone quarried in the Isle of Portland.

Pre-Raphaelites: a group of painters who, about 1848, sought to return to the style of painters before Raphael (Millais, Burne-Jones, Holman Hunt etc.).

Presbytery: the part of a monastic church east of the choir.

Principal rafter: stronger rafters dividing the roof-structure into sections.

Purbeck marble: an expensive shelly limestone from Purbeck, Dorset, often polished.

Purlin: horizontal timbers parallel with the ridge of the roof supporting the rafters.

Putto (pl. putti): a small boy or cherub.

Quatrefoil: an ornament divided by cusps into four lobes.

Queen-post: see Roof.

Quoins: dressed stones at the angles of a building.

Rebus: a pun, or play on words.

Recessed spire: a spire recessed within a parapet.

Rendering: plastering of an outer wall.

Reredos: an ornamental screen or hanging on the wall behind the altar.

Respond: a half-pier carrying one end of an arch and bonded into a wall.

Reticulated tracery: see Tracery.

Retrochoir: an extension of a church to the east of the high altar.

Ridge-piece: see Roof.

Rococo: the last phase of the Baroque style, prevalent on the continent *c.*1720–1760.

Romanesque: another name for Norman and Anglo-Saxon architecture, defined by round arches and vaults.

Rood: a Cross bearing the body of Jesus, flanked by the Virgin Mary and St. John.

Rood loft: a gallery on top of the rood-screen.

Rood screen: a screen at the junction of nave and chancel bearing the Rood.

Roof: Arched brace: inclined curved timbers, strengthening collar- or hammer-beams.

    Collar-beam: a tie-beam applied higher up the slope of the roof.

    Double-framed: the use of longitudinal members (ridge-piece, purlins), the rafters then being divided into stronger principals and weaker subsidiaries.

    Hammer-beam: a horizontal beam projecting from the wall bearing arched braces.

    King-post: an upright timber connecting a tie- or collar-beam to the ridge-beam.

    Queen-post: a pair of upright timbers placed symmetrically on a tie- or collar-beam connecting it with the rafters above.

    Ridge-piece: a longitudinal timber forming the ridge of the roof.

    Scissor-brace: a timber supporting the common rafters above the level of the collar-beams.

    Single-framed: a roof composed entirely of transverse members, not tied longitudinally.

    Trussed-rafters: a pair of common rafters pegged together at the ridge and stabilised by a linking collar-beam and bracing.

    Wagon roof: the appearance of the inside of a canvas over a wagon, obtained by closely set arched braces, the roof being panelled or plastered.

    Wall-post: vertical posts placed against the side walls, supporting arched braces.

Rose window: a circular window with tracery radiating from the centre.

Rosette: a rose-shaped ornament.

Rustication: large blocks of masonry separated by sunken or chamfered joints.

Sacristy: a room housing sacred vessels, treasures etc.

Saddleback: a tower roof with two gables.

Saltire cross: an equal-limbed diagonal cross.

Sanctuary: the area around the high altar.

Scagliola: an imitation marble, made of cement and colouring matter.

Scallop: decoration on the under surface of a Norman capital in which a series of truncated cones are elaborated.

Scissor-brace: see Roof.

Sedilia: recessed seats for priests in the south wall of the chancel.

Sexfoil: an ornament divided by cusps into six lobes.

Single-framed: see Roof.

Soffit: the ornamental underside of an arch, canopy, ceiling, etc.

Sounding-board: a canopy or tester over the pulpit.

Spandrel: the space between the curve of an arch and enclosing mouldings.

Splayed-foot: see Chamfer.

Squinch: a supporting arch displayed across an angle between two walls.

Squint: an oblique hole cut in a wall or pier to enable the altar to be seen from afar.

SS collar: a collar awarded to those in the service of John of Gaunt, Duke of Lancaster in the late 14th century.

Stiff-leaf: Early English type of foliage of many-lobed shapes, on capitals etc.

String-course: a projecting line of moulding running horizontally round the walls of the church or tower.

Stucco: plaster-work.

Sunken star: an early Norman ornamental motif.

Tester: a canopy or sounding-board over the pulpit.

Three-decker pulpit: a pulpit, with clerk's stall and reading-desk below.

Tie-beam: a horizontal timber connecting the feet of the rafters in a roof.

Tierceron: a secondary rib in a vault, springing from the intersection of two other ribs.

Tower arch: an arch usually at the west end of the nave opening into the ground floor of the tower.

Tracery: rib-work in the upper part of a window.

    Curvilinear: tracery consisting of curved lines.

    Geometrical: consisting of circles or foiled leaf-shaped circles.

    Intersecting: each mullion branches into two curved bars.

    Plate: an early form in which openings are cut through the stone in the head of the window, often producing a Y shape.

    Reticulated: in which circles are drawn at top and bottom into ogee shapes producing a net-like pattern.

Transept: transverse portion of a cross-shaped church.

Transitional: the style of building in which Gothic pointed arches exist alongside Norman architecture, typical of 1160–1200.

Transom: a horizontal bar across the opening of a window.

Tree of Jesse: in which the genealogy of Jesus is traced back to Jesse, father of King David.

Tree of Life: the motif of a tree sometimes found on Norman tympana.

Trefoil: an ornament divided by cusps into three lobes.

Triforium: an arcaded wall-passage or blind arcading facing the nave at the height of the roof of the aisle, and below the clerestory.

Triglyphs: blocks with vertical grooves in the Doric frieze.

Triptych: a set of three painted panels, hinged together.

Trumpet: a development of scalloped capitals in which each scallop assumes a concave or trumpet shape.

Trussed-rafters: see Roof.

Tufa: a limestone formed by spring-water laden with calcium carbonate bubbling through the rock.

Tuscan columns: one of the classical orders of architecture.

Tympanum: the space over the lintel of a doorway and below the arch above.

Undercroft: a vaulted room below a church.

Vault: an arched roof or ceiling.

    Fan-vault: in which all the ribs springing from their origin are of the same length and curvature and equidistant from each other.

Venetian window: a window with three openings, the central one arched and wider than the outer ones.

Vesica: an oval, with pointed head and foot.

Volute: a spiral scroll, found on Ionic capitals, and also on Norman capitals.

Voussoir: a wedge-shaped stone used in the construction of an arch.

Wagon roof: see Roof.

Wall-plate: a timber laid longitudinally on the top of a wall.

Wall-post: see Roof.

Water-leaf: simple leaf pattern found in late Norman capitals.

Wimple: a veil folded round a woman's head, neck and cheeks.

Wind-braces: pairs of small arched braces joining the purlins and the wall-plate in a roof.

Y-tracery: see Tracery, plate.

Zigzag: Norman geometrical decoration found on arches etc.

Bibliography

Betjeman, J. *Collins Guide to Parish Churches of England and Wales*, 1980, Collins

Bigglestone, P. in *The Gale of Life*, 2000, Logaston Press

Blair, P.H. *Anglo-Saxon England*, reprinted 1997, The Folio Society

   The Book of Saints Sixth edition, 1989, Cassell

Borenius, T. and Tristram, E.W. *English Medieval Painting*, 1927

Brandwood, G.K. *Temple Moore: An architect of the late Gothic Revival*, 1997, Paul Watkins

Cautley, H.M. *Suffolk Churches and their Treasures*, 1937, Batsford

Cave, C.J.P. *Roof Bosses in Medieval Churches*, 1948, Cambridge University Press

Cheetham, F. *Alabaster Images of Medieval England*, 2003, Boydell Press

Clifton-Taylor, A. *English Parish Churches as Works of Art*, 1974, Oxford University Press

   The Pattern of English Building, 1987, Faber and Faber

Colvin, H. *A Biographical Dictionary of British Architects 1600–1840*, 3rd. Edition, 1995, Yale University Press,

Cox, D.C. *Sir Stephen Glynne's Church Notes for Shropshire*, 1997, The University of Keele

Cox, J.C. and Harvey, A. *English Church Furniture*, 1907, reprinted 1973 EP Publishing

Cranage, D.H.S. *An Architectural Account of the Churches of Shropshire*, 1884–1912, Wellington

Crossley, F.H. *English Church Craftsmanship*, 1941, Batsford

   English Church Design 1040–1540 A.D., 1945, Batsford

Curl, J.S. *Georgian Architecture*, 1993, David and Charles

   Victorian Churches, 1995, Batsford/English Heritage

Domesday Book: Shropshire, 1986 Phillimore

Drake, C.S. *The Romanesque Fonts of Northern Europe and Scandinavia*, 2002, Boydell Press

Eastlake, C.L. *A History of the Gothic Revival* (1872), With an introduction by J.M. Crook, Leicester University Press (1970)

Ekwall, E. *The Concise Oxford Dictionary of English Place-names*, 1960, Clarendon Press

Esdaile, K.A. *English Church Monuments 1510–1840*, 1946, Batsford,

Foster, R. *Discovering English Churches*, 1981, British Broadcasting Corporation,

Friar, S. *A Companion to the English Parish Church*, 186, Bramley Books

Ganderton, E.W. and Laford, J. *The Stained and Painted Glass of Ludlow Parish Church*, 1961

Gardner, A. *A Handbook of English Medieval Sculpture*, 1937, Cambridge University Press

Gelling, M. *Place-Names in the Landscape*, 1984, Dent

   The Place-names of Shropshire, Part 1, 1990, English Place-Name Society

   The West Midlands in the Early Middle Ages, 1992, Leicester University Press

Gethyn-Jones, E. *The Dymock School of Sculpture*, 1979, Phillimore

Gittings, C. *Brasses and Brass-Rubbing*, 1970, Blandford Press,

Glynne, Sir Stephen *see* Cox, D.C.

Greenhill, F. A. *Incised Effigial Slabs*, 1976, Faber and Faber

Grossinger, C. *The World Upside-down: English Misericords*, 1997, Harvey Miller Publishers

Grounds, D. *A History of the Church of St. Laurence, Church Stretton*, 2002, Logaston Press

Harbison, R. *The Shell Guide to English Parish Churches*, 1992, André Deutsch

Harrison, M. *Victorian Stained Glass*, 1980, Barrie and Jenkins,

Harrison, M. and Waters, B. *Burne-Jones*, 1989, Barrie and Jenkins

Hartwell, C. *Pevsner Architectural Guides: Manchester*, 2001, Penguin Books

Henderson, W. 'The Church of Ashford Carbonell', *Quarterly Journal of the British Archaeological Association*, Vol. XXXIX, Part III, 1883

Higgins, M.C. in Raguin, V.C. *The History of Stained Glass* (see below)

Hinde, T. (ed.) *The Domesday Book*, 1985, Hutchinson

Hird, N. in *The Gale of Life*, 2000, Logaston Press

Hodgetts, G. Personal communication, 2001

Hopkinson, C. and Speight, M. *The Mortimers, Lords of the March*, 2002, Logaston Press

Howell, P. and Sutton, I. *The Faber Guide to Victorian Churches,* 1989, Faber and Faber

Ionides, J. *Thomas Farnolls Pritchard of Shrewsbury*, 1999, The Dog Rose Press

Jeffery, P. *The Collegiate Churches of England and Wales*, 2004, Robert Hale

Jenkins, S. *England's Thousand Best Churches*, 1999, Penguin Books

Jones, A. *A Thousand Years of the English Parish*, 2000, The Windrush Press

Kemp, B. *English Church Monuments*, 1980, Batsford

Klein, P. *The Misericords and Choir Stalls of Ludlow Parish Church*, 1986

Knowles, D. and Hadcock, R.N. *Medieval Religious Houses in England and Wales*, 1971, Longman

Leonard, J. *Shropshire Parish Churches*, 1991, Breedon Books
    Staffordshire Parish Churches, 1995, Breedon Books

Leonard, J and Wilson, A. in *The Gale of Life*, 2000, Logaston Press

Marks, R. *Stained Glass in England during the Middle Ages*, 1993, Routledge

Marks, R. and Williamson, P. (eds.) *Gothic Art for England 1400–1547*, 2003, V and A Publications

Mercer, E. *English Architecture to 1900: The Shropshire Experience*, 2003, Logaston Press

Moffett C. 'Archaeological Investigations at the Anglo-Saxon Church of St. Andrew, Wroxeter: 1985–86'. *Trans. Shropshire Archaeological and Historical Society* vol. lxvi, 1989

Moran, M. *Vernacular Buildings in Shropshire*, 2003, Logaston Press

Morris, R. *Churches in the Landscape*, 1989, Dent

Munby, J. in *Gothic Art for England 1400–1547*, edited by R. Marks and P. Williamson, 2003, V and A Publications

Pevsner, N. *Shropshire* in *The Buildings of England* series, 1958, Penguin

Platt, C. *The Abbeys and Priories of Medieval England*, 1984, Secker and Warburg

Raguin, V.C. *The History of Stained Glass*, 2003, Thames and Hudson

Redundant Churches Fund *Churches in Retirement*, 1990, HMSO

Rodwell, W. *Church Archaeology*, 1989, Batsford/English Heritage

Rowley, T. *The Shropshire Landscape*, 1972

Sewter, A.C. *The Stained Glass of William Morris and His Circle*, 1974, Yale University Press

Stanford, S.C. *The Archaeology of the Welsh Marches*, 1991, Stanford

Stavridi, M. *Master of Glass Charles Eamer Kempe 1837–1907*, 1988, John Taylor Book Ventures for the Kempe Society

Sullivan, M.R. Personal communication, 2003

Summerson, J. *Architecture in Britain 1530–1830*, 9th Edition, 1993, Yale University Press

Taylor, H.M. and Taylor, J. *Anglo-Saxon Architecture*, 1965, Cambridge University Press

Theobald, P. in *The Gale of Life*, 2000, Logaston Press

Thurlby, M. *The Herefordshire School of Romanesque Sculpture*, 1999, Logaston Press

Trinder, B. *A History of Shropshire*, 1983, Phillimore

Tristram, E.W. *English Medieval Wall Painting: the Twelfth Century*, 1944, Oxford University Press (reprinted 1988, Hacker Art Books)

Tyrell-Green, E. *Parish Church Architecture*, 1924, S.P.C.K.

Vallance, A. *English Church Screens*, 1936, Batsford

Victoria History of Shropshire: Vol. II 1973; Vol. VIII 1968; Vol. X 1998; Vol. XI 1985, Oxford University Press

Watson, M. and Musson, C. *Shropshire from the Air*, 1993, Shropshire Books

Whiffen, M. *Stuart and Georgian Churches outside London*, 1947, Batsford

Whinney, M. *Sculpture in Britain 1530–1830*, 1988, Penguin Books

White, R. in *The Gale of Life*, 2000, Logaston Press

White, R. and Barker, P. *Wroxeter – Life and Death of a Roman City*, 1998, Tempus Publishing

Williamson, P. *Medieval and Renaissance Stained Glass in the Victoria and Albert Museum*, 2003, V and A Publications

Wilson, C. in *Gothic Art for England 1400–1547*, 2003, V and A Publication

Zaluckyj, S. *Mercia: the Anglo-Saxon Kingdom of Central England*, 2001, Logaston Press

Zarnecki, G. *Later English Romanesque Sculpture 1140–1210*, 1953, Tiranti

References

Chapter 2 Origins
1. Hird, 2000, 1.
2. White and Barker, 1998, 106.
3. Blair, 1995, 123.
4. Hillaby, J., 'The Origins of the Diocese of Hereford', *TWNFC*, 1976, 16-52
5. Ekwall, 1960.
6. Ekwall.
7. Hinde, 1985, 11.
8. Domesday Book: Shropshire.

Chapter 3 Medieval Churches
1. Clifton-Taylor, 1987, 99.
2. Mercer, 2003, 10.
3. Foster, 1981, 69.
4. Wilson, 2003, 98.
5. Foster, 1981, 161.

Chapter 4 Monastic Foundations
1. Knowles and Hadcock, 1971.
2. Graham, cited by Platt, 1984, 22.
3. Platt, 1984, 32.
4. Knowles and Hadcock, 1971.

Chapter 5 Post-Reformation Churches
1. Colvin, 479.

Chapter 6 Towers and Spires
1. Mercer, 2003, 82
2. Friar, 1996, 455.

Chapter 7 Porches
1. Cautley, 1937, 48.

Chapter 8 Roofs and Vaults
1. Cranage, 169.
2. Moran, 2003, 352.

3. Munby, 2003, 381.
4. Friar, 1996, 388.

Chapter 10 Fonts
1. Cranage, p.1118.
2. Drake, 2002.
3. Leonard, 1995, 49.
4. Mercer, 2003, 31.
5. Drake, 2002, 13.
6. Thurlby, 1999, 148; Drake, 2002, 14.

Chapter 11 Memorials and Monuments 1250–1870
1. Kemp, 1980, 15.
2. Greenhill, 1976, 3.
3. Gittings, 1970, 20.
4. Gittings, 1970, 21.
5. Based on Gittings, 1970, 94.
6. Whinney, 1964, 68.
7. Kemp, 1980, 150.
8. Whinney, 1988, 163.
9. Whinney, 1988, 198.
10. Whinney, 1988, 261.
11. Whinney, 1988, 303.
12. Pevsner.

Chapter 12 Stained glass and wall-painting
1. Higgins, 2003, 36.
2. Williamson, 2003, 9.
3. I am indebted to Michael Pitchford for the details of churches containing Kempe glass, and for information about H.W. Bryans.
4. Sewter, 1974, 6.
5. Harrison and Waters, 1989, 26.
6. Harrison, 1980, 72.
7. Stavridi, 1988, 88.

Chapter 13 Rood-screens and lofts
1. Vallance, 1936, 82.
2. Vallance, 1936, 44; Crossley, 1941, 61.

Chapter 14 Pulpits, Pews and Chancel furnishings
1. Cox and Harvey, 1973, 255.
2. Grossinger, 1997, 128.

Chapter 15 The north-west – Oswestry and Ellesmere
1. Moran, 2003, 369.
2. Moran, 2003, 369.
3. Ionides, 1999, 224.
4. Ekwall.
5. Harbison, 1992, 215.
6. Jenkins, 1999, 575.
7. Howell and Sutton, 1989, 72.
8. Ekwall.
9. Clifton-Taylor, 1986, 60.
10. Moran, 2003, 111.
11. Gelling, 1992, 70.
12. Ekwall; Gelling, 1992, 106.
13. Vallance, 1936, 82.
14. Ekwall.
15. Cranage, 786.

Chapter 16 The north-east – Whitchurch and Market Drayton
1. Cox, 1997, 21.
2. Cranage.
3. Ekwall.
4. Ekwall.
5. Gelling, 1992, 68.
6. Mercer, 2003, 69.
7. Newman and Pevsner, 2006, 300
8. Gelling, 1992, 69.
9. Mercer, 2003, 279.
10. Whinney, 1988, 261.
11. Newman and Pevsner, 2006, 446
12. Summerson, 1953, 110.
13. Ekwall.
14. Brandwood, 1997, 75.
15. Gelling, 1992, 68.
16. Mercer, 2003, 59.
17. Gelling, 1984, 60.
18. Hartwell, 2001, 199.
19. Colvin, 1995, 882.
20. Whiffen, 1947, 26.

Chapter 17 Central Shropshire – Baschurch and Myddle
1. Gelling, 1992, 72.
2. Gelling, 1992, 75; Watson and Musson, 1990, 32; Stanford 1991, 113.
3. Gelling, 1992, 181.
4. Gelling, 1984, 173.
5. Ekwall.
6. Gethyn-Jones, 1979, 54-5.
7. Moran, 2003, 37.
8. Gelling, 1992, 91.

Chapter 18 East Shropshire – Newport and Shifnal
1. Gelling, 1984, 176.
2. Gelling, 1992, 97.
3. Whinney, 1964, 411.
4. Greenhill, 1976, 176.
5. Curl, 1995, 76.
6. Gelling, 1984, 154.
7. Drake, 2002, 12.
8. Gelling, 1992, 5.
9. Cranage.
10. VCH XI, 169.
11. Whinney, 1988, 437.
12. Newman and Pevsner, 2006, 326
13. Jeffery, 2004.
14. Ekwall.
15. Ionides, 1999, 283
16. Ekwall
17. Tyrell-Green, 1924, 151.
18. Cranage.
19. Marks, 1993, 182.
20. Grossinger, 1997, 128.
21. Cheetham, 2003, 201.
22. Gittings, 1970, 60.
23. Greenhill, 1976, 176.

Chapter 19 Shrewsbury
1. White and Barker, 1998, 41.
2. Ekwall.
3. White and Barker, 1998, 98.
4. Taylor and Taylor, 1965, 32.
5. Mercer, 2003, 1.
6. Tyrell-Green, 1928, 155
7. Greenhill, 1976, 263
8. Ekwall, 1964, 158
9. Howell and Sutton, 1989, 93.
10. Ekwall.

11. Cranage.

12. Ekwall.

13. Moran, 2003, 352.

14. Harbison, 1992, 221.

15. Jeffery, 2004.

16. Church guide.

17. Curl, 1993, 134.

18. Summerson, 1953, 327.

19. Moran, 2003, 33.

20. Betjeman, 1980, 356.

21. Jeffery, 2004.

22. Whiffen, 1947, 53.

23. VCH II, 106.

24. The Book of Psalms.

25. Moran, 2003, 33.

26. Ionides, 1999, 220-223.

27. Cranage.

28. Mercer, 2003, 45.

29. Cheetham, 2003, 152.

30. Moffett, 1989; White and Barker, 1998.

31. Taylor and Taylor, 1965, 694.

32. White and Barker, 1998, 138..

33. White and Barker, 1998, 141.

34. Esdaile, 1946, 52.

35. Whinney, 1988, 129.

Chapter 20 Telford

1. Gelling, 1984, 59.

2. VCH XI, 172.

3. Ekwall.

4. VCH XI, 263.

5. Pevsner, 1955, 158.

6. VCH X, 289.

7. VCH XI, 268.

8. VCH XI, 281.

9. Cranage.

10. VCH XI, 91.

11. VCH, XI, 62.

12. Wesley, quoted by Cranage, 206.

13. VCH XI, 130.

14. Newman and Pevsner, 2006, 480.

15. Gelling, 1984, 10.

16. VCH XI, 171.

17. VCH XI, 192.

18. VCH XI, 194.

19. VCH XI, 241.

20. VCH XI, 299.

21. Ekwall.

22. Gelling, 1992, 182 (b?)

23. VCH XI, 320.

24. Ionides, 1999, 281.

25. VCH XI, 331.

Chapter 21 West Shropshire – Pontesbury

1. Ekwall.

2. Jones, 2000, 112.

3. VCH II, 47.

4. Ionides, 1999, 242.

5. VCH VIII, 219.

6. Gelling, 1992, 128.

7. VCH VIII, 225.

8. VCH VIII, 213.

9. Friar, 1996, 117.

10. VCH VIII, 290.

11. VCH VIII, 329.

12. Ekwall.

13. Jones, 2000, 111.

14. Ionides, 1999, 236.

15. Newman and Pevsner, 2006, 600.

16. VCH VIII, 326.

17. Moran, 2003, 352.

18. Mercer, 2003, 44.

19. VCH VIII, 330.

Chapter 22 Church Stretton and the Stretton Hills

1. VCH VIII, 7.

2. Trinder, 1983, 43.

3. Ionides, 1999, 279.

4. Ekwall, 1960, 39.

5. White and Barker, 1998, 142.

6. Ekwall.

7. VCH II, 38.

8. VCH VIII, 125.

9. Gelling, 1984, 219.

10. Morris, 1989, 267.

11. VCH VIII, 139.

12. Ionides, 1999, 219.

13. Grounds, 2002.

14. Moran, 2003, 111.

15. White and Barker, 1998, 142.

16. Whinney, 1988, 453.

17. Ionides, 1999, 271.

18. Kemp, 1980, 139.

19. VCH VIII, 77.

20. VCH VIII, 55.

21. Moran, 2003, 38.

22. VCH VIII, 145.
23. Gelling, 1992, 15.
24. VCH VIII, 99.
25. Mercer, 2003, 39.
26. Moran, 2003, 452.
27. VCH VIII, 108.
28. VCH VIII, 117.
29. Greenhill, 1976, 275.
30. VCH VIII, 159.
31. Mercer, 2003, 39.
32. VCH VIII, 168.

Chapter 23 Corvedale and Wenlock Edge
1. Taylor and Taylor, 1965, 49.
2. VCH X, 232.
3. Woods, T; cited by Zaluckyj, 2001, 98.
4. Gelling, 1980, 104.
5. VCH X, 250.
6. VCH X, 151.
7. Ekwall.
8. Mercer, 2003, 48.
9. Newman and Pevsner, 2006, 245.
10. Gelling, 1992, 180.
11. VCH X, 322.
12. Jeffery, 2004.
13. VCH X, 135.
14. VCH X, 340.
15. Glynne in Cox, 1997, 52.
16. Cranage.
17. Ekwall.
18. Mercer, 2003, 18.
19. Gelling, 1992, 49.
20. Cranage.
21. Greenhill, 1976, 287.
22. Crossley, 1941, 53.
23. Taylor and Taylor, 1965, 526.
24. Ekwall, 415.
25. VCH X, 185.
26. Gelling, 1992, 14.
27. VCH X, 450.
28. Tristram, 1944.

Chapter 24 The lower Severn Valley – Bridgnorth
1. Kemp, 1980, 115.
2. Whinney, 1988, 135, 138.
3. Ionides, 1999, 238.
4. Kemp, 1980, 150.

5. Thurlby, 1999, 104.
6. Marks and Williamson, 2003, 389.
7. Thurlby, 1999, 99-104.
8. Marks, 1993, 139.
9. Gelling, 1984, 53.
10. Hopkinson and Speight, 2002, 132.
11. Jenkins, 1999, 572.
12. A.R. Green, cited by Vallance, 1936, 14.
13. Drake, 2002, 13.
14. Greenhill, 1976, 212, 252.
15. Greenhill, 1976, 177.
16. Borenius and Tristram, 1927.
17. Ekwall, 239.
18. Ekwall.
19. Gelling, 1984, 114.
20. Gelling, 1984, 240.
21. Cranage.
22. Ionides, 1999, 283.
23. Esdaile, 1946, 109.
24. Mercer, 2003, 31.
25. Ekwall.

Chapter 25 Bishop's Castle and Clun Forest
1. Leonard and Wilson, 2000, 131.
2. Bigglestone in *The Gale of Life*, 2000, 169.
3. Church guide.
4. Moran, 2003, 354.
5. Moran, 2003, 352.
6. Sullivan.
7. Ekwall.
8. Mercer, 2003, 54.
9. Cox and Harvey, 1973 reprint, 132.
10. Cranage.
11. Pevsner.
12. Ekwall; Gelling b.
13. White, 2000, 31.
14. Cranage.
15. Moran, 2003, 39.
16. Gelling, 1984, 114-121.
17. Gelling, 1984, 175.

Chapter 26 The Clee Hills
1. VCH X, 120.
2. Gelling, 1992, 90.
3. Ekwall, 1960, 17.
4. Greenhill, 1976, 23 and 262.
5. Hopkinson and Speight, 2002.

6. Cranage.
7. Leonard, 1991, 10.
8. Watson and Musson, 1993, 73.
9. Ekwall.
10. Ekwall.
11. Whinney, 1964, 376.
12. Ekwall, 278.
13. Rowley, 1972.
14. Mercer, 2003, 64.
15. Mercer, 2003, 88.
16. Cheetham, 2003, 150.
17. Newman and Pevsner, 2006, 319.
18. Grounds, 2002, 98.
19. Ekwall.
20. Cranage.
21. Eyton.
22. Ekwall, 1964, 423.
23. Mercer, 2003, 294.
24. VCH X, 391.
25. Taylor and Taylor, 1965, 580.
26. Mercer, 2003, 67.
27. Marks, 1993, 89.
28. Mercer, 2003, 31.
29. Zarnecki, 1953, 14.
30. Thurlby, 1999, 149.

Chapter 27 The south – Ludlow

1. Henderson, church guide.
2. Ekwall.
3. Stanford, 1991, 5, 113.
4. Jeffery, 2004.
5. Mercer, 2003, 332.
6. Newman and Pevsner, 2006, 187.
7. Mercer, 2003, 30.
8. Speight, M. church guide.
9. Mercer, 2003, 62.
10. Ionides, 1999, 234.
11. Rodwell, 1989, 144.
12. Tyrell-Green, 1924, 170.
13. Sullivan.
14. Marks, 1993, 190, 194.
15. Whinney, 1988, 86.
16. Clifton-Taylor, 1986, 102.
17. Gardner, 1937, 309.
18. Klein, 1986.
19. Grossinger, 1997, 134.
20. Cave, 1948, 199.
21. Marks, 1993, 164.
22. Kemp, 1980, 74.
23. Marks, 1993, 164.
24. Quoted by Kemp, 1980, 80.
25. Gelling, 1992, 66.
26. Cranage.
27. Ionides, 1999, 33.
28. Taylor and Taylor, 1965, 570.
29. Mercer, 2003, 3.
30. Moran, 2003, 111.

Index

Philippa 298
Ralph de 303
Roger 303-304
Morton **119**
Morville 9, 19, 21, 63-64, 270, 272, **278-280**
Much Wenlock 46, 72, 103, **258-260**, 267
Munslow 9, 45, 65, 71, 84, 105, 250, **260-261**
Muxton **168**
Myddle 72, 148, **153-154**
Myndtown – see Mindtown
Mytton family 111
Mary 263
Thomas and Elizabeth 72, 231

Nash 44, 99, **313**
Nash, John 30
Neale, J.M. 32
Nedeham, Sir Robert & Lady 72, 126
Neen Savage 45, 98, **313-314**
Neen Sollars 44, 77, 312, **314-315**
Neenton **315**
Neo-Norman churches 33, 116
Nesfield, William Eden 29, 126
Nesscliff Hospital 24
Netherwood, Robert 188
Sarah 188
Newbery, R.J. 89
Newcastle on Clun **298**
Newport 50-51, 93, 94, **168-169**
Hospital 24
Newport, Francis, 1st Earl of Bradford 202
Sir Richard 72-73, 202
Newtown 99, **136**
Nicholson, A.K. 89
Thomas 29, 173, 288, 294, 303
Norbury 44, **298-299**
Norman architecture 12-15, 40
chevron ornament 9, 53-55
decorative work 53-57, 60-65
North, Herbert 188
Norton, Bonham and Jane 257, 312
John 74-75, 169
Norton in Hales 75-76, **136**

Oakengates **211**
Oakeley family 296
O'Connor 89, 289
Offa, King 7
Offa's Dyke 8
Ogee arch 16

Oldbury **280**
Onibury 9, 45, 48-49, 101, **334**
Onley, John 72, 200
Onslow, Speaker Richard 187
Oswestry, Holy Trinity 44, **119**
Hospital 23, 24
St. Oswald 6, 75, 107, **119-120**
Ottley family 244
William and Mary 71
Owen, Catherine 80, 237
Judge 74, 237
Martha 237
Roger 80, 237
Sir Roger 74, 237
T.E. 206
Thomas 29
Oxford Movement 32

Paget, James 191
Palmers' Guild 328, 330, 331
Parker, Reverend John 29, 115
Richard 202
Parr, Thomas 221
Parry, Blanche 175
Nicholas 134
Payne, Edward 89
Henry 89
Peada, King 6-7
Pearce, William 89
Pearson, Andrew 268
John Loughborough 36, 107, 127, 128, 138, 185, 186
Pemberton, Thomas 261
Pembrugge, Sir Fulke de 69, 175
Lady Isabella de 69, 174, 175
Penda, King 6
Penson, Thomas 33, 116, 119
Peplow 37, 66, 94, **136-137**
Perpendicular architecture 12, 17-18, 25, 42, 50, 58
Petton 29, 66, 79, 101, 102-103, 107, **154-155**
Pevsner, Sir Nikolaus 4
Phillips, Richard 121
Pigot, Harriet 81, 161
Pilkington 898
Pitchford 2, 13, 67-68, 71, 103, 107, **244-245**
Pitchford, Sir John de 244-245
Pitt, Dorothy 334
Plowden, H. 72
Plowden Hall 72

Severn

by Richard Hayman

It was on an island in the Severn in 1016 that Cnut and Edmund settled their competing claims to the throne of England, and it was at the Severn that the English formally recognised Llywelyn ap Gruffudd as the Prince of Wales. From the Iron Age to the Second World War, regimes have built fortresses and other defences to ensure their control over the Severn and, throughout the Civil Wars, Royalists and Parliamentarians fought bitterly for possession of it. Three of Britain's finest bridges were built over the river – the medieval Welsh Bridge in Shrewsbury, the 18th-century Iron Bridge and the modern Severn Bridge, all of which have transcended their practical functions to become icons of their age. Along the riverbank are also the smaller details of history, the redundant slipways, stone quays, canal interchanges, mills and warehouses, all of which are remnants of once vibrant riverside industry. But there are also a Roman city, numerous churches and one of Britain's finest cathedrals, all of which are where they are because of the river, and all evidence of how powerfully the river has drawn human life to its bank.

This book explores the many ways in which the river has become part of our culture, including eating its fish, navigating it, mythologizing it and drowning in it. It is about when and why the river mattered, and why it still matters.

Paperback, 272 pages, over 120 colour and 20 b/w illustrations. Price: £15

Saints & Sinners of the Marches

by Michael Tavinor

'Saints and sinners are not always that far apart' maintains Michael Tavinor in this new anthology. Taking 366 characters from the Marches area of England and Wales – one for each day of the year – the dean of Hereford introduces us to some of the men and women who have made a difference to the area and often deserve to be better remembered. Saints there certainly are, not least Hereford's own saints Ethelbert and Thomas Cantilupe, and sinners too – who would argue with Roger Mortimer, ruthless war-lord of the 14th century? But most of the characters are 'in between' – artists, writers, bishops, deans, musicians. Here we find Thomas Parr, reputed to be the oldest man who ever lived when he died in 1635; Richard Tarlton, court jester to Elizabeth I; Private Jones, a brave holder of the Victoria Cross, whose grave faces a different way because he committed suicide – and unexpected figures such as Cardinal Wolsey who was once dean of Hereford, even if he didn't ever come to the cathedral.

Each page of the book consists of biography, then a poem or piece of prose either by the person described or focusing on what he or she represents.

The text is greatly enlivened by the drawings on each page by Sandy Elliott. These seek to draw out of the text some of the humour, sadness and challenge of the many and varied characters presented.

Hardback, 400 pages, 366 b/w illustrations, text printed in red and black. Price: £20

Also from Logaston Press

The Herefordshire School of Romanesque Sculpture
by Malcolm Thurlby

This book, first published in 1999, has been much enlarged and extended. The new edition is almost double the length, is in a larger format, is printed in colour and includes a history of the Anarchy in Herefordshire by Bruce Coplestone-Crow.

This vibrant collection of work was carved between *circa* 1134 and 1155 by a group of sculptors who, it would seem, had received their initial training at Hereford Cathedral. This book explores their work, considering the careers of the two main sculptors, the role of the patrons, the sources of inspiration, the coming together of the work of the sculptor with that of the metalworker and the illuminator and painter, and the intended meaning behind some of the imagery. The sculptors were working on or near the front line between the opposing factions supporting Stephen or Matilda: strange as it may seem, the patrons of the work were also warlords.

Paperback (with flaps), 320 pages, 400 colour photographs. Price: £17.50

Shropshire Almshouses
by Sylvia Watts

Almshouses, in the shape of early 'hospitals', have been a feature of Shropshire from the 12th century, but the majority of the nearly 40 surviving almshouses were founded in the 17th and 19th centuries, and the most recent in 1955. An Introduction surveys the architectural trends and also looks at the provision of almshouses across the county and how it compared with other parts of the UK, whilst the Gazetteer looks at each group of almshouses in detail, including the personalities of the founders, the degree of social control to which the residents were subjected, and the ways which those residents found to evade the rules and regulations.

Paperback, 144 pages, 50 colour and 15 /w images ISBN 978 1906663 31 5 £12.95

The Shropshire Home Guard
by Bernard Lowry

The Home Guard was formed in 1940 in response to the threat of an invasion of Britain that would involve German paratroop attacks aided by fifth columnists as had happened in Belgium and Holland. Shropshire was included in these plans, not least because it was feared that spies could be present anywhere in the country, and it was feared that the invasion might well come through Ireland directed towards the north Wales coast. The story is drawn from records held in Shropshire Archives and stories told by former members. It thus combines official documents and orders with personal accounts of what it was like to be a member —and what did and didn't happen in practice.

Paperback, 128 pages with 45 black and white illustrations. Price: £10

The Drovers Roads of the Middle Marches
by Wayne Smith

This is the story of the men who until as recently as the 1930s used to walk with their sheep and cattle out of Wales along the ancient trackways to the markets and fairs of England. The journeys were carefully judged – too slow and the expenses of feeding and accommodating men and beasts would mount, too fast and the animals would lose condition. Taking the easier routes meant the expense of turnpikes and tollgates, but going the long way round cost time. Droving was a steady trade, and the drovers were often entrusted with commissions and even money to be taken to London, a practice from which the first banks developed. Tell-tale signs of droving routes can still be discerned in the landscape in the pine trees and ponds that marked the routes, and the names of farms, houses and inns. Wayne Smith describes the routes the drovers took, and includes sections in 16 circular walks, all illustrated with his own photographs.

Paperback (with flaps), 176 pages, 50 colour and 12 b/w photos, 17 maps. Price: £10

Vernacular Buildings of Shropshire
by Madge Moran

This book brings together Made Moran's work, with the exception of the area around Whitchurch which was covered in her earlier publication *Vernacular Buildings of Whitchurch and Area and their occupants*. Initial chapters track the changes from buildings designed with defence in mind to first-floor halls. Cruck buildings are given their own chapter, as are box-framed and jettied houses, roof construction, the transitional house, wallpaintings and dendrochronology. Ludlow, Shrewsbury and Much Wenlock are given a series of chapters, followed by a gazetteer for other settlements.

Paperback, 592 pages, over 1,500 b/w drawings and photographs. Price: £25

The Folklore of Shropshire
by Roy Palmer

Shropshire's folklore is presented in a series of themed chapters that encompass landscape, buildings, beliefs, work, seasons, people, music and drama. In the eleven chapters the county's rich store of folklore unfolds in a way that allows you to dip into what most intrigues, or to read from start to finish. Roy Palmer is nationally known for his researches into folklore, and has written accounts of the folklore of several counties on both sides of the southern Welsh border, along with various anthologies.

Paperback, 352 pages, over 250 b/w illustrations. Price: £12.95

The Story of Shrewsbury
by Mary de Saulles

Shrewsbury has a rich history, having been a frontier town and a centre of England's thriving medieval woollen industry sited on a major trading river. As such it witnessed conflict which led to a series of fortifications – elements of which remain today – and visits by many of England's medieval kings. More visible remains are in the timber-framed buildings erected by the merchants made wealthy by trade, exploiting their position through the formation of guilds. Wealth was also brought to the town as a result of the abbey, which was also the early industrial hub of the city, with its building work, craftsmen and mills. It was also the site of two early parliaments.

In the Georgian period the town began to exert its influence as the county town, where the gentry came to spend their leisure time at the various entertainments, and stroll on the promenades. But not all was gentility, nor was the fashionable 'season' all elegance, for the river encouraged the establishment of industries, from noxious tanyards in the medieval period, to equally troublesome leadworks and noisy cloth and spinning enterprises.

With the coming of the railways, suburbs grew and the economy further diversified and education gradually spread from the confines of Shrewsbury School and various charitable institutions. After the Second World War, the town's rich architectural heritage was threatened by redevelopment. The book ends with a consideration of recent developments in the nature of the town and what it indicates for the future.

Paperback, 272 pages, 120 colour and 100 b/w illustrations. Price: £15

A Guide to Slow Travel in the Marches
by Les Lumsdon

The Guide is structured around eight key towns – Welshpool, Oswestry, Shrewsbury, Church Stretton, Ludlow, Hereford, Llandrindod Wells and Abergavenny – which can act as bases for exploration, with suggested tours from each using trains and buses. Each section includes a guided walking tour of the main town, with places to look out for or to step inside, followed by descriptions of suggested journeys to places worth visiting in the surrounding area, with walking tours of the destinations also usually included. As well as public transport links, for each place there are suggestions for cycle rides and walks, some taking a few hours, others a whole day or even days. The guide also lists places to eat and imbibe, for it is natural for the slow traveller to enjoy local food and drink; indeed, the UK's Slow Food movement is well represented in the Marches. The section for each location includes a list of extras such as farmers' markets, local activities and festivals, as well as a selection of useful local publications and websites.

Paperback, 240 pages, 30 colour and over 100 b/w photos and 20 maps. Price: £10